Souls With Longing

Souls With Longing

Representations of Honor and Love in Shakespeare

Edited by
Bernard J. Dobski and Dustin A. Gish

LEXINGTON BOOKS
Lanham • Boulder • New York • Toronto • Plymouth, UK

Published by Lexington Books
A wholly owned subsidiary of The Rowman & Littlefield Publishing Group, Inc.
4501 Forbes Boulevard, Suite 200, Lanham, Maryland 20706
www.lexingtonbooks.com

Estover Road, Plymouth PL6 7PY, United Kingdom

British Library Cataloguing in Publication Information Available

Library of Congress Cataloging-in-Publication Data

Souls with longing : representations of honor and love in Shakespeare / edited by Bernard J. Dobski and Dustin A. Gish.
    p. cm.
    Summary: "*Souls with Longing* focuses on representations of honor and love in the plays and poetry of William Shakespeare. The contributors to this collaborative volume reveal how Shakespeare's representations of the longing for and pursuit of honor and love in his characters teach us about who we are, what we desire, and why. Shakespeare's works thus vividly represent a grand pageant of souls with longing which holds sway over our political, moral, and romantic imaginations."—Provided by publisher.
    Includes bibliographical references and index.
    ISBN 978-0-7391-6541-6 (hard)—ISBN 978-0-7391-6542-3 (pbk.)—ISBN 978-0-7391-6543-0 (electronic)
    1. Shakespeare, William, 1564-1616—Criticism and interpretation. 2. Honor in literature. 3. Love in literature. I. Dobski, Bernard J., 1972– II. Gish, Dustin A., 1969–
    PR3069.H6S68 2011
    822.3'3—dc23   2011030998

Printed in the United States of America

Read him, therefore; and again, and again:
And if then you do not like him, surely you are in
some manifest danger,
not to understand him . . .

And so we leave you to other of his Friends,
whom if you need,
can be your guides: if you need them not, you can
lead your selves, and others.
And such Readers we wish him.

—Epistle Dedicatory,
"To the Great Variety of Readers,"
First Folio Edition of Shakespeare's Works
(London, 1623)

Contents

Acknowledgments

Most of the chapters in this volume originated as papers delivered at a conference on "Love and Honor in Shakespeare" at Assumption College in fall 2009. The conference itself emerged from the intellectual inspiration of Nalin Ranasinghe at Assumption College, who noticed the intimate interplay between themes of love and honor in Shakespeare's works and the aims and purposes of liberal education, and who encouraged us to organize a gathering of scholars and friends that might do justice to both. For the considerable institutional and financial support required to make possible the conference, we would like to thank the Office of the Provost at Assumption College as well as The Fortin and Gonthier Foundations of Western Civilization Program, directed by Geoffrey Vaughan. Generous assistance was also provided by the Intercollegiate Studies Institute (ISI) to sponsor one of the two keynote addresses at the conference.

The genesis and publication of such a collection rests upon the kindness and support of many individuals. We would like to acknowledge, above all, the contributors to this volume (and the conference), who patiently attended to our frequent questions and requests in assembling and editing their chapters for the volume and whose deep appreciation for Shakespeare and his works is eloquently exhibited in their writings, past and present. We have learned much about love and honor in Shakespeare from them. Paul Cantor deserves particular thanks. He eagerly agreed to be a part of this project in its earliest stages and continued to offer us indispensable guidance as we organized both the conference and this volume. James Kee and William Morse at the College of the Holy Cross provided helpful comments on the editors' contributions at important stages in the project as well. In preparing the manuscript for publication, we would also like to thank the editorial staff at Lexington Books for their interest in and support of the volume, as well as the anonymous reviewers for their helpful comments. Joseph Parry and Erin Walpole guided us through the entire process, consistently offering technical and editorial support that improved the quality of the final product.

Finally, we want to acknowledge the patience and support of both our families. From beginning to end, our wives and children have quietly acquiesced in our absence during the long hours of conversation, planning, and preparation that led up to the publication of this volume. Souls with longing also have bodies in need of sustenance; for the nourishment of both the soul and body, we owe immense debts of gratitude to our families. This volume testifies to the sacrifices they made in the service of human wisdom, a theme worthy of its own Shakespearean poetry. Their love we honor in dedicating this volume to them.

~

Prologue

~

Shakespeare's Souls with Longing

Bernard J. Dobski and Dustin A. Gish

We discover in the works of William Shakespeare the wisdom of a poet whose art charms and entertains, even as it educates us. In the "eternal lines" of his plays and poetry, Shakespeare conjures a vivid gallery of characters for his audience and readers.[1] His representations of human beings are as true to life as any nature has conceived, perhaps more true. We may wonder if there is a Falstaff or a Hamlet or a Cleopatra living in our midst from whom we can learn as much as we can from the characters that inhabit Shakespeare's works. Through sustained reflection on his characters, we become keenly aware of our humanity and thus come to know ourselves more profoundly. Audiences and readers, for centuries, have read Shakespeare's poetry and beheld his plays with awe and pleasure, and still do.[2] Shakespeare indeed fascinates us, for he educates us even as he entertains us. A thoughtful editor once wrote that the works of this "poet of nature" constitute "a faithful mirror" of manners and life, and that Shakespearean characters "act and speak by the influence of those passions and principles by which all minds are agitated, and the whole system of life is continued in motion."[3] His writings represent for us the grand spectacle of being human—a pageant of souls with longing in whose wake we ceaselessly follow.

Among the diverse aspects of the human condition on display in his works, we are drawn in particular to Shakespeare's representations of dominant passions and soaring ambitions which are so compellingly rendered as to lead us to discover their causes and consequences in the soul. Our natural longings for both honor and love are two of the causes or principles that animate our souls and keep our lives in perpetual motion, while holding out to us the hope of respite and rest. Striving towards the honorable or beloved, we deem honor and love to be good insofar as each promises us a form of completion and self-sufficiency, satisfaction and transcendence. Through his representations, Shakespeare invites us to search out the subtle contours and grand arc of our own hopes and desires. In his plays and poetry, he reveals the cords that bind our souls to those objects which we long to possess, and which in turn we expect will nourish us. His works stage for our entertainment and consideration characters defined by how they conceive and pursue honor and love, yearnings that distinguish them as individuals. Shakespeare always reminds us as well of the context within which his characters—and we—seek honor and love.[4]

I

What hath Shakespeare wrought? Why do we see ourselves and our longings, writ large and yet intimately familiar to us, in his figures? The abiding popularity of Shakespeare's works is evident in the influence of his plays on film and television, as well as the steady performance of his plays annually on stages in theaters and parks, in and beyond the English-speaking world.[5] Shakespeare remains one of our most cherished cultural touchstones. The representations he has made exert an undeniable, if perhaps not fully acknowledged, hold upon our romantic, moral, and political imaginations. Despite efforts to recast the human in modes derived from theoretical paradigms of modern and post-modern thought, we are yet unable to escape from our nature and therefore remain indebted to Shakespeare for his portraits of us.[6]

That the judgment of much contemporary scholarship on or about Shakespeare should be at odds with a popular taste for his plays and poetry is troubling. Running against the grain of scholarly opinion, a few commentators continue to declare Shakespeare the most creative person in history, the author of our modern conception of the human—and for good reason.[7] Evidence for this view is found in the extraordinary performative legacy of Shakespeare's substantial body of work, translated into more languages than even Shakespeare could imagine. But perhaps the greatest proof that Shakespeare's characters are alive and well is the vitality with which the full spectrum of human souls is observed in his work. Has a person yet been born whose soul has not, in some decisive respect, already found its pattern or form in one of his characters? The range of human possibility seems both revealed in and circumscribed by his wisdom and art: Shakespeare appears to be at once the creator and prophet of our humanity. What, we wonder, is the source of this Shakespearean wisdom, the font from which such genius springs?

If indeed Shakespeare has invented us—or rather, shapes and molds us through his poetry in the image of his own characters—we must imagine that he has done so without neglecting that inquiry into human nature that reveals to the poet the defining qualities and limitations of being human. To plumb the depths of human nature is to explore the human soul and its constitution, along the way grappling with the permanent questions associated with our humanity, those moral and political problems that define our lives in common. Such an inquiry, the fruits of which are apparent in his works, transcends the traditional distinctions separating poetry and philosophy. The richness of Shakespeare's characters reflects the quality of his intellect; his knowledge and understanding of the truth about what is, and therefore about human beings, renders Shakespeare as much a philosopher as a poet.[8] That knowledge reflects our nature and is translated through his poetic art into living images which simultaneously appeal to and educate the audience before the stage as well as the reader in his study. What, then, do we learn about ourselves and our world by observing and reading Shakespeare's works? Shakespeare, as artist and thinker, offers a comprehensive education. His wisdom rests upon the fundamental insight that all human beings *as* human beings have a share in our common humanity—a universalism which refuses to deny, and is highly attentive to, difference and distinction.[9] For what he teaches touches upon the whole of human affairs, upon what being human fully entails.

Shakespearean characters are no more or less fantastic or fictional than we ourselves are. What issues from his poetic imagination does not exceed what we may fashion about and for our own lives through the working of our romantic, moral, and political imaginations. The world in which Shakespeare's characters dwell is one commensurate with our own, although it is perhaps superior insofar as the vicissitudes of fortune and randomness of chance can be traced back to an author's guiding hand and intellect. While a few characters seem to partake of an illusory being—Macbeth's witches, Ariel, Puck, or ass-headed Bottom—and thus would appear to exceed the bounds of the possible for human life, we nonetheless bear witness to the power of his art which works its true magic not by begging for a willing suspension of our disbelief, but by embarking on such flights of fancy in order to unsettle us; to test our conviction that we have a firm grasp on what is real and what is not about ourselves and the world around us. Shakespeare, by means of his art, projects his imaginings back upon our lived experience, letting us judge for ourselves the truth of what we have discovered about human nature in his works.[10] He thus ornaments the truth in order to reveal it; his abstractions from the familiar bring forth what is present but all too often concealed within our quotidian existence. By revivifying the mundane, Shakespeare shakes the ground of our preconceived opinions and prepares us to see and rethink ourselves.[11]

With his poetry, which educates our mind even more so than it caters to our imagination, Shakespeare carries us beyond the confines of the ordinary and thereby provides access to those aspects of ourselves and our lives in common that we might otherwise tend to forget or neglect. The power of his imaginative art is not only a function of creative genius, but implies knowledge of the fundamental alternatives available to us as human beings in our quest to live our own lives well. Through the unforgettable representations in his plays and poetry, Shakespeare reads us— perhaps better, and more definitively, than we read him or his creations.[12] But Shakespeare can only help us to know and understand ourselves in the fullest sense if his art works within those limits imposed by the human associations, moral and political, that we construct and inhabit. It is only through the recognition and observance of such limits that Shakespeare can illuminate those human longings—especially for honor and love—that drive us, literally and figuratively, into the arms of others.

II

Shakespeare's works taken as a whole exhibit a variety of private and public alternatives around which we might orient our lives: religious piety, political greatness, the pursuit of honor, poetic expression, familial duty, romantic and erotic transports, philosophy or contemplation. Shakespeare's plays therefore survey the paths to happiness which beckon human beings. Yet his articulation of those possibilities are never presented abstractly, in a vacuum, but always within, and often in tension with, a framework of circumstance, whether political, religious, or social. As with the inescapable dramatic context of Shakespeare's texts, the choice of framework exhibits the richness and diversity of his inherited traditions: *political* (ancient Athens or Rome, republics or empires, divine-right monarchies or modern liberal states), *religious* (pagan, Christian, Jewish, Muslim, or secular), and *social* (civil societies grounded in classical virtues, Medieval feudalism, Renaissance humanism, or modern European liberalism).[13] Such backdrops set the stage for our reflections on the character of great passion and ambition, and the manner in which our deepest longings are shaped by, and shape, the world around us. [14]

The dramatic context of each play highlights for the reader the impact of the longings for honor and love on marriages, families, religious belief, political activity, the law, justice, the role of prudence in politics, and the need for moderation in erotic affairs. Audiences and readers of Shakespeare are thus invited by the structure of his work to apply the principles, teased out and examined in his fiction, to their own existence. Shakespeare invites us to map out the psychology of his characters as it emerges from their experience—from what they say and do as well as from what is said and done to them—against our own experiences, and the experience of the longings in our own souls. His art stages, more clearly than we might see them for ourselves, our longings and their aims or ends, as implied by their trajectories— aims or ends perhaps intuited by passion, but grasped only dimly, if at all, by reason. By virtue of this art, Shakespeare helps us to evaluate the coherence of our passions, the character and integrity of our pursuits. Perhaps this helps to explain why some his most memorable characters live at the extremes, in one sense or another, as we see (for example) in his portraits of Cleopatra, Cordelia, Rosalind, Portia, Falstaff, Henry V, Caesar, Richard III, Macbeth, Iago, or Hamlet. Such extremes however are not to be confused with abstract ideals that are simply to be admired and emulated, or despised and shunned. Rather, these characters tend to embody grand expansions of admirable yet dangerous human qualities, or peculiar aberrations of otherwise healthy hopes and desires. These figures are much more than ideograms representing a single moral, political, or social perspective; they bring to life what is attractive as well as repulsive within us, and are so designed as to draw us more deeply into an engagement with ourselves through Shakespeare's works and thought.

The representations to which Shakespeare provocatively directs our attention demonstrate the power and allure of great passion and ambition whose modern currency is too often devalued, if not entirely collapsed by contemporary theories that diminish or ignore the purchase which such longings have upon our souls, by translating (or rather mistranslating) the pursuit of honor and love into reductive terms of self-interest, utilitarian calculation, individual preferences rooted in custom, prejudice, social Darwinism, or cultural materialism.[15] Whether in towering figures of ambition incarnate— Coriolanus, Julius Caesar, Henry V, Lady Macbeth, Richard III—or through pairs of tragic lovers who make themselves (especially in death) into lasting monuments of overwhelming passion—Antony and Cleopatra, Romeo and Juliet, the Phoenix and Turtle-dove; Shakespeare insists that our powerful longings for honor and love receive their due. Even his seemingly more moderate portraits of devoted honor-lovers (like Brutus, Portia, and Hotspur) or passionate lovers (like Lucentio and Bianca, or Desdemona and Othello), which can be and often are mistaken for stylized romantic images, contain the seeds of the unflinching critique of honor and love fleshed out in his figures of Iago or Falstaff—the latter an exemplar of that materialism and hedonism which, in the name of realism, makes a mockery of both honor and love.[16]

Shakespeare's representations invite us to seek a more coherent account of our longings and thereby to moderate and reconcile (insofar as possible) the hopes whence they arise. Such a response to Shakespeare's characters would be consistent with the longing for transcendence that inevitably draws human beings to meditate upon beautiful works of art. And so we are drawn to Shakespeare's plays and poetry even as his work elicits and refines such longings. Our attention falls upon the tension evoked in those Shakespearean characters pursuing honor or love, and we are led to ponder the effect that the mutual influence and interplay of these longings have on the action of the play. Shakespeare does not propose to explain away or resolve this tension through his plays, however. He does not represent such longings for honor and love as mere "problems" in need of solutions—and, as a result, we flourish by engaging with and contemplating them, thereby seeing with greater clarity the architecture of the human soul. It is on account of this capacity for illumination that we see Shakespeare's characters—however perfect or deficient or excessive they may seem—as more vibrant and alive than even the audiences and readers whose self-understanding is being informed and interrogated by his representations.

The humanity of Shakespeare's compelling portraits of honor-seekers and lovers who fall into the embrace of others makes them even more attractive. Consider the "immortal longings" of Cleopatra, longings which at once occasion and impossibly complicate the consummation of her great love for Antony. Even while "eternity was in [their] lips and eyes," the lovers' embrace precipitates war with Octavian Caesar and the world of Rome—and ends in death.[17] Inseparable from their immortal longings, which are conceived as true elixirs for their souls, there is a darker potion whose toxin emanates from the interweaving of the love between Cleopatra and Antony, with their longing to have the honor which must attend their unrivaled amorous displays, even as it dooms their romance. For these lovers find the chief satisfaction of their private longing in their public display of romance; ever the political masters, they take as much pleasure from being honored for their love as they do from the invigorating charms of their beloved. The longings that bind them together in private also demand, for their fullest expression, the political stage afforded by Antony's rule over the Roman empire, which is to say, the known world.[18] Despite proclamations to the contrary, the immortal longings so radiantly represented by the intoxicating love between Cleopatra and Antony are not enough, are ultimately insufficient. As these lovers realize (perhaps one lover sooner than the other), the condition for satisfying their longing for immortal glory is purchased at the expense of their present love. To be free to love as they desire, they must conquer a world whose inhabitants (living or dead) will perpetually honor them for it.

Shakespeare thus embodies, through the tragic paradox in souls with such longings, the tension between, on one hand, the desire to transcend this world through private happiness and passionate love (*eros*) and, on the other hand, the desire to attain honor and immortal glory through a spirited attachment (*thumos*) to this world. For a reconciliation of this tragic antithesis, we might look to Shakespeare's representation of this tension within Christian marriage at least insofar as Christianity obscures or absolves the tragic demands made by politics for the here and now, not to mention the exalted hopes for erotic love in a hereafter. Love chastened by Christian marriage might escape pagan excess, but risks doing so at the expense of the public realm which loses its luster as our attraction to affairs in *this* world necessarily gives way to those of another. The prospects for a Christian resolution to the problem of *eros* are called into doubt by the grim endings—for lovers and their cities—in Shakespeare's romantic tragedies, especially *Romeo and Juliet*. What, then, are the prospects for honor?

In the character of Julius Caesar, Antony's great predecessor both in honor and in love, Shakespeare depicts an alternative path to Cleopatra's immortal longings. This route eschews the apparent contradictions that doom the Egyptian queen and her Roman lover. While Caesar, too, divines an apotheosis through a kind of martyrdom, he still chooses the path of politics, not love—and does so intentionally, with articulate constancy, hence not tragically. Pursuing honor in its most problematic aspect as a quest for glory,[19] the imperially minded Caesar seems to foresee in his sacrifice the means whereby he can achieve that undying fame which surpasses his rivals for republican honor (from the elder Brutus, founder of the Republic, or Coriolanus, to Cicero or his own "best lover" and assassin, Brutus). That Caesar's political pursuits are more consistent than Cleopatra's erotic yearnings however does not make them any less troubling. After all, his pursuit of glory is not limited to the private realm; his efforts to attain everlasting renown help to undermine the moral integrity of Rome, introducing an imperial calculus that robs the republican order of both its liberty and its law-abiding character. In considering Shakespeare's Roman plays in general, are we not led to wonder whether such longings, however conceived and directed, are at odds with life itself? Does such passion require the sacrifice of life? Is the individual quest for greatness always at odds with those limits that are necessary for healthy politics? Does the tragic character of the Roman plays reflect the "lust in action"—torn between highest aspirations and brutality in exhaustion—of an unrestrained classical pursuit of honor and love?[20]

Turning from Shakespeare's pagan plays to the Christian plays, we witness an expansion of Roman boundaries, as the old world yields to a new empire. Under the sway of universalizing religion, a world within beckons the spirited and erotic Shakespearean characters. The invitation to turn inward rather than to conquer the "world without"—the realm of politics— leads them to care for and cultivate both body and soul in the heavenly light of a "world above." Shakespeare shows how Christianity can soften, if not resolve, tensions aroused by the "immortal longings" which were essential to the vitality of his pagans and yet, in the end, the source of their tragedy. Shakespeare's more ordinate, although still passionate, lovers (like Kate and Petruchio, Rosalind and Orlando, Portia and Bassanio, or Beatrice and Benedick) eventually retreat into the private realm of domestic pleasure and virtue, far from the public stage. Within the bounds of a Christian marriage, Shakespeare's heroines also rise as the educators and rulers of their husbands. But the prospects for the happiness of Christian lovers who marry and still anticipate or maintain a share in political rule—the Princess of Aquitaine and Berowne, Isabella and Duke Vincentio, Viola and Duke Orsino, Miranda and Prince Ferdinand, Katherine of Valois and King Henry V—are subjected to lingering doubts or tainted by great misfortune.

Even if Christianity demotes grand political ambition in favor of otherworldly devotions, Shakespeare seems to hold out hope for a greatness wedded to Christian piety—in the character of Henry V, arguably the greatest statesman to grace his stage, heralded by the Chorus as both a "conquering Caesar" and "the mirror of all Christian kings."[21] Of course, this King Henry, unlike his unfortunate heir (Henry VI), is no Christian ascetic devoid of ambition; his greatness is in no small part due to this fact as well. In his English histories, Shakespeare depicts the emergence of such a pinnacle of princely ambition within the framework of a particular political order that challenges the demotion of political life affected by Christianity and abetted by a corrupt clergy. Does the constitutional monarchy of Shakespeare's Christian England thus revive the possibility of political greatness entertained by the classical views of *eros* and *thumos*? The plausibility of this suggestion would need to be tested: The limited success of Christianity in the private realm to restrain erotic longing is represented in proportions both comic (Christopher Sly, Touchstone, Audrey) and tragic (Romeo and Juliet, the Poet and the

"Dark Lady" of his Sonnets). When it comes to the public realm—whether due to the weak-willed moralism of Richard III's victims, the tortured consciences of Macbeth and his Lady or Alonso, the excessive piety and disdain for this-worldly rule of Henry VI, or the pensiveness of "good" Prince Hamlet—Shakespeare invites us to reconsider the tragic consequences caused by the inherent limitations of even Christianity to control and shape human ambition on a grand scale.

Such difficulties, grave as they are, do not lend Shakespeare's work an air of resignation. Rather, his works seem to offer for our consideration an alternative perspective—one which resists a strict adherence to the moral and political virtues associated with either the classical or the Christian models of human life even as it respects both the vitality of the classical world and the moral and ethical limits reflected in Christian piety. This perspective is one which is in tune with the moral and spiritual roots common to the classical and Christian worlds, but tries to find a home for our immortal longings within this world, without thereby reducing the beautiful or noble to the vulgar, or interpreting the high in terms of the low. Such a perspective, which is neither classical nor Christian but which seeks to do justice to what is true in both, emerges when we study the speeches and deeds of his more prudent or philosophical characters, such as Portia of Belmont, Duke Vincentio, Theseus, or Prospero.[22] Whatever conclusions we are tempted to draw about Shakespeare's own judgments with respect to these characters and the alternative modes they embody, he makes our pursuit of honor and love, and satisfaction of our longings, an abiding theme of his works.

III

The authors of the chapters in this volume offer exemplary reflections on the education to be derived from studying representations of honor and love in Shakespeare, especially insofar as the lessons that are taught by his plays and poetry illuminate the yearnings which not only attend, but perhaps also embellish or distort, our very conceptions of honor and love. Each takes a direct approach to the works of Shakespeare, affirming a method of interpretation which has more in common with Hamlet (Shakespeare's own literary critic: "The play's the thing . . .") than with the critics who predominate in the secondary literature and fashion readings based on contemporary literary theories. The contributors to this volume foreground Shakespearean characters for study, rather than push them into the background, as much Shakespeare scholarship today tends to do.[23] And their arguments attend above all, although not exclusively, to Shakespeare's representations of human beings whose souls yearn for distinction and fulfillment through honor and love.

We open the volume with wide-ranging reflections on honor and love which help to lay the foundation for the examinations of honor and love to follow. John Alvis studies the concern for honor in Shakespeare as a moral conundrum, since the benefits of cultivating reputation must be balanced against the dramatized costs thereof. The profit margin so to speak, Alvis concludes, depends upon the character of the regime within which honor-seeking preoccupies the minds of the more spirited public figures in such different regimes as republics (Rome), monarchies (England, France), and commercial polities (Venice). John Briggs queries the plays to discover if we sufficiently appreciate the degree to which love and honor are bound to interact and become volatile, for example, in Shakespeare's *Romeo and Juliet*. He explores the play's structure to see how its tragic force derives from a deep chemistry of love and honor working its way into our hearts and memories— and wonders whether in this play, or any other play, Shakespeare devises a curative remedy or a deleterious poison for what ails our souls.

The following two pairs of chapters, as well as the first, reflect upon the ideals and aims in our pursuit of honor and love, and how our longings are mediated by the conventions within which these pursuits inevitably take place. Paul Cantor reads *As You Like It* as a satire on courtly love and one of Shakespeare's most self-consciously literary works, one in which Shakespeare develops a critique of the Elizabethan pastoral and Petrarchan love poetry so influential in his day. By juxtaposing the three pairs of very different lovers in the play, he argues, Shakespeare shows how the problems posed to love might be better addressed by blending natural simplicity with a sense of courtly refinement. Laurence Nee in his chapter on *A Midsummer Night's Dream* focuses our attention on Theseus' political concern for the disorderly effect of erotic love, poetry, and the desire for self-sufficiency upon public peace and prosperity. When the young lovers and tyrannical Bottom return to Athens from the natural realm of the forest, the danger posed to the political order by their natural longing for transcendence must be governed not by anachronistic Christian imagery or Bottom's dream, but by Theseus' moderating statesmanship.

Carol McNamara highlights the relation of individual desires to the common good in her reading of *Troilus and Cressida* as an account of how political rule becomes disordered when private motives drive public ends. With reference to the invocation of Aristotle in the play, she shows how Shakespeare judges the immoderate loves of the three Trojan brothers, Hector, Paris, and Troilus—their love of honor, shame of dishonor, and reckless pursuit of their passions—to be the root cause of their tragic failure to adopt a prudent political and military course for Troy. Bernard J. Dobski, in his chapter on the character and career of Henry V, explores how Prince Hal's friendships with Falstaff and Ned Poins allow him to interrogate the nature of his own political ambitions. Through his representation of these two friendships, Shakespeare indicates the imperative by which this scandalous and deeply ambitious royal learns to cover himself in enduring glory: combine Machiavellian prudence with a Christian respect for the political and moral limits governing man.

The next three chapters illuminate darker dimensions of love and honor in Shakespeare, showing the problems with their pursuit when one attempts either to transcend human nature through Christian self-denial or to dominate a realm through the radical assertion of will. In his treatment of *Romeo and Juliet*, David Lowenthal explores the way Christian piety can distort the traditional or romantic view of love. The tragedy of this play's star-crossed lovers originates in the unbending piety of the friar whose ascetic insistence on sexual purity paradoxically gives rise to a Romeo torn between manliness and effeminacy, and a secular political order incapable of stiff opposition to the Church. Only Juliet, tutored by her nurse, preserves a natural constancy in her love for Romeo, which is grounded in a properly ordered sexual love, free from the pietistic extremes of Christianity. In *Macbeth*, however, Carson Holloway finds no natural solution to the problem of demonic evil embodied by the play's protagonist and his Lady. In their irrational pursuit of political power, this couple ruthlessly seeks and obtains a "good" that destroys their souls and prohibits them from reliably securing their interests even as they fulfill their ambitious desires. Shakespeare's portrait of a tyranny that "repudiates reasoning" in favor of a willful and self-destructive violence anticipates by nearly four hundred years the blood-soaked ideologies that wracked the twentieth century. Leon Craig, in his chapter on *Richard III*, similarly exposes the deep wickedness arising from an inordinate love of honor inflamed by a deformed *eros*. He argues that the *eros* in the misshapen Richard is actually drained of all sexual desire, for women or men. Once un-tethered from the physical objects of erotic longing, the Duke of Gloucester hunts a cold, limitless tyranny over human beings as such, with an eye to the conquest of all of Britain, Ireland and France.

The final pair of chapters returns us to reflection on Shakespeare and his art, offering an explicit engagement with Shakespeare's own activity—and rule over his audience and readers—as an artist and thinker. In reading *The Tempest*, Dustin Gish sees Shakespeare working out in his Prospero the inherent limitations of even a benevolent, enlightened effort to resolve the political problem of rule over the unwise and irrational. Prospero's desire for justice, he argues, unbound by a respect for the limits of our human nature and united with the god-like power promised by natural science, distorts his love of wisdom into the basis for rule which is a species of tyranny. Only the education in being human that Prospero receives through the action of a play which he ostensibly controls frees him from that crime for which, in the end, he begs pardon. Glen Arbery guides us through the plays in a search for Shakespeare's own commentary on the performative aspect of his work. It is the theatrical dimension of the concern for public honor, he argues, that allows us to grasp the genius that defines Shakespeare over, against his representations of honor-loving characters. In seeing how Shakespeare, unlike his Brutus, Antony, Cleopatra, or Macbeth, survives the public shame of tragic honor through his willingness to play "a motley to the view," we gain deeper insight into the role played by the stage itself in his dramatic work.

Representations of honor and love in Shakespeare are not limited to the characters in his works for the stage, though these portraits are sketched out in compelling detail. Shakespeare also offers reflections on our longings in his poetry—and not only in lengthy works as *Venus and Adonis* and *The Rape of Lucrece*, where the themes of honor and love are intertwined and openly on display. In the brief codas that appear in the Epilogue and conclude this volume, we hear the poetry of Shakespeare sounded on the question of honor and love. George Anastaplo interrogates the enigmatic lovers in Shakespeare's *The Phoenix and Turtle*, reminding us of the paradoxical attempt by lovers to satisfy their longing by the sacrifice of individuality in a union with another: to live and die in the arms of a beloved, and so to honor, in perpetuity, the virtue of love in the extreme. The intensity of such a constant love—one that "bears it out even to the edge of doom" (Sonnet 116)—while beautiful and true, may yet preclude the possibility of two becoming one in self-forgetting union, or their love bridging the gap between mortal and immortal. Scott Crider concludes the volume with a reading of Shakespeare's Sonnets and the lyrical will which voices them. He contends that the effort by the Speaker to achieve a double securing of love and honor for his beloved (first the Fair Youth, then the Dark Lady) establishes a monument to both the flourishing and the shame of his loving. This lyricism testifies to the love of the beautiful that elevates souls and the carnal desires that drive bodies, and does so by preserving them together in a medium which defies the ravages of age and death: passion, poems, and poet merge and become immortal in a lyric state.

Through his representations of honor and love, Shakespeare brings to life before our eyes souls with longing, and through our study of such souls we gain insight into the human soul itself and come to a deeper appreciation of the motives and motions therein that compel us to embrace as well as rival one another. As the chapters in this volume bear witness, it is by examining these representations of honor-seekers and lovers in Shakespeare's works that we come to grips with, and better understand, our own expectations and desires with respect to our various associations and communities— ranging from the quotidian and the conventional, to the extraordinary and the extreme, from the private and intimate to the political and the grand. For as the plays and poetry of Shakespeare amply demonstrate, the study of such representations of honor and love is one means by which our own romantic, moral, and political imaginations can accomplish their work. Such studies therefore become a necessary prolegomena to the discovery of human nature itself, the ultimate ground of Shakespeare's own thought and wisdom.

Notes

1. Shakespeare, Sonnet 18.

2. Ben Jonson's prefatory poem to the First Folio (see Appendix A) trumpeted Shakespeare's immortal glory: "He was not of an age, but for all time!" John Milton, in his first published poem, a sonnet attached to the Folio's second edition, declared that Shakespeare had constructed "a live-long Monument" for himself in his plays. John Dryden, in his *Essay of Dramatic Poesy* (1668), proclaimed "the Divine Shakespeare"—of all poets, ancient and modern—in possession of "the largest and most comprehensive soul."

3. Samuel Johnson, "Preface to Shakespeare" (1765), in *Johnson on Shakespeare: Essays and Notes Selected and Set Forth . . . by Walter Raleigh* (London, 1908) 9–63, 11–12.

4. Allan Bloom, *Love and Friendship* (Simon and Schuster, 1993) 393: "The survey of the human spirit, which is what Shakespeare's plays taken together are, instructs us in the complex business of knowing what to honor and what to despise, what to love and what to hate."

5. One contemporary scholar attributes the dominant legacy of Shakespeare to his gift of poetic invention, the richness, originality, and astonishingly polysemous quality of his language, and his sway over generations of great writers, and not only in English: Jonathan Bate, "The Mirror of Life: How Shakespeare Conquered the World," *Harper's Magazine* (April 2007) 37–46.

6. William Faulkner, in his 1950 speech accepting the Nobel Prize for Literature, observed that the "young man or woman writing today" must leave "no room in his workshop for anything but the old verities and truths of the heart, the universal truths lacking which any story is ephemeral and doomed—love and honor and pity and pride and compassion and sacrifice."

7. Paul Johnson, "Shakespeare: Glimpses of an Unknown Colossus," in his *Creators* (Harper Collins, 2006) 49–76. See Harold Bloom, *Shakespeare: The Invention of the Human* (Riverhead Books, 1998) xviii–xix: "[One] might contend that Shakespeare's originality was in the *representation* of cognition, personality, character. But there is an overflowing element in the plays, an excess beyond representation, that is closer to the metaphor we call 'creation.'" Shakespeare's art, Bloom contends, is "so infinite that it *contains* us, and will go on enclosing those likely to come after us." Allan Bloom argues that Shakespeare chooses not to "create" but rather to explore human nature and the wonders of nature itself; see A. Bloom 1993, 270, 393–394: "The movement" in his plays "is from nature to art to nature"—but in his writing them, Shakespeare accomplishes "a perfection of nature." Samuel Johnson, in his "Preface," remarked that his characters "are the genuine progeny of common humanity, such as the world will always supply, and observation will always find." Ralph Waldo Emerson, in his *Representative Men* (London, 1850), concluded that "the wise Shakespeare" wrote in "his book of life . . . the text of modern life, the text of manners; he drew the man of England, and Europe, the father of the man in America . . . he read the hearts of men and women, their probity, and their second thoughts, and wiles, the wiles of innocence, and the transitions by which virtues and vices slide into their contraries" (130). Such exalted praise of Shakespeare seems outrageous, but may turn out to be "plain truth rather than effervescent hyperbole." David Lowenthal, *Shakespeare and the Good Life: Ethics and Politics in Dramatic Form* (Rowman and Littlefield, 1997) ix.

8. See the "Introduction" to Allan Bloom, with Harry Jaffa, *Shakespeare's Politics* (Basic Books, 1964; University of Chicago Press, 1986) 1–12. See also Allan Bloom, "Political Philosophy and Poetry" and "A Restatement," *American Political Science Review* 54/2 (1960) 457–64 and 471–73; Howard White, *Copp'd Hills Toward Heaven: Shakespeare and the Classical Polity* (Martinus Nijhoff, 1970) 1–24, 141–53; Lowenthal 1997, vii–xii; cf. David Bevington, "A Natural Philosopher," in his *Shakespeare's Ideas* (Blackwell, 2008) 1–14.

9. Scott Crider, in *With What Persuasion: An Essay on Shakespeare and the Ethics of Rhetoric* (Peter Lang, 2009), argues that Shakespeare's plays teach "a universal ethics of rhetoric" which holds to "the mean between universalism and difference," such that the Shakespearean canon can become for contemporary culture a "shared text of virtue" and a "supplement" to the Bible and modern liberalism (1–7, 179–87). See Harry Jaffa's "Foreword" to John Alvis, *Shakespeare's Understanding of Honor* (Carolina Academic Press, 1990) vii: "Shakespeare's plays, taken as a whole, provide us with what we might call a history of civilization." See also Harry Jaffa, "The Unity of Tragedy, Comedy, and History: An Interpretation of the Shakespearean Universe," in *Shakespeare as Political Thinker*, eds. John Alvis and Thomas West (Carolina Academic Press, 1981; ISI Books, 2000) 29–58.

10. Samuel Johnson argued in his "Preface" (14) that Shakespeare's plays "are occupied only by men, who act and speak as the reader thinks that he should himself have spoken or acted on the same occasion: Even where the agency is supernatural

the dialogue is level with life. Other writers disguise the most natural passions and most frequent incidents; so that he who contemplates them in the book will not know them in the world. *Shakespeare* approximates the remote, and familiarizes the wonderful; the event which he represents will not happen, but if it were possible, its effects would probably be such as he has assigned; and it may be said, that he has not only shewn human nature as it acts in real exigencies, but as it would be found in trials, to which it cannot be exposed. This therefore is the praise of *Shakespeare*, that his drama is the mirror of life." On the human limits to the pursuit of first principles, see Aristotle, *Nicomachean Ethics* I.4 (1095b1–3): "One must begin from what is known; but this has two meanings, the things known to us because familiar and the things known simply. Perhaps we, at any rate, ought to begin from what is known to us."

11. See A. Bloom 1993, 269: "Shakespeare seems to be the mirror of nature and to present human beings just as they are. His poetry gives us the eyes to see what is there." See also C. S. Lewis, *An Experiment in Literary Criticism* (Cambridge University Press, 1961) 141: "My own eyes are not enough for me, I will see through those of others. Reality, even seen through the eyes of many, is not enough. I will see what others have invented. Even the eyes of all humanity are not enough. . . .[I]n reading great literature I become a thousand men and yet remain myself. . . . I see with a myriad eyes, but it is still I who see. Here, as in worship, in love, in moral action, and in knowing, I transcend myself; and am never more myself than when I do."

12. See A. Bloom 1993, 269–70; H. Bloom 1998, xx.

13. On the variety of political regimes in Shakespeare, see A. Bloom 1964, 8–12; Howard White, "Politics in Shakespeare," in *Antiquity Forgot: Essays on Shakespeare, Bacon, and Rembrandt* (Martinus Nijhoff, 1978) 5–30. See also the essays in: Alvis and West 2000, esp. John Alvis, "Introductory: Shakespearean Poetry and Politics," 1–27; *Shakespeare's Political Pageant*, eds. Joseph Alulis and Vickie Sullivan (Rowman and Littlefield, 1996); *Shakespeare's Last Plays*, eds. Steven Smith and Travis Curtright (Lexington Books, 2002); *Perspectives on Politics in Shakespeare*, eds. John Murley and Sean Sutton (Lexington Books, 2006). To read Shakespeare as a political thinker is neither to politicize him or his work, nor to interpret his plays through the distorting lens of history, theory, or ideology: for example, cf. *Political Shakespeare: New Essays in Cultural Materialism*, eds. Jonathan Dollimore and Alan Sinfield (Manchester University Press, 1985); Andrew Hadfield, *Shakespeare and Renaissance Politics* (Arden, 2003); *Shakespeare and Early Modern Political Thought*, eds. David Armitage, Conal Condren, and Andrew Fitzmaurice (Cambridge University Press, 2009); Robin Wells, *Shakespeare's Politics: A Contextual Introduction* (Continuum, 2009, 2nd edition).

14. See Appendices B, C, and D.

15. See Paul Cantor, "Shakespeare—'For All Time'?," *The Public Interest* 110 (1993) 34–48; "Shakespeare At Liberty," *The American Conservative* (April 2011) 38–41.

16. See Jaffa 1990, vii–viii; Alvis 1990, 5–6, 14–18. Harold Bloom (1998, 315–18) asserts that the want-wit, whored-out, besotted hero-villain of *Merry Wives*

of Windsor is merely a false, pseudo-Falstaff. But the play unveils the debased farce of "Sir John in love," and a Falstaff plagued and humiliated by his own harsh realism. Shakespeare would have us "Minding true things by what their mockeries be" (*H5* IV.Chorus.53). See Crider 2009, 66–68; cf. A. Bloom 1993, 401–10.

17. Shakespeare, *Antony and Cleopatra* V.ii.273–274, I.iii.35–37. See A. Bloom 1993, 297–325, 396; see also Paul Cantor, *Shakespeare's Rome: Republic and Empire* (Cornell University Press, 1976) 155–83.

18. See Cantor 1976, 184–208; Jan Blits, *New Heaven, New Earth: Shakespeare's Antony and Cleopatra* (Lexington Books, 2009).

19. Alvis 1990, 10. See Aristotle, *NE* IV.3 (1123b15–21); cf. I.5 (1095b22–32), VIII.8 (1159a13–27), and IX.9 (1169b3–10).

20. Shakespeare, Sonnet 129. Shakespeare's "The Rape of Lucrece" and *Titus Andronicus* expose the savage extremes of heart and mind in Rome, and its crimes against nature or barbarism. See George Anastaplo, "Shakespeare," in his *The Artist as Thinker* (Swallow Press, 1983) 15–61. The philosophy found in Shakespeare's Athens may pose an alternative to Rome and to Christianity when it comes to arbitrating between *eros* and *thumos*; see White 1970, 23–24. This alternative has its problems, as we learn from the erotic mischief and uneasy conquests in *A Midsummer Night's Dream*. For a survey of Shakespearean love-plots tempered by orthodox Christian views on sexual conduct and marriage, see Bevington 2008, 15–41.

21. Shakespeare, *Henry V* V.Chorus.23, II.Chorus.6. By kindling a national love of honor which conjoined Roman virtue and the pursuit of greatness with Christian piety and ceremony, Henry sought to found a modern monarchy. See Alvis 1990, 248–50.

22. To see Shakespeare's best regime, John Alvis points to Shakespearean rulers who personify the self-confident magnanimity of the commanding figure in Sonnet 94 and who also possess the requisite qualities of justice and self-knowledge (1990, 250; 2000, 138). See White 1970, 10: "What men honor, what men hold to be good, is the distinctive feature of any regime."

23. H. Bloom 1998, 737–45.

~

Chapters

"I'll have grounds more relative than this—
the play's the thing . . ."

Hamlet II.ii.583–84

1

~

Shakespeare's Understandings of Honor

Morally Absolute, Politically Relative

John Alvis

I propose a beginning in the effort to investigate Shakespeare's understanding of honor as a motive subject to moral scrutiny and as a phenomenon within politics subject to regulation with a view to the common good. To make a start I must raise several questions the determination of which strikes me as a condition for understanding Shakespeare's principles in the way his poetry instructs us to make inferences from poetic particulars to general conclusions. The questions I pose bear upon a concern to grasp how Shakespeare guides us in considering honor-seeking, first, morally and by reference to an ideal order within the individual human soul. The "absolute" of my title refers to this dimension of the subject. The relativistic dimension will occupy me thereafter. By "relative" I mean a Shakespearean understanding of the part played by honor-seeking relative to particular political regimes. Aristotle said that, speaking generally, political life is chiefly concerned with honor. A regime distinguishes itself from others by what it honors, and a political society distributes offices and power in accord with its estimate of what should be esteemed. Shakespeare distinguishes such communities as Britain, Rome, Scotland, and Venice by reference to this principle. Yet because I contend Shakespeare thinks of honor not as absolutely but only provisionally a worthy object of choice, this relative understanding embraces also what the dramas depict regarding various institutions regimes have relied upon for regulating and channeling ambition toward the common good. This chapter can aspire to no more than making a start because to the questions it raises my answers must be provisional—though I trust suggestive—since my examination of the regimes Shakespeare has depicted in his plays must confine itself to Rome and England. These political orders Shakespeare has presented with more particularity than one finds in his portrayal of other polities. Both the Roman setting and the British we find have drawn the dramatist's attention at beginning, middle, and end of his career. Yet to make more than a beginning one would need to take account of the constitutions and institutions peculiar to other civil societies encountered in the plays and poems.

To infer reliably regarding how the plays dispose us toward honor requires attending to related issues equally fundamental. First, what I should think most important to decide is whether one can discover in Shakespeare's works a conception of the divine in terms of which cultivating honor could find its proper place among endeavors either enjoined or proscribed by religious faith. Does such a conception of what a divine authority may require regarding honor lie within Shakespeare's own convictions as distinct from notions evident in characters he depicts? It is not obvious that the sonnets, the narratives, or the dramas display a Shakespearean belief in divinities, or in the one God held by Jews, Christians, and Islamists to be supremely divine to the exclusion of every other pretender. "Nothing" I mean forthrightly asserted in such manner as Milton, say, by declarations in his own person makes evident his subscribing to belief in the God of Abraham, Isaac, and Jacob. One finds Shakespeare making no confession of belief of that sort. In a few instances the plays may stage classical pagan divinities (Hymen, Diana, Jupiter, Hecate maybe), yet these odd intrusions seem fanciful extrusions, not solemn theophanies suggestive of intent to convey and to inspire reverence. Even so, the absence of professions of faith seems not to settle the issue in the negative. Why not? For one thing regarding belief we expect some basis upon which to draw inference one way or the other because Shakespeare causes his characters to make so much of *their* belief or, in some instances, of their disbelief. Hamlet consults his faith in a God who creates, oversees individual conduct, and punishes or rewards in an afterlife; Richard of Gloucester apparently moves from disbelief to a despairing conviction of his own damnation. Edmund of *King Lear* dismisses belief in boasting his allegiance to a Nature conceived as first moving efficient cause as well as final cause, since he equates both efficient and final causes with power. Lear himself first appears to believe in classical gods, subsequently comes to speak of a single Deity ("God's spies") and at the end seems in doubt of any supervening divinity. At times Lear also speaks of Nature as though that principle is—or ought to be— supremely authoritative. For that matter so does Shakespeare in the sonnets, although even in the same sonnet he may refer to an ordaining "Heaven" operating in tandem (Sonnet 94).[1] In the pre-Christian setting of *King Lear* an Edgar disguised as a madman speaks in the manner of a Christian fearing tormenting devils, whereas in his proper mind, he fabricates a miracle in order to deceive his father into belief that gods have prevented his suicide, an act of desperation which, so Edgar swears, a demon had provoked. Prospero also contrives to make others believe in supernatural judges who are punishing sins and requiring amendment. Does Prospero himself believe in "providence divine," a phrase he once employs in conversation with Miranda (though he also attributes a widely disposing power to "fortune"), or does he merely think it proper to induce such trust in his young daughter? Pious Gonzalo attributes to divine plan ("the gods have chalked our way") the play's propitious outcome which, however, has actually been arranged by Prospero's contrivances. Except to the audience in his Epilogue, Prospero himself does not pray. Has Shakespeare, then, created Edgar and Prospero in order to remind us of a perennially available philosophic alternative to piety of any sort? Does he thereby endorse the position that no religious faith is true altogether and none simply false, but all useful to the wise skeptic? One desires to know whether the question must be pursued beyond merely noting Shakespeare's grasping the importance to poets and rulers of understanding the uses and abuses afforded by religion, the importance of taking beliefs regarding the supernatural into account. I suspect but cannot establish that Shakespeare identifies the Supreme Being with the God of whom one speaks rightly only when one attributes to him actions consistent with the sovereignty implied in the phrase "Nature's God." That is to say nature faintly personified but solely for the purpose of connoting an agency best imagined as producing the operations of a rational being unaffected by passion. Human beings are images of God in the sense of their being imperfect similitudes, that is to say sufficiently reasonable to surmise what form complete rational self-governance would take but themselves capable of no more than a scant approximation of such completion.

A complete understanding of what constitutes wisdom with respect to pursuit of honor depends upon resolving this theological question. For if there exists such a Supreme Being as the patriarchs and prophets claim to have heard or that which the Christian evangelists claim to have witnessed, pursuit of honor would seem to be at best a distraction from the one thing needful. Alternatively, how would things stand if divinity should be conceived, not as a Supreme Person but as a principle best discerned in thinking what reason would be if perfectly devoid of passion? On that reckoning honor-seeking would still be a distraction from perfecting reason. Any ambition other than an all-consuming desire to understand would impede that fulfillment of reason via contemplative activity which the old philosophers conceived to be human finality. Seeking honors would, however, deserve a higher estimate than the Hebrew or Christian scriptures encourage. Attaining honor would amount to a good subjoined to a more authoritative purpose. That is, it would be a good provided it should be employed to enlarge the rule of reason. Presently this last thought will deserve further attention.

If my first query lies some distance beyond, a second I will pose comes nearer my pay grade. Can one deduce Shakespeare's concept of the nature of the human soul? Would a rehabilitated version of an ancient view suffice? A promising working thesis one might devise by considering a commonplace that could be gleaned from any one of several Platonic dialogues or from remarks by Cicero in his *Tusculan Disputations*.[2] This classical moral psychology produces the familiar schema of a tripartite psychic hierarchy. Soul is the principle of self-motion. The soul's motion at any particular moment of choice will be determined by the interplay of three influences. Taking these in ascending order, the passions give a certain impetus varying in kind and intensity according to the chooser's bodily constitution and habitual character. A second influence one finds exerted by the special emotions attributed to spiritedness, an array of associated emotions by which a person feels indignation, ambition, and will to dominate. A third influence upon both making a decision and determining means of executing choice is the non-emotional cause identified with reason in one of reason's two modes of activity. A soul operating in accord with its best constitution succeeds in governing its passions and spirited emotions by its reason. This is the ideal human condition productive of self-motion proceeding from self-knowledge. Self-knowledge, in turn, amounts to knowing what one is in the light of what one ought to be.[3] But Shakespearean drama either depicts characters that make their choices while in a condition well short of ideal, or depicts souls closer to the ideal yet so situated as having to contend with others more distant than themselves from rational self-government. A Shakespearean drama provides us with rational treatment of human beings conducting themselves more or less irrationally, or rationally merely in the sense of calculating effectively upon means to ends, ends themselves dictated by passion or spirited emotions. We learn the right order of souls by coming to perceive many derangements of that order together with rare positive exemplars, the latter chiefly if not exclusively confined to comedies: Prospero, Duke Vincentio, perhaps Theseus and Belmonte's Portia.

The two *Henry IV* plays and *Henry V* testify to this psychic dynamic in the manner Virgil had adopted for presenting Aeneas, Dido, and Turnus when he had dramatized in all three characters a psychomachia setting a rational principle contending with both spirited and fleshly impulses while assigning to Aeneas the preeminent degree of reason, to Dido erotic passion in ascendant degree, in Turnus spiritedness dominant over reason. In the three plays just mentioned Shakespeare distributes these three contending faculties among separate characters. In each case one of the three dispositions predominates; in Falstaff intemperate bodily passions, in Hotspur spiritedness heedless of calculation; in Henry Monmouth spiritedness submissive to cool reckoning. Henry IV shares with his son a superior capacity for calculation, but in the father cunning presides over a flagging ambition whereas the son puts forethought in service to an honor-seeking spiritedness that proves sovereign over filial devotion, friendship, patriotism, and justice. Once the drunkard, whoring and avaricious Falstaff suffers Hal's rebuke at the end of the second play, his fraction of a soul must be reprised in the several scoundrels who were his friends and who tag along with Henry V to France. Hotspur slain in combat by Henry Monmouth bequeaths his share of the tripartite soul to the braggart French. In all three plays the plot advances to a climax predestined by the young prince proceeding through scenes setting Henry's plan to "attract more eyes" in counterpoint with unworthy alternatives represented by tavern-friends (*epithumia*), warrior-antagonist (*thumos*) and father (cold calculation). This design adapts the format of medieval morality plays to a secular version thereof, substituting as its aim personal self-conquest in place of sanctity: replacing Everyman with monarch-*in-potentia* overcoming propensities toward un-princely conduct soliciting him in three "Tempters," personifying so many exemplars of false teachers. In place of discovering God's grace the young prince should acquire a soul well-tempered by the classical standard of moderation (*sophrosyne*). *Henry IV, Part 1* concludes with Hal triumphant over Hotspur and over bad companion Falstaff as the prince-in-making exploits that in himself which resembles Hotspur to overcome Falstaff while employing the calculating opportunism of his father to conquer the part of himself which resembles the vainglorious rebel leader. Add Hal's making use of Falstaff's satire against the usurper Bolingbroke (e.g., Harry cannot claim blood kinship with his father if he hasn't a stomach for thievery; the usurping king's scepter is a dagger) and one might suppose Shakespeare has devised a manual for the preparation of princes in an era of skepticism. Hal realizes his father's usurpation has discredited respect for the claim that royal authority enjoys divine protection, seeks indeed to publicize the lesson while assured that his personal strength and wit will suffice to restore the authority which had once rested upon widely voiced but untrustworthy and now exploded conventions. His father's liability will serve as the dull foil against the background of which his own merit will shine all the more stunningly.[4]

Such a reading of the Henry plays has its proponents yet it must confront a difficulty that appears when one asks whether Prince Harry's prefabricated reformation indicates his devotion to justice or merely discloses a self-command he has possessed all along, yet a self-mastery as serviceable to unjust rule as to justice. None of Shakespeare's sources had attributed to the young scofflaw this scheme of premeditated reform. The one soliloquy in which Harry explains himself to himself confides his intent to simulate lawlessness in order to "arouse more wonder" by the pretense of his having suddenly acquired responsible sobriety. Since Henry Monmouth refers on two subsequent occasions to his plan of simulation we must take it seriously. Moreover, we may sense Hal takes no satisfaction in his celebrated dissipations. He enjoys Falstaff's company only when it affords him opportunity for a combat of wits. The competition answers to his delight in victory whatever the field of exercise. Thus Hal can find even in Eastcheap enjoyments, which, while simulating dissipation, actually satisfy his taste for spirited exertion. Shakespeare's refinement upon the classical conception of psychic dynamics lies in his recognition of the utility for advancing spirited ambition afforded by pretending low vice. As a dramatist he knows, as does Hal, that "nothing pleaseth but rare accidents." This is in keeping with his sensitivity to theatricalism as a component of public life. That all the world's a stage no one knows better than Henry Monmouth.

Yet Shakespeare further resembles the classical moralists in discerning the political costs incidental to a reputation for viciousness even if the vices be counterfeit. Hal's pretense of lawlessness and dissipation encourages lawlessness in earnest from common thieves as well as rebellion on the part of subjects who fear such a prince's succeeding to the throne. Then, since the pretense largely constitutes the heir-apparent's preparation for rule, one has to wonder whether Hal has set himself to crave ever more spectacular *coups de theatre* as that which he has first contrived. Where does the king go from here? Eliot's first tempter failing to revive in Thomas Becket a taste for diversions he had indulged in youth says in parting he will leave the Archbishop to his "higher vices." Shakespeare similarly directs attention to the problem of enlisting spiritedness in the service of justice and confining it to that function. In the *First Alcibiades* and again in *The Republic* Plato's Socrates takes on the task of educating high-spirited young noblemen because he grasps that although anger of the sort occasioned by indignation over injustice belongs to spirited souls, their love of honors and victory at times promotes, but with equal probability at other times opposes, justice.

The concluding scene of *Henry IV, Part 2* displays Hal's submitting himself to the Lord Chief Justice after having boxed the ears of this highest officer of the law after the king. Yet a cloud of uncertainty still occludes the "reformed" Prince, now King, because this turnabout Harry has seized as yet another wonder-arousing spectacle securing his accession and attendant glory without cost to himself. *Part 2* ends without having established the new king's capacity for promoting justice in circumstances wherein he cannot expect spectacular glory. To my mind the final play of the tetralogy answers the question of Henry's devotion to justice in the negative. *Henry V* depicts a brilliant self-mastering leader conducting a war unjust in its aims and big with predictable troubles for victorious England, troubles Shakespeare had already depicted in the first tetralogy and to which he has the Chorus make allusion in an Epilogue appended to this final play of his Henriad.

I should mention another feature common to Shakespearean characterization and classical moral psychology, this too accompanied by a Shakespearean refinement. The better known version of the classical teaching I have been expounding maintains that reason governs passion not directly but in partnership with spiritedness. The spirited emotions aiming at honor or at avoiding shame join with reason to subdue appetites that look no farther than immediate sensual pleasures or avoidance of pain. Diverging from this predominant view, Shakespeare appears to consider spiritedness more disruptive of reason than the bodily passions.[5] More thorough-going in disruption than mere sensualists, spirited souls precipitate the large commotions, the wars, assassinations, usurpations, revenges, and sexual intrigues dramatized in Shakespeare's tragedies and histories. Their harm begins within individual souls and extends to societies. Ambition, anger or indignation, and will to prevail over others inflict disorder within the individual intellect together with ruin upsetting civic order, upheavals more terrific than the nuisances sensuality precipitates. For one Falstaff whose drinking, lusting, and thieving disturb the peace we see a dozen instances of murders, tortures, foreign and civil wars, mass proscriptions, corruption of law, and depredations upon property caused by ambition, will to power, or even patriotic anger (Brutus's) directed against ambition (Caesar's). Mark Antony afflicts himself with inconstancy and inflicts harm upon others not from simple lust but from desire to arouse admiration for the singularity of his and Cleopatra's glamorized public display of their love. Falstaff's incontinence, in itself merely harm on the small scale, does not take on real consequence until Prince Hal exploits his company and low amusements to advance a scheme for cornering a market in fame. Macbeth desires not power simply but the honor that attaches to exercising power. He more regrets loss of honor than the loss of wife and heaven. By thus calling into doubt the idea that spiritedness inclines to ally with reason does Shakespeare part company with a classical teaching he otherwise supports? Or, alternatively, does my impression owe simply to a dramatist's having chosen to populate his stage with characters whose choices are of the sort to generate momentous political consequences?

A related issue arises from noting two distinct meanings of *reason* or the *rational*. To exercise reason in relation to the other sources of the soul's activity is to conduct one's self rationally, to achieve self-government, as commonly said. But we also designate with the same word the faculty employed in science, in theoretical speculation, by which we understand grasping the nature of things. To what degree does the latter, speculative science, depend upon the former, moral excellence? Is the desire to know itself subject to regulation on behalf of some super-ordinate moral obligation, or is an all-consuming intellectual desire the one unregulated regulator? Does discerning the natures of things require first subduing passion and spiritedness? Or, to reverse the question, can one act in accord with justice if one does not seek to know natures and that order of the whole referred to as Nature? One derives from the plays a sense of the dramatist's conviction that doing justice requires intelligence in addition to benevolence. Does good government require a discernment wider or beyond prudence, require an understanding more theoretical than what consists with wise management? Equally crucial with regard to Shakespeare's portrayal of public figures who impress us with their practical intelligence, to what extent is self-knowledge enabling self-direction dependent upon knowing the nature of things? Is moral excellence dependent upon excellence in the realm of theory? The example afforded by Prospero's studies would seem to deny Shakespeare's having considered the two functions of reason to be identical. Prospero says his preoccupation with cultivating science—even though the science had been the "liberal arts"—so undermined his governance that it provoked evil ambition in his brother and caused his dukedom to lose its liberty. Then, does Shakespeare give precedence to practical intelligence over theoretical? Or is it rather that the practical does depend upon the theoretical but only if the theoretical can keep mindful of politics while attending to studies apparently remote from politics? Something more than Prospero's personal safety seems at stake, since, if the security of the contemplative were the only concern, Prospero could remain on his isle with or without his daughter, continue to have his needs provided by Caliban and rough magic, and live solely for those joys of unimpaired contemplation extolled by philosophers as otherwise disparate as Plato from Machiavelli? Then have I inverted the hierarchy Shakespeare actually has suggested? Is it that reason as governing has priority over reason as knowing essences or universals? Or, is it that Shakespeare has Prospero return to Milan and rule because Shakespeare thinks theory itself defective—precisely as theory—until completed by actual political rule, in Prospero's case completing a virtue not yet attained?

Connected to this question one perceives another. Cicero says he diverges from Plato by his maintaining that some men can govern passion without invoking spirited emotions to assist reason. Cicero says he never knew Scipio Africanus to exhibit anger even in the midst of combat. Does Shakespeare conceive such self-sufficing reason in Prospero? At the crisis of the play Prospero says he is disturbed and his daughter says she has never seen him more so. Yet we have earlier witnessed him pretending to feel anger. Does he do so now for the benefit of Ferdinand, his chosen son-in-law and presumably his chosen successor? Does Shakespeare's Caesar experience either fear or anger as observers believe he does, or does he coolly fabricate and dissimulate? In the instances just cited does the psychic chain of command proceed, not immediately from reason governing spiritedness which, in turn, regulates passion, but directly from the reason—a platonic charioteer revised, holding the reins of just one pinto horse representing spirited and passionate impulsions together?

Of that I am not certain, nor can I help much with a more vexing question: namely, when reason governs, never mind whether directly or indirectly calling on spiritedness for assistance, to what does reason look? No Shakespearean evidence occurs to suggest reason takes its bearings by reference to hyper-uranian ideas, as Plato's Socrates speculates on one occasion. Hobbes would say calculation looks to the satisfaction of the last appetite felt prior to choice. Of this alternative likewise we lack dispositive evidence though Shakespeare depicts an abundance of unreflective characters to which the Hobbesian account would seem to apply. With some of the more thoughtful characters we are uncertain as to what the last passion preceding choice may be, whereas in the few most thoughtful, passion may seem never to exercise imperious command over reason.

The reader will have already grasped the connection between the queries I have thus far proposed, on the one hand, and, on the other, the problem of determining a Shakespearean understanding of honor. "Honor" designates with a single word two quite different, sometimes even opposed, dispositions. Honor in the sense of repute, credit, fame, glory, human respect one must consider a thing relative, that is, relative to what attracts praise from whatever body of opinion the seeker of fame has chosen to pass judgment on his plea. Honor in the sense of the deservedly honorable carries the meaning of an absolute standard of worth, what intrinsically warrants esteem whether or not it attracts opinion favorable to its possessor. A person who is honorable in this sense may be indifferent to honor in the sense of favorable opinion.

If his demonstrated merit should confirm him in this self-estimate, we recognize him for the self-respecting, great-souled, or magnanimous man. Sonnet 94 appears to present such a figure in its first eight lines. Caesar's North Star speech just prior to his slaying envisions a great-souled ruler as immoveable as the mind depicted in the sonnet. Yet cannot self-respect be groundless? As for Shakespeare's conception of what might qualify for the intrinsically honorable, would it not be the case that to determine in what it consists we should need to answer some of the questions previously posed? Must we not determine especially what constitutes for Shakespeare that good, truth, or standard by looking to which reason governs the other elements of the soul? Reason as self-control seems to function negatively, by imposing restraints. But is there no positive impulsion, nothing to stir reason so as to set it moving, and moving toward some desirable good itself beyond restraint? Moreover, if we find that Shakespeare invites allegiance to a Supreme Being, would it not be necessary in order to arrive at a self-respect grounded in right judgment that the self-examining soul know the nature of that Being? If that Supreme Being equates with the Biblical Jehovah or with Jesus, self-respect, must be regarded as, so to speak, beside the point. For Jew, Christian, or Moslem the point lies in keeping oneself constantly mindful of the necessity of deferring every honor, redirecting every credit to God. Such is the meaning of the first of the two commandments which on the authority of both Deuteronomy and Jesus contain the entire law of God. Great deeds and virtues attributed to such figures as Abraham, Jacob, Moses, or David in truth belong to the God of Israel. Nothing of Deuteronomy's injunction alters for followers of Jesus who himself yields all glory to the Father. St. Paul says of properly disposed Christians "Our glory is the testimony of our conscience" (II Corinthians 1:12). But even conscience must not credit itself but rather yield all praise to the divine grace which implants and sustains conscience. Among Shakespeare's characters the one and only spokesman for such a view will be found in Henry Monmouth who decrees death for those of his soldiers who should presume to claim any part of the honor of the victory at Agincourt. This from the leader who prior to that conflict had inspired his men to a combat miracle by promising them lifelong fame and membership in a select brotherhood sharing his royal blood.

Harry displays the practical wisdom of speaking as if all depends on God, but only after exertions conducted in the belief that all depends on oneself. Neither will one discover the speaker of the sonnets anywhere disposed to practice the self-abnegation counseled in the gospels and by Paul. Shakespeare as sonneteer goes the length of assuring his beloved of deathless fame on the strength of his confidence of the fame in prospect for these sonnets. But of course since the beloved will never be named he must find what satisfaction he can in imagining that nothing other than these monuments of ink to Shakespeare's own excellence will outlive him. Anxiety for honorable standing in the eyes of others appears to figure in the same degree that love figures as a concern among all men and women, pagan, Christian, or Jew, of ancient eras or modern, Roman, British, French, or Italian. Honor-seeking can show as conspicuously in women as in men: Volumnia, Lucrece and Cleopatra match almost any male aspirant in their desire for renown. Scholarly learning attracts the interest of noblemen only in a single play, wherein certain leisured aristocrats renounce love of women to set up a college of scholar wannabes. Yet they found their think tank not for the sake of knowledge itself but to acquire the celebrity they suppose attends the learned. Only in a single play does Shakespeare focus his plot on middle-class characters, but in that play the wives of Windsor are merry because they secure their wifely honor by contriving a series of humiliating deceptions they inflict upon the titled Sir John Falstaff. Descending to the groundlings, neither Roman nor British commoners are self-starters in pursuit of recognition, but they can be roused to spasms of ambition by their betters and do dependably respond to shame. Love and honor impel human beings with about equal force equally universal in extent as well as comparably diverse in application.

Shakespeare's plays depict the effects of honor-seeking upon the individual soul and, at the same time, upon the common life of civil societies. Taking first the operation of the impulse upon the individual soul, I propose an accounting of effects by a cost-benefit assessment. What comes to sight from considering what ambition seeks and placing in the balance what it must pay to enjoy the benefit ambition has projected for itself?

I think we see the ledger emerging in this way: The person who sets his bearings by honor's star expects, and may achieve, the virtues men agree should earn honor while he raises his sights above petty concerns. Such a soul may enjoy thereby the liberty one identifies with self-sufficiency, yet still win the friendship of others engaged in similar efforts, and taste in prospect a sort of personal immortality in the minds of future ages. Credit in other men's eyes gives assurance of worth, bestows power, with power greater security for those one loves as well as some means of assisting those more distant who deserve support. Credit enables action and enlarges the scope of effectual action. In a Lucrece we see love for honor produce courage, a wider sense of responsibility, and a keener practical intelligence; in a Coriolanus ambition produces patriotism and contempt for ease and trifling pleasures; in a Brutus love of honor sustains attachment to the common good and the friendship of superior men; in an Antony nothing but honor's residue keeps alive valor, hardiness, and generosity. Honor sustained or sought for supports in a Hotspur valor, contempt for dishonesty and resistance to usurped authority; in a Falconbridge, manly independence; in a Katherine of Aragon, feminine independence; in a Henry V, military and political genius; in a Hamlet, restored respect, however transient, for the obligations of a prince; in a Duke Vincentio, a resolve to reform his city; in the Windsor wives, a spirited defense of domestic integrity.

On the debit, honor's attractions exact their costs in undermining self-knowledge, independence, and justice. Self-knowledge—if understood to consist in perceiving what one is against the measure of what a human being ought to be—suffers from courting the unreliable measure of opinion. So suffers also independence. Coriolanus seeks to be self-sufficient yet a selfless servant of his country. But because he mistakes honor for a great-souledness that can subsist without striving for repetitions of public approval he renders himself vulnerable to a populace and tribunes who refuse their approval, and inflexibly attached to contention with fellow citizens. Brutus seeks to resolve a difficult political crisis by consulting what he thinks public opinion expects of him rather than by giving due thought to those conditions that indicate the republic cannot be resurrected, then declines sensible means to an end dubious enough in its aim because he wants to maintain a reputation for purity of motives. Though not a hypocrite he thrusts back opportunities for self-knowledge preoccupied as he is with causing others to think well of him and on that basis thinking well of himself. Antony and Cleopatra are similarly preoccupied with calling a world to witness the singularity of their life of love such that their governance suffers as well as their love which languishes when it cannot draw upon the excitement provided by public display. Hotspur's mind full of ambitions for military distinction cannot serve him in his other capacity as coordinator of a rebellion and judge of men. Hamlet admires the ambitious Fortinbras with such misguided emulation that he forgets the Norwegian's unjust march against Hamlet's country and in dying gives his consent to Denmark's losing its independence to this bravo. He thereby proves more successful in assisting the foreign prince to avenge his father against Hamlet's own father than he has been in avenging his own father against his father's murderer. Henry Monmouth conducts a war unjust to France and not wise for the welfare of his own realm in order to provide an opportunity for his glory to surpass the spectacular exhibitions he has contrived for himself in the several overturning of expectations he has arranged for himself in the three previous plays. Does Shakespeare suggest that pursuit of honor is indispensable yet an unreliable ally of justice and prudence? Indispensable nonetheless because no other motive proves so effective for attaching spirited souls to public life? Does Shakespeare then agree with St. Augustine who thought he disparaged Roman virtues by imputing to Romans the motive of self-glory? Alternatively, does Shakespeare agree with the imputation but not with Augustine's blanket disparagement? And, if so, is it because he rates the public life more highly than Augustine, or because his faith in higher purposes is less assured than Augustine's?

The reader might conclude from the foregoing that I am proposing the dramatist conducted in his plays an argument with himself over the worthiness of cultivating reputation. So I am, yet not the sort of self-debating that enjoys running up to a blank wall. Think of it rather as an investigation leading to the issue of the need for identifying by what wisdom the energy derived from this universal human desire may be regulated for the perfection of the soul and the good of souls associated in civil societies. Even without definitive answers to the questions earlier posed we may profit from considering briefly what I have called this relative aspect of Shakespeare's thoughts upon honor.

If the spirited impulse be thus universally distributed what then can one recognize to be relative and various in Shakespeare's portrayal of honor? Honor proves to be from play to play relative to the varied character of political regimes depicted therein. The nature, costs, and benefits of the universal disposition Shakespeare shows to be relative to the particular form of political sovereignty that obtains in the regime depicted in any particular play.

Shakespeare has depicted the fortunes of two regimes over a course of time sufficient to reveal interdependencies between political institutions and the pursuit of honor. Rome in both republican and imperial eras, Britain, a monarchy in process of fundamental change, are his chosen settings for plays written in the early, the middle, and as well in the last years of his career. These plays together with one narrative poem Shakespeare has set, moreover, early, middle, and late in the respective histories of the two regimes. The beginning and end of Rome he considers and depicts Britain prior to its Christian era and extending up to the reign of Henry VIII with a forecast of the mode of rule initiated by Elizabeth. Of the two sets of plays, one can say, as Shakespeare has had one of his Romans say: "Honor is [his] story." The Roman republic he imagines to have been founded upon a noblewoman's resentment of dishonor suffered from the son of a tyrant. Junius Brutus exploits her indignation to change Rome's constitution, extending the personal revenge to a political indignation against monarchy. Viewed in process of extemporizing institutions in the time of Coriolanus and then in retrospect from the crisis depicted in *Julius Caesar*, we see the principle that informs the Roman republic. Republican constitution, law, and education look to realize a conception of justice one may express in the formula: limitation of will maintained by competition for honors. Limitation of will follows upon a premise that all men without institutional restraints incline to partisan mischief and that the arbitrariness of tyrants licenses criminality in the sovereign. Roman republicans reject monarchy because they will not expose themselves to the risk of kings degenerating to tyrants. Their conception of rule of law envisions a condition in which no citizen should suffer subjection to the arbitrary will of others while the citizenry collectively are kept safe from rulers enforcing their arbitrary will. The republic exists for the sake of denying anyone authority to say—as Shakespeare's Caesar on one occasion asserts: "The cause is in my will." A plural executive, a legislative authority shared by a Senate acting only in concert with popular ratifying assemblies, popular vote on chief executives nominated by the Senate, written laws, and the vetoes and interpositions entrusted to the tribunes, all these provisions evolving in response to several historical crises answer to the purpose of shackling the partisan and arbitrary. The achieved result republican Romans extol as their liberty. This constitution has a soul, a principle of self-movement relying on a renewable source of energy. Competition for honors constitutes the animating principle. Not just any distinctions command esteem in Shakespeare's Rome. Excellence in science or the fine arts never attracts notice among the republicans Shakespeare presents. Roman religion produces nothing resembling the saintliness for which a few Christians will come by such wide renown as they will acquire, though not by the saints' desire. The strange notion of there being an excellence in sexual love appears only once the Empire has come to pass and even so Antony and Cleopatra are viewed as exotics. Chastity, fidelity, and patriotism earn distinction for Lucrece, Virgilia, Volumnia, Valeria, and Brutus's Portia because these attainments support the public good. Service to the republic, whether service be shown in fields military, political, or domestic, continues to provide the only occupation deserving of praise so long as the republic endures. Even partisanship suitably confined can sustain this constitution. Shakespeare's patricians enjoy expressing contempt for commoners, but so long as the class preens its snobbery the individuals comprising the class keep themselves safe from descending to demagoguery. The republican patrician Casca supposes the demagogue Caesar must faint away from the collected halitosis emitted from an adulating plebeian crowd. Once a preeminently successful patrician general overcomes the snobbishness he takes in with his mother's milk, the republic must perish. Coriolanus thinks his honor depends upon his despising commoners. Brutus has something of the common touch but would not be a Caesar (though one voice in a crowd he momentarily captivates shouts he should). Pompey seems to have tried but Caesar beat him. Cassius might descend to rise if he had not been beaten in a previous war. Caesar stoops to conquer armed with requisite military prowess and party machinery. Alternatively, one can say once the republic has become an empire in its extent it has created thereby conditions for a single extraordinary man combining military with party leadership to terminate competition for honors by definitively surpassing all competitors. Caesar has contrived so to live, and perhaps has devised so to die, that he institutionalizes his name, thereby arranging perpetuity for his redirecting all public honors to himself.

If one should conclude as I do that the constitution Shakespeare has attributed republican Rome manages for five centuries to regulate ambition in a manner conducive to securing a durable independence together with liberty under law, and unprecedented security for individual rights, one would infer Shakespeare means to commend a republican form of government.

That inference leads to my final questions, these regarding Shakespeare's portrayal of England's constitution during an era extending from King John to Henry VIII. Does Shakespeare's England possess means of channeling ambition comparable to those he has attributed the Roman republic? Evidently not. Shakespeare's depiction of the British monarchical constitution seems to make it quite distant from that of the Roman republic because the basis of claims to distinction voiced or assumed by Shakespeare's Englishmen appear almost always personal and remote from serving public good, as distinct from promoting family interests or the personal interests of other noblemen, including monarchs.

Yet my further question must venture somewhat beyond the bounds ordinarily observed by literary criticism: does England seem so distant from Roman consciousness of and devotion to a res publica because it was so, in fact, or because Shakespeare has by omission misrepresented the British constitution of the era he has dramatized? A virtual absence of Parliament as a feature of England's constitution only just less important than the monarch is the omission or suppression to which I refer. So rarely do the history plays make mention of Parliament and so little is made of the legislative body on the few occasions it receives notice that it is fair to say Parliament has no dramatic presence. Its scant nominal presence just suffices to cause one to notice the institution's effectual absence. If we had no record on which to rely save the Shakespeare Histories we would not know that Parliament was divided into a House of Lords and a House of Commons. A sharp ear for one remark made by an Archbishop in a single scene of a single play (*Henry V*) might produce an inference that a certain body of men called Parliament had some role in publicly deliberating upon legislation, yet one could infer nothing regarding the authority of that body relative to the king's authority. No Shakespearean king appears before a Parliament or is reported to have done so, or proposes he will, or regrets he has or has not. No Shakespearean king—save one (see *2H4* V.ii.134, V.v.103)—ever mentions Parliament. All the more striking the anomaly when one takes account of English jurists writing in the era Shakespeare has depicted. These writers emphasize rule of law and the coordinate role of Parliament with monarch in making laws. For this reason Fortesque concludes his Britain of the fifteenth century realizes Thomas Aquinas' model of a royal and political regime, "political" here meaning pertaining to a *polity*, Aristotle's term for a mixed regime, or subsequent ages would say, a republic.[6] Sir Thomas Smith, Elizabeth's favored legal scholar explicitly categorizes Britain as a "res publica" in the title he gives to his well-known legal commentary and in that work maintains sovereignty to be vested in Parliament.[7] Although it should be noted that such declarations were usually attended by the reservation that Parliament to be complete must provide for the presence of the king in its sessions and that of course the members are convened by royal writ and can be dismissed by him, even so the jurists cannot be held to have treated the deliberative body as though it did not share sovereignty with England's monarchs.

It must remain a matter of conjecture why in rendering several crises of his country's history spanning more than two centuries Shakespeare should have thought proper to have drawn a veil over an essential feature of the nation's constitution. It could be that he has intended thereby to assert a view of effectual truth in opposition to professions "officially" sponsored. However much Englishmen take comfort in supposing they live under laws collegially produced, in truth Parliament's role counts for next to nothing in comparison to less public determinations devised by kings and their court favorites. Or, to conjecture from the opposite quarter, it may be an attentive element of the audience he expects to carry home from the theater a lesson subsequently to be espoused by Whigs. Misrule is the massive impression conveyed by the ten Histories. Hence for champions of a stronger Parliament the plays would admonish with the lesson: observe what Englishmen suffer from arrogant as well as from weak monarchs who have sought to evade their responsibility to act in concert with a representative deliberative body. Whatever may account for Shakespeare's distortion, his Englishmen are neither good Romans honor-loving yet regulated by sound political institutions, nor good Christians contemptuous of honor-seeking but thereby the more devoted to rectitude before the eyes of a God who sees all and requires righteousness. They desire to be well thought of as much or more than Shakespeare's Romans do. But for Shakespeare's English nobility honor takes the form of precedence in the favors bestowed by the monarch. The dispensing of honor is thus all too personal, the grounds upon which honor is claimed or conferred are often far from clear. Absent Parliament the pursuit of honors among Shakespeare's Englishmen appears to have neither a proper field for its exercise nor a means for such regulation as would channel ambition toward promoting the safety and good of the realm. When we observe Shakespeare's Romans we do seem to learn something of Rome. Whether we learn something equally reliable about the English constitution by reading Shakespeare's Histories depends it seems upon resolving the question of his intent in his apparent infidelity to what actually was.

Notes

1. Sonnet 146 with its lament over a soul held captive by a "sinful" body and with its concluding adjuration to seek immortal life appears to attest conventional Christian spirituality. Yet its tenor, if orthodox, does not seem to carry over to any of the other 153 poems of the sequence. Moreover, immortality may even here refer to durable fame earned by poetic excellence or to living eternally in contemplating timeless truth. In any event the poem conveys no sense of devotion to a personal deity.

2. I have in mind similar discussions of a tripartite soul to be found in the three Platonic dialogues *Republic*, *Phaedrus*, and *Timaeus*. There are some differences in the three versions, and it is unclear to me whether one of the three accounts is to be preferred, or, indeed, if what is common among the three should be taken as a Platonic doctrine. A tradition of commentary has accorded Platonic "doctrinal" status to the three-part schemata. See, for instance, Plutarch's reference to the horses of the soul in his *Life of Marcus Antonius*.

3. Paul Cantor has proposed Shakespeare's assortment of characters in *The Tempest* intends to display the classical psychic divisions with Prospero embodying reason speculative and practical, Ariel and Ferdinand spiritedness, and Caliban, Stephano, Trinculo the bodily passions requiring government. See "Prospero's Republic: Shakespeare's Politics in *The Tempest*," in *Shakespeare as Political Thinker*, eds. John E. Alvis and Thomas G. West (ISI Press, 2000, revised edition) 241–60. I suggest the relevance of this assumption to Shakespearean characterization generally in the dramas, narrative poetry, and the sonnets. The notion seems to me to account for more than either the theory of humors or a modern psychology that professes to treat the dynamics of the mind independently of moral judgments.

4. Once Bolingbroke has become the monarch we see in the two plays named for his reign that the burdens of royal office appear to place him in a new light. The scheming opportunist of *Richard II* now in private conversations with his son acknowledges himself to have been such, referring to his "bypaths and indirect crook'd ways" for which he prays "O God forgive" (*2H4* IV.iii.313, 347). Then, as

he approaches death, his grief has combined with genuine fear for the future of his subjects in the lawless reign he anticipates from his successor. Bolingbroke may be unique among Shakespeare's kings for moral improvement upon acquiring power. As for his wisdom, the legislative plan he bequeaths his son for creating a new order of noblemen from taxes levied on ecclesiastical holdings arguably rests upon a basis more just and farsighted than the war Henry V finances and seeks to legitimate by bribing Archbishops with the promise of preventing his father's tax legislation, then being deliberated in Parliament.

5. In this respect Shakespearean moral psychology resembles Virgil's portrayal of spiritedness in the *Aeneid* (i.e. in his depicting of Dido, Turnus, and Aeneas), as well as Cicero's account in *Tusculan Disputations*. I may misunderstand Plato's Socrates, since I am assuming his assertion that the spirited emotions draw upon reason implies that spiritedness is more docile to reason than the lower passions. Yet my assumption does not follow of necessity from the partially rational character Socrates attributes to the spirited part of the soul. Similarly, from the same assumption I may have misunderstood Aristotle. These are issues requiring a more thorough sifting than can be attempted here.

6. Sir John Fortesque, *On the Laws and Governance of England*, ed. Shelley Lockwood (Cambridge University Press, 1997) 49. A similar claim for Parliament is found in Thomas Bracton, *De Legibus et Consuetudinibus Angliae*, ed. George Woodbine, tr. Samuel E. Thorne (Belknap Press of Harvard University, 1968) 33.

7. Sir Thomas Smith, *On the Commonwealth of England* II.1. Given the likelihood that in writing his *Richard III* Shakespeare acquainted himself with Sir Thomas More's narration of the events Shakespeare incorporates in his play, he would have encountered in either More's Latin or English version the statement that the authority of Parliament is "complete and absolute." See *The Complete Works of Thomas More*, tr. and ed. Daniel Kinney (Yale University Press, 1986) Vol. 15: 320.

2

~

Love, Honor, and the Dynamics of Shakespearean Drama

John C. Briggs

For purposes of teaching great works of literature, and for the sake of teaching oneself—perhaps to regain what once seemed within one's grasp but has now proven elusive, misunderstood—it is sometimes necessary to resort to themes and topics that are out of fashion not only with students but also the greater part of recent literary scholarship, even out of fashion with oneself. Asking about the relation of love and honor in Shakespeare's plays, and in particular the bearing of love and honor on the dynamics of the plays' power to move us, risks the appearance of naiveté, even complacency. But when formerly widespread assumptions about love and honor fall into disuse and obliquity, a good deal of reconstructive energy needs to be devoted to rehabilitate them so that the plays can be read and experienced as fully as possible. Sometimes only then can students and jaded scholarly imaginations absorb and judge scenes, characters, and whole plots.

To the sophisticated eye, such an approach is vulnerable to the charge of oversimplification. The topical pairing of love and honor, evoking an array of questions about the relation between *eros* and *thumos*, or the nature of emotion and virtue, tends to come across these days as willfully traditional, old hat, esoteric, conducive to habits of self-indulgent literary appreciation. It seems insufficiently heuristic or theoretical, and not clearly useful for making the world a better place. If it cannot meet such criticisms, a traditional or neo-traditional criticism that invokes love and honor will not only fail to meet theorists' skepticism; it will not confront many students' certainty that their own experience or ignorance of love and honor is authoritative, or their complementary conviction that there is nothing sure but live-and-let-live relativism. What is to keep interpretation of any play of Shakespeare from these extremes, including the academic disposition to look for agendas, symptoms, or historical forces in place of complex trajectories of character, passions, and ideas? A modern psychology of instincts and biases, for whatever help it offers, is not clearly superior to older ways of grasping psychological depth and moral / political complexities that are generated by the tension and complementarity of *thumos* and *eros* in Shakespeare's dramaturgy.

I

The pairing of love and honor as framing ideas for a collection of essays on Shakespeare's plays also evokes a way of understanding characters' motivations and aspirations in terms of political life as well as psychology. Love and honor are not only opposites in a sense; they are by their nature (though in what precise ways it is our task to inquire) accountable to one another. As love draws toward marriage, it engages political understandings, sanctions, and incentives regarding a particular polity's conception of marriage. In *Romeo and Juliet*, for example, the alliance of families is of course a crucial political strategy. The Prince's cousin Paris (we assume with the Prince's permission and perhaps encouragement) proposes marriage to Juliet under circumstances that might help defuse the Montague / Capulet feud with the bond of a ruler's blood. The Friar dares to attempt a direct alliance of the warring parties, which he says he must at first conceal until political circumstances are favorable to revealing it. Unfortunately, each strategy undermines the other for reasons related to the tension between love and honor in Verona. If we do not take seriously the implications and political importance of such marital alliances, we miss many of the rich potentialities of Shakespeare's Verona. Missing the power of love to challenge, explode, or secure those alliances, we risk losing even more.

To ask directly about love and honor in Shakespeare increases the chances of rediscovering important things: the play's revelations of personality, the springs of action in the play's plot, and the consequent trajectories of Shakespearean character that have proven so enduringly moving to generations of audiences. When critical approaches go along with critical fashion by looking immediately for hidden motives and mechanisms, or by so problematizing character that each dramatic person in the play is a crisscrossing of social influences and psychological forces, instead of (not in addition to) a dynamic of thought, choice, action, and circumstance, they miss or downgrade the plays' persistently edifying and curative popularity. In ignoring the nature and dynamic of honor and love in those dramas, they are unlikely to consider that dynamic as a wellspring of character and political life. The interplay of irascible, yet honor-loving *thumos* and sexual, yet high-aspiring *eros* forms and tests character and polity in play after play: comedy, tragedy, history, and romance.

Some things are so large, or so taken for granted in these dramas, that sophisticated modern criticism is frequently tempted to ignore them, or to dismiss them as discredited conventions. Today, anger is stigmatized as a clinical condition. It is "OK" to be mad, but anger that is not approvable moral anger is now likely to be considered a form of psychosis or criminal rage. The Aristotelian idea that anger is driven by a sense of justice, and hence a sense of honor in defending justice—whether or not thumotic passion is well- or ill-directed—is alien to modern sensibilities. Ancient imaginations knew the type of the wrathful madman perhaps better than moderns do, for they knew Achilles. By contrast, the modern tendency (in peacetime, at least) to reject the traditional possibility of the legitimacy of war for honor's sake militates against seeing war when it plays a non-baleful role in Shakespeare's plays. Not just war but the ubiquity of war in Shakespeare's works easily goes unnoticed, along with the framing power of war to color character and action. The comedies are as likely as the tragedies to share in this pattern: not only in response to the presence of war but as dramatic motions influenced by the potentialities of anger and honor-driven conflict. Without an acknowledgement of the deep psychological grounding of warlike, honor-loving qualities in a variety of characters and polities in circumstances that challenge and form them, our reception of Shakespearean action risks becoming incoherent.

War is not the only thing. As Mars courts Venus, or rivals her, love is its problematic complement in pre-modern understandings of human possibilities. The destructive power of love can invade almost any plot—not only in the tragedies (for example in Cleopatra's ruination of a willing Antony and Lady Macbeth's seduction of her husband's honorable inhibitions), but in the comedies and tragicomedies (as in Prospero's old self-undoing love for his brother Antonio, another Antonio's love-thwarting love for Bassanio in *The Merchant of Venice*, and the near-murderous passions of multiple pairs of lovers in *A Midsummer Night's Dream*).

War is arguably the more commonly unacknowledged, lurking reality that frames almost all the comedies as well as the tragedies. Indeed it is often a formative cause—not merely a color—of the plays' comedic power. Think how much *All's Well that Ends Well* would change without the scourging drama of the frivolous yet challenging Italian wars. Consider *Measure for*

Measure without the lingering effects of war, followed by a long abusive peace and the prospect of a resumption of hostilities. Questions of honor, precedence, and competitive prerogatives not only provoke jousting, duels, and incipient warfare between groups as soon as the action begins. They inhere in, exercise, elevate, and deform characters and plots. Though in recent films and stage productions the seriousness of the war-frame is often ignored, reduced to innocuous parody, or hyped as gratuitous violence, the implicit martial frame—even if it exists only in the rumor, memory, or imagination—draws upon, and draws out, greater and baser possibilities of character and action.

When love and war mix seemingly unrestrainedly in Shakespearean drama, the disastrous result is evident: deformation and tragedy (*Othello, Macbeth, Antony and Cleopatra, Lear*), or the self-undoing satire of *Troilus and Cressida*, though even in these cases the persistent frame of war *adds* significance to, even *makes* significant, plots ostensibly driven by erotic energies. When war is a looming possibility yet strangely alienated from the action, as in *Measure for Measure, Hamlet* and *Timon of Athens*, it is the almost un-admitted, missing element—the factor kept in the background yet a contributor to the conflict and the resolution.

Shakespearean comedy is often rightfully characterized as festive, con-ciliatory, conducive to the ceremonies of courtship and marriage. War is by no means welcome, and is kept more or less at a distance, for it threatens to shift comedy's foundations. But the prospect of war also engenders, as well as lurks behind, Shakespeare's comic weddings, the byplay of lovers, and the rivalry of suitors. It is not only risked in the dangerous passages of courtship; it is calmed and bridled by reconciliation and comity between rival families and within the souls of the lovers. Often it threatens, as in the last scenes of *Twelfth Night*, to wreck everything at the moment of resolution. Or it enforces a sense of urgency in the proceedings: In Act V of *As You Like It*, we see that Rosalind's plots of courtly testing and reconciliation have been racing against the threat of invasion and civil war. But war also lends a vital ardor to love. The last minute eruption of Duke Orsino's jealousy toward Viola, which issues threateningly from a wounded sense of honor, is also a manifestation of ardent love. The near-miraculous appearance of Olivia's look-alike brother turns that mixture of passions away from violence and self-damage toward a profession of love, which would not come to be, or be itself, without this incorporation of Orsino's expressed capacity for jealousy and retribution.

For Shakespeare, one of the most striking mythic memories of war amidst the offices of peace would have been the famous battle between the human guests and the centaurs at the wedding of King Pirithous, as preserved in Ovid's *Metamorphosis*. Shakespeare of course was schooled in that text. In *A Midsummer Night's Dream*, Bottom proposes that the mechanicals play that battle before the Duke of Athens and his Queen on their wedding night.[1] The ludicrous suggestion is tellingly indecorous. The Duke turns him down: a little play about the famous violent desecration of a king's nuptials (complete with mass rape and slaughter) would be a silly outrage.[2] And yet in another sense it would resonate with the wedding of the moment: Theseus has recently defeated the distinctively warlike Amazon Queen—now his Queen—in a battle of one kingdom against another. She is not quite subdued as the action of the play begins. There must be a wedding, and a consequent discipline of delay that would be incongruous were Hippolyta a mere war-captive. Is the ceremonious pause then merely a conqueror's vanity? Hippolyta and Theseus continue their rivalry—much as Oberon and Titania and the lovers in the forest do, with some danger of cataclysm in nature, or lovers' violence. The royals are partners in the peacetime equivalent of war: the hunt. Their banter over the calls of one another's hunting dogs is a conciliatory, competitive engagement with each other's martial resources. The treaty of their matrimony will be sealed, or lost to disorder, partly through their rivalrous, mutual love of the hunt.

The centaurs of Thessaly, whom Bottom and his friends promise to play for the Duke, did not attack—in Ovid's tale—the wedding from without. They were honored guests and therefore part of the proceedings. Their natures mixed, at least at first, with those of their hosts.[3] As partly uncivilized relatives of the Queen, the centaurs were however unused to drink, and became inebriated. They wrecked the proceedings, their lusts intent upon carrying off the women as their own at all costs. Their centaurish natures, which were graphic reminders of their hosts' dual natures of base and higher elements, mixed with the wedding drink of reconciliation so as to destroy the ceremony's delightful, risky work. The ceremony's magnanimity and erotic sublimation, well-suited to the reconciliation of disparate families, deteriorated into rage and sexual license joined as mutually debasing allies.

The centaurs' outrage not only burst the confines of ceremony; it threatened the foundation of the kingdom. Killed or exiled from Thessaly, the defeated manhorses lived on in poetical allusion to their war and defeat. Modern tourists can see how they persisted in the ancient imagination when they visit the restored Parthenon in Nashville, Tennessee, where their battle with the king's relatives adorns the base of the throne of Athena. The armed goddess, if we believe the scholars who reconstructed her, presided serenely over the scene of carnage, as though acknowledging, embodying, and resolving humanity's divergent potentialities for marriage and mayhem, alliance and misalliance.

Elsewhere in Shakespeare, the intertwinings of love and honor compose a variety of moving plots, as well as forms of character that live on in repetitions of reading and attending. If they are alive to those interactions, audiences are more likely to return to the plays, seeking to shake and temper memories of Shakespearean trauma and relief.

Recall Lear's resolve in the first scene to hold to his kingly word of honor, in the face of his love for Cordelia. In that decaying lordliness, he defies the love that most moves him. The magnitude of his vehement insistence upon honoring his own command is hardly comprehensible without an audience's awareness of his *love* for Cordelia and the high stakes of honor that accompany his division of his kingdom. His political ambition to neutralize France and frustrate civil war by favoring Cordelia with the largest, most powerfully allied portion of Britain becomes a perverted, desperate love—a poisonous cordial he pours into his own ear. The force of the play has much to do with these two things together: on the one hand, Lear's idea of honor (as in the king's words, which, once declared, cannot be taken back) and its potentially ennobling, then twisted power over his love for Cordelia; on the other, the power of that love to ruin his rule. Like Lear we cannot take in the one without the other, though unlike Lear we have the mixed privilege of a feeling witness who is yet distanced enough from the wreck to reflect upon its paradoxes, and the faint though immediately fading possibility that he might have peacefully succeeded.

Think now of the play of love and honor in *Measure for Measure*, in which Isabella, in the process of disciplining herself to be devoted to the Church by taking on the habit of a nun, fiercely defends her honor against Angelo but then submits in silence to the Duke's proposal of marriage at the end of Act V. Whether that silence is self-conscious, honorable consent, or virginal resistance is of course an important question. Is her resistance the re-expression of her preliminary vows as a novice in God's service, or should it be taken as a defense of her maiden honor, which paradoxically might be consistent with the married love that the Duke offers her? Her tentative entry into the convent, with all its rites of purification, involves the gradual taking on of a habit of honorable devotion in preparation for marriage to Christ. When the Duke doffs his disguise as a friar and proposes to her, he is appealing to her awareness, consistent with that process, that her worldly and religious senses of honor have been humbled by new claims of love and what might be the higher honor of becoming espoused to her Lord—whether it be to Christ or to the sometimes designedly Christ-like Duke of Vienna. This is one of the deep problems of that problem play that intrigues and baffles us, that draws us in and warns us off. We are offered the chance to undergo longing and uncertainty about the nature of marriage when marriage is presented as a sacrament of compelling *and flawed* erotic, political, ethical, and religious aspirations.

In *Much Ado About Nothing*, what better variation on this theme of paradoxical relations between love and honor than Beatrice's love-test for Benedict: "Kill Claudio," she declares, in that moment bringing about one of the most striking, disturbing, humorous turns in the play. Benedict will presumably show his love by acting honorably. But what does this mean? He is being asked to destroy Claudio as a result of Claudio's claim of honor against Hero, whom Claudio loves. Hero's apparent loss of honor has spurred Claudio to take revenge upon her precisely because he loves her and sees the honor of their love threatened. If he had succeeded, Benedict would have of course won Beatrice's love—and confirmed her love for her friend—yet only by destroying Hero's chance of recovering her own honor, and her Claudio.

What recovers the situation in *Much Ado* for comedy is not just the Friar's stratagem of fabricating Hero's death. It is the emergence of a deeper interplay of love and honor. The play turns upon Claudio's self-consciously *honorable*, ritualized display of grief for the sake of his lost love, and his publicly resolved submission to marriage so honorable he does not see or wish to see the face of his bride—all the while entering into what he thinks is not possible: the recovery of his lost love in the honorable—though because it is honorable, the most erotically promising—wedding to her look-alike sister, who turns out to be Hero herself transformed by these honorable, erotic acts of grief and the loving Friar's canny stratagem to save Hero's honor. We do not need to disentangle these things to notice their mutually reinforcing appeal to our sympathies amidst the rich, fraught fabric of conflicts they generate. We never completely forget the potentially lethal combinations of love and honor exhibited in many sinister turns earlier in the play. But the comedy mitigates those turns by exercising them almost on the verge of war, not only between lovers but also between characters fresh from real armed conflict, allies in war who, as we have seen, are capable of falling into cruel hatreds.

In all these works of Shakespeare, and in many more if we had time to think of them, the relation of love and honor cannot be adequately felt or described as a mere coincidence, an arbitrary interplay of differences, or a direct conflict of opposites. More importantly, it is often an interaction that contributes mightily to each play's tragicomic structure and impact—its cathartic power as a working out of the dynamics of characters caught and propelled by their choices in plots of comic and tragic possibilities.

II

In *Romeo and Juliet*, we have one of Shakespeare's most fraught, and most moving instances of this phenomenon. In its first scene we see combative wits not sure whether they want to fight or fornicate with their rival clan— insistent upon their martial honors and power over the opposite sex yet not sure whether their martial and sexual fantasies are separate, or even whether they bode murderous or conciliatory impulses. Their witty outbursts manifest a giddy sense of limitlessness mixed with foreboding. It seems as though the liberation of spirit and *contemptus mundi* that mix within the Christian dispensation have somehow heightened the thumotic and erotic impulses of even minor characters in Shakespeare's Verona. They are full of life while courting death. The dangerous conflicts and concordances of love and honor in such an environment, arising within young men of extraordinary ardor and high spirits, infect not only Juliet but also the Friar, and even her aged father. We rarely witness such a sustained, ubiquitous power of doing and undoing elsewhere in Shakespearean drama.

In two other, crucial scenes outside the explicit love plot, the pattern reaches heights of development and cathartic power that tell us something important about the action of the play as a whole, and why it maintains its hold on us. The first is the fight between Mercutio and Tybalt, which ends with Romeo's selfless, defective intervention, the death of his friend, and consequently, Romeo's fatal confrontation with Tybalt. The scene would devolve into melodrama were it not for Mercutio's expansive superiority to his surroundings: the force of his presence, which momentarily joins the company of Falstaff and Hamlet.

It is the ingenious range and rage of that presence that is most memorable, deriving as it does from Mercutio's free and intuitively probing friendship with Romeo—a friendship of great promise not only because Mercutio is the Prince's kinsman but because his affection seems to grow the more he wittily swaggers in the Verona street. Witnessing that interaction within and between Mercutio and Romeo, one wonders whether Mercutio's enlarging, insistent idea of friendship (which Romeo understands better than others)—might nobly rival or save the overall action of the play rather than help doom it. As a cousin of the Prince rather than the warring families, one who freely mixes thumotic rivalry, bawdy affection, and high-minded friendship, he is also a powerful mitigating agent whose character and action work temporarily to moderate the forces of love and honor threatening the lovers and Verona itself.[4] When that spirited love falls victim to Tybalt's underhanded sword, inadvertently aided by Romeo's lovingly incompetent intervention, it is Juliet who takes on Mercutio's mantle so that it can be fashioned for the sake of a love even more radical in its combination of spirited valor and *eros*. Juliet incorporates and purifies, with mortal speed, his mercurial devotion.

The complementary example of loving hate is Romeo's confrontation with Paris just outside Juliet's tomb. It is another interaction of love and honor that holds us suspended between reconciliation and death. Both men act to protect Juliet from desecration. Romeo accosts Paris with a magnanimous lover's plea to let him enter the tomb without fighting. Paris, who we have seen nobly wooing Juliet and who, we know, has no grudge but a desire to honor and protect, dies as prelude to Romeo's end.

Romeo at first avoids the duel; but his counterpart insists, as Romeo himself would in Paris's position. Romeo's rash act of honorable defense sharpens and accelerates his erotic yearning to join Juliet. There Juliet will herself die in the noble Roman way for the sake of her erotic calling. Thus the aspirations of love and honor complement and undermine one another. The lovers' ability to feel and project these cooperative contradictions— combined with their articulate grasp of their condition of being in the throes of those contradictions—makes for a catharsis of fear and pity that we too undergo, at a distance, the more we take in the rich ordeal in them, as well as its nearly successful, then lethal resolution. Insofar as their deaths bring peace between the warring families and within audiences touched by the lovers' passions, the ensuing armistice is an acknowledgement of complicity in a noble waste. Freedom from the play's erotic, thumotic entanglements has entailed a loss.

But this is not enough. We need an account of Friar Lawrence's contribution to the conflict of love and honor leading to the end just described, an analysis of how his work weaves itself into the characterizing relations of love and honor that form of the play. What is to be said, in particular, of the Friar's Christianity and its working conception of honor and love? To what extent do these things underlay and complete the play's mythos, its animating plot?

The Friar is of course Shakespeare's individualized representative of Love's party on Earth: of the Christian dispensation bringing love to a supposedly deed-centered, honor-driven, warlike, highly political world of Judaic piety and Roman virtue. The Friar is no Old Testament Judge or king. He has no official standing in the Veronese Prince's court. In fact we never see him outside his cell until the disastrous last scene, when his panic at being exposed as a political agent in the city's affairs is so great it causes him to abandon Juliet in the tomb.

In one sense, then, the Friar's vocation profoundly disempowers him, removing him physically and philosophically from the Prince and from the work of governing Verona. On the other, however, his active representation of the Christian legacy empowers him to act from above, for the over-arching good of Love. We see him unhesitatingly involved in all the play's intimate affairs of the heart, which no one else but the lovers themselves can enter: Romeo's agony over Rosalind, then over Juliet; the lovers' private resolve to end their lives; their secret joining—in their swift marriage and even (as directed) on the wedding night; as well as Paris's charged diplomatic negotiation with Juliet. On a mission that transcends the usual inhibitions, the Friar has the power—and uses it in the knowledge that he has it—to influence the course of Verona's politics through counsel, secret ceremonies, plots, and a potion. The counsel includes, of course, directions to Juliet about how to lie (see IV.i.89–90), even though it is Juliet whom Shakespeare presents as capable of preserving her honesty even when she is interrogated by her parents.

That these machinations of spiritual and Machiavellian intervention help bring on—indeed effectuate—disaster should not prevent us from noticing how the Friar's ideas of love and honor comment upon and explain a good deal about his actions. His discourse about plants and human nature indicates that he intends to bring peace to Verona by joining and tempering both love and honor, not by suppressing one, or exiling either from the another. Most notably, the Friar does not purpose to eliminate from Romeo or from Verona the thumotic desire for distinction that can foster conflict, for he several times chides Romeo for abandoning it, and bases the substance and timing of his secret plot on the families' and the Prince's continuing desire to defend honorable marriage. By seeking to balance *thumos* with love in an honorable marriage, he plots for an honorable political as well as erotic union so revolutionary in its joining of opposites, so irreversibly blessed and consummated, and so well-timed in its disclosure, that Verona's warring families and the Prince must certify it and so end their broils.

In the Friar's well-worn but still suggestive commentary on herbs and Romeo's condition, we learn that nothing is so vile it does not possess "some special good," nothing so good that if "strain'd from that fair use," it "[r]evolts from true birth" (II.iii.1–22). If "[v]irtue itself turns vice, being misapplied/ And vice sometime by action" is "dignified" (21–22), both love and honor are shriven and implicated in human virtue and folly, depending upon how they are applied and used. "Opposed kings"—"grace and rude will"—encamp in man, and the "worser" must be suppressed. But that "worser"—rude will—is found in love and honor both. (21–22, 29). Each has a will that must be tempered. Thus the Friar condemns Romeo's disabling infatuation with Rosalind as a dotage, the product of his willful imagination and appetitive will. He arranges the secret wedding of Romeo and Juliet without any proof—or any attempt to secure proof—that Romeo's love for Juliet is anything different. When he thinks of his plan, it is the wedding itself and its political impact that will discipline that will and the vices of Verona. Together, love and honor will temper each action of the will to make something good.

This joining of erotic and honor-seeking aspirations is apparently what the Friar has in mind when he commands Romeo to "love moderately" (II. vi.14). It is the result of acting well as an honor-loving man and loving husband, even though the rigors of exile have thrown Romeo's fiery love into cold despair on the brink of suicide. Where Romeo would kill himself rather than suffer the torments of indefinite separation—and (as we sense in his vehemence) rather die than undergo the profound indignity of that separation given the absolute claims of his love—the Friar would have him act like a man by combining his tempered will as a lover with the moderation of his willful fury. He must do both:

Hold thy desperate hand!
Art thou a man? Thy form cries out thou art;
Thy tears are womanish, thy wild acts [denote]
The unreasonable fury of a beast.
Unseemly woman in a seemly man,
And ill-beseeming beast in seeming both. (III.iii.108–11)

III

In the end, of course, the Friar fails. His counsel to the lovers as well as his plan for their reunion miscarry. Love and honor destroy rather than temper one another. He is undeniably instrumental in the lovers' deaths. Taking the path of honor in his disgrace after his cowardly flight from Juliet's side, he speaks truly and thoroughly within the limits of the scene about his contributions to events, and condemns himself as the "greatest" among those the Prince has called "parties of suspicion" (V.iii.222–23). More, he says he is willing to be executed if he is found instrumental for "aught in this." Whatever lesser sanction might be due an accessory, he says he will accept death if he is found to be implicated. Rather than claim his end was Love and his means forgivable, he submits to the judgment of his worldly ruler. The political imperatives of the Prince's rule, including the need to preserve his honor as the preserver of Verona's peace, reassert themselves.

And yet rather than focusing on the Prince's judgment, which we never hear, the conclusion of the play reintroduces the tension and interaction of love and honor by explicitly combining worldly and poetic justice. With measured, conditional clemency, the Prince reassures the Friar by remembering his past services in a persistent, present-perfect tense: "We still have known thee for a holy man." There is no guarantee of immunity from punishment—"Some shall be pardon'd, and some punished" (V.iii.308)—and yet honor and love together strangely reassert themselves in the grander, perhaps ultimately unconvincing, scheme of poetic justice. In this larger sense, poetic justice has punished both Veronese houses for their faction-mongering. They have lost their heirs and stand condemned by evidence of a loving bond which, despite or because of its disastrous end, now seems greater than their rivalry. The Prince too has suffered, with a loss of kinsmen that punishes him for his failure to end the fighting: "All are punished" (V.iii.292–95).

Before the Prince speaks, closure has already been effected by fortune and, paradoxically, the Friar's plot, which has accidentally (and, if we are uncharitable, recklessly) led to the lovers' deaths. The Friar's goal of making Love prevail over warring claims of honor has been achieved, though at a cost that would make monstrous any man's plan to achieve it in the way it has unfolded. The patriarch's reconciliation in the last scene is a ceremony of grief. Is this then a triumph of love?

In the end the play frames the judgment of the Prince and of the play overall as though it were an elusive balance—of love and honor within each character and the intricacies of plot, of political justice weighed against political clemency, and of worldly justice and clemency weighed against some kind of heavenly judgment and forgiveness. I have argued elsewhere[5] that this balance, affected by the way the play molds its sources, is especially arduous and strangely pleasing. It is a cathartic drama whose tenor and impact would not be possible without its rendering of the lovers' climb toward death and the belated, heartbreaking reconciliation that ensues. The play is a tragedy after all, though we have to wonder, taking a cue from Samuel Johnson's Preface, whether Shakespeare in fact turned even this play, as he did many others, into a tragicomedy. As a tragedy it raises deep philosophical and political questions about the strengths and weaknesses of Verona's regime, and of the cross-purposed characters of Shakespeare's Veronese. In this light, the validity of a tragicomic triumph of Love over the tomb is barely conceivable. And yet without Shakespeare's working out of the plots and personalities that are stimulated and tested by these influences—especially in their sensitivity to the mutual claims of love and honor—these philosophical questions would pale. In that working out of these things—largely through Shakespeare's augmentation and departure from his sources—love reappears where honor prevails, and honor where love controls.

This distinguishing play of love and honor, once it is incorporated into teaching and interpretation, appeals to students' and older audiences' experience as well as to the intuition that there must be something more. It removes disabling inhibitions about the play's remoteness, and activates a sense of wonder at what is inspiring because it is somehow deeply familiar and yet beyond us. For the older set, perhaps jaded by dozens of performances and reinterpretations, a recognition of the claims of love and honor in Romeo and Juliet increases the likelihood that the play will call out to be seen and read again and again.

Notes

1. "'The Battle with the Centaurs,' to be sung / By an Athenian eunuch to the harp" (V.i.44–45).

2. Theseus also tells him that he has told Hippolyta the story *already*, to draw attention to his ancestor Hercules, the victor over the raging beasts: "That have I told my love, / In glory of my kinsman Hercules" (46–47).

3. In Castiglione's *Book of the Courtier*, a touchstone of chivalrous conduct, or Sidney's *Arcadia*, from which Shakespeare probably drew his references to centaurs, the idea of courtly perfection is embodied in a man's seemingly effortless chivalry, his masterful blending with his horse.

4. His appropriately named companion, Valentine, is mentioned in the action but does not appear. Mercutio's actual partner in this action is Benvolio, whose prominent intervention in the street brawl of Act I is the complementary work of a good-willed, moderately warlike man working to temper angry claims of honor. Together, Benvolio and Mercutio are catalysts of a peaceful, spirited resolution of Verona's inner and outer conflicts.

5. John C. Briggs, "*Romeo and Juliet* and the Cure of Souls," *Ben Jonson Journal* 16 (May 2009) 281–303.

3

The Spectrum of Love

Nature and Convention in *As You Like It*

Paul A. Cantor

I

As You Like It is the prototypical Shakespearean romantic comedy in its structure.[1] The play begins in a world of sterile and deadening convention, with the older generation tyrannizing over the younger. The oppressed characters must flee to a more natural world, which takes the form of a forest, much as in *A Midsummer Night's Dream*. Released through their encounter with nature from the stranglehold of convention, the youthful characters are able to work out their problems. In particular, they manage to free themselves from the false conceptions of love they have inherited from society, thereby making possible a set of four marriages at the end of the play. This resolution prepares the way for the characters to return to civilization and be reintegrated into society. Thus, the plot of *As You Like It* allows Shakespeare to examine the rival claims of nature and convention,[2] of primitivism and civilization, of the country and the court. In literary terms, this process takes the form of interrogating a long-standing literary convention, the pastoral ideal. As always in dramatizing a clash of forces, Shakespeare does not simply opt for one side over the other.

The characters in conventional positions of power at the beginning of *As You Like It* are presented as usurpers, overturners of the natural order. The play initially seems to suggest that the natural order would be benevolent, if only the force of convention did not tamper with it. Duke Frederick has usurped the throne from his older brother, Duke Senior, the original and rightful duke, the duke by birth. Oliver, by mistreating his younger brother

Orlando, has chosen to disregard the will of their father, who wanted to nurture all his sons, to have each one brought up well. As the play opens, Orlando complains that he is not getting the education he deserves. Contrary to their father's intentions, his brother is bringing him up like a beast:

> For my part, he keeps me rustically at home or (to speak more properly) stays me here at home unkept; for call you that keeping for a gentleman of my birth, that differs not from the stalling of an ox? His horses are bred better. (I.i.7–11)[3]

Complicating matters from the beginning, Shakespeare suggests that nature does not intend human beings to live like beasts. Somehow human nature is different from animal; to be human is to be educated and civilized. As we will see, As You Like It shows what is wrong with the court, while portraying what is healthy about the more natural world of the forest. Still, the basic premise of the play is that human beings are at home in civilization—only in a civilized community can they fully develop their nature. In short, from the beginning Shakespeare denies a simple opposition between nature and civilization.[4] However fitfully and confusingly, nature points human beings to a civilized state.

But misguided and evil actions can thwart the benevolent intentions of nature. Human beings create an order that does not correspond to the natural order, introducing arbitrary distinctions by means of their customs. That is the focus of Orlando's complaint to Oliver:

> The courtesy of nations allows you my better, in that you are the first born, but the same tradition takes not away my blood, were there twenty brothers betwixt us. I have as much of my father in me as you, albeit I confess your coming before me is nearer to his reverence. (I.i.46–51)

Even here, when he criticizes custom, Orlando does not reject it completely. He is willing to allow some legitimacy to the traditional authority of the older brother over the younger. Orlando only claims that custom goes wrong when it totally disregards the facts of human nature.

Shakespeare is dealing here with the broader political problem he takes up throughout his history plays, where it takes the form of the disjunction between the king by convention and the king by nature.[5] Often the man who sits on the throne by inheritance, for example Richard II, has less of a genuinely kingly nature than a man not born to the office, for example Henry Bolingbroke. Shakespeare presents a comic image of this problem at the beginning of As You Like It in the wrestling match. Charles the wrestler is the champion, acknowledged by this community as the king of his sport, and everybody assumes that he can defeat any opponent. Conventional opinion especially scorns Orlando. As the youngest of the challengers, he seems the least likely to dethrone the champion. But in contrast to the situation in politics, in wrestling an objective and unambiguous test of virtue exists. When Orlando defeats Charles in fair combat, he provides a powerful image of youthful natural energy overturning conventional forms of authority. Orlando's wrestling victory is a kind of mock revolt, a symbol of overthrowing the ruler. Charles is in fact associated with both representatives of conventional authority in the play. He is the Duke's champion and also has made a secret pact with Oliver to kill Orlando. The Duke is thus not happy to see Charles beaten. Understanding that this conquest is a challenge to his authority, he ends up in effect banishing Orlando as a result.

Shakespeare uses the wrestling match at the beginning of As You Like It to reveal the way in which society fears the natural strength of the young, and in particular the way Oliver resents his younger brother's virtuous nature:

> I hope I shall see an end of him; for my soul (yet I know not why) hates nothing more than he. Yet he's gentle, never school'd and yet learned, full of noble device, of all sorts enchantingly belov'd, and indeed so much in the heart of the world, and especially of my own people, who best know him, that I am altogether mispris'd. But it shall not be so long, this wrastler shall clear all. (I.i.164–72)

In a parallel to this plot development, Duke Frederick objects to his daughter Celia's friendship with Rosalind, the daughter of Duke Senior, whose rule he has usurped. Convinced that Celia should resent Rosalind's virtue, Frederick wants to separate the two young women. But Celia holds up their bond as an ideal:

> If she be a traitor,
> Why, so am I. We still have slept together,
> Rose at an instant, learn'd, play'd, eat together,
> And whereso'er we went, like Juno's swans,
> Still we went coupled and inseparable. (I.iii.72–76)

In a syntactical image of perfect unity, Celia asserts her identity with Rosalind: "thou and I am one" (I.iii.97). Her father's attempt to interfere with this friendship epitomizes the insistent tendency of authority to try to destroy everything good about the young. That is why in As You Like It, the young must flee the world of authority and convention, in the hope of reversing its distorted values:

> Now go we in content
> To liberty, and not to banishment. (I.iii.137–38)

As Shakespeare repeatedly suggests at the opening of the play, the conventional values of society are not necessarily the true values. In fact they overturn the genuine order of virtues, as Orlando's old servant, Adam, explains to him:

> Know you not, master, to some kind of men
> Their graces serve them but as enemies?
> No more do yours. Your virtues, gentle master,
> Are sanctified and holy traitors to you.
> O, what a world is this, when what is comely
> Envenoms him that bears it! (II.iii.10–15)

The arbitrariness of the conventional order of society is the subject of the long dialogue between Celia and Rosalind about fortune and nature. They present society as a realm in which fortune prevails. The distribution of positions of authority is merely a matter of chance, and genuine differences in human nature are ignored and concealed: "Fortune reigns in gifts of the world, not in the lineaments of Nature" (I.ii.41–42). When the court jester Touchstone joins their conversation, he further emphasizes the arbitrariness of custom. In a passage that anticipates the role of the Fool in *King Lear*, Touchstone bitterly complains about his inability to speak the truth in a social world ruled arbitrarily by convention:

> *Celia.* You'll be whipt for taxation one of these days.
> *Touchstone.* The more pity that fools may not speak wisely what wise men do foolishly. (I.ii.84–87)

Act I of *As You Like It* depicts all that is wrong with the world of conventional authority, thereby making it possible for the audience, as well as the characters, to appreciate the freedom of the forest world.

II

Once the action is transposed to the Forest of Arden in Act II, Duke Senior gives an eloquent statement of the pastoral poetic ideal. Pastoral poetry was very popular in the Elizabethan period, practiced by court poets such as Sir Philip Sidney and Edmund Spenser.[6] Set in a rustic world of shepherds and shepherdesses, and celebrating their simple, peaceful life, this kind of poetry was attractive to the hypersophisticated world of Queen Elizabeth's court. It offered a contrast to and relief from all the intrigue, slander, infighting, and backbiting of Elizabethan court life. In pastoral poetry, typically a figure from the court is introduced into a rural world, thereby allowing the author to weigh the values of the court against the values of the country.

Duke Senior speaks on behalf of the virtues of country life:

> Now, my co-mates and brothers in exile,
> Hath not old custom made this life more sweet
> Than that of painted pomp? Are not these woods
> More free from peril than an envious court?
> Here feel we not the penalty of Adam,
> The seasons' difference, as the icy fang
> And churlish chiding of the winter's wind,
> Which when it bites and blows upon my body
> Even till I shrink with cold, I smile and say
> "This is no flattery: these are counsellors
> That feelingly persuade me what I am."
> Sweet are the uses of adversity,
> Which, like the toad, ugly and venomous,
> Wears yet a precious jewel in his head;
> And this our life, exempt from public haunt,
> Finds tongues in trees, books in the running brooks,
> Sermons in stones, and good in everything. (II.i.1–17)

Happy to escape the pressures of politics, Duke Senior relishes his banishment. Life in the country is safer and also freer. Above all, he is now relieved of the burdens of office. He confirms what we have seen in Act I—that the court is a world of intrigue and deception. Duke Senior particularly emphasizes one advantage of the rustic world—the absence of flattery. In the court, the ruler is continually surrounded by yes-men, who never cease speaking of how great he is. The courtiers refuse to tell the ruler any unpleasant truths because he can always punish them for being the bearers of bad tidings. But as Duke Senior points out, nature has no need to flatter man. And the hostile elements teach the Duke that he *is* a man. The fact that he can suffer cold reminds him that in his body he is no different from other human beings. Here again *As You Like It* anticipates *King Lear* and the lesson Lear learns in the storm, that he is "not ague-proof."[7]

Thus Duke Senior views his banishment as an opportunity to grow in wisdom. When he speaks of finding books and sermons in nature, he recognizes the fact that losing his political power has given him greater access to truth. The people he encounters in the rustic world are simpler than courtiers and therefore less capable of deceiving him. In the more natural world of the forest, hostility is out in the open and thus easier to handle. Once liberated from the world of the court, people drop the charade of false politeness and speak their feelings openly to each other:

> Jaques.   I thank you for your company, but, good faith, I had as lief have been myself alone.
> Orlando. And so had I; but yet for fashion sake I thank you too for your society.
> Jaques.   God buy you, let's meet as little as we can.
> Orlando. I do desire we may be better strangers. (III.ii.253–58)

The candor of this exchange is refreshing, especially when compared to the enforced and empty formalities of the court.

In the forest world, the natural elements set a standard of honesty. When the weather is nasty, it does not try to conceal its hostility beneath a veneer of flattery. Several of the songs in the play express this idea:

> Here shall we see
> No enemy
> But winter and rough weather. (II.v.6–8)
> Blow, blow, thou winter wind,
> Thou art not so unkind
> As man's ingratitude. (II.vii.174–76)

However hostile nature may become, at least it does not betray human trust. In the Forest of Arden Shakespeare portrays a pastoral world in which human beings may suffer, but their mistreatment of each other is no longer the primary cause. Shakespeare entrusts the best statement of the pastoral ideal in all its honesty and modesty to the old shepherd Corin:

> Sir, I am a true laborer: I earn that I eat, get that I wear, owe no man hate, envy no man's happiness, glad of other men's good, content with my harm, and the greatest of my pride is to see my ewes graze and my lambs suck. (III.ii.73–77)

The pastoral ideal appears to be a sane and healthy alternative to the corruption of the court. But does Shakespeare completely endorse it? A simple rustic life may sound attractive to jaded, decadent courtiers, who have had too much of the sophisticated life in court. But life in the country can be dull and boorish. Shakespeare complicates *As You Like It* by making a literary ideal confront reality. He juxtaposes an idealized vision of rustic life with a more realistic portrayal. This complexity is already evident in Duke Senior's opening speech, in which he begins celebrating nature with praise of "old custom" (II.i.2). Even on the simplest level of interpretation, the Duke's speech makes an important concession. The banished courtiers had to become accustomed to the forest before they could appreciate it. Initially it must have seemed hostile and dangerous to them, and it took them awhile before they could benefit from their new surroundings. This pattern applies to all the new arrivals in the forest in the play; at first they do not celebrate it as a liberating world, but find it uncomfortable and even frightening.

But the deeper revelation of Duke Senior's opening speech is that he and his companions have brought old custom with them into the world of nature. The artifacts of civilization remain everywhere he looks; he finds books in the running brooks and sermons in stones.[8] In short, these are civilized courtiers entering an uncivilized world. Having already had the benefits of a courtly upbringing, they are educated and refined people, who were not forced to grow up in the forest. The true rustics we meet in the play, such as Audrey and William, are crude, dumb, and unrefined. Touchstone has great fun with them, as he gets to play the man of the world with them. In a typical exchange, he exposes their simplicity:

Touchstone.	Is thy name William?
William.	William, sir.
Touchstone.	A fair name. Wast born i' th' forest here?
William.	Ay, sir, I thank God.
Touchstone.	"Thank God"—a good answer. Art rich?
William.	Faith, sir, so so.
Touchstone.	"So, so" is good, very good, very excellent good; and yet it is not, it is but so, so. Art thou wise?
William.	Ay, sir, I have a pretty wit.
Touchstone.	Why, thou say'st well. I do now remember a saying, "The fool doth think he is wise, but the wise man knows himself to be a fool." (V.i.20–32)

Evidently growing up in the forest does not naturally foster intelligence or the ability to articulate one's thoughts. That is why Orlando is surprised when he meets Rosalind dressed up as Ganymede: "Your accent is something finer than you could purchase in so remov'd a dwelling" (III.ii.341–42). The Forest of Arden exposes a disjunction that, as Shakespeare was to reveal later in his career, has deeply tragic possibilities. In order to develop human potential fully, especially to sharpen one's faculties, one must grow up in the world of the court, but it is decadent and corrupting. To lead the happy, healthy, simple life of the country, one seemingly has to sacrifice all forms of sophistication, those that lead to corruption but also those that refine human nature.

As You Like It certainly criticizes courtly life in the name of the pastoral ideal. But at the same time it criticizes rustic life in the name of the civilization of the court.[9] The pastoral world is not as completely peaceful as it initially may seem to be. Indeed, almost the first thing we learn about the banished courtiers is that they must kill in order to survive.[10] Duke Senior has to admit that they must murder the forest animals for food:

> Come, shall we go and kill us venison?
> And yet it irks me the poor dappled fools,
> Being native burghers of this desert city,
> Should in their own confines with forked heads
> Have their round haunches gor'd. (II.i.21–25)

For all their efforts to adapt to country life, the courtiers remain intruders in the forest and never really belong in this world. In fact, having been banished as a result of a usurpation, they themselves become usurpers in the forest. This irony is not lost on Jaques:

> The melancholy Jaques grieves at that,
> And in that kind swears you do more usurp
> Than doth your brother that hath banish'd you. (II.i.26–28)

Moreover, in the indifference of the deer to the slaughter of one of their number, Jaques discovers in the forest a mirror image of the cruelty of court life.

The inhabitants of the Forest of Arden do not always live up to the pastoral ideal. Some, as we have seen, are stupid; some are downright nasty, and fail to behave the way they are supposed to according to literary convention. When Rosalind and Celia first arrive in the forest, they are looking for a place to rest and ask help from a stock figure in pastoral romance, a kindly old shepherd. But it turns out that Corin comes, not from the pages of Edmund Spenser's poetry, but from the real world of English tenant farming. He is forced to tell the young ladies: "My master is of churlish disposition" (II.iv.80), and because Corin is responsible to his master, he cannot help Rosalind and Celia. Far from being hospitable, Corin's master is in the process of liquidating his assets and hence unwilling to aid strangers. Thus the young women are forced to buy the rural property, and fortunately for them they have the requisite civilized gold with them. Rarely in literature do we get this kind of insight into the economics of the pastoral world. Those who dwell in the Age of Gold are not supposed to have to deal in real gold.[11]

The most basic problem with the forest world is that it may not nurture humanity on the level of mere physical needs. In Act II, scene iv, Adam and Orlando, having found nothing to eat in the forest, have reached the brink of starvation. The court is a world of superfluity and conspicuous consumption, and this luxury is potentially corrupting. When people have too much, they get flabby, both physically and spiritually. But not to have enough can be equally damaging and distorting to human nature. Bringing human beings face-to-face with physical necessity can reduce them to the level of beasts. Shakespeare shows this outcome comically in Act II, scene vii, when Orlando interrupts the picnic of the banished courtiers with his sword drawn. This situation is potentially tragic, suggesting that ordinary men will kill for food if they are starving. But the episode is made lighthearted by the context, as Duke Senior quickly reduces the matter to a mere lack of etiquette:

> Art thou thus bolden'd, man, by thy distress?
> Or else a rude despiser of good manners,
> That in civility thou seem'st so empty? (II.vii.91–93)

Orlando is chastened by this rebuke:

> You touch'd my vein at first. The thorny point
> Of bare distress hath ta'en from me the show
> Of smooth civility. (II.vii.94–96)

Orlando elegantly talks his way out of trouble, but notice the implication of his comment: on the lowest level, the level of bare necessity, nature is antithetical to civility.[12] Reducing men to bestial hunger, nature can make them too concerned with their bodily needs to care any longer about the refinements of civilization, among them morality. Fortunately for Orlando, he is not really in the state of nature in a Hobbesian sense, as he himself recognizes: "I thought that all things had been savage here" (II.vii.107).

This scene once again suggests that Shakespeare is not setting up a simple opposition between nature and civilization. Rather he is holding up the ideal of a civilized state of nature, suggesting that it is natural for human beings to live in civil society. In the utopian world of his comedy, Shakespeare points toward an ideal synthesis that gives us a standard by which to measure the deficiencies of real political communities and especially the tragic disjunctions between nature and convention they normally embody.[13] Accordingly, *As You Like It* exposes the limitations of both court life and country life. The most profound comment on the subject is given to the Fool in the play, Touchstone. As his name suggests, he tests the value of everything in the world of the play. As a fool, Touchstone constantly provides reversals of perspective, reminding us that the wisdom of the world is but foolishness. For example, he continually deflates false ideals by calling attention to the limits of human beings as bodily creatures: "I care not for my spirits if my legs were not weary" (II.iv.2–3).[14] With his comic undercutting of false ideals, Touchstone adds an element of realism to the romance world of *As You Like It*. By exposing the rudeness of country life, he prevents us from being taken in by the pastoral ideal. The rustics betray their limitations in their inability to appreciate his wit, while he continually laments how much he misses the sophistication of the court.

But in one way Touchstone enjoys his banishment to the forest. The stupidity of the rustics allows him to show off, as they mistake him for a true man of the world, and solemnly solicit his opinion of their pastoral existence. Corin asks: "And how like you this shepherd's life, Master Touchstone?" (III.ii.11–12). True to his role as the fool, Touchstone gives a profoundly nonsensical answer:

> Truly, shepherd, in respect of itself, it is a good life; but in respect that it is a shepherd's life, it is naught. In respect that it is solitary, I like it very well; but in respect that it is private, it is a very wild life. Now in respect it is in the fields, it pleases me well; but in respect it is not in the court, it is tedious. As it is a spare life (look you) it fits my humor well; but as there is no more plenty in it, it goes much against my stomach. (III.ii.13–21)

Touchstone's paradoxes brilliantly encapsulate the ambivalence of the pastoral ideal as Shakespeare presents it.[15] The Fool can see what is good in rustic life, especially by comparison with the court, but he also sees what is lacking in the country. He likes being alone, but as a professional fool he misses having a public to appreciate his antics. He likes being closer to nature, but at the same time he misses the lively entertainments of the court. He finds life in the forest healthy—it keeps him lean—but it provides little to please his stomach. The virtues of the pastoral life turn out to be inseparable from its defects.

Although he philosophically sees both sides of the issue, in the end Touchstone chooses to speak up for the virtue of the court, and tells Corin that he is damned for never having experienced courtly sophistication:

Why, if thou never wast at court, thou never saw'st good manners; if thou never saw'st good manners, then thy manners must be wicked, and wickedness is a sin, and sin is damnation. Thou art in a parlous state, shepherd. (III.ii.40–44)

But Corin has an answer to this charge:

Not a whit, Touchstone. Those that are good manners at the court are as ridiculous in the country as the behavior of the country is most mockable at the court. You told me you salute not at the court but you kiss your hands; that courtesy would be uncleanly if courtiers were shepherds. (III.ii.45–51)

Each world, the court and the country, has its own standards, its own customs. Problems arise only when someone tries to act like a courtier in the country or a rustic in court, thus exposing the limitations of either world. The ideal would be to combine the natural simplicity of the country with the refinement and sophistication of the court.[16] But because of the problem of education, this synthesis turns out to be very difficult. It is not easy to be simple and unaffected if you have grown up in the court, since, as Touchstone's conduct shows, the great temptation of any courtier is to put on airs. At the same time, it is difficult to be refined if you have grown up in the country because it does not offer the models of sophisticated behavior readily available in the court.

III

The general problem of combining rustic simplicity with civilized refinement turns out to be the specific problem with love as portrayed in As You Like It. True love is revealed to be a medium between the rudeness of the country and the decadence of the court. Shakespeare examines in detail three pairs of lovers in the course of the play: Orlando and Rosalind, Silvius and Phebe, Touchstone and Audrey. This spectrum of lovers serves to define the nature of true love. Orlando and Rosalind emerge as the Aristotelian mean between the extremes of Silvius and Phebe on the one hand and Touchstone and Audrey on the other.[17] The love between Touchstone and Audrey is too rustic and uncouth, a purely physical attraction.[18] By contrast, the love between Silvius and Phebe is overly refined and idealized. They play the game of courtly love, with Phebe cast as the proud disdainful mistress and Silvius as the despairing young lover. In short, as their names suggest, they are characters straight out of pastoral love poetry. The problem is that they are in a real forest with real sheep, and end up looking ridiculous, like fictional characters trying to live in the real world. They seem to have gotten their idea of how to behave as lovers out of books, and must learn to become more realistic about love.[19] Touchstone and Audrey go to the opposite extreme. There is no genuinely romantic element in their love; he wants to marry only because under the circumstances it seems the practical thing to do. These two love pairings serve as poles to help define the true love of Orlando and Rosalind. They turn out to be more realistic than Silvius and Phebe, but more romantic than Touchstone and Audrey. Their task is to learn how to combine realism and romance in love. Shakespeare presents love as something physical, rooted in the body and its desires, which cannot be ignored. At the same time, however, love is something spiritual, with a refining power that lifts humanity above the level of the beasts.[20] That refinement is the result of certain love conventions taught by civilization, which link love to poetry. In dramatizing the love of Orlando and Rosalind, Shakespeare shows the way they learn to combine elements of nature and civilization, both spontaneity and cultivation of emotion.

The young shepherd Silvius is clearly a stock romantic lover, straight out of the pages of Petrarch's sonnets. The figure of the young man who worships his beloved from afar, with no hope of being granted her favors, had a long and distinguished literary pedigree by the time Shakespeare wrote his romantic comedies. The pedigree stretched all the way back to the twelfth century in France, when the lyrics of the troubadours introduced the idea of courtly love into European literature.[21] Transposed into the new genre of chivalric romance in such poems as the *Lancelot* of Chrétien de Troyes, stories of knights in shining armor devoted to their fair mistresses swept the world of secular literature in the High Middle Ages. At the turn of the fourteenth century, Dante spiritualized the idea of courtly love in his *La Vita Nuova* and later carried it to new heavenly heights in his presentation of his lady Beatrice in his *Divina Commedia*. His Italian successor Petrarch established the conventions of romantic love poetry in his sonnets addressed to his ideal woman, Laura. He inaugurated a vogue of writing love sonnets that penetrated every corner of Europe, eventually reaching England in the second half of the sixteenth century, and culminating in the great sonnet sequences of Sir Philip Sidney, Edmund Spenser, and, of course, Shakespeare himself.[22]

The figure of Silvius is a late avatar of this romantic love tradition, presenting himself proudly as a lover in despair:

No, Corin, being old, thou canst not guess,
Though in thy youth thou wast as true a lover
As ever sigh'd upon a midnight pillow.
But if thy love were ever like to mine—

As sure I think did never man love so—
How many actions most ridiculous
Hast thou been drawn to by thy fantasy? (II.iv.25–31)

Silvius sounds just like Romeo when he talks to Friar Lawrence: no older man can understand the power of his love; he is unique in his passion (just the way every poetic lover claims to be).[23] When we next see Silvius, with the shepherdess Phebe, he is in the standard situation of Petrarchan love poetry and pastoral romance, begging his disdainful mistress to love him:

Sweet Phebe, do not scorn me, do not, Phebe;
Say that you love me not, but say not so
In bitterness. The common executioner,
Whose heart th' accustom'd sight of death makes hard,
Falls not the ax upon the humbled neck
But first begs pardon. Will you sterner be
Than he that dies and lives by bloody drops? (III.v.1–7)

Mouthing the clichés of Petrarchan love poetry, Silvius speaks this way because he believes that this is how a man in love behaves. But entreating Phebe not to scorn him is exactly the way to elicit her disdain. Naturally she plays along with the game Silvius initiates. If he wants her to be the disdainful mistress of Petrarchan love poetry, why not indulge his fancy? She enjoys seeing the spectacle of a man groveling at her feet.

The one encouraging sign at this point is that Phebe is evidently more realistic than Silvius. Taking his metaphors literally, she shows how ridiculous they are:

Lie not, to say mine eyes are murtherers!
Now show the wound mine eye hath made in thee;
Scratch thee but with a pin, and there remains
Some scar of it; lean upon a rush,
The cicatrice and capable impressure
Thy palm some moment keeps; but now mine eyes,
Which I have darted at thee, hurt thee not,
Nor I am sure there is no force in eyes
That can do hurt. (III.v.19–27)

Phebe does not trust poetry, which in her view makes false claims about the world. At this point Rosalind in her disguise as Ganymede breaks in to speak on behalf of the real world. She recognizes that Phebe is playing the part of a great beauty, but she questions whether the shepherdess is really all that beautiful. She warns Phebe that beauty is in the eyes of the beholder, which in her case means Silvius. Phebe's charms will not work on the person she thinks is Ganymede:

> No, faith, proud mistress, hope not after it.
> 'Tis not your inky brows, your black silk hair,
> Your bugle eyeballs, nor your cheek of cream
> That can entame my spirits to your worship.
> You foolish shepherd, wherefore do you follow her,
> Like foggy south, puffing with wind and rain?
> You are a thousand times a properer man
> Than she a woman. 'Tis such fools as you
> That makes the world full of ill-favor'd children.
> 'Tis not her glass, but you that flatters her,
> And out of you she sees herself more proper
> Than any of her lineaments can show her. (III.v.45–56)

Speaking of the virtue of self-knowledge, Rosalind gives Phebe some practical advice, urging her to settle for what she already can have in Silvius:

> But mistress, know yourself, down on your knees,
> And thank heaven, fasting, for a good man's love;
> For I must tell you friendly in your ear,
> Sell when you can, you are not for all markets.
> Cry the man mercy, love him, take his offer. (III.v.57–61)

Ordering Phebe "down on your knees," Rosalind works to restore balance by reversing the stock poetic situation of the man abasing himself before a woman. Although her use of the commercial language of selling and markets may seem crass and mercenary in the context of a love affair, Rosalind is just trying to introduce some realism and practicality into the lives of two people who have clearly been carried away by an artificial literary ideal.

Rosalind is trying to help Silvius and Phebe, but as usual in comedy at first she makes matters worse. Phebe falls in love with Rosalind in her disguise as Ganymede, revealing the perversity of love; as Rosalind points out: "He's fall'n in love with your foulness—and she'll fall in love with my anger" (III.v.66–67). Actually wanting love to be difficult, young people are always secretly searching out, and creating their own, obstacles to erotic fulfillment. Phebe longs for a more romantic situation than Silvius offers her. She does not want to marry the boy next door, even though, or rather precisely because, he is the logical mate for her. She requires the romantic escapade of falling in love with Ganymede in order eventually to reconcile her to the obvious choice in love.

The plot works to bring about a reversal of the typical roles of man and woman in Petrarchan love poetry. To appreciate how Silvius feels, Phebe has to experience what it is like to pursue Ganymede unsuccessfully. She even quotes Christopher Marlowe's poem *Hero and Leander* to express her feelings, thereby revealing how much her behavior derives from literary models:

Dead shepherd, now I find thy saw of might,
"Who ever lov'd that lov'd not at first sight?" (III.v.81–82)

Phebe must learn for herself what it is to be disdained in love, and when she finds out that Ganymede is really Rosalind in disguise, she decides that marrying a woman would be a little too exotic for her. Thus by the end of the play she is willing to make do with the homegrown love she scorned at the beginning. She realizes that Silvius' devotion to her is what really matters in love: "Thy faith my fancy to thee doth combine" (V.iv.149–50). In order to be united at the end of the play, Silvius and Phebe have had to recognize the artificiality of the roles they have been playing, roles largely derived from love poetry. In short, they both have had to learn how to be more realistic about love.

That is not the problem for Touchstone; his affair with Audrey is never in danger of being called a storybook romance. He has too great a sense of humor ever to let himself play the stock part of a lover. With his ironic detachment from life, he cannot take love too seriously and is self-conscious about his amorous role:

I remember when I was in love, I broke my sword upon a stone, and bid him take that for coming a-night to Jane Smile; and I remember the kissing of her batler and the cow's dugs that her pretty chopp'd hands had milk'd; and I remember the wooing of a peascod instead of her, from whom I took two cods, and giving her them again, said with weeping tears, "Wear these for my sake." We that are true lovers run into strange capers; but as all is mortal in nature, so is all nature in love mortal in folly. (II.iv.46–56)

Touchstone is in effect a parody of a lover, deliberately aping the folly of young men like Silvius.

He behaves the same way when Rosalind finds Orlando's love poetry in the forest. Touchstone starts reeling off parody verses:

If a hart do lack a hind,
Let him seek out Rosalind.
If the cat will after kind,
So be sure will Rosalind. . . .
Sweetest nut hath sourest rind,

Such a nut is Rosalind.
He that sweetest rose will find
Must find love's prick and Rosalind. (III.ii.101–4, 109–12)

With his ribald puns, Touchstone points to the natural, animal aspect of love, reminding Rosalind that love involves physical desire and is not all idealized romance. Thus when Touchstone himself falls in love, he does not have any illusions about what he is doing. Trapped in a forest, he comes across a healthy goatsmaid and concludes that a little loving is in order.

But in a reversal of the normal pattern of courtship, Touchstone imagines Audrey to be worse than she really is. Rather than being overly idealistic about his love, he is overly cynical, evidently realizing that, if he claims too much for his beloved, he may be disappointed. But if he expects little or nothing from her, then he may be pleasantly surprised. His strange view of romance produces perhaps the weirdest love duet in the history of poetry:

Audrey.   Well, I am not fair, and therefore I pray the gods make me honest.
Touchstone.   Truly, and to cast away honesty upon a foul slut were to put good meat into an unclean dish.
Audrey.   I am not a slut, though I thank the gods I am foul.
Touchstone.   Well, prais'd be the gods for thy foulness! sluttishness may come hereafter. But be it as it may be, I will marry thee. (III.iii.33–42)

Most men want a beautiful and faithful wife; Touchstone wants just the opposite. His decision to marry Audrey comes across as a complete non sequitur, until one realizes how his principle of lowered expectations in love operates.

He finally explains his decision to Jaques:

As the ox hath his bow, sir, the horse his curb, and the falcon her bells, so man hath his desires; and as pigeons bill, so wedlock would be nibbling. (III.iii.79–82)

Touchstone presents marriage as something natural in the sense of something animal. As a result of bodily urges, human beings pair off the way animals do. In short, for Touchstone it is the mating season. Hence he might as well take Audrey as anyone else. Marriage is not a solemn occasion for him and it does not arouse deep emotions in him.[24] His candid attitude toward marriage is refreshing, as he reduces wedlock to its bare essence:

Come, sweet Audrey,
We must be married, or we must live in bawdry. (III.iii.96–97)

It turns out that Audrey is being practical about love too. Touchstone is her passport to the world of the court: she desires "to be a woman of the world" (V.iii.4–5). She was originally supposed to be married to William; by comparison with such a clod, Touchstone looks like a great man to her.

Of course Audrey may be a little disappointed when she gets to court and finds out what Touchstone's social status really is. But in truth Touchstone and Audrey are made for each other, as no less than Hymen, the god of marriage, proclaims:

> You and you are sure together,
> As the winter to foul weather. (V.iv.135–36)

Storms may be on the horizon for the marriage of Touchstone and Audrey. Jaques gives them two months, and, ominously, Touchstone originally did not seem too concerned about the validity of his marriage, anticipating that he might wish to see it dissolved (III.iii.90–94). His story reveals how hollow marriage looks when devoid of virtually all romance and all poetry.

IV

Orlando and Rosalind avoid the extremes of either Sylvius and Phebe or Touchstone and Audrey. There *is* poetry in their romance, but they do not act simply like characters out of books. Because they do not become captives of conventional roles as lovers, they do not allow poetry to take over their lives. What saves them from a life of romantic cliché is Rosalind's playfulness and her refusal to get locked into a single role.[25] She manifests this tendency from the very beginning of the play when she tells her friend Celia: "From henceforth I will [be merry], coz, and devise sports. Let me see—what think you of falling in love?" (I.ii.24–25).[26] As long as Rosalind thinks of love as a game, she can maintain her spontaneity as a lover. And she meets Orlando in an unconventional setting for young lovers, namely at a wrestling match. Although they do follow the customary romantic pattern of falling in love at first sight, they have a hard time communicating initially. Orlando cannot respond to Rosalind's overtures with the conventional language of a lover; to his dismay, he is tongue-tied in her presence:

> Can I not say, I thank you? My better parts
> Are all thrown down, and that which here stands up
> Is but a quintain, a mere lifeless block. (I.ii.249–51)

This scene is very different from the first meeting of Romeo and Juliet, who have all the poetry of love at their fingertips and find themselves immediately speaking to each other in sonnet form. Conventions do not always stand in the way of love; sometimes they serve a useful romantic purpose by casting a spell of refinement over the basic physical facts of eros. Rosalind has to teach Orlando how to be a lover and that means in practice teaching him the language of love. She must give him the means of expressing his love, but without making him lose touch with his natural quality as a lover, his spontaneity. The problem is clear in their initial meeting: Orlando freezes in a conventional romantic situation.[27] He evidently cannot talk to Rosalind as Rosalind, and as a result their love seems to have little chance of developing. The comic way out of this impasse is for Orlando to get to know Rosalind and learn how to deal with her in circumstances that will liberate him from the prison of romantic stereotypes.

That is why the long interlude in the Forest of Arden becomes crucial to the blossoming of their love. The new and more natural environment frees Rosalind and Orlando from their conventional roles. In their changed situation, the ordinary rules of social conduct no longer apply, and in particular their inherited social positions cease to be a factor in their interaction. They are able to work out their romantic problems by playing roles. Orlando cannot talk freely to Rosalind but he can talk to her in her disguise as Ganymede, even when she as Ganymede pretends to be Rosalind. By the same token, once Rosalind is disguised as a man, she too acquires a new freedom in talking about love.[28] In short, if Orlando and Rosalind cannot effectively talk to each other as man-to-woman, they will learn to do so as man-to-man. Trying to communicate in a conventional romantic situation, in which they are locked into standard sexual roles, they find that they are freighted with a great deal of emotional baggage, which holds them back from speaking freely to each other. Orlando is especially paralyzed, given his set ideas about how a young lover should speak in the presence of his beloved. The interchanges between Orlando and the person who appears to be his new male friend—Ganymede—are much more relaxed and straight-forward, free of stock romantic responses.[29] As Shakespeare does in several of his comedies, he seeks to remake romantic love on the model of friendship.[30] He suggests that in effect Orlando and Rosalind need to get to know each other as friends—free of the pressures of a conventional romantic situation—before they can become true lovers. As is clear in the case of Rosalind and Celia at the beginning of the play, friends of the same sex can form a deep bond, and speak to each other freely and honestly. Shakespeare hopes to recapture something of this freedom and honesty of friendship in the relations between man and woman by liberating them from the artificiality of conventional romantic posturing.

Once Orlando gets to the forest, he is transformed into a poet and even starts pinning sonnets to trees:

Hang there, my verse, in witness of my love,
And thou, thrice-crowned queen of night, survey
With thy chaste eye, from thy pale sphere above,
Thy huntress' name that my full life doth sway.
O Rosalind, these trees shall be my books,
And in their barks my thoughts I'll character,
That every eye which in this forest looks
Shall see thy virtue witness'd every where.
Run, run, Orlando, carve on every tree
The fair, the chaste, and unexpressive she. (III.ii.1–10)

Where was all this poetry in Act I when Orlando needed it to respond to Rosalind's romantic overtures to him? But in many ways, his verbal facility here is no better than his earlier silence. This love poetry is extremely conventional—to the point of being trite. When Orlando proclaims "these trees shall be my books," he sounds like Duke Senior in Act II and raises the same difficulty. He is bringing convention into the forest world, threatening to turn nature into convention.[31] He provides a perfect image of the artificiality and sterility of the Petrarchan lover.[32] Still unable to talk to Rosalind as a real woman, he can achieve satisfaction only in poetry.[33] In Act I he was tongue-tied in her presence; here in Act III he pours out poetry to express his love, but only in her absence. Orlando is still not getting any message across. As so often happens in this play, he must find a happy medium—a position between silence and stilted poetry.[34]

In fact, Orlando need not cast himself in the conventional poetic role of the despairing lover. Rosalind already loves him, precisely for his being a healthy young male. After all she met him at a wrestling match and presumably was attracted by his virile athleticism. Rosalind tries to tell him that he needs to break out of romantic stereotypes. In her disguise as Ganymede, she can say what propriety would forbid her to say as Rosalind. She can be romantically aggressive in a way that would be unacceptable for a woman according to the social conventions of her day (we have already seen that Orlando has difficulty dealing with a forward woman). She tries to encourage Orlando by describing the attributes of a conventional lover in unappealing terms:

A lean cheek, which you have not; a blue eye and sunken, which you have not; an unquestionable spirit, which you have not; a beard neglected, which you have not (but I pardon you for that, for simply your having in beard is a younger brother's revenue); then your hose should be ungarter'd, your bonnet unbanded, your sleeve unbutton'd, your shoe untied, and every thing about you demonstrating a careless desolation. But you are no such man; you are rather point-device in your accoustrements, as loving yourself, than seeming the lover of any other. (III.ii.373–84)

Rosalind is trying to tell Orlando that instead of the standard brand of despairing lover, she wants a man with self-respect, who shows it by taking care of his appearance.

The twists and turns of the plot give Rosalind a chance to test Orlando in a make-believe situation. Unable to trust him fully, she does not know if his deeds will live up to his words. Accordingly she imposes trials upon him; for example, she wants to see if he will be punctual. Punctuality may seem like a trivial issue for young lovers, but it actually goes to the heart of the fundamental issue of whether Orlando is willing to deal with Rosalind as a real woman, not a poetic projection—as an independent person whose needs he must take into account.[35] In a subtle but forceful way, Rosalind is trying to train Orlando to be a proper husband.

In particular, she wants to give him a trial run at a proposal, knowing full well that this will be the hardest task for him:

Come, woo me, woo me; for now I am in a holiday humor, and like enough to consent. What would you say to me now, and I were your very Rosalind? (IV.i.68–71)

She carefully teaches him the right approach, showing him where he goes wrong:

Orlando. I take some joy to say you are, because I would be talking of her.
Rosalind. Well, in her person, I say I will not have you.
Orlando. Then, in mine own person, I die. (IV.i.89–92)

In speeches that alternately echo Touchstone and Phebe, Rosalind warns Orlando against using stale poetic language, pointing out how artificial his rhetoric is:

No, faith, die by attorney. The poor world is almost six thousand years old, and in all this time there was not any man died in his own person, videlicit, in a love-cause. Troilus had his brains dash'd out with a Grecian club, yet he did what he could to die before, and he is one of the patterns of love. Leander, he would have liv'd many a fair year though Hero had turn'd nun, if it had not been for a hot midsummer night; for, good youth, he went but forth to wash him in the Hellespont, and being taken with the cramp was drown'd; and the foolish chroniclers of that age found it was—Hero of Sestos. But these are all lies: men have died from time to time, and worms have eaten them, but not for love. (IV.i.94–108)

By taking Orlando's metaphor literally, Rosalind shows how ridiculous the conventional language of love poetry is. In exaggerating the power of love, the poets lie. Rosalind cautions Orlando to be more realistic about love, and above all to break out of the conventional Petrarchan association of love with death. Unlike Juliet, Rosalind is not eager to have a husband who is always ready to rush into death to prove the power of his love for her. Her rejection of the extremism of Petrarchan poetry is one reason her story follows a comic, rather than a tragic, path.

Suddenly Rosalind changes course: "now I will be your Rosalind in a more coming-on disposition" (IV.i.112–13), and reveals to Orlando another aspect of love. He has seen the disdainful, chaste mistress; now he will see the other extreme, the woman who is too easy to get:

Orlando. Then love me, Rosalind.
Rosalind. Yes, faith, will I, Fridays and Saturdays and all.
Orlando. And wilt thou have me?
Rosalind. Ay, and twenty such.
Orlando. What sayest thou?
Rosalind. Are you not good?
Orlando. I hope so.
Rosalind. Why then, can one desire too much of a good thing? (IV.i.115–24)

Rosalind keeps working to get Orlando to appreciate a happy medium in love, a woman who is not too disdainful but who also does not come on too strong.

Finally Rosalind arrives at the crucial part of educating Orlando—she must show him what marriage will really be like. Lovers in Petrarchan lyrics seldom think about or discuss this aspect of romance, either ignoring it completely or assuming that marriage will be just like courtship, a form of "eternal love." Rosalind suggests otherwise:

Rosalind. Now tell me how long you would have her after you have possess'd her.
Orlando. For ever and a day.
Rosalind. Say "a day," without the "ever." (IV.i.143–46)

Once again, Rosalind is telling Orlando to cut the poetry, especially the hyperbole, and understand the reality of marriage—above all the fact that a real man and a real woman must deal with their marriage on a day-to-day basis, and not try to dwell in an artificial dream world of eternal love.[36] Moreover Rosalind points out how differently lovers behave once they actually get married:

> No, no, Orlando, men are April when they woo, December when they wed; maids are May when they are maids, but the sky changes when they are wives. I will be more jealous of thee than a Barbary cock-pigeon over his hen, more clamorous than a parrot against rain, more new-fangled than an ape, more giddy in my desires than a monkey. I will weep for nothing, like Diana in the fountain, and I will do that when you are dispos'd to be merry. I will laugh like a hyen, and that when thou art inclin'd to sleep. (IV.i.146–56)

Rosalind's persistent use of animal imagery, a tendency she shares with Touchstone, reflects her attempt to de-idealize Petrarchan poetry and to destroy its illusions about love. Orlando is shocked at this honest vision of marital discord:

> *Orlando.* But will my Rosalind do so?
> *Rosalind.* By my life, she will do as I do. (IV.i.157–58)

Rosalind cautions Orlando against entering marriage with any false expectations of wedded bliss. She wants him to realize that he will be marrying a real woman, not a poetic image, and will have to learn to adapt to her everchanging moods.

In the utopian world of comedy, Rosalind and Orlando get to work out their problems before marriage. In particular they have a chance to act out their roles as husband and wife when they are not yet taking them seriously because they are only playacting. This luxury permits a harmonious resolution to any discord they experience. Indeed in *As You Like It* all the lovers are miraculously brought together in harmony at the end, as Rosalind magically solves all the difficulties. The lovers seem to have gotten themselves into a hopelessly tangled mess, but all riddles are solved and all problems are resolved once Ganymede is revealed to be Rosalind. To ensure that the comic spirit prevails, Shakespeare also quickly resolves all the political problems. Oliver and Duke Frederick simply repent and reform. First Orlando saves Oliver's life in the forest, thus producing a change of heart in his older brother. Something similar then happens with Duke Frederick, who, coming to annihilate Duke Senior, experiences a religious conversion. With all potential conflicts in the play thus resolved, everyone can be united at the end. Even Oliver joins in the marriage festival, as he miraculously falls in love with Celia. At the quadruple wedding that results, Hymen himself shows up to celebrate:

> Wedding is great Juno's crown,
> O blessed bond of board and bed!
> 'Tis Hymen peoples every town,
> High wedlock then be honored. (V.iv.141–44)

Hymen thus reveals the social function of marriage—to repopulate the community. The most basic principle of Shakespeare's comedies is that, from the point of view of society, romantic love should be directed toward marriage, and hence sexual reproduction and the renewal of the community; marriage "peoples every town." This understanding of the natural function of love between the sexes provides the basis for sorting out the romantic confusions of *As You Like It*. It explains, for example, why Rosalind cannot end up paired with Phebe, or even with her old friend Celia for that matter.[37] In Shakespeare's comedies, the potentially disruptive and confusing power of eros is contained through the institution of marriage, and directed toward generation in the service of the regeneration of society.[38] At the end of *As You Like It*, everyone who wants to can return to civilization, but it will be a more natural civilization, freed from the arbitrary tyranny of custom.[39]

V

Shakespearean comedy may appear to be far removed from the serious world of Shakespearean tragedy, with its political complexities and profound exploration of the conflict between the individual and the community. But as we have seen, *As You Like It* raises many of the same issues Shakespeare deals with in his tragedies, above all the tension between nature and convention. In many respects, *As You Like It* offers the comic counterpart of the tragic world of *King Lear*. In its lightly sketched political setting, *As You Like It* develops the same contrast Shakespeare was soon to grapple with far more seriously in *King Lear*: between a courtly world of moribund conventions and a more natural world that seems both liberating and threatening.[40] In their counterpointed romances, Shakespeare's characters in *As You Like It* enact a drama that raises the issue of nature and convention in terms of love. Shakespeare presents convention as a negative force in love when it locks young lovers into sterile and artificial poses, cutting them off from genuine spontaneity of emotion and from the natural fulfillment of their erotic urges in marriage and procreation. But as he does when he treats the issue politically, Shakespeare does not simply reject the role of convention in love or present it as the complete antithesis of nature. In order to rise above the level of mere animal urges, eros requires the civilizing power of convention to refine it into something higher in its aims. *As You Like It* portrays a process in which the lovers are not simply freeing themselves from the power of convention but rather learning to overcome its tendency to artificiality and to bring it more in harmony with nature.

In short, just because some conventions of love poetry are exposed as artificial and unnatural does not mean that all such conventions are equally bad, and human beings can do without conventions entirely when it comes to the relations between the sexes. Shakespeare juxtaposes the story of Touchstone and Audrey with that of Silvius and Phebe to make this point clearer. By ridiculing all idealism in love and going to the opposite extreme of presenting it as no better than the coupling of animals, Touchstone does not solve the problem of romance. In fact Shakespeare hints that these two extreme views of love are inextricably linked. Silvius' artificial manner of courting gives romantic love a bad name, and encourages Touchstone to regard all poetry in love as ridiculous. An overly idealistic view of love tends to breed its inverted image, an overly cynical view.[41] Disillusioned with love as a result of asking too much of it, a young man may plunge into the opposite extreme of denying it any value. Locked into all-or-nothing attitudes, Shakespeare's lovers have trouble finding a middle ground. Love must have an infinite value or it has none at all.

Neither extreme captures the complex nature of human love, which is a mixture of the higher and the lower aspects of human nature, the spiritual and the physical. Human beings are not simply animals, and they manifest their higher nature in their efforts to distinguish true love from mere sex. To do so, they need social conventions, such as the legal institution of marriage and the custom of courting. The courting rituals of one society may look artificial, unnatural, and even ridiculous to another society. And yet all human societies do have their courting rituals, patterns of behavior imparted to their youth in order to guide them toward marriage. In that sense, courting rituals may be said to be natural to human societies, even though the form they take in a given society will be arbitrary and hence may look "unnatural" to another society.[42]

Thus it is no accident that in English we refer to the ritual patterns that direct youth toward marriage as *courtship*. We may think that love, being sexual, should be linked to the country, but it turns out in *As You Like It* that the distinctively human form of love is associated with the court. With the rustic figures Silvius and Phebe behaving like courtly lovers, Shakespeare presents love as a "trickle down" phenomenon. Learning to imitate the elegance and sophistication of their social superiors, lovers take their models of how to behave from high society. This can, as we have repeatedly seen, introduce an element of artificiality into their behavior, but it can also work to elevate their love above the purely animal level and give it the refinement it needs.

It is crucial, therefore, to the effect of As You Like It that the characters plan on returning to the conventional society of the court at the end of the play, as symbolized by their entering the world of married life. Many Marxist and feminist critics reject the idea that marriage provides a proper resolution and a happy ending to As You Like It. Hugh Grady, for example, writes sarcastically: "Of course the play ends with a monumental celebration of marriage as the inevitable and proper vessel for the cultivation of eros." He objects to "the tendency of 20th-century criticism of Shakespearean comedy to privilege the conclusion of plays over the dissonances and contradictions of the works' 'performative comedy.'" He goes on to argue that "the final emphasis on marriage, so overwhelming as a plot-structure device, is destabilized by several different kinds of 'supplements' to marriage in the play," including the epilogue spoken by the boy actor who plays Rosalind.[43] According to this understanding, because we finally learn that the woman who pretended to be a boy in As You Like It was in reality a boy all along, we are left with a dizzying sense of the artificiality of all roles in human life ("gender-role instability, the promiscuity of desire"[44]); nothing is natural in the human world, not even the distinction between the sexes; all is conventional.

In this kind of reading, As You Like It, far from attempting to sort out natural from artificial forms of love, simply shows that all forms of love are artificial, as witness the pervasive role playing in the drama. These critics can actually point to a champion of their views within As You Like It, and his name is Jaques. In what is the most famous passage in the play, his set piece on the Seven Ages of Man, Jaques does in fact claim that all human life is merely role playing:

> All the world's a stage,
> And all the men and women merely players;
> They have their exits and their entrances,
> And one man in his time plays many parts. (II.vii.139–42)

As several critics have commented, it is extraordinary how often this "Seven Ages of Man" speech is lifted completely out of context and offered as Shakespeare's own view of human life.[45] But as a dramatist, Shakespeare never speaks to us directly in his plays, and this speech is in fact heavily ironized by its dramatic context. For one thing, as Jaques finishes his speech by mocking old age, Adam enters to refute visually the claim that men of his years are necessarily feeble.[46] Elsewhere in the play, Shakespeare goes out of his way to have one character after another criticize Jaques—Touchstone, Duke Senior, Orlando, Rosalind—and expose the limitations of his point of view.[47]

But the "Seven Ages of Man" speech can be refuted purely on internal grounds.[48] As a comprehensive account of human life, it obviously fails because of what it omits. Jaques finds human life meaningless only because he leaves out everything that gives human life meaning. His speech is the outpouring of a lonely, detached man, who views life as an outsider and sees it as a series of lonely, detached roles, one following after another, with no connections and no continuity. As several critics have noted, what the speech most conspicuously omits is the possibility of marriage and having children—precisely what normally supplies connections and continuity to the lives of most human beings.[49] Jaques comes up with his jaundiced view of human life as merely role playing only by ignoring what As You Like It in the end offers its characters as the way out of their dilemmas, namely marriage. Marriage may seem to be just another convention, but in his comedies Shakespeare presents it as something real, in contrast to the artificiality of Petrarchan love. Silvius and Phebe will achieve nothing as long as they try to live in the unreal world of poetry; once they marry, they will enter the social world and get down to the real business of human life, which in the terms of Shakespearean comedy is raising a family.[50]

In Shakespeare's comedies role playing is a temporary means for coming to terms with life, not life itself. One can work out one's romantic problems by adopting different roles in a kind of holiday spirit, but in the end, Shakespeare shows, one must settle down to the realities of married life, as we have seen Rosalind teaching Orlando. As Mera Flaumenhaft says of Rosalind: "her disguise is nothing like the roles Jaques describes. . . . She always knows the difference between her female self and her boy's persona. It is clearly a temporary device, and she uses it only to accomplish her purpose. She is and wants to be a woman."[51] Acknowledging the provisional character of role playing, Shakespeare clears a separate space for it in a kind of alternative universe in his comedies, such as the Forest of Arden in As You Like It or the wood outside Athens in A Midsummer Night's Dream. In a comedy, the characters must leave their normal everyday world, with all its conventions and stock responses, and enter a utopian space in which the ordinary rules of life no longer apply. Through disguises and other confusions of identity, they are free to discover something new about themselves. But after exploring alternatives to their ordinary, conventional lives, they must return to the world they came from, reoriented and reinvigorated by their holiday experience, but prepared to resume a place in conventional society. A character like Jaques, who persists in believing that all life is merely role playing, will be unable to settle down into a conventional role and reintegrate into society. Accordingly, this melancholy figure refuses to join in the fun and the celebration at the end of As You Like It, and insists on going off to accompany Duke Frederick in his religious retreat. Jaques is an inveterate outsider and a malcontent.

Thus critics like Grady can take little comfort from having Jaques champion their views within As You Like It. It turns out that Shakespeare has built into the play a refutation of the idea that life is merely role playing by attributing it to the one persistent spoilsport in the comedy, a figure whose views are contradicted by the action and the other characters in As You Like It. Grady admits that he reaches his conclusions only by not privileging the end of Shakespeare's comedy. But the end of a play is integral and vital to its meaning. For example, one cannot know for sure if a given play is a comedy or a tragedy until one sees whether it has a happy or a sad ending. That is a concrete illustration of the fact that the end of a play necessarily shapes our understanding of its meaning as a whole. Grady refuses to accept the idea that, as a comedy, As You Like It moves toward a natural end dictated by the genre. He wants to stay with the "dissonances and contradictions" in the middle of the play, as if the whole purpose of a comedy were not precisely to resolve such tensions at the end. One might connect Grady's refusal to recognize that a drama moves toward a natural end (fulfilling the nature of its genre) with his refusal to accept marriage and sexual generation as the natural end of eros (fulfilling human nature). As a modern, and specifically a Marxist, thinker, Grady would like to eliminate the concept of "the natural" entirely. He views all human life as merely conventional because for him, as a Marxist, it is always the product of historical circumstances and hence a social construct.

Shakespeare shows in As You Like It that he is just as aware as any contemporary thinkers of the problem of conventions in human life. But unlike them, he does not respond by rejecting all conventions; rather he tries to discriminate between those conventions (such as marriage) that serve a function in society and those (such as Petrarchan love) that are dysfunctional in social terms. Much of As You Like It is devoted to criticizing certain forms of poetry as artificial, but let us not forget that Shakespeare is himself a poet and the play a form of poetry. Shakespeare is trying to shape a new form of poetry about love that will be more suited to the needs of society than the high-flown but unreal flights of the Petrarchan lyric. In *As You Like It*, this reformed poetry includes an unusual amount of prose as a way to counteract the way poetry often takes flight, and to bring it back down to earth. Shakespeare shows that the best love poetry will include a healthy dose of prose.[52] In fact, *As You Like It* suggests that true love poetry takes the form of a happy medium between elaborate verse and straightforward prose.

Thus, in *As You Like It* the problem of love is ultimately a problem of poetry. Love is a poetic ideal and even at times a poetic myth; lovers learn what it is to love from reading poetry; they derive their notions of how to behave as lovers from literary models.[53] Thus, however seductive the dream of erotic spontaneity may be, love can never become purely "natural" in the sense of doing completely without all conventions. Love depends upon communication, and communication requires language, which is inevitably a matter of convention; indeed love seems to require a peculiarly literary language for communication, and that literary language is highly conventional.[54] But *As You Like It* suggests that, just as in politics, there are degrees of conventionality in love. No love can be purely "natural," but that does not mean that we cannot usefully discriminate between the highly artificial and hence sterile love of the Petrarchan lyric and the more spontaneous and genuine love Rosalind and Orlando struggle to achieve.[55] For Shakespeare, some gap between nature and convention is inevitable; serious problems arise only when the gap widens so far that convention completely loses touch with nature. A perfect example of this negative development can be found in Petrarchan love poetry: the convention of the despairing lover and his remote, disdainful mistress is wholly at odds with the basic and natural function of procreation in love. Shakespeare's romantic comedies in general and *As You Like It* in particular constitute a fundamental and thoroughgoing critique of the Petarchan poetic ideal and an attempt to reform it in the direction of a more natural conception of the relation between men and women, one that integrates love into the community by restoring its compatibility with the social institutions of marriage and the family.

Shakespeare's critique in his romantic comedies of the ideal of love upheld in the Petrarchan poetry of the Renaissance links up with his critique in his history plays of other cultural survivals from the Middle Ages, such as the chivalric and crusading spirit that continued to influence Renaissance politics. In his critique of the ongoing impact of medieval literary ideals on the life of his day, Shakespeare shows remarkable affinities with the program of Cervantes in *Don Quixote*. The two greatest authors of the age were united in their determination to expose the danger of allowing remnants of medieval poetry and romance to supply a false guide to life in love as well as in politics. Although both Shakespeare and Cervantes gave us enduring images of romantic love, they basically succeeded in ending the centuries long pan-European vogue for Petrarchan poetry by exposing its artificiality and unreality—and thereby making their audiences laugh it to death.[56] Together *As You Like It* and *Don Quixote* constitute a remarkable case of art setting out to remedy the problems created by life imitating art.

The treatment of love in *As You Like It* offers a microcosm of the problem of nature and convention in Shakespeare, and sheds light on what he is doing in his tragedies, especially *King Lear*. Shakespeare's tragedies and comedies grow out of the profound paradox of the human condition: man is that animal whose peculiar nature it is to live by conventions he himself creates.[57] The particular set of conventions by which a given community of human beings lives will always be to some extent arbitrary, but that they will live by some conventions is natural to them as human beings. The challenge in this paradoxical situation is to recognize that some conventions may be more natural than others in the sense of being more appropriate to the functioning of people together in a community, more in harmony with their development and fulfillment as human beings. Shakespeare accepts this challenge in *As You Like It*, and interrogates a variety of conceptions of love, testing one against another, to see which best integrates love into the fullness of human life and above all into life in the human community. That is the sense in which *As You Like It* explores the question of which conventions of love are more natural, and in particular attempts to bring the conventions of love poetry more in harmony with human nature. In thus exploring the problem of nature and convention in love, *As You Like It* prefigures Shakespeare's more daring attempt to explore the problem of nature and convention in politics in his tragedies.[58]

Notes

1. On the form of Shakespearean comedy, see Northrop Frye, *A Natural Perspective: The Development of Shakespearean Comedy and Romance* (Columbia University Press, 1965), esp. 72–117; C. L. Barber, *Shakespeare's Festive Comedy* (Meridian, 1963), esp. 3–15 and, for *As You Like It*, 222–39.

2. For a discussion of the interplay between nature and convention in the family relations in the play, see Joseph Alulis, "Fathers and Children: Matter, Mirth, and Melancholy in *As You Like It*," in *Shakespeare's Political Pageant: Essays in Politics and Literature*, eds. Joseph Alulis and Vickie Sullivan (Rowman and Littlefield, 1996), esp. 38–48.

3. All quotations from Shakespeare are taken from *The Riverside Shakespeare*, ed. G. Blakemore Evans (Houghton Mifflin, 1974); act, scene, and line numbers are incorporated into the text.

4. On this point, see David Bevington's introduction to *As You Like It* in his edition, *The Complete Works of Shakespeare*, Fourth Edition (HarperCollins, 1992), esp. 290: "Civilization at its best is no less necessary to the human spirit than is the natural order of the forest." See also Anne Barton's introduction to *As You Like It* in Evans 1974, 366, and Ronald R. Macdonald, *William Shakespeare: The Comedies* (Twayne, 1992), 87, who says of the play: "its apparently opposable categories are not simply placed over and against one another . . . but actually in-here in one another, with each member of such a relationship deriving its ground and means for being from its opposite number. Nowhere is this dialectical situa-tion clearer than in what may seem to be the central opposition of the play as a whole, the great and apparently watertight categories of culture on the one hand and nature on the other. A little consideration will show that the play makes it remarkably difficult to sort out its various elements unequivocally according to this distinction."

5. On this issue, see my chapter "Shakespeare's *Henry V*: From the Medieval to the Modern World," in *Perspectives on Politics in Shakespeare*, eds. John A. Murley and Sean D. Sutton (Lexington, 2006) 11–31. See also Jan Kott, *Shakespeare Our Contemporary*, tr. Boleslaw Taborski (W. W. Norton, 1974) 276.

6. For the relation of Shakespeare's comedies to the pastoral tradition, see Thomas McFarland, *Shakespeare's Pastoral Comedy* (University of North Carolina Press, 1972), esp. 3–48, for the general relation of comedy to pastoral, and 98–121, for a specific discussion of *As You Like It*. See also Marjorie Garber, *Shakespeare After All* (Random House, 2004) 438–41.

7. *King Lear* IV.vi.105. For the parallels of *As You Like It* to *King Lear*, see *Narrative and Dramatic Sources of Shakespeare*, ed. Geoffrey Bullough (Routledge and Kegan Paul, 1958), Vol. II: 153. See also Garber 2004, 444.

8. See A. C. Nuttall, *Shakespeare the Thinker* (Yale University Press, 2007) 231: "Even as he condemns language, the Duke is turning everything into language." See also Garber 2004, 444.

9. See McFarland 1972, 114: "The shepherd's world is somewhat criticized as against the court; the court is somewhat criticized as against the shepherd's world."

10. See Kott 1974, 278, and Derek Traversi, *An Approach to Shakespeare* (Anchor, 1969), Vol. I: 311.

11. See Kott 1974, 279.

12. See Traversi 1969, 313.

13. Shakespeare could have encountered the idea of such a synthesis in the most famous pastoral romance of his day, Sir Philip Sidney's *Arcadia*. Sidney describes his pastoral world this way: "As for the houses of the country . . . they were all scat-tered, no two being one by the other, and yet not so far off as that it barred mutual succour: a show, as it were, of an accompanable solitariness and of a civil wildness" (*The Countess of Pembroke's Arcadia*, ed. Maurice Evans [Penguin, 1977] 70). The paradoxes of an "accompanable [sociable] solitariness" and a "civil wildness" take us to the heart of the complex idea of nature in *As You Like It*.

14. On Touchstone's role, see Mera J. Flaumenhaft, "Is All the World a Stage? Marriage and a Metaphor in *As You Like It*," in Murley and Sutton 2006, 86.

15. See Barber 1963, 227.

16. See Bevington 1992, 290.

17. This point has been made by many critics of the play: see, e.g., Barber 1963, 223; Bevington 1992, 289; Garber 2004, 459–62; Albert Gilman in the introduction to his edition of *As You Like It* (New American Library, 1963) xxviii; Alan Brissenden in the introduction to his edition of *As You Like It* (Oxford University Press, 1993) 17, 35; and Maurice Charney, *Shakespeare On Love and Lust* (Columbia University Press, 2000) 37–38.

18. See Jean Howard in the introduction to *As You Like It* in *The Norton Shakespeare*, ed. Stephen Greenblatt (W. W. Norton, 1997) 1594.

19. The presence of the hypersophisticated lovers Silvius and Phebe in the forest world is one more indication that "nature" is not simply opposed to "civilization" in *As You Like It*. The supposedly natural world is already civilized; courtly manners have penetrated the forest. On this point, see Macdonald 1992, 88–89. Terry Eagleton points out: "The rustic lovers speak with rhetorical artifice. . . . We cannot speak of a simple antithesis of country and city" (*William Shakespeare* [Basil Blackwell, 1986] 91). More generally, Nuttall says of *As You Like It*: "The celebrants of the pastoral ideal are poets, and poetry is itself art, not nature" (2007, 228).

20. On love as mediating between the "materialistic" and the "spiritual," see Flaumenhaft 2006, 82.

21. For two classic studies of courtly love and its literary heritage, see C. S. Lewis, *The Allegory of Love: A Study in Medieval Tradition* (Oxford University Press, 1936) and Denis de Rougemont, *Love in the Western World*, tr. Montgomery Belgion (Pantheon, 1956).

22. On the spread of Petrarchanism, see Gordon Braden, *Petrarchan Love and the Continental Renaissance* (Yale University Press, 1999).

23. See Garber 2004, 459–60.

24. See Barber 1963, 231–32.

25. On the importance of Rosalind's capacity for role playing, see Macdonald 1992, 95–100.

26. Later Rosalind says: "I'll prove a busy actor in their play" (III.iv.59).

27. See Bevington 1992, 290.

28. See Brissenden 1993, 36, Barton 1974, 366, and Flaumenhaft 2006, 84.

29. See Garber 2004, 458.

30. The tension between romantic love and friendship is an important theme in Shakespeare's earlier comedies, such as *Two Gentlemen of Verona*, *Love's Labor's Lost*, *A Midsummer Night's Dream*, and *The Merchant of Venice*; the comedy most fully devoted to showing romantic love remade on the model of friendship is *Twelfth Night*.

31. See Macdonald 1992, 101.

32. See Howard 1997, 593–94.

33. See Garber 2004, 457: "Orlando needs to be brought into direct contact with Rosalind, to stop thinking of her as some idealized, unreal lady. . . . He needs to speak to her rather than about her."

34. See Bevington 1992, 290: "Orlando must learn from Rosalind that a quest for true understanding in love avoids the extreme of pretentious mannerism as well as that of mere artlessness."

35. On the importance of punctuality, see Flaumenhaft 2006, 85.

36. On this point, see Flaumenhaft 2006, 87.

37. See Nuttall 2007, 239: "Shakespeare chose to make comedy revolve around procreation. There was then no question of homosexual marriage, and such unions are infertile."

38. Shakespeare could find the importance of linking love with marriage in his principal source for *As You Like It*, Thomas Lodge's pastoral romance *Rosalynde* (1590). There the shepherd Coridon complains about the way courtly lovers disdain marriage when he speaks to the cruel shepherdess Phoebe: "if all maidens were of her minde, the world would growe to a madde passe; for there would be great store of wooing and little wedding" (Bullough 1958, II: 225). On the importance of generation in *As You Like It*, see Flaumenhaft 2006, 88.

39. See Macdonald 1992, 104: "The play thus moves from the tyrannical imperatives of Frederick's court to the playful subjunctives of the forest, and if the conclusion foreshadows a return, we have some assurance that it will be a return to a court where the impulse to tyrannize will be checked by a better understanding of the many forms tyranny can take." See also Traversi 1969, 308.

40. On this issue, see my chapters "Nature and Convention in *King Lear*," in *Poets, Princes, and Private Citizens: Literary Alternatives to Postmodern Politics*, eds. Joseph M. Knippenberg and Peter A. Lawler (Rowman and Littlefield, 1996) 213–33; "*King Lear*: The Tragic Disjunction of Wisdom and Power," in Alulis and Sullivan 1996, 189–207; and "The Cause of Thunder: Nature and Justice in *King Lear*," in *King Lear: New Critical Essays*, ed. Jeffrey Kahan (Routledge, 2008) 231–52.

41. One can observe this process at work in *Romeo and Juliet* in the way Romeo's overly idealistic love provokes Mercutio's cynicism on the subject.

42. On the importance of courting in *As You Like It*, see Flaumenhaft 2006, 84–86.

43. Hugh Grady, *Shakespeare's Universal Wolf: Studies in Early Modern Reification* (Clarendon Press, 1996) 208.

44. Grady 1996, 209. Feminist critics offer *As You Like It* as evidence for their claim that sexual identity is socially constructed. See, for example, Jean E. Howard, "Cross-dressing in *As You Like It*," in Gilman 1963, 198: "In my view, the figure of Rosalind dressed as a boy engages in playful masquerade as, in playing Rosalind for Orlando, she acts out the parts scripted for women by her culture. Doing so does not release Rosalind from patriarchy but reveals the constructed nature of patriarchy's representations of the feminine and shows a woman manipulating those representations in her own interest, theatricalizing for her own purposes what is assumed to

be innate, teaching her future mate how to get beyond certain ideologies of gender to more enabling ones." Howard is correct that Rosalind's role playing helps free Orlando from certain harmful social stereotypes, but the question remains whether Shakespeare believes that sex is simply gender—that is to say, a social construction, not a natural fact. For Howard sexual roles are purely conventional and not at all natural. Shakespeare's comedies, however, appear to rest on certain biological givens, such as the fact that women can bear children and men cannot.

45. See, e.g., Macdonald 1992, 98 and Traversi 1969, 324.

46. See Barton 1974, 367; Garber 2004, 452; Traversi 1969, 325.

47. See Barton 1974, 367–68.

48. For a thoroughgoing analysis and critique of the "Seven Ages of Man" speech, and a probing discussion of Jaques' character, see Flaumenhaft 2006, 71–78. See also Traversi 1969, 325–28.

49. Flaumenhaft (2006, 74–75, 77) is very astute on the importance of marriage and Jaques's failure to refer to it in his "Seven Ages of Man" speech.

50. Let me emphasize that I am talking here about the view of life Shakespeare presents in his comedies. He views matters quite differently in his tragedies, where he takes the perspective of his extraordinary heroes and heroines, not that of ordinary humanity. The kind of extreme Petrarchan love ridiculed in the comedies is taken very seriously in *Romeo and Juliet*, where Shakespeare explores the possibility of a love that transcends conventional categories and goes against the demands of society. Nevertheless, he does show that the price one pays for this kind of heroic love is death, and in that sense even *Romeo and Juliet* may be said to caution against the path of Petrarchan love.

51. Flaumenhaft 2006, 84. See also Macdonald 1992, 99: "Rosalind's foolery is a temporary measure aimed at moving Orlando off the dead center of romantic lover. Once this has been accomplished, she exchanges her ironic detachment for emotional investment in the world once again, although it is a world substantially transformed by her own irony."

52. That this problem transcends Shakespeare's historical moment is shown by the way it comes up in Jane Austen's 1818 novel *Persuasion*, when her heroine, Anne Elliot, criticizes Captain Benwick's obsession with romantic poetry: "he repeated, with such tremulous feeling, the various lines which imaged a broken heart, or a mind destroyed by wretchedness, . . . that she ventured to hope he did not always read only poetry; . . . she ventured to recommend a larger allowance of prose in his daily study" (*Persuasion*, ed. D. W. Harding [Penguin, 1965] 121–22, end of Chapter 11).

53. Today books have been supplemented by movies and television in providing romantic models for youth, but the basic principle remains the same. Instead of imitating courtly aristocracy, young people now copy movie stars (the aristocracy of the modern democratic world).

54. See Macdonald 1992, 87–88.

55. As Flaumenhaft says, "Some customs seem more appropriate to our nature than others" (2006, 96–97). See also Macdonald, who speaks of how the "characters

come to examine attitudes and postures, rejecting those that are found to be dishar-monious with human nature and embracing, often in modified form, those that are found to be harmonious" (1992, 86).

56. Various forms of romantic love and romantic love poetry obviously survived the comic critique of Shakespeare and Cervantes; some of their own characters, including Romeo and Juliet, as well as Don Quixote and Dulcinea, have becomes archetypes of romantic love in our culture. The fact that Jane Austen still felt a need to make fun of the poetic excesses of romantic lovers in the early nineteenth century is evidence of the survival of the romantic ideal. Nevertheless, the kind of extreme Petrarchan love poetry still very much in vogue in Shakespeare's and Cervantes' day was dealt a death blow by their humor. Other factors contributed to its demise, but we should not underrate the importance of two writers of the stature of Shakespeare and Cervantes setting out to ridicule Petrarchan poetry into extinction.

57. On the connection between *As You Like It* and *King Lear* in terms of the nature/culture binary, see Eagleton 1986, 90–91.

58. This chapter is a revised and expanded version of a paper entitled "The Touch-stone of Nature: Politics and Love in *As You Like It*," given originally at the 1998 Annual Meeting of the American Political Science Association in Boston. Since writing the first draft of this chapter, I have read extensively in the criticism of *As You Like It*, and find myself in the—for me—unusual position of agreeing with the majority of it. In general, critics seem to agree in their interpretations of *As You Like It* in a way that is quite unusual for Shakespeare scholars (with the notable exception of the Marxist and feminist critics I discuss in this chapter). There are no great criti-cal controversies about the characters, as there are, for example, in the debates about Shylock in *The Merchant of Venice* or Falstaff in the *Henry IV* plays, or, most famously, in the case of Hamlet. Some disagreements have developed over the characters of Jaques and Touchstone—they both have their champions and their detractors—but by and large critics have come to very similar conclusions about Shakespeare's treatment of love in the play. Perhaps the schematic arrangement of the three pairs of lovers at the center of the play is so obvious in its intent that even Shakespeare scholars cannot find it in their hearts—or their minds—to argue about how *As You Like It* should be interpreted. Among the critics who develop arguments very similar to mine, often citing the same passages, I particularly recommend the work of Barber, Barton, Bevington, Flaumenhaft, Garber, Macdonald, and Traversi.

4

~

Pagan Statesmanship and Christian Translation

Governing Love in A Midsummer Night's Dream

Laurence Nee

Shakespeare's A Midsummer Night's Dream playfully portrays the struggles of two sets of young lovers against the "sharp" customs and laws of the city of Athens (I.i.162).[1] An analysis of their attraction to one another reveals, however, that their expectations of love's rewards are inherently tragic. The pagan statesman, Theseus, recognizes the power of, and limits to, the lovers' desires and attempts to moderate them in light of what is naturally possible. Denying that these limitations are inherent to love, the Christian mechanicals attempt to purge love of its tragic elements through their play-within-the play. While their comic transformation of Pyramus and Thisby is never staged, Bottom enacts their intentions through his dream and its unperformed epilogue. By presenting for the audience's consideration a comparison of Theseus' statesmanship with the mechanicals' intentions, A Midsummer Night's Dream depicts nothing less than the pagan and Christian responses to the problem posed by love.

The Dual Nature of Love

From its opening word, A Midsummer Night's Dream vividly depicts the problematic nature of love. Athens' Duke, Theseus, has forcibly taken his future bride, the Amazon Hippolyta, and longs to enjoy her "[n]ow." Theseus openly acknowledges injuring Hippolyta when he "wooed" and "won" her "love" with his sword (I.i.17). While Hippolyta has been conquered by the force of Theseus' sword, he speaks as if he has been conquered by another force: the internal necessity of satisfying his "desires." Wedding harsh images of rape to his thirst for immediate gratification, Theseus initially presents love as the violent compulsion to satisfy bodily lust.

This initial impression must be tempered, however, by Theseus' restraint. Another longing, as strong if not stronger than his lust, restrains it. Wishing to "wed [Hippolyta] in another key," Theseus willingly delays his "nuptial hour" four days until the new moon appears and brings his "triumph" (I.i.18). According to Theseus' simile, like a stepmother who precludes a "young man" from enjoying his "revenue," the slow natural cycle of the moon delays Theseus' harvesting and enjoyment of the fruits of his conquered field. Theseus recognizes both that the moon moves according to a fixed, knowable order and that analogous, regular motions govern the waxing and waning of his own passions. Of all the lovers in the play, he alone recognizes, and acknowledges, that he desires both sexual gratification and restraint. Despite the depth of his self knowledge, he offers no account why an erotic lover might desire or exercise such restraint.

Such an account emerges in the young Athenian lovers' speeches, which testify to the dependence of "true love" upon restraint. Interrupting Theseus' nuptial plans to "stir up . . . merriments" and "reveling," Hermia's father, Egeus, abruptly calls upon the Duke to enforce the "ancient privilege of Athens." As Theseus tells Hermia, this "privilege" should deify Egeus as "a god" whose ordering imprint shapes her otherwise formless wax. As if exercising his property rights, Egeus may bestow her as he sees fit (I.i.46–51). He wills that she marry Demetrius, who previously loved Helena. Hermia, however, loves Lysander and would die rather than resign herself to her father's "will."

As a result of Theseus' prompting, Hermia and Lysander are left alone to recount for each other the tales and histories that depict the divine attributes of "true love." From these poetic accounts, the young lovers learn that the "course of true love never did run smooth."[2] It is "customary" for "true lovers" to bear a "cross," which may take the form of differences in blood or age, the opposition of friends, or the horrors of war, sickness, and death. Comparing themselves to these "true lovers," Hermia and Lysander see in the "cross" of Athens' "ancient privilege" a testament to the truth of their love.

The young lovers embrace these "crosses" because such restraints transform the character of their love (I.i.199). The lovers' ability to endure these crosses heightens their expectations of what love can provide. According to Lysander's account, mere love is "momenta[r]y," "swift," "brief," and "short as any dream," nothing more than a bodily urge or an impulse of the "spleen" (I.i.143–45). In contrast to such passing bodily fancies, "true love" endures and fills lovers with the hope that, through their restraint and constant devotion to their beloved, they can escape the variable world of desires. The strong temptation to reduce the lovers' willingness to bear these "crosses" to mere delayed gratification must be moderated by their own accounts of their love; they do not experience their sacrifices in this way. In keeping with their deepest longings, they believe that their sacrifices are free from the benefits enjoyed from gratifying desires like lust.

Restraint or endurance also transforms the nature of the beloved. As Helena attests, true love can "transpose" "base and vile" inconstant lust into the "form and dignity" of an enduring religious devotion. In doing so, true love simultaneously transforms the beloved from a mere object of lust into a "god," before whom the lover offers "prayers" (I.i.197, 232; II.i.203). While Egeus' divinity arose from the absolute obedience he demanded, Lysander looks god-like because of his liberality. Lysander bestows numerous gifts upon Hermia without receiving any immediate benefit for doing so; he appears, like a god, not merely to be able to restrain his desires, or needs, but to be free from them. With Lysander's transformation, Athens is reduced in Hermia's mind from "a heaven unto a hell," which she willingly abandons along with her family and friend. Seeking to emulate the divine restraint of her beloved, Hermia vows to "dote[ ] in idolatry" upon Lysander like a chaste "nun" who worships in a "cloister" (I.i.47, 52, 70–71, 109, 205–7; cf. II.ii.56–59). Believing that their beloveds are like gods, lovers embrace restrained "true love" and hope that, in imitating the character of their beloveds, they too can become like gods, transcend their variable, transitory mortality, and find the enduring satisfaction of their desires.

As the lovers' hopes imply, lovers only endure these restraints or crosses for the sake of some future benefit. Lovers may starve themselves for an evening, but expect to feast on their "lovers' food" tomorrow. The paradox of the lovers' sacrifice is structurally embodied in the last two lines of the scene. In the penultimate line, Helena will deliberately "enrich" her "pain" by telling Demetrius where Hermia has fled. But, in the final line, she reveals that she willingly does so in the hope that his "sight" will turn "back again" to her (I.i.222–23, 250–51). Lovers' sacrifices, therefore, are not selfless. While they do sacrifice in the short-term, they expect to gain in the end from these acts of temporary denial. Despite their underlying desire for gain, they do not see what motivates them and continue to experience their sacrifices as selfless acts.

The gain or reward which lovers like Helena long to receive is the love of their beloveds; lovers especially long to be loved for what they have sacrificed and endured for the sake of their beloveds. Comparing and contrasting lust to hunger, as frequently occurs in the play, the nature of this longing to be loved can be seen. Like the restrained Theseus, the "starv[ing]" Hermia and Lysander will display "patience" and endure the "trial" of being deprived of their "lovers' food." Just as the hungry may "starve" themselves for some period of time, so too may lovers restrain their lust. But as the example of the fawning "spaniel" Helena painfully shows, lovers deeply long to be loved, wanted, and desired in turn by their beloveds. Although she could relieve her hunger by consuming an apple, or other similar "food," Helena cannot overcome her "starv[ation]" for her "lovers' food" simply by physically gratifying her lust. The "food" which lovers crave includes more than mere physical gratification; it includes the beloveds' voluntary reciprocation of lovers' affection. While the hungry are indifferent to whether an apple "consents" to be eaten, Theseus' restraint demonstrates that lovers are not satisfied simply to take, "force," or consume their beloveds (I.i.134–42, 150–55, 222–23).

Seeking to be loved, lovers compete against all those who also desire their beloveds' affection. Lysander and Demetrius, who are great imperial warriors in Plutrach's *Lives*, violently compete in Shakespeare's play for honors on love's battlefield. These competitions begin with verbal sparring but culminate in ferocious battles, which might have ended in death if not for the intervention of the fairies (cf. III.i.401–11). Theseus' attempt to transfer the passion which previously expressed itself through the "sword" into the new "key" of love is symbolically represented through the name of his servant who will help to bring about this transformation—Philostrate, or the lover of war (I.i.12). The longing to be loved proves so strong that it will even wrench apart the play's only friends. Hermia and Helena once shared "counsel sweet" on beds of "primrose" and "grew together" into "one heart" by singing "one song" in "one key" but are transformed by Lysander's variant affection into "thie[ves]" and "counterfeit[s]" seeking to steal into each other's marital bed (I.i.216–20; III.ii.198–219, 282–88). Born of the desire to be loved by the beloved, rivalry arises as the handmaiden of love.

When lovers have not been loved for bearing crosses for their beloveds, or when their beloveds bestow their affection on another, these lovers become angry and cry for justice. Just as Lysander claims to be "as well derived" and "possessed" as Demetrius, Helena, in denouncing the injustice of Demetrius' neglect of her, alleges that she is as "fair" as Hermia (I.i.99–103). Since Athens and her citizens judge the two to be equally "fair," Demetrius "errs" in "doting" on Hermia precisely because of Helena's constant, patient devotion to him—even as his "oaths" to her "melt" away and she recognizes that love is "blind" (I.i.230–5, 242–45). So great is her devotion to Demetrius that Helena willingly subjects herself to "expense" for him. She ends her soliloquy by promising to inform Demetrius of Hermia's flight and, thereby, "to enrich" her own "pain" for his sake (I.i.104, 249–50). Surpassing the restraint of the hungry Hermia or Theseus, or even the liberality of Lysander, Helena willingly harms herself for the sake of Demetrius. While she cannot see what motivates her sacrifice, her anger betrays her expectation that lovers who suffer for the sake of their beloveds have justly merited the love of their beloveds.

Lovers like Helena also remain blind to the paradox contained within their claims to justice. If their beloveds are like gods, then they are also without need, including the need to be loved or to have their own goodness or "lovability" confirmed. These gods would know that they are good. If lovers were without need, then they would not need to be loved by their beloveds. Being deficient, they do need to have their goodness confirmed through their beloveds' love. Therefore, in their very claim to merit their beloveds' love, the lovers testify to the fact that they are not worthy of being loved by beloveds who are divine. If they were god-like, these lovers would no longer love or need to be loved in turn.

In their minds, though, these lovers merit being loved. To merit being loved, lovers must be free. The moon receives no reward for waxing and waning. Theseus demonstrates his freedom by willingly restraining his lust before the cycles of the moon, which "wither[s]" the crops of his "revenue" and "linger" the satiation of his need (I.i.4–6). Hermia "must starve" because of the "cross" which she endures deprives her of Lysander's "food." While Hermia's freedom arises from her resistance to the external "yoke" of her father's "sovereignty," Theseus' self restraint points to an internal freedom which is born from his ability to delay the immediate satisfaction of a desire or need (I.i.81–82). Surpassing Hermia or Theseus's endurance of their crosses, Helena displays her freedom by voluntarily enriching or increasing her "pain" for the sake of Demetrius. So strong is Hermia and Helena's longing to be free that, like chaste nuns who cage themselves in a "cloister," they voluntarily forsake the "distilled" pleasures of "earthlier" happiness and choose a "cold" and "fruitless" existence (I.i.65–77). Lovers long to display their freedom in this way to avoid being reduced to their "spleen." Without acts of restraint and denial, their "actions" will be the product of brief, arbitrary, and involuntary desires which will dissolve as quickly, and will strike as arbitrarily, as lightning passes between heaven and earth. Hoping to be loved, lovers attempt to display their merit by restraining these compulsory desires and freely "starving" themselves for the sake of their beloveds.

The strength or power of the lovers' desire to be free does not, however, establish that they are. Egeus, Hermia, Theseus, Helena, and Lysander all testify that the desires of lovers are shaped by poetic fables and fantasies (I.i.32–35, 67–68, 132–34, 233–37; cf. V.i.195–99). Amidst his narrative of how the "cunning" Lysander filched his daughter's heart, Egeus notes that "unhardened youth" is vulnerable to "strong prevailment" which can steal the impression of a young lover's "fantasy" (I.i.30–38). Echoing Egeus' warnings about the fickleness of love, Theseus advises Hermia to "question [her] desires, know of [her] youth, [and] examine well [her] blood" before so quickly and unwaveringly rejecting her father's "will" (I.i.67–68). Hermia herself testifies to love's variability by recalling the "false" Aeneas who, like countless lovers before and since, broke his "vows" to the gods and his beloved Dido (I.i.173–74). Revealing that such promises are no more lasting than snow before a flame, the "show'rs of oaths" which Demetrius promised to Helena "dissolved" and "did melt" once he felt the "heat" of Hermia's beauty (I.i.245).

The power and variability of lust and the inability of lovers to contain it through oaths and other testaments to restraint also emerge in the woods. Hermia and Lysander flee to the woods because his "dowager" aunt will provide the "revenue" for their escape and, unlike Theseus' restraining "dowager," will facilitate the gratification of their desires (I.i.156–58; cf. I.i.5–6). The transformation of the "dowager" prefigures the release of Lysander's previously restrained desires. When Hermia and Lysander next appear, his "cunning" speech is employed not to tell tales of true love but, rather, to seduce his beloved into sharing his "bed" (II.ii.35–65). Hermia's nightmarish dream foreshadows the inconstancy of Lysander's affections which "alter" from Hermia to Helena (II.ii.61, 145–56).

Outside of the protection and restraint of the city, the prospect of rape also reemerges. The cold Demetrius chastises the "ill counsel" Helena displays in leaving the safety of the city and committing "the rich worth of [her] virginity" to "one that loves [her] not" (II.i.214–19). His sober warning assumes a more ominous tone as he leaves her "to the mercy of wild beasts" and promises to do her "mischief in the woods" if she continues to follow him (II.i.227–37). Despite the harshness of his words, they have an air of rational calculation. His presentation of rape is muted. Demetrius is not Helena's lover. Devoid of lust for her, he does not need to restrain himself; his apparent restraint is indifference. Given the violence that emerges at the end of the lovers' time in the woods, it is not clear whether a lover could restrain himself here. The woods recall—albeit in this muted way—that, despite the lovers' deepest hopes, they may not be able to restrain the compulsory desires which Theseus described in his opening lines. As a result, the possibility of lovers attaining a god-like freedom from such variable, transitory motions may only be found in "tales."

The problem of freedom reveals the dual and paradoxical nature of love and what lovers desire. In its initial appearance in the play, love longed for physical gratification and for restraint. In their account of the tales of true love, the young Athenian lovers reveal that they restrain their desires in the hope that bearing such "crosses" will transform their lust into something divine. According to these tales, true love persists, even when desires must be denied or pain endured. Able to endure, true love distinguishes itself from that "spleen-like" lust, which is compulsory, momentary, and fleeting. By enduring and denying their desires, lovers resemble their divine beloveds, who themselves are liberal and free from the needs which characterize temporal, embodied beings.

Lovers, however, hope to be loved for the sacrifices they make. They long to have their divinity confirmed through the reciprocity of their beloveds' love. They believe that they merit this love because of the restraint they display and the sacrifices they make. By displaying their freedom from need and deficiency, lovers believe that they show themselves to be whole or complete, like their divine beloveds, and, hence, are entitled to be loved by them. When they are not loved in turn, lovers grow angry and decry the injustice they suffer.

The longing to be loved illuminates the problem of love. The lovers' account of the tales reveals that what appeared as a tension between gratifying lust and restraint is, in fact, a tension between the lovers' desire to gratify their bodily desires and a desire to be free from these very desires—to be like a god. By longing to fulfill both desires, the lovers raise the question of whether their desires are incommensurable. If, as one critic of the play has suggested, comedy is characterized by the "reconciliation and the satisfaction of desire," then the opening scene of A Midsummer Night's Dream poses the question of whether love is inherently tragic.[3]

The Mechanicals' Art: Forging Love Anew

The question of whether love is inherently tragic is immediately reintroduced in the next scene by the mechanicals who attempt to transform Ovid's tragic tale of Pyramus and Thisby into a comedy which they hope to perform before the Duke on his wedding day. The Ovidian source of their play-within-the play raises the identical issues about love which the opening scene of A Midsummer Night's Dream brought forth.

Despite the similarity of themes, a critical difference between the two presentations of these issues emerges: the lovers in the opening scene are pagan aristocrats; the mechanicals are presented as a sect of Christian priests.

The mechanicals are male artisans who are not members of the Athenian nobility. Wives, mothers and children are noticeably absent from their group. In rewriting *Pyramus and Thisby*, they purge the family from the play.[4] The absence of women may account for why they are not lovers. Like the clois-tered nuns of whom Theseus anachronistically speaks, the mechanicals also appear to be "cold" and "fruitless" (I.i.71–73). Finally, they bear the names of principal figures from the Christian tradition: (Saints) Peter, Nicholas, Francis (of Assisi), and Thomas (Aquinas).

Confronted with Ovid's story, in which young lovers also flee their city in order to escape the obstructing authority of their parents, the mechanicals at-tempt to rewrite *Pyramus and Thisby* in order to remove the causes which im-pede lovers, lead to their deaths, and provoke fear in "ladies." To alleviate this fear, the mechanicals focus on extracting from *Pyramus and Thisby* the images and sounds that will frighten the ladies. The "roar" of the imaginary lion in the play, they say, will certainly "fright the ladies out of their wits" and prompt them to "shriek" (I.ii.64–70). Even the mere sight of a lion on stage "is a most dreadful thing" for "ladies" to behold since it is the most "fearful wildfowl" (III.i.25–31). The ladies, moreover, "cannot abide" seeing Pyramus' suicide and so need a "more better assurance" to "put them out of fear" (III.i.15–20). Seeking protection from this "parlous" (perilous) image, Tom Snout invokes the Virgin Mary (III.i.12).[5] While their concern for the ladies initially appears only altruistic, the mechanicals are also concerned with preserving their own lives. If the ladies endure a fright, then the mechanicals will be punished with death. Thoughtful poets, the mechanicals note—three times—that they will surely "hang" if they offend their audience (I.ii.68–74).

To protect the "ladies" and themselves, the mechanicals embark on a crusade to change *Pyramus and Thisby* in four critical ways. The task of imple-menting these changes is so daunting that Peter also prays to the Virgin Mary to bless and assist their efforts to transform this tragedy into a "lamentable comedy" (I.ii.11).[6] Bottom first recommends the elimination of Pyramus' suicide (III.i.9–11). In Ovid's tale, Pyramus kills himself because he believes Thisby is dead; finding him dead, she stabs herself. By eliminating Pyramus' suicide, Thisby will have no cause to take her own life and both lovers will be saved (cf. V.i.143–148). The second change would remove the fear caused by the lion. As Bottom's prayer for "God" to "shield" the mechanicals from the staged lion implies, the mere image of a lion poses such a frightening threat to life that it terrifies even the mechanical playing the role (III.i.28; cf. V.i.177).

While the first two changes purge the play of images of death or threats to life, the third and fourth changes insert examples of art's ability to overcome nature's indifference, to control nature, and to ensure that the lovers satisfy their desires. Pyramus and Thisby cannot meet unless the moon provides light for them to find each other. Theseus previously indicated, however, that the moon does not cycle through its phases in accordance with human desires. The mechanicals believe that they can overcome the indifference of nature: by looking in an almanac, they can track the course of the moon and learn when it will provide light (III.i.49–50). When knowledge of the workings of nature proves insufficient, they create a man-in-the-moon to provide artificial light (III.i.55–57). With the fourth change, the mechanicals ensure that the only remaining "obstacle"—the wall—no longer impedes the lovers (cf. I.ii.54–59). To the degree to which the wall is an image for the customs, "privilege," and "law" of the city, what previously separated the young Athenian lovers is transformed in the play-within-the play into a man, who now facilitates the consummation of Pyramus and Thisby's sexual desires (cf. V.i.180, 189, 200). The play will comfort the audience by showing art's ability to replicate and control nature and to ensure that lovers can satisfy their desires.

The impetus for the changes seems to be the mechanicals' "materialist bias."[7] In contrast to the young Athenian lovers who fail to refer to their lust in the opening scene, the mechanicals indulge in sexual jokes and refer to venereal diseases (cf. I.ii.84–96; V.i.169–180, 200). Love, in their account, appears to be nothing more than bodily gratification. Failing to discuss "true love," they give no account of the young lovers' longing to enjoy a god-like freedom from such desires. The mechanicals also extract the play-within-the-play's testament to "true love": the suicides of Pyramus and Thisby. Hermia's praise of suicide, in the opening scene of A Midsummer Night's Dream, illuminates its relationship to true love. By twice expressing her own willingness to die rather than live without Lysander, Hermia indicates that her life would be unbearable without her beloved (I.i.79, 173). While her lust could be gratified with another "food," her need to be loved by her divine beloved could not be satisfied if he were to die.

In expunging suicide from their play, the mechanicals betray their belief that lovers do not naturally desire to possess god-like perfection or goodness and to have this goodness confirmed through the love of a divine beloved. The materialism of the mechanicals leads, paradoxically, to their belief that the lovers' desire for "true love" is the unnatural product of dangerous images. As the frequent references to sight in the opening scene indicate, the perception of lovers is formed by the accounts which they hear or read (I.i.55–56, 132–33). Love may "transpose" things "base and vile" into "form and dignity" but love's power to do so arises from the tales or histories which transform lust into "true love" (I.i.132–34, 232–33). Denying that tales and stories of true love appeal to a natural longing in lovers, the mechanicals contend that the "ladies" only suffer "parlous" fear as a result of potent and hazardous images imprinted on their imaginations. The mechanicals thus seek to remove these images and replace them with edifying ones that promise lovers that they will be able to gratify their other, natural desires perpetually. If the mechanicals succeed, then love will no longer be tragic. If their understanding is correct, and lovers only long to have their desires perpetually gratified, then the philanthropic poet would provide the fearful with an image of bodily immortality and the permanent satisfaction of desire. Bottom's god-like translation into the fairy realm provides this image.

Ironically Fulfilling Love's Longings: Bottom's Translation

A complete vision of the mechanicals' efforts to remove the tragic elements of love would include an image of a lover saved from his "mortal grossness." The play the mechanicals perform for the Athenian lovers not only fails to present such an image but remains a tragedy. The changes they intend to make are never fully implemented: the wall and moon are added but Pyramus and Thisby still commit suicide, which the prologue does not amend (V.i.143–48, 295–301, 340–42). The mechanicals do not implement all the proposed changes because they cannot "rehearse" (III.i.69). While the mechanical's play-within-the play does not provide a complete picture of their attempt to transform love from a tragedy to a comedy, this image can be found in Bottom's translation—his assumption, in ass-like form, into the fairies' realm.[8]

There are at least three reasons why Bottom's "most rare vision" can be understood to replace the mechanicals' unperformed comedy (IV.i.203). Examining the structure of the third act of A Midsummer Night's Dream reveals that Bottom's translation literally takes the place of the mechanicals' rehearsal of the transformed Pyramus and Thisby (III.i.69, 99). In addition, the two principal features of the dream are analogous to the two sets of substantive changes the mechanicals intend to make to their play-within-the play. After the "spirit" Puck gives Bottom an "ass head," the weaver sings to prove that he is not afraid (III.i.111). Awoken by his singing, Titania, whose eyes have been anointed with the juice of the love-in-idleness flower, sees him, thrice declares her love for him, and promises him two bountiful gifts (III.i.135, 149; IV.i.44; cf. III.i.165, 195). She gives him "fairies to attend" to his desires (III.i.150). These beneficial spirits gratify four of his five senses, but in fact they principally gratify Bottom's "chief humor"—his longing for tyrannical power, which is satisfied by the mastery he exercises over the fairies who obey his every will and whim (IV.i.1–33; cf. I.ii.24). She also promises to "purge" him of his "mortal grossness" so that he will become "like an airy spirit" (III.i.153–54). Through the combination of these two promises, Bottom will be able to satisfy his desires not only now, or in the near future, but also for all time.

Finally, Bottom's dream is intended to serve the same purpose which the mechanicals' changes were intended to serve. By eliminating frightening images of death and adding comforting images of art's power to satisfy human needs, the mechanicals hope to allay the ladies' fears. By providing the audience with an account of beneficent fairies who promise to relieve "mortal grossness" and eternally satisfy all mortal desires, Bottom believes that his "epilogue" will relieve these same fears. For this reason, Bottom attempts to "sing" the "ballet of this dream" after Thisby's death. If Bottom is correct, then an audience who could "see the epilogue" of his translation would be "perfectly joined together in the same mind and in the same judgment" that life is not short and unsatisfying (IV.i.212–17).[9]

The frequent references in the scenes depicting Bottom's miraculous translation to passages from the Epistles of St. Paul also support the claim that Bottom's translation provides an image of a lover saved from his "mortal grossness."[10] According to the use of the word in the extant English versions of St. Paul's text, a human being who is "translated" is "taken up bodily into the presence of God without dying" (cf. I.i.191; III.i.113; III.ii.31).[11] As was the case with the Biblical Enoch, translation liberates Bottom from his "mortal grossness," allows him to dwell with the spirits, and affords him the opportunity to experience a "most rare vision."[12]

Whereas Peter Quince and Puck use a critical Pauline term—"translated"—to describe Bottom's experience, Bottom's account of his dream parodies St. Paul's claim that the "foolishness" of the Holy Spirit is superior to the "wisdom" of the "princes of the world" and the "prudent" (IV.i.209–217; cf. I Corinthians 2.9–10, quoting Isaiah 64.3).[13] St. Paul argues in his First Letter to the Corinthians that those who know that their "base" and "despised" "flesh" must perish live "in weakness, and in fear, and in much trembling" (I Cor. 1:27–28, 2:3)—like the "ladies" in the audience or Minyas' daughters in Ovid's Pyramus and Thisby. Trapped within the deficiencies of the body, the senses, and reason, they cannot know the "power of God," which is the only means to "save" human beings from this fearful fate (I Cor. 1:18, 21). God's power is most radically expressed in Christ crucified and his "cross," which is a "stumbling block" to the Jews and "foolishness" to the Greeks (I Cor. 1:17–19, 23; 2:8). Through this "cross," death, and hence fear, is overcome.

Because the "mystery" of the "cross" and Christ's miraculous resurrection cannot be "known" through the senses, the "wisdom of God," remains "hidden" from the "wise," who know only through sensory experience (*I Cor.* 2:5–7). In contrast to "the wisdom of this world," the "wisdom of God" is revealed through the Holy Spirit, which surpasses reason by remaining independent of the limited capacities of the senses.

In parodying St. Paul's argument, Bottom claims that he had this "most rare vision" because his senses were transformed—his eyes heard; his ears saw; his hands tasted; and his tongue conceived. Whereas in St. Paul's account the senses are transcended through the power of the Holy Spirit, Bottom's senses are preserved, albeit in a new and transformed way. St. Francis of Assisi called his body an "ass" (cf. III.i.97).[14] In contrast to St. Paul's account, Bottom is able to experience this "vision" because he becomes an ass or all body. As a result of his translation, Bottom conceives through his tongue; his reason becomes the mere expression of his hunger or taste. As Peter Quince exclaims, Bottom is "monstrous"—an image of nothing more than his translated body (III.i.99).

Because his vision depends upon the preservation and transformation of his body, Bottom cannot rationally convey his dream to other human beings, who still depend upon their sensory experience. As a result, his dream remains "past the wit of" the mechanicals or the audience; they can only come to believe, or opine, the account he provides them. Bottom notes that a man would be "but an ass if he [were to] go about to expound this dream" (IV.i.205). Given what has been said about being an "ass," Bottom claims that only one who is all body, devoid of reason, would "expound" or believe such "foolishness." St. Paul, at the end of his account, claims that the Holy Spirit reveals the "bottom" of God's secrets.[15] With his name playfully recalling St. Paul's claim, Bottom gets to the "bottom" of the fairies' world as a result of the mischievous "spirit" Puck, who is the minion of the king of the spirits, Oberon.[16] While promising to cure fear through this rare vision, Bottom's dream may at its "bottom" be mere "foolishness."

The dream's image of the lover is "foolish" for at least three reasons: it demonstrates the incoherence of the lovers' conceptions of the divine and the body; it presents lovers with an image of a gratified tyrant; and it encourages lovers to equate their immediate desires with what is fitting or just. The divine as presented in the dream is incoherent. Titania and Oberon fail to account for why a self-sufficient god-like being without need would or could serve lovers (see, for example, II.i.64–80). In Bottom's dream, Titania needs to love and be loved and, thus, is as incomplete as the lovers are. In their need to imagine "some bringer of [their] joy," lovers also imagine an anthropomorphized god and fail to recognize that what is truly divine would be free from the needs and desires which characterize them (V.i.19–20). Seeking to preserve lovers' desires, the dream presents Bottom as both relieved of his "mortal grossness" and still eating, drinking, and "scratching." The dream provides no account of why a lover who has attained a god-like condition would still have bodily needs which require satisfaction. The presence of these desires within this vision does suggest, however, that the lovers want to satisfy their desires eternally; they do not want to transcend them.

The dream, therefore, shows that the mechanicals' proposal is impossible. Lovers fear death and the cessation of desire that it brings. Seeking to overcome death, they long for the eternal preservation, and gratification, of their bodily desires. This longing can only be satisfied if their bodies are made immortal. The idea of bodily immortality is, however, "foolishness." If immortality necessitates the absence of change or perfection, then an immortal "body" would be without change or motion. Bodily desires are, though, characterized by their change and motion. Lovers incoherently long for an unchanging changeable body. They hope, as well, for a beneficent god who would be both unchangeable and able to change by acting to remove their "mortal grossness." Lovers, therefore, long in a doubly incoherent way: they seek to become god-like and yet to gratify perpetually their bodily desires; they imagine a god who is both perfect and yet needs, and acts for, human beings.

Bottom's dream also presents a dangerous image of a gratified tyrant. Peter alleges that there is "not a man in all Athens able to discharge Pyramus but" Bottom. According to this claim, only Bottom can play the lover. Yet, to the degree to which Bottom can be said to be a lover, he only plays the role as an actor. While Titania pursues Bottom with "the soul of love," Bottom has no interest in loving Titania (II.i.182). Although she repeatedly declares her love for him, he never reciprocates. Instead of proclaiming his love, he calls her love unreasonable and corrects her praise of his wisdom and beauty (III.i.136–49).

According to Bottom, his "chief humor" is for tyranny, not for love (I.ii.19, 24; IV.ii.7–8). He consistently displays this "humor" through the play. In his first words in the play, Bottom commands Peter Quince; he attempts to play all the roles; he orchestrates the changes in the play; and, during the performance, he corrects Theseus (I.ii.2–3, 14–15, 45–67; III.i.16, 33–35, 52–54, 63–67; V.i.183–86). While in the fairy world, Bottom indulges his humor by mastering those who serve him. Taking more pleasure in ruling Titania and the other fairies than in eating the relishes they bring, Bottom metaphorically longs to ingest more than mere food—he longs to consume or incorporate these spirits or to conform them to his "will."

Through the recounting of his dream, he hopes to gratify this "humor" permanently. By providing the audience with his dream, he imagines himself surpassing the divine hero Hercules, to whom he compares himself. Bottom's dream will break the "gates" of hell and mar the "fates" which rob human beings of their lives, frustrate their desires, and foster their fears (I.ii.25–33; cf. V.i.279–83). By relieving their fears, Bottom will become the greatest benefactor of human beings and as a result be "preferred" above all others (IV ii.37). Giving his dream "permanence," he will become the perfect tyrant: eternally served by all he has benefited.[17]

This picture of Bottom's tyrannical humor clarifies the ways in which Bottom is distinguishable from the young Athenian lovers. Unlike these young lovers, Bottom never loves another; he never restrains his desires or sacrifices for the sake of a beloved. There is no indication that he desires to emulate or become a divine beloved as these young lovers do. As a result, there is no indication that he believes that anything outside of, or beyond, himself is desirable, except as a means to gratify his existing desires. While repeatedly eating during his translation, Bottom's tastes remain pedestrian: he "desirest to eat" merely oats, hay, and dried peas. Despite the fairies' offer to "fetch" more ornamented foods, Bottom would "rather have" his "great desire" gratified and the fairies not "stir" him (III.i.160–62; IV.i.10–17, 31–38). Bottom desires nothing more than what he already wants. He needs no "jewel" or ornamentation; he desires no relishes for his foods. He believes his desires are sufficient; they do not need amendment or supplementation. Just as Bottom does not wish to amend his culinary desires with relishes, so too he does not want to amend his erotic desires with a beloved. While he desires to have others serve him, he does not want to be "loved" for he has no desire for the sacrificial or restrained relishes which come from longing to be worthy of being loved by a god-like beloved.

Bottom is distinct from the young Athenian lovers in another critical, psychological way. Failing to exercise restraint, Bottom transforms all of his servants into indistinguishable tools to gratify his desires. The god-like Titania, though unloved by Bottom, is his unloved gratifier. His varying attachments to Peaseblossom, Cobweb, Moth and Mustardseed are determined by their respective ability to relieve whatever need he has at that moment (III.i.176–190). In contrast to Bottom, Hermia's chastity, that is, her ability to restrain her desires, is for the sake of keeping Lysander "virtuous" (II.ii.59). She would enter a nunnery to ensure only Lysander would receive her "virgin patent" (I.i.79–82). He is her god-like beloved. She restrains herself for him to receive what only he can provide her—a confirmation of her goodness, as proven by his love for her.

If Bottom's dream were propagated, all beloveds would become expendable, serving simply to gratify the appetites of the lovers. Any apparent restraint exercised by the lovers would be for their sake. Lovers who sought to be relieved of their "mortal grossness" might practice their chastity on any number of beloveds to earn the god's reward. The suicide that marked the "true lovers" of the tales would be unnecessary, as the beloved is no longer the indispensible way to confirm the lovers' goodness. Bottom's dream would bring about a critical psychological shift in lovers: they would no longer experience their restraint as sacrifice for their god-like beloveds. Instead, restraint would become a temporary, calculating way to gain greater, future rewards, and beloveds would be transformed into indistinguishable means for gaining rewards. If the dream were promulgated, the possibility of experiencing and understanding restraint, as the young Athenian lovers do, would be destroyed.

Finally, by presenting an image of a "lover" who is satisfied with his own desires as they are, Bottom's dream "foolishly" depicts what is just or fitting as equivalent to the gratification of immediate desires. Believing that he is a god, Bottom calls his servants worshipers (III.i.173–74). Acting on this belief, Bottom assumes that his immediate desires, and hence their satisfaction, must be good. As a result, what is fitting or just becomes the mere satisfaction of his "will"—the rule of the god-like strongest.

Bottom's notion of what is fitting or just recalls Athens' "ancient privilege," which allowed Egeus to "dispose" of Hermia according to his "will" (I.i.42–45; cf. IV.i.178). According to the unstated implications of Egeus' claim, if he sought to recover a sword he had lent to another, were mad, and intended to harm himself with this same sword, it would be unjust for the borrower to withhold the sword from him or lie about its whereabouts. Egeus denies that justice arises from what reason can know about what is fitting or beneficial. Given the variability of the lovers' desires, and their propensity to desire what is often harmful to them, the play repeatedly shows that the implied premise of Egeus' claim—that his immediate desires always benefit him—is false. If nature is hostile or indifferent to lovers, then they may have longings which are impossible, or hazardous, to satisfy. To know what is fitting for them, lovers would need to use their reason to look beyond their immediate desires to try to discern if they should, and how they might best, be gratified. Theseus' restraint suggests that there may be goods which do not appear to satisfy lovers' immediate needs. His advice to the obstinate Hermia provides a clue as to how these goods might be found: the wise use reason to govern their desires in light of what is fitting and most likely to make them "earthlier happy" (I.i.76).

Despite the fact that both locate what is just or fitting in the "will" of the stronger, Bottom's dream is much more dangerous than Egeus' "ancient" claim. Although both characters are spoken of as gods, Bottom alone has the additional authority of revelation to ensure that his "will" is gratified. If Bottom's dream were to be openly preached and believed in Athens, his "will" would be absolute and justice would become the gratification of his divinely sanctioned desires. As inconstant and often dangerous lovers show, their immediate desires are frequently opposed to what is fitting or beneficial to them. Bottom's dream, however, presents an image of tyranny fulfilled. In addition to presenting an incoherent notion of lovers and gods, his dream would impress upon the audiences' imagination a powerful image of earthly happiness rooted, not in reason, but in the gratification of immediate desires. Bottom, therefore, is an image of deified appetite, which ungoverned by reason would rule tyrannically over the human being.

Pagan Wisdom: Governing Love through Theseus' Statesmanship

Given the danger posed by Bottom's dream, Theseus' decision to show the mechanicals' kindred play-within-the-play to the young lovers appears foolish (IV.i.215–17). The temptation to dismiss his decision must be tempered, however, by the picture of his wisdom which emerges from his first appearance in A Midsummer Night's Dream. Of all the lovers, he alone recognizes the dual character of his own love—his desire both to gratify his lust and to restrain it. His apparent "foolishness" must also be reconsidered in light of the fact that he not only knows and governs himself and his love but also wisely governs nearly all of the events which transpire within A Midsummer Night's Dream. In the opening scene, Theseus announces his intention to establish a new order (I.i.16–19). While constrained by the old law, he is not absolutely so and augments it to the degree that seems possible at the time (I.i.41–45, 65–66). After the events in the woods change Demetrius, Theseus "overbears" Egeus and the old law (IV.i.178–79). With the father's authority thus overruled, Egeus disappears from the play. By this act, Theseus does what the mechanicals intend to do: he ensures that a would-be tragic tale of love ends comically.

With respect to Theseus' choice of the mechanicals' play-within-the play, he is similarly in control. Bottom informs the other mechanicals that Theseus has "preferred" their "comedy" even before Philostrate has presented the options (IV.ii.32–37). After returning to the city, Bottom sees Theseus and presumably informs him not only of his translation but also the mechanicals' failure to "rehearse" (IV.ii.34–35). Theseus, therefore, knows that the play which the mechanicals perform will not be their revised, comic version of *Pyramus and Thisby*, but will be a tragedy in which the principal characters die (V.i.56–58, 301, 341, 352–53; cf. IV.ii.41–42). Theseus also changes the way the play will be viewed by adding his own prologue, which supersedes Peter Quince's.

Theseus treats the mechanicals seriously and seeks to control them. His seriousness arises from his intimate knowledge of the woods and the potential affect of the events which occur there on Athens. Unlike Bottom and the mechanicals, the lovers do not see fairies or a translated ass. In recounting their events in the woods, the lovers do not mention any "bringer" of "joy" or "fear" (IV.i.186–98; cf. V.i.19–22). In relating the lovers' account of the events, Hippolyta also fails to mention a "bringer" (V.i.1, 23–27). Given these silences, Theseus's remarks to Hippolyta about the "lunatic, the lover and the poet" cannot be based upon the lovers' report. Instead, he must rely on what he has heard from Bottom, or what he knows. Since Bottom did not encounter the lovers while in the woods, Theseus must know about the woods and what transpires there. By noting that an "oak" bears Theseus' name, the mechanicals suggest that what transpires in the woods also falls under the Duke's control. Unlike the land whose revenue he is denied, the woods are the Duke's property; he knows them and enjoys their fruits when they flower (I.ii.99).

Due to Theseus' governance of the mechanicals' play, it does not have the same effect on each lover. As Hermia and Helena watch in silence, Lysander and Demetrius see a comedy, whereas Hippolyta perceives a tragedy. Replying to Philostrate's objection to his choice, Theseus instructs the young lovers to focus on the intention of the mechanicals and not the action of the play or the content of what is said (V.i.81–84, 89–105). By doing so, Theseus causes the young men to see the mechanicals as well-meaning buffoons and to treat their play as an object of ridicule. The importance of neutralizing the influence of the mechanicals on Lysander and Demetrius is suggested by their names. In Plutarch's *Lives*, Lysander and Demetrius are great enemies of Athens. The Spartan Lysander inflicts a naval defeat on Athens that precipitates her defeat in the Peloponnesian War. Lysander corrupts Spartan virtue through wealth and his "excessive liberality" and corrupts Athenian liberty by suppressing popular government and installing the oligarchic rule of the thirty. Although indifferent to oaths, he is said to be the first Greek whom the cities worshiped as a god.[18] The "wild beast" Demetrius is also impious. In addition to corrupting the Mysteries, he pollutes the Parthenon with his "profane" sexual escapades. He is deified as a god as well, ornamenting himself with robes which suggest that he rules the cosmos and taking as his model Bacchus. With respect to lust, Demetrius has "the worst character of all the princes of his time."[19]

Through the characters of Theseus, Lysander, and Demetrius, Shakespeare recalls and presents simultaneously three critical figures from Athens' history whose relationship to erotic love affected her founding, the death of her political liberty, and the corruption of her religion. Through his statesmanship, Theseus attempts not only to re-found Athens so that erotic love has a place within the city but also to neutralize the threats erotic love poses to Athens—threats symbolized by Lysander and Demetrius. His efforts appear successful. The formerly feuding Lysander and Demetrius now laugh together. While their historical namesakes erotically pursued empire and divinization, these young lovers seek objects for their erotic love in their beloved; their wars are fought in the bedroom and not on the battlefield. Like Philostrate, they have been transformed from lovers of war to lovers of mirth and merriment. Whereas the historical, oligarchic Lysander destroyed Athenian democracy, his namesake views the mechanicals as well intentioned and harmless parts of the city. Although the historical Lysander corrupted Spartan virtue through Persian gold, his namesake ignores the mechanicals' materialism and embraces the moderate restraint which accompanies "true love."

Greater importance, however, should be placed on the way in which Theseus' comments blind the young men to the impiety of the mechanicals' play. While A Midsummer Night's Dream does not speak frequently of the city's gods, it does refer to the pagan pantheon and the temples in which they are worshiped (IV.i.179, 197; V.i.177). The telling of Pyramus and Thisby in Ovid is an act of impiety. Three "ladies" recount the tale instead of worshiping Bacchus. Bottom's dream is another act of impiety—the denial of the old pagan gods, like "Jove," in favor of the new divinities revealed through his vision. In Plutarch's Lives, Lysander and Demetrius both display a two-fold impiety. In addition to undermining the accepted religious practices—by disregarding oaths and desecrating sacred space and rites—they seek to replace the old religion with a new one which is predicated on their own divinity. Theseus' prologue renders Bottom's evangelists laughable, however. Through this act of statesmanship, Theseus prevents Lysander and Demetrius from learning from the mechanicals how to undermine Athens' existing religion and establish themselves as gods.

The historical examples of Lysander and Demetrius draw attention to what the effect of propagating Bottom's dream would be—the dream would replace the old religion of Athens with a new faith that has Bottom as its deified prophet. Bottom's prophecy is the deification of desires and their immediate gratification. While Athenian religion is infrequently mentioned in the play, it can be said to leave room for reason. Athens allows for reason's moderate discernment of what is beneficial, in contrast to Bottom's immoderate prophecy, and hence allows for Theseus' wise statesmanship. If the Athens of Theseus fosters reason's governance of erotic love, then Athens' decline is seen most clearly in the threat which Lysander and Demetrius represent—unrestrained erotic love which finds its satisfaction in the deification of the tyrant and his desires.

In contrast to the young men, the women do not mock the play. Hippolyta, the woman who initially experiences love as only injury and force, comes to empathize with or feel pity for Pyramus, a man who calls on the furies to kill him when he believes his beloved is dead (V.i.209, 279–85; cf. IV.i.46). This moment appears to be the other "key" which Theseus hoped would ornament their wedding: an awakening in her of a notion of a "true love." As a result of his ability to ensure the play affects different audiences differently, Theseus once again surpasses what the mechanicals had hoped to accomplish: he renders the play simultaneously "merry" and "tragical" (V.i.58).

Theseus also allows Hermia and Helena to watch the play-within-the-play in silence, a silence they have maintained since leaving the woods (cf.V.i.84). In their final remarks, Hermia had noted that she sees "with parted eye, [w]hen everything seems double," and Helena had described this double seeing in the following manner: "I have found Demetrius like a jewel, [m]ine own and not mine own" (IV.i.187–91). Prior to this point in the play, all the characters—except Theseus—were blind to the dual nature of love; thereafter, the two young women have an eye which is "parted" or cleft, and so capable of seeing two distinct facets of something at once.

Hermia and Helena now see their beloveds as somehow both their "own" and not their "own"—or as linked to their desires, and yet independent of them. To describe the shift that has occurred in their seeing, Helena compares her beloved to a jewel (IV.i.189–91). Unlike the goods which gratified Bottom, a jewel cannot be tasted, smelled, heard, or touched—in the sense of providing sexual gratification—by lovers. Like Theseus' wisdom, the jewel can become the lovers' "own" only insofar as it can be known or seen, even while it remains visible to others. The jewel is never possessed or ingested—incorporated into the lovers as Bottom's gluttony suggests. Lovers who long for this jewel do not dwell simply in their private, immediate desires; attracted to the jewel, these lovers are drawn to an object which must remain other than them.

Lovers see in the jewel the perfect, unchanging character which they also ascribe to their divine beloveds. The jewel beautifies lovers who wear it;

adorned with a jewel, they appear to acquire the attributes of the jewel or to become jewel-like. In this way, the jewel appears to "benefit" lovers as they expect their divine beloveds to do. Despite these similarities, the jewel and the god-like beloved remain fundamentally distinct. Lacking desire and volition, the jewel does not need to be loved and cannot love. Because the jewel cannot love, the benefits lovers enjoy from the jewel are not bestowed as just rewards for the lovers' merit and sacrifice. The relationship of the jewel's lovers to the jewel is no longer economic or characterized by exchange—as if lovers sacrifice for a divine beloved and it owes them love in return. Therefore, the jewel's lovers would not sacrifice for the jewel; their love is not the "true love" found in the tales that the young Athenian lovers recite. The admiration of the jewel's beauty by its lovers in the absence of all hope and expectation that it will love them in return is the most important part of love which the so-called lovers in the play overlook.

Lovers desire the jewel for its pure pleasures. Unlike taste, which is preceded by the pain of hunger or thirst, sight is not accompanied by an analogous pain. Lovers take untainted pleasure in seeing an object which is whole, self-sufficient, and complete—that is, beautiful. Wearing the jewel, lovers become beautiful. Looking upon their own beauty, lovers enjoy pleasures which are analogous to seeing the jewel.

The jewel then does not gratify in the way that the food Bottom consumes does. Like the relishes which Bottom rejects, the jewel is not necessary (cf.III.i.151; IV.i.36–37). Just as his hunger can be satiated through plain oats, so too can unornamented clothing relieve the pain caused by the cold. In ornamenting themselves with the jewel or adding relishes to their food, lovers do not aim to gratify merely the desires which rule over Bottom. While they become warm and eat, these lovers also beautify themselves by directing their desires beyond mere gratification. Through ornamentation, these lovers come to approximate, and participate in, the divine completeness which they see in the beautiful jewel or relish. In addition to enjoying the sight of beauty for its own sake, these lovers are pleased when their desires participate in divine completeness to the greatest degree possible for mortals. Like Theseus' wisdom, the beautiful jewel pleases when seen and when it ornaments its lovers.

The jewel, therefore, is a reasonable image of the proper object of erotic love. In desiring the jewel, lovers experience the pure pleasure of sight. In ornamenting their other desires with relishes, they come to approximate the completion, self-sufficiency, perfection, and, hence, goodness of the jewel. Seeing their beauty, these lovers do not need to have their goodness confirmed by a beloved; they know they are good. While they are not gods, they have approximated divinity to the greatest degree possible for human beings. In doing so, they have avoided the incoherencies which beset those lovers who sought to gratify perpetually their immediate bodily desires. The jewel's lovers do not seek such gratification; rather, they long to beautify their desires.

The serious statesman leaves a place for such lovers in the city, knowing that the wise governance of the city depends upon them. Although Demetrius' variable affection previously shattered their friendship, they are here again one—"two artificial gods" united in one counsel, key, song, flower, or heart through wisdom (III.ii.192–219). Like their namesakes, the Hermes-like Hermia and Helena, who is translated in the woods into Helen, through their wisdom or double vision, are the beautiful intermediaries between the divine things and lovers.

Although the events in the woods are edifying for the young women, they pose a serious threat to Athens if Bottom's experience there comes to be known. Theseus, in his greatest act of statesmanship, twice prevents Bottom from speaking his dream as an epilogue (V.i.348, 354). As a result of Theseus' advice Lysander and Demetrius laugh at the mechanicals' blundering performance. Even if the mechanicals' shared dream were to be spoken, its doctrine would not be taken seriously (cf. IV.ii.30). In the place of Bottom's dream, Theseus offers his own account of the fairies (V.i.355–62). In the statesman's account, the fairies do not serve Bottom's private, tyrannical "will" but, rather, visit the shared beds of loves to bring them "rightly revels and new jollity."

Bottom's dream must be silenced; it undermines and denies the authority of reason. From the perspective of reason, his vision is utter "foolishness." Despite its "foolishness," the vision would give Bottom power over other human beings, who would want the perpetual gratification of their desires which the dream promises. Given its potential power, the dream would bestow on its prophet unlimited authority—authority surpassing Egeus' at the beginning of the play—and, as a result, would subjugate all Athenians to his "will." As Bottom says, no one who speaks this dream would be a "true" Athenian (V.i.215; cf. IV.i.212–13, IV.ii.29).

If promulgated, the image of the translated Bottom would foster a dangerous notion of the human being. Bottom's eyes, which allowed him to see or know for himself, are transformed into a vehicle for hearing, or relying upon the opinion or account of others. He now conceives, or thinks, according to his tastes, or his desires for food and drink. His reason relies on hearing the best ways to satisfy his body's desires or needs. While he was translated, four of his five senses were satisfied; sight was not (cf. IV.i.1–30). Unlike the young women who have come to see the jewel, Bottom is incapable of "see-ing" as Theseus does. Bottom's dream also strips the head of its rationality; it is ass-like and driven by the passions of a beast. The dream would, therefore, deprive lovers of an image of the human being between an ass-like animal and a god-like tyrant.

In Plutarch's *Lives*, Theseus, the legendary founder of Athens, engages in a similar act of statesmanship. His foundation of a new political order is predicated on his slaying of the Cretan Minotaur. Unlike the centaur, which has the body of a horse and the reasoning mind of a human being, the Minotaur has the body of a human being and the impassioned head of a bull—the animal associated with Bacchus. Theseus' slaying of the Minotaur in Plutarch is analogous to his slaying of this image of human beings in Shakespeare's *A Midsummer Night's Dream*.[20] As he also does by eliminating the plays about drunken centaurs, Bacchanals, and the death of learning, Theseus' metaphorical slaying of Bottom's dream neuters the potential effect of this powerful image on the audience and protects the status of reason. Guided by reason, human beings can question their immediate desires and inquire after those goods that might make them "earthlier happy" (I.i.76). To foster in them the desire for these goods, the statesman Theseus replaces Bottom's narcissistic dream with the social and communal dancing of couples (V.i.353).

Shakespeare's Statesmanship: Governing the Fairies in the Woods

Praise for Theseus' statesmanship must be tempered, however, by the play's ending. While the silence of Hermia and Helena casts a dark shadow over the play's final act, it is the fairies' final blessing which draws our atten-tion to the precarious nature of the resolution promised by the marriages.[21] Oberon vows that "the issue" created in the bride-beds of these lovers shall forever "be fortunate" (V.i.398). The issue of Theseus and Hippolyta is Hippolytus, who is killed by the amorous Phaedra—yet another stepmother playing a prominent role in *A Midsummer Night's Dream*. The fairies intend for good fortune to preside over these couples but are unable to fulfill their intention.

According to the fairies' description of themselves, they are the personi-fication of natural forces. Human beings, seeking to understand why hos-tile, fear-inducing, chance events occur in nature, imagine a first cause—a "bringer of that . . . fear." When human beings spill a drink or slip off a chair, they imagine that Puck has mischievously undermined their intent

(II.i.32–58).[22] When nature appears hostile to their needs, they imagine that the feuding Titania and Oberon are the "parents and originals" of their problems (II.i.81–87).[23] When human beings enjoy natural blessings, they also imagine "some bringer of that joy" (V.i.19–20).[24]

Contrary to lovers' imaginings, nature is not intentionally concerned with them; it can benefit or destroy—it can appear comic or tragic. Its forces do, though, accidentally benefit. When prudent statesmen recognize what has occurred and how to use it, they can direct nature's blessings to bring great goods to their people. When the fairies touch Demetrius' eyes with the "juice" from the love-in-idleness flower, thereby ensuring that the desires of the lovers are in accord, Theseus overthrows the old law, and Egeus' claims, thus allowing A Midsummer Night's Dream to end comically (II.i.166–68; cf. I.i.41–45, 65–73).

The statesman's "solution" cannot, however, be permanent. To see why, it is necessary to return to the source of both Shakespeare's A Midsummer Night's Dream and the mechanicals' play-within-the play: Ovid's Pyramus and Thisby (Metamorphoses 4.1–201), a tale which reveals the place and power of Bacchus in nature and human life.[25] Both plays attempt to transform this tale of Pyramus and Thisby from a tragedy into a comedy.[26] Pyramus and Thisby is the first of three tales told by the daughters of Minyas to pass time while they perform Minerva's household tasks. Choosing to "stay at home [and] violate [Bacchus's] holy day," they work at their looms instead of participating in his "sacred orgies." In working at their looms, and in the tale they tell, the daughters display their preference for Minerva (Athena), the goddess of weaving, over Bacchus. The young lovers in the tale die as a consequence of their decision to follow their desires and to disobey and abandon their families. Love, according to the tale, must be restrained by the authority of the family and given expression in the household. In addition to telling this tale and refusing to participate in Bacchus' festival, the daughters go so far as to "dare to say he's not Jove's son." This declaration makes explicit what their failure to participate implied—that the recitation of Pyramus and Thisby is an act of impiety, for which the three daughters are punished: they are turned into bats and forced to dwell in "the woods; since they detest the day." After they are punished, "the name of Bacchus . . . gained great fame."

In the Ovidian tale, the aspect of erotic desire symbolized by Bacchus is decried for its destructive effects on the young lovers; it brings "orgies," divides them from their families, and precipitates their deaths. In A Midsummer Night's Dream, Bacchus' influence extends beyond young lovers. The conflict between Oberon and Titania concerns a "changeling boy" from India, whose mother was a "vot'ress" of Titania's "order" (II.i.118–45). This language recalls Ovid's description of Bacchus: the god is said to be "eternally a boy" who has "won the Orient where . . . sun-scorched India is bathed by Ganges" (4.10–20). The disorders within nature and among the lovers are attributable to Bacchus, who is aligned with the Queen of fairies in opposition to their King. Since the blessing of the lovers' beds requires a restoration of harmony in the fairy realm, Bacchus must become Oberon's "henchman." With the juice of the love-in-idleness flower, Oberon induces Titania to surrender the Bacchus-like boy to him and ends her maternal devotion to him (II.i.68–80, 121, 137; IV.i.87–92).

The difficulty in seeing the true character of nature—the life-giving but destructive forces of the god Bacchus in her—can be found most clearly in the mechanicals. Bacchus is associated with wine, bulls, agriculture, winnowing fans, and resurrection—which all recall the coming into being and passing away of life.[27] The mechanicals, however, are devoid of such associations. They are never associated with the most basic reminders of the cycle of life: offspring, who are linked to the Athenian aristocrats at the beginning and end of the play. Despite being artisans, there is no farmer among them.

Bottom's profession as a weaver recalls Athena, not Bacchus. Because he assumes the ass-head, which comically replaces the frightful bull-head of the Minotaur in Plutarch's "Life" of Theseus, Bottom might be thought to represent the mechanicals' pious acknowledgement of Bacchus. If so, it must be with the following qualification. Bacchic resurrection describes the general cycle of life in nature; while a particular ear of corn may die, its seeds give life to a new generation of corn. Although fostering hope in individual immortality, Bacchus recalls the general cycle of life and does not ensure the resurrection of any particular human being. Bottom's dream presents the taming of this general cycle of life through personal resurrection. In his dream, both aspects of the erotic longing are satisfied: he individually retains the motions of his bodily desires, which he is promised will be perpetually satisfied, and yet personally becomes a god, who is purged of his "mortal grossness." The dream promises to bring into accord the lovers' longing for a permanent, intelligible order and their longing for the motion of life, which is represented in their quest to gratify perpetually their desires. Bottom's dream is "foolish" because it claims that the tension between Athena and Bacchus can be resolved and is not a permanent feature of nature.

The irresolvable nature of this tension would imply that a statesman could not govern the phenomenon of Bacchus. Oberon's use of the love-in-idleness flower must, however, moderate this initial impression. While Bacchus and the fairies come from the east, the "love-in-idleness" flower is "western" (II.i.69, 166). Its name is a synonym for the "pansy," whose root is *pensée* in

French, which translates as thought, reflection, or meditation.[28] The "love-in-idleness" flower is an image of reason.

This claim, however, lacks precision. According to Oberon's account, the flower did not originally possess power over would-be lovers (see II.i.155–68). The flower's purple color—the color of royalty and rule—came into being as a result of the moon's affect on Cupid's arrow. Oberon indicates that the arrow only fell upon its intended path, and upon the flower, when it crossed the "chaste" beams of the "moon" which "quenched" its "fiery shaft." The purple "love-in-idleness" flower arises when a "milk-white," "little western flower," Cupid's arrow, and the quenching beams of the moon are united. While the western flower is an image of pure reason—milk-white and un-tainted by erotic love—and Cupid's arrow is erotic love with enough power to "pierce" even the heart of a "fair vestal" virgin of the west, the two only unite in and through the power of the moon. What, then, is the moon?

The question of how to represent the moon dominates the play.[29] At the beginning of A Midsummer Night's Dream, Theseus indicates that he knows that the moon waxes and wanes according to a fixed cycle or order. The moon's regularity and its intelligibility are found in the constancy of its motion, not rest. Its fixed cycle, however, is not believed to control the motions of this celestial body alone; it is also traditionally said to govern human desire. The references to human sexuality which fill the opening scene highlight the connection, and tension, between the moon's cycle and lust. According to Theseus' simile, just as the land's capacity to bring forth "revenue" reflects the fixed cycle of the seasons, so too does a woman's fertility mirror the fixed cycle of the moon. If a woman's lust surges during the most fertile period of her cycle, then her "will" would be strongest during this time.[30] Like farmers who work the land or parents who desire children, lovers who long for the consent of their beloveds cannot act when they "will." Their desires must be governed by natural cycles. As the image of Bottom's gluttony indicates, the tyrant opposes natural limitations and seeks to have his desires gratified when he "wills." When dominated by unrestrained lust, he will resort to rape to gratify his desire. As the allusions to rape in the play's opening lines recall, however, Theseus' desires do not accord with this natural cycle or with Hippolyta's "will." If, however, he intends to win Hippolyta's "will" and "wed" her in "another key," Theseus must sublimate his desires to the moon's cycle.

The flower's royal or ruling color comes about after erotic love, redirected by the moon, wounds the "herb." While the object of rational inquiry is like a jewel, reason is like a flower—it participates in generation and decay. As a result, reason remains in potency, and cannot rule, until it is "wounded" by erotic love. Erotic love is too unruly until it is quenched by the order of the moon and comes to be contained within the flower which is reason. The moon does not, therefore, attempt to purge erotic love of lust, as the "true," young Athenian lovers do; nor does it allow this desire to rule lovers, as the image of Bottom's enslavement to his passions suggests. Rather, the moon provides the means by which reason might order or govern these desires so that lovers might rule over them and direct them to what is beneficial. The purple, ruling flower is the union of reason and erotic love: reason ruling erotic love; or, erotic love ruled by reason. This love-in-idleness flower comes into being when reason takes as its guide for how to govern the passions the regularity and order in the motions of nature.

The comfort provided by this account of the love-in-idleness flower must be tempered, however, by Theseus' claim that the mechanicals' depiction of the man-in-the moon is their "greatest" error (V.i.241–43). The mechanicals' innovation ascribes will or agency to the moon; according to their image, there is literally a "man" in the moon, directing it. As a result, what is naturally unchangeable, the motions of the moon, is now presented as changeable and under the sway of human "will." Theseus' criticism is in keeping with the play's characterization of the fairies: they work through "nature," in order to perfect or complete its intentions (V.i.405–14). There is no indication that they have a will independent of it. The moon's cycle represents an order in nature which reason can apprehend and use as a guide to govern desires. The fixity of the moon's cycle appears problematic in light of Theseus' opening remarks that indicate the moon's indifference, if not hostility, to lovers. According to Oberon's account, the ruling flower only comes into being once the moon quenches erotic love. If the moon's cycle is fixed and indifferent to lovers, then the moon cannot be relied upon to quench Cupid's arrow. Since the flower requires the aid of the moon's beams to come into being, the indifference of nature appears to preclude reason's governance of the lovers' erotic desires.

Theseus' public depictions of the limitations of the moon must be tempered by what he tells us about the poet's power to shape the imagination (V.i.12–22) and what Oberon says about the flower's birth. Oberon reminds Puck of the events that preceded the coming into being of the "love-in-idleness" flower: "once I sat upon a promontory / And heard a mermaid, on a dolphin's back, / Uttering such dulcet and harmonious breath / That the rude sea grew civil at her song, / And certain stars shot madly from their spheres / To hear the sea-maid's music" (II.i.148–54). Oberon's recollection makes clear that the purple flower was born in conjunction with a poet's art. Like the composite "mermaid" who rides between sea and air, "the poet's eye," according to Theseus, "doth glance from heaven to earth, from earth to heaven."[31] Just as the mermaid delivers her "song" while carried between realms by a dolphin, the poet is carried between realms by imagination, and the images it forms are its songs. These images carry riders from the formless matter of the sea into the air, where spirits purged of "mortal grossness" dwell (III.i.153–54). Theseus thus claims that the poet's "pen" embodies these "unknown" and "airy" "forms" of heaven in the images the poet crafts on earth.

In describing the poet's greatest "trick," Theseus testifies to the power of the poet's art. Comprehending a "bringer" of human "joy" and "fear," the poet constructs images of first causes that account for human passions. Transforming the way in which the world is seen, these images cause bushes to be "supposed" bears. In Oberon's account, the mermaid's song is so powerful that it controls nature: it calms the "rude sea" and causes stars to shoot "madly" from their proper spheres. Given its power over the sea, the song is like the moon, which Titania calls the "governess of floods" (II.i.103); the image of the moon has the same power as the moon itself. As the other references to singing in A Midsummer Night's Dream show, the song is also the means by which lovers come to encounter, or resemble, the divine (I.i.30–31; III.i.123; III.ii.203–11; IV.i.27–29). A poet who can cause the stars to leave their orbit can change the way in which the audience sees the moon. Through his "song," the poet can overcome the indifference of nature, and create beautiful and reasonable ordering images that will attract the lovers' desires to what is beneficial.

In A Midsummer Night's Dream, the clearest example of the poet's power over nature, or his audience's perception of nature, is Shakespeare. Throughout his play, Shakespeare constantly "disfigures" the moon. This disfigurement reveals the "power and problematic nature of poetry"—it "has the power to make us forget that the representation or imitation may even be a distortion of what is."[32] In his dependence upon the flower to rectify the discord in nature and among the lovers, Oberon reveals the extent of the poet's power. Nature cannot complete its intentions without the poet's art.

The question of the play is, then, not whether to represent nature but how it should be represented: rationally or foolishly. A Midsummer Night's Dream can be said to be the most rational depiction of the Athena-Bacchus tension, which lies at the root of the tension embedded within erotic love.[33] As with Theseus' orchestration of the mechanicals' play-within-the-play, Shakespeare's statesmanship shows how the wise poet can slay the maddening, foolish fears of lovers so that they might embrace the night and love in the most jewel-like way. When Helena speaks of her friendship of "counsel" with Hermia, she describes how, "like two artificial gods," they "created both one flower" (III.ii.203–4). Like these "gods," Shakespeare creates a flower which will shape the ways in which his audience will view nature and love. In A Midsummer Night's Dream, the poet-statesman is Shakespeare; the play his "love-in-idleness" flower.

Notes

1. The Riverside Shakespeare, ed. G. Blakemore Evans (Houghton Mifflin, 1974). This chapter has benefited from the thoughtful comments and suggestions of Matthew Clarke, B. J. Dobski, Dustin Gish, Rafe Major, and Lise van Boxel.

2. In the mechanicals' play, Pyramus and Thisby also view their love through the prism of the tales of true lovers (V.i.195–99).

3. Russ McDonald, "Introduction," A Midsummer Night's Dream (Penguin, 2000) xxxiv.

4. In the reformed play-within-the-play, the characters of Thisby's mother, Pyramus' father, and Thisby's father, who are to be played by Robin, Snout, and Quince (I.ii.54–59), are replaced by the moon, the wall, and the prologue (cf. IV.i.178–79).

5. McDonald 2000, 34n12.

6. McDonald 2000, 13n11.

7. McDonald 2000, xli.

8. The word "translated" occurs four times in Shakespeare's corpus. Three of the four instances occur in this play (I.i.191; III.i.119; III.ii.32; cf. Merry Wives of Windsor I.iii.54).

9. See St. Paul, I Corinthians 1:10; cf. AMND IV.ii.28–30.

10. The importance of death and resurrection to St. Paul can be seen in his first appearance in the New Testament (Acts 7:54–60).

11. On the use of the word "translated" in the versions of Paul's Letters to the Colossians (1:13) and to the Hebrews (11:5) that were available to Shakespeare in English Bibles, see The New Testament Octapola, ed. Luther A. Weigle (Thomas Nelson and Sons, 1946) 1130–31, 1272–73.

12. On Enoch, see The New Bible Dictionary (Eerdmans Publishing Co, 1962) 377–78; cf. Elijah, II Kings 2:1–11.

13. McDonald calls Bottom's translation "a parody of a religious epiphany" (2000, xxxiv).

14. C. S. Lewis, The Four Loves (Harvest Books, 1988) 101.

15. The Tyndale and Great Bibles indicate that the Spirit reveals the "bottome" or "botome" of God's secrets (I Cor. 2:10). See Weigle 1946, 932.

16. In the play, the word "spirit" is used synonymously with fairy (II.i.1, III.i.147).

17. McDonald 2000, xliii.

18. Plutarch, Lives of the Noble Greeks and Romans, tr. John Dryden (Modern Library Edition, 1992), Vol. I: 585–86, 588–89, 596, 639–40.

19. Plutarch 1992, Vol. II: 458–61, 446–47, 452–53, 472, 537.

20. See Plato's *Phaedo* 58b-c; Jacob Klein, "Plato's *Phaedo*," in *Lectures and Essays* (St. John's College Press, 1985) 375–78. In his claims for the soul's immortality presented in this dialogue, Socrates slays a related image of human beings: that we are passionate beasts enslaved to the paralyzing fear of death.

21. According to McDonald (2000, xxxv, xlvii), the fairies' final blessing stimulates "doubt about whether joy at the happy ending is actually warranted." Recalling "the Ovidian sequel to the marriage of Theseus and Hippolyta," their doomed son Hippolytus, a "disturbance beneath the surface" is seen indicating that "everything is more complicated than it first appears."

22. Puck has the "attributes [of] those human accidents and errors that defy logical explanation" (McDonald 2000, xxxvii).

23. The fairies give intelligibility "to the changes that afflict human beings, changes which would otherwise be either inexplicable or else, without the dream, would be too cruel or too hard to speak of." Leo Paul S. de Alvarez, "Poetry and Kingship: Shakespeare's *A Midsummer Night's Dream*," in *The Arts, Society, Literature*, ed. H. Gavin (Bucknell University Press, 1984) 178.

24. In order to see the critical importance, and effect, of Shakespeare's distinct presentation of the fairies, compare his fairies to those described by Thomas Hobbes and John Locke. Both authors warn of the "ecclesiastical dominion" that is predicated upon the tales that old wives and poets tell about fairies—tales that deprive men of their reason: Hobbes, *Leviathan* IV.47.21, 23, 28, 32; Locke, *Some Thoughts Concerning Education* §138. I am indebted to Rafe Major for this insight.

25. Shakespeare probably relied upon Arthur Golding's 1567 translation of the *Metamorphoses*. *Riverside Shakespeare* 1974, 217. All references to the *Metamorphoses* here are taken from the Golding translation reprinted by Paul Dry Books (2000). According to McDonald (2000, xxxvi), the play "contains allusions to the Bible and more indirect echoes of humanist versions of some major Platonic texts. But the most potent of all literary influences is Ovid's *Metamorphoses*."

26. Shakespeare also rewrites the story of *Pyramus and Thisby* as a tragedy: *Romeo and Juliet*. See Plato, *Symposium* 223d.

27. James Frazier, *The Golden Bough* (Penguin, 1996) 465–68; cf. Pausanias, *Guide to Greece* (Penguin, 1979), Vol. I: Bk. 1, Ch. 24, §§ 4–5.

28. McDonald 2000, xlii, 23n168.

29. Alvarez 1984, 175.

30. Given the similar length of the two cycles (about 28 days), it was thought that menstruation, which lasted about "four days," occurred around the new moon (ending the old cycle and beginning the new), while ovulation peaked with the full moon (mid-way through the cycle).

31. Herodotus I.23–24; see Seth Benardete, *Herodotean Inquiries* (St. Augustine Press, 1999) 15–16, citing Plato, *Republic* 453d9–11.

32. Alvarez 1984, 176. To cite one example of poetry's ability to make the audience forgetful of "what is," the play occurs during a new moon and in a period of darkness that should prevent the characters from being able to see. In playing this

trick, Shakespeare surpasses the mechanicals whose man-in-the moon is too literal and noticeable to the audience.

33. The rationality of the play can be seen in its title, chiastic structure, and distribution of poetry and prose among the characters. The title indicates that the play's events occur on the shortest night of the year, or the most rational, illuminated day, making its dream the most rational dream for which one could hope, that is, if reason were able to order human affairs in light of the most beneficent conditions nature could provide. See Alvarez 1984, 159–60, 178–79.

∼

5

Private Goods and Public Neglect in Shakespeare's Troy

Carol McNamara

Throughout much of the recent scholarly commentary on *Troilus and Cressida*[1] runs an effort to explain the complicated themes and the strange tensions of the play through the imposition of a theory or structure external and sometimes even alien to the play itself. James O'Rourke employs "the Hegelian master-slave dialectic" in an effort to explain "the negation of the woman in traditional heterosexuality." Linda Charnes looks to Freud for a starting point and Daniel Juan Gil uses theories of "homosociality" to clarify the behavior of the play's warriors.[2] While these interpreters offer insights of interest, the results of their theorizing often serve either to over-complicate or over-simplify the meaning of the play. More importantly, most neglect the very guidance that Shakespeare's text explicitly offers us towards providing a theoretical framework for understanding *Troilus and Cressida*. To understand the true relationship between *eros*, honor and political rule, Shakespeare provides an Aristotelian framework for his play.[3]

Shakespeare's use of Aristotle's discussion of the subjects of honor, youth and reason focuses our attention on the nature of political rule in *Troilus and Cressida*. The play is chiefly the story of how political rule is disordered when private motives drive public ends. War is a profoundly public endeavor that requires a collective effort to achieve the common end of victory but individuals often fight for private reasons, sometimes incompatible with the good of the city. On the public level, the Trojan fight to retain possession of Helen, queen of Sparta, is a fight for the collective glory of Troy. Yet, how the city as a whole benefits from possessing Helen is unclear; in fact, only the harm Helen's presence inflicts is palpable. The military threat to Troy is directly connected to Helen's presence within its walls and without her, Troy would sit unmolested by the Greeks. But the Trojan leadership continues to argue that the glory with which Helen endows Troy is worth the fight. The public fight for glory does not, however, explain the private motives for continued war with Greece. It is the private passions of the Trojan nobles, the reckless pursuit of honor, and the private satisfaction of sexual desires, all unrestrained by reason or prudence that dominates the decision for war. The private benefit to Paris, Helen's lover, in carrying on with the war is obvious, but private ends drive other Trojan War participants too. Shakespeare's Hector fights the war contrary to his own reason and judgment about what is just and good for Troy, for the sake of individual honor. King Priam embraces the youthful passions of his younger sons as a ruling principle. Troilus, the younger brother of Paris and Hector, pursues the war for the dual purposes of winning personal approbation and immortal glory for Troy, but he is often distracted from fighting the war by his private desire for Cressida. The tension we see in Troilus' dueling passions reflects the divisions within the city of Troy.

My argument is that Shakespeare employs the love story of Troilus and Cressida to examine the passions that explain the genesis and nature of the Trojan War. This use of the two young lovers, and not a mere adherence to the Chaucerian tradition, explains Shakespeare's choice to dedicate the title of his play about the Trojan War and its great heroes to Troilus and Cressida, despite the fact that they appear in the play together as lovers only on the evening of their consummation and the morning of their parting (III.ii and IV.ii).[4] Through his portrayal of Troilus and Cressida individually, Shakespeare explores the weaknesses of human nature: the false allure of honor, the destructive power of the passions and the necessity of calculation. Troilus has the emotional and moral character of the young man Aristotle describes in his *Rhetoric*, whose youth inclines him to impulsive actions for the sake of sexual gratification and the honor of his society, vacillating between the one and the other, according to his current desires and circumstances. Cressida also succumbs to her desires but her behavior is governed more by calculation. She tells us frankly about her experience of the inconstancy of men, with the result that, like Aristotle's older man who has seen many things go wrong, she is less hopeful for the future and more suspicious.[5] Because it is the Trojan and not the Greek side that is destroyed by the decision to fight for Helen, this chapter considers Shakespeare's discussion of the Trojan court in particular as emblematic of the difficulties encountered by political regimes in which passion and pride, not reasonable laws and wise leadership, prevail.

The argument of this chapter proceeds by examining first Shakespeare's presentation of Troilus's youthful *eros* and love of honor, and how they mirror the ethos of the Trojan regime and its leaders, Paris, Hector and Priam. Then, the chapter will consider the character of Cressida. She is reviled for her infidelity but perhaps she is no more fickle than Troilus. Cressida trades her heart for security, but Troilus risks the good of his state for an empty glory and a kiss. In the end, Shakespeare shows us through the characters of Troilus and Cressida how the privileging of the passions over reason, and private motives over the public good lead inevitably to the destruction of Troy.

The Two Sides of Troilus

Shakespeare's Prologue enters the scene armed for battle, to explain the causes of the Trojan war, speaking in a mighty Homeric manner of the Greek "princes orgulous . . . their high blood chafed," gathered in a great and serious cause to pursue "cruel war" against the strong walls of Troy (Prologue.1–8).[6] And yet we learn that the cause of the war is no great affair of state, not a territorial dispute, nor a clash of political principles, but the refusal of the Trojans to return "the ravished Helen, Menelaus' queen," who was abducted from Sparta and who now "with wanton Paris sleeps" (Prologue.9–10). The Prologue suggests that Helen has been abducted against her will from Sparta. The Greek princes, banded together in a moment of unity, have traveled to Troy to take Helen back by force. The Prologue, thus, informs us that the causes of the Trojan War are rooted in the human passions, in Paris' unbridled erotic desire, and in the desire for honor on both sides, the Trojan desire to defend the treasure they have taken, and the Greek desire to restore to King Menelaus what is his and defend Greek honor.[7] As a result, we are left to doubt from the start that, despite the high spirits with which the conflict began, its cause is indeed worth "the chance of war" (Prologue.31).

Our impression from the Prologue that the war's worth is questionable is immediately reinforced by our introduction to Troilus. Homer mentions Troilus once and only briefly, as one of the noblest of Priam's sons, "whose delight was in horses."[8] Shakespeare makes more of Troilus as a passionate and spirited young man who represents the two sides of Troy: he is a lover like his "wanton" brother Paris, but, like Hector, also a lover of honor. Later in the play, Ulysses, who proves to be a wise judge of character, comments on Troilus' nature to Agamemnon. He is

. . . a true knight,
Not yet mature, yet matchless firm of word,

Speaking in deeds and deedless in his tongue;
Not soon provoked, nor being provoked soon calmed;
His heart and hand both open and both free.
For what he has he gives; what thinks, he shows;
Yet gives he not till judgement guide his bounty,
Nor dignifies an impair thought with breath;
Manly as Hector, but more dangerous . . . (IV.v.96–105)

Ulysses observes that Troilus possesses the noble and bold qualities of youth that make him both an admirable and dangerous opponent. Like the noble young man in Aristotle's *Rhetoric*, Troilus is open and trusting because he has not yet been cheated. He is a lover of honor because he desires distinction and even superiority. But when slighted or betrayed, as Troilus is by Cressida, he is driven to great indignation at the injustice that he suffers. In fact, Troilus' one experience with betrayal is enough to undermine his innocence. Ulysses judges that Troilus has great potential for valor and even careful judgment but he also sees the force of Troilus' youthful passions, which drive him to pursue his decisions, once taken, with fierce determination.[9] He evaluates Troilus as more dangerous than Hector because once provoked, he is not soon calmed. Aristotle explains that the combination of hot temper and a sanguine view of the future make the young more courageous for: "the hot temper prevents fear, and the hopeful disposition creates confidence."[10] Shakespeare illustrates this point through the contrast between Hector and Troilus on the battlefield: whereas the gentlemanly Hector will pause to allow his fallen opponents to fight another day, prolonging the sport of war, Troilus will fight to the end. Ulysses, who has a reputation for deception and scheming, has clearly judged that Troilus' youthful valor could be of use to him in his plan to bring the Trojan War to a speedier conclusion.[11]

Troilus is the first character we meet in *Troilus and Cressida*. We learn from Troilus from the start that he is not "master of his heart" (I.i.5). He is so much in love that he can do little but think of "fair Cressida" (I.i.32), the woman of his desires, who is "stubborn-chaste against all suit" (I.i.93). Shakespeare uses his portrait of Troilus as a young man unable to govern his desires as emblematic of the Trojan War, a war instigated by the abduction of a woman by an ardent young prince. It is, furthermore, significant that Troilus' declaration of love for Cressida focuses on her physical beauty (I.i.50). When Troilus describes his frustrated sexual longing for Cressida to her uncle Pandarus, he imagines her in the most exotic of settings: "Her bed is India; there she lies, a pearl. / Between our Ilium and where she resides./ Let it be called the wild and wand'ring flood" (I.i.94–98). Allan Bloom argues that Troilus has the examples before him of durable marriages, those of Priam to Hecuba and Hector to Andromache, but it is the example of Paris and Helen that looms large for him.[12] Young men, Aristotle explains, are particularly swayed by their sexual desires, concerning which they exhibit no self-control. Aristotle explains these desires as "changeable and fickle," violent while they last, but quickly over.[13] Troilus' youthful inclinations are reinforced by the standard set by Paris and Helen, and supported by the entire city of Troy, which celebrates the indulgence of the passions (II.i.173–90).

The immoderate nature of Trojan leadership is reflected further in Troilus' behavior. We learn from Troilus that he is so distracted by his unrequited love that he has remained within the walls of Troy that day, feeling unable to fulfill his responsibilities on the battlefield against the Greeks. While Troilus is under the soft influence of love, he elevates the private above the public; the war against the Greeks seems of no great importance to him. He asks: "Why should I war without the walls of Troy that find such cruel battle here within" (I.i.2). For him, the alarum and sounds of the war are "ungracious clamors" and "rude sounds" (I.i.93). "[M]ad in Cressida's love" (I.i.53), it appears to him, there are "fools on both sides" and that it is madness to paint Helen with their blood each day. Troilus insists he cannot fight for Helen who, he complains, "is too starved a subject for my sword" (I.i.94). Here, we meet the amorous Troilus, who resembles more the erotic Paris and less the honor loving Hector. Hector too has private doubts about the war but he is a man who values his honor above all else, even above truth, a fact he concedes in the Trojan War council, and apparently above his love for his wife, who is unable to persuade him to remain home from battle on the day of his death (II.ii.189). By contrast, Paris eschews honor for *eros*. He thinks little of abdicating his responsibility on the battlefield, to idle away the hours with Helen (III.i.130). The fact that their lusty deed is the immediate cause of the war seems not to weigh heavily upon Paris or Helen, whose participation in the affair seems more voluntary than the Prologue suggests. Paris tells Helen that he loves her "above thought," a love in no way subordinated to or moderated by reason, or even honor (III.ii.158). Shakespeare fashions the erotic side of Troilus in Paris' image to demonstrate how seductive and destructive the example set by Paris is of the common good. For while Paris' slavery to his passion has led Troy to war, his passion keeps him from defending it. If Troilus and others follow Paris's erotic example, the battlefield will be empty and Troy undefended. It may be due to some awareness that Hector fights to defend his *eros* that Paris entreats "Sweet Helen . . . To help unarm our Hector," with her "white enchanting fingers" (III.ii.143–45). Perhaps it is his hope that Helen will persuade even Hector of her worth to Troy.

Shakespeare indicates, however, that the doubt Troilus expresses concerning the worthiness of the war's cause, the defense of Helen, raises pressing questions. Why should Troilus risk his life on the battlefield for Helen when it is only Paris who benefits intimately from Troy's possession of her? Why should Troilus not devote his attention to the pursuit of his own love for Cressida? In fact, why should the men of Troy generally risk their lives, and indeed the very existence of the city of Troy, just to keep Helen for Paris? Even if the city perceives Helen not just as a lover of Paris, but as a beautiful ornament adorning the whole city, should this suffice to justify the risks and sacrifices involved in her defense?

Despite the serious questions raised by the opening scenes, it is noteworthy that the tone is rather light and even comic at times. It stands in sharp contrast to the solemn epic character of the prologue, not to mention Homer's *Iliad*. Shakespeare's immediate purpose is, no doubt, to expose the youthful self-dramatization of Troilus' young passion but what accounts for the continuation of this comic air deep into the play, especially on the Trojan side? In fact, it is not clear from Shakespeare's account that any of the war's participants take the fighting and winning of the war very seriously. Agamemnon informs us that the war has endured for seven years and yet the Greeks have so far fallen short in their purpose (I.iii.12).[14] The result is an army disgruntled to the point that they are willing to participate in the deceptions of Ulysses to provoke Achilles' reentry into battle.

On the Trojan side, we have observed in Troilus a certain insouciance about the course of the war perhaps because while the Greeks have shed some blood, they have not yet done lasting harm to Troy. When Aeneas encounters Troilus within the city's walls, he encourages him to take to the battlefield where "good sport is out of town today!" Troilus, in response, surprises us by his instant willingness to abandon his romantic brooding to pursue "sport abroad" with Aeneas (I.i.112). Shakespeare mocks the determination of the knightly Trojan and Greek aristocrats to fight a serious war over a woman, however beautiful, for sport and honor, while apparently putting all other reasonable political considerations aside. The political realm in Troy is dominated by the private goods of *eros* and honor and not the public good. Troilus' character and actions reflect these priorities.

The Trojan Court: Troilus and
Hector and the Problem of Honor

Shakespeare brings the nature of political rule in Troy directly under scrutiny with his presentation of the Trojan War council. King Priam opens the session with the most recent proposal from the Greek camp. If the Trojans agree to return Helen,

> . . . all damage else,
> As Honor, loss of time, travail, expense,
> Wounds, friends, and what else dear that is consumed
> In hot digestion of the cormorant war,
> Shall be struck off . . . (II.ii.3)

In return for Helen, the Greeks will end their rapacious war and forget all offense. It seems reasonable that without offering an opinion of his own, old Priam should first solicit counsel from Hector, the first soldier among the Trojans.[15] Hector prefaces his advice with the disclaimer that "no man lesser fears the Greeks" than he does, so concerned is he with the preservation of his reputation for fearless courage in battle. Nevertheless, Hector presents himself initially as the voice of prudence on the Trojan council when he explains that "modest doubt is called / The beacon of the wise" (II.ii.15–16). Hector very reasonably advocates the return of Helen, arguing that she is neither worth the sacrifice of the lives she costs to keep, nor the great risk of destruction to Troy. And so, it is still more puzzling that, despite his sound and prudent counsel, Hector concludes with a question that opens the matter up for debate, with the invitation to Troilus and Paris to persuade him that Troy should not return Helen: "What merit's in the reason which denies/ The yielding of her up" (II.ii.24)?

Troilus had complained to Pandarus that at "Priam's royal table" he struggled to conceal his love for Cressida from the judgment of Hector and Priam (I.i.27). His behavior at the war table echoes Aristotle's description in the *Rhetoric* of the young man's moral and emotional qualities: the young "are shy, accepting the rules of society in which they have been trained, and not yet believing in any other standard of honor." In addition, Troilus displays the "exalted notions" about noble deeds that Aristotle attributes to youth, who "have not yet been humbled by life or learnt its necessary limitations."[16] The result is that under the influence of his immediate social circumstances and in the absence of his lover, Troilus no longer appears pacified by Cressida's love but instead, in response to Hector's challenge, argues vigorously in favor of continuing the war against the Greeks. At court, Troilus endeavors to reconcile the private good of Paris with the public good of Troy. He argues that it is not merely the possession of Helen, but the honor of Priam and Troy which are at stake in this war. When Hector reasserts that Helen "is not worth what she doth cost / The holding," Troilus responds "What's aught but as 'tis valued" (II.ii.51–53)? Men assign value in response to their desires and attachments, according to Troilus. The passions are the source of human loyalty and nobility. Reason is the stuff of ignoble calculation and base self-preserving interest. Because the Trojans as a whole have decided that Helen is of value to them, a value confirmed by the Greek determination to launch "above a thousand ships" for her recapture (II.ii.82), they must continue the fight for her no matter what the cost. In response, Hector argues that worth is not relative to the "particular will" of the "prizer," the individual who places value, but that the nature of each person or thing determines its value objectively. To proceed as Troilus suggests, is "mad idolatry." Hector's argument is that Troy can rationally calculate Helen's value and decide whether her worth is equal to the dangers Troy endures to possess her. The difficulty is that the argument over Helen's worth is ultimately beside the point: neither Troilus nor Hector truly values Helen but only the honor the possession of her represents.

We see, then, that the Trojan warriors fight for the Greek Helen as "a theme of honor and renown / A spur to valiant and magnanimous deeds" (II. ii.201–2). Troilus has, as Aristotle would say, "exalted" ambitions for Troy. If the Trojans beat down their Greek foes, Troilus believes "fame in time to come will canonize" the Trojans and Troy will win eternal glory by defeating Greece (II.ii.202).[17] Troilus argues that the defense of Helen provides a means to achieving this great fame and glory for Troy. Richards argues that Troilus here becomes "the reflective apologist of Honor, a theme and cause . . . in which he easily triumphs over Helenus . . . and even over Hector himself."[18] But why does Troilus link honor and immortal fame? Are the valiant and magnanimous deeds done to keep Helen and win honor truly noble, especially if the possession of her is itself unjustified? And do honor and immortal fame ensure the happiness of the individual or the good of the state?

The answer to this last question is elucidated by Achilles' reflections in Homer's *Odyssey* on his premature death. Achilles casts doubt on the value of immortal fame when Odysseus (Shakespeare's Ulysses) later encounters him in Hades. Odysseus praises Achilles' godlike honor among the Greeks and his power over the realm of the dead. But Achilles tells him that he "would rather follow the plow as a thrall to another man, one with no land allotted him and not much to live on, than be a king over all the perished dead." Languishing among "the senseless dead men," Achilles is apparently less enthusiastic about immortal glory than he was in life.[19] Homer's Achilles concludes that the imagined good immortal glory brings is illusory; perhaps a life well-lived consists in private happiness, if not obscurity. For his part, Aristotle argues that honor is not worthless when it is the goal of truly courageous deeds; truly courageous men act as the circumstances and courage demand in order to achieve a noble end regardless of the honor they receive, while it is those who care about reputation and the avoidance of shame who value honor most of all.[20]

Like Homer, Shakespeare exposes the irrational basis of the argument for honor when he has Troilus himself dismiss "fears and reasons" in favor of "Manhood and honour" (II.ii.32). As Aristotle makes clear, the heroic young, like Troilus, are dazzled by the idea of the magnificent at a time when death seems far away. They are unwilling to consider the possibility that eternal glory may be illusory for all but perhaps the great Achilles, who despite his after-death misgivings, certainly achieved immortal fame. Troilus' argument is empty of compelling "reasons," as his brother Helenus points out, and does not answer, but merely dismisses as unmanly, Helenus' most vital question: "Should not our father bear the great sway of his affairs with reason" (II.ii.34–35)? Troilus' response to Helenus shares something with the Aristotelian gentleman's argument for virtue: he asserts simply without further explanation that the Trojans fight for honor for its own sake and that it is noble to do so.[21] Like Aristotle's young man from the *Rhetoric*, Troilus "would always rather do noble deeds than useful ones."[22] But a courageous man who performs a truly noble deed always acts in the right way and as reason directs him, according to Aristotle.[23] As Bloom points out, however, reason does not fare well in the Trojan court where what is perceived as noble and beautiful, rather than what is rational and good for the city, receive the highest regard. Bloom argues that Troilus "stands foresquare for the noble and the splendid and seems certain that they cannot defend themselves against reason, if reason is credited. Reason cannot prove that the sacrifice of life in defense of a woman's honor is preferable to safety and comfort."[24] But does the rejection of what Troilus considers base expedience and utilitarianism leave noble, irrational self-aggrandizement or even self-sacrifice as the only political alternative? In an inchoate way, we may respond to Troilus' passion and determination as admirable but when we consider further that it leads not to the public good at all but directly to the utter destruction of Troy, our admiration diminishes. Reason can defend necessary military action and perhaps even self-sacrifice in a truly noble and good cause but not irrational self-destruction.

Troilus' passionate and public support for the cause of the war and the pursuit of glory should perhaps surprise us. Earlier we saw that Troilus and Paris, lost in love, neglected the war, but now, we see Troilus seem to forget his desire for Cressida while in pursuit of honor. We had earlier a strong indication of Troilus' impulsiveness when he abandoned his pining for Cressida for the sport of battle. Here, Hector diagnoses Troilus' impetuosity as a symptom of his youth. He explains that the superficiality of Troilus' and Paris' arguments in favor of the war reveal that they are "not much / Unlike young men, whom Aristotle thought / Unfit to hear moral philosophy" (II.ii.165). Because they are informed more by "hot passion of distempered blood" than by a "free determination / Twixt right and wrong" (II.ii.166-171). In the *Nicomachean Ethics*, Aristotle explains that "a young man is not equipped to be a student of politics; for he has no experience in the actions which life demands of him." Since a young man is apt to pursue "all his interests under the influence of his emotions, his study will be pointless and unprofitable, for the end of this kind of study is not knowledge but action." Only a man who has received an all-round education, and who regulates his desires and actions "by a rational principle," is a good judge of the things he knows.[25] Aristotle's argument is that the inclinations of a young man should not guide the political affairs of the city.

As Hector contends, Aristotle's accounts in the *Ethics* and the *Rhetoric* of the young man's limitations describe Troilus accurately. Troilus is governed by his emotions. One moment he is wholly ruled by his private desire for Cressida: under the influence of love, the war against Greece pales in importance. The next moment, Cressida is forgotten in his spirited longing for individual honor and "a promised glory" for all of Troy (II.ii.204). Hector's "discourse of reason" can do nothing to "qualify" or moderate the "madly hot" blood of the "youthful Troilus" (II.ii.113). Troilus is interested not in knowledge, but in arguments that support his call for action. Only as a result of living and experience, as Aristotle suggests, could Troilus learn to govern his emotions and to act with prudence and moderation. Richards argues that Troilus achieves self-government by the end of the play, when he witnesses Cressida's betrayal of their love vows. Ulysses, following a plan to provoke Troilus' youthful ire, leads him to the place where, hidden, he watches Cressida choose the attentions and protection of the Greek Diomedes over her love for Troilus (V.ii). Richards points out that when Ulysses suggests Troilus depart from the scene of Cressida's infidelity, "lest your pleasure should enlarge itself to wrathful terms" (V.ii.38),[26] Troilus in due course responds: "Fear me not, sweet lord. / I will not be myself, nor have cognition / Of what I feel. I am all patience" (V.ii.64). Richards' Troilus is "true" to Cressida and self-controlled in his anguish, but is he self-controlled in his ultimate response to the tragedies that befall him?[27]

The end of the play signals the end of Troilus' youthful trust and hopefulness: with Cressida, he suffers his first devastating disappointment: Cressida's betrayal undermines Troilus' romantic reveries, and Hector's death compels him to accept that his great hopes for Trojan glory are illusory. Instead, Troy will be remembered ignominiously for its misjudgment and defeat at the hands of Greece. But Troilus engages in no real reflection in his moment of despair. His quite natural reaction to these first experiences of disillusionment is to seek comfort in personal vengeance against Cressida's Greek lover, Diomedes, and against the "great-sized coward" Achilles, on Hector's behalf (V.ii.165; V.x.30). Aristotle tells us that the young overdo everything: "they love too much and hate too much."[28] Similarly, Troilus is not tempered by his experiences but, like Achilles avenging Patroclus' death, aroused by passionate rage. After observing Cressida with Diomedes, Troilus returns to the battlefield to reinvigorate the action of the war. He chides Hector for his "vice of mercy" for the gentle chivalry with which he permits Greeks felled by his "fair sword" to "rise and live." When Hector responds nobly that "tis fair play," Troilus reminds his brother all too ominously that the battle is real:

Let's leave the hermit Pity with our mothers
And when we have our armours buckled on,
The venomed vengeance ride upon our swords,
Spur them to ruthful work, rein them from ruth. (V.iii.45–49)

Observing Troilus on the battlefield, Ulysses describes his actions:

Mad and fantastic execution,
Engaging and redeeming of himself
With such a careless force and forceless care
As if that luck, in very spite of cunning,
Bade him win all. (V.v.38–42)

When Troilus is on the battlefield, he forgets all pity and prudence in pursuit of victory. It is Ulysses, who has manipulated both the Greek camp and Troilus towards reengagement in the war with the ultimate objective of bringing it to a swift conclusion. Bloom helpfully suggests that Ulysses intentionally demystifies Troilus' "romantic ideals" by revealing to him the truth of Cressida's betrayal. Ulysses cruelly compels Troilus to see clearly through the illusion that fighting for love is a wise endeavor. Troilus sees clearly something of which Hector remains unaware to his mortal detriment: wars are not sport but violence undertaken for the sake of victory in a worthwhile cause. It is blindness to this knowledge that leaves the noble Hector susceptible to

Achilles' devious tactics. Shakespeare shows us that Achilles kills Hector in a way that Troilus thinks ignoble and cowardly. We don't know if Shakespeare concurs with Troilus' judgment of Achilles' baseness but he does ask us to consider whether this really matters for, in the end, Hector is dead, Troy is lost and Achilles receives immortal glory for his deeds. Ulysses dangerously calculates that the disillusioning of Troilus will save more Greek lives by ending the war sooner than his jealous wrath will cost.[29] Certainly, Troilus' rage is a predictable response from a young man betrayed by love and distraught by loss but is it the appropriate response of a prince who bears responsibility for soldiers and a city, a duty of which the trusted and wise Aeneas reminds him but to little avail (V.xi.10)? In the end, with Aristotle's guidance, Shakespeare shows us that the young Troilus is not to blame for Troy's predicament. Instead, it is the imprudent judgment of Troy's mature leaders, Priam and Hector, who behave like Aristotle's young men, which allows the individual pursuit of pleasure and honor to trump the very survival of the city. Troy's own leaders are thus responsible for Troy's destruction.

Hector and Ulysses: Honor and Expedience

Hector is chief among Troilus' role models and yet it is Hector who lets Troilus and Troy down most of all. Hector does not follow his own reasonable advice to return Helen to the Greeks and thereby end the war. He argues against Troilus and Paris that Troy's determination to pursue the war is not only unreasonable, but also unjust. For natural justice demands that all men be given what is owed to them, and a wife belongs legally and morally to her husband. Paris' abduction of Helen is an erotic indulgence, which offends and corrupts this law of nature, the law that binds together a wife and her husband. As a result, Hector concludes that,

> If Helen, then, be wife to Sparta's king,
> As it is known she is, these moral laws
> Of nature and of nation speak aloud
> To have her back returned. Thus to persist
> In doing wrong extenuates not wrong
> But makes it more heavy. (II.ii.174–188)

Hector believes that justice and morality are on the side of the Greeks and that it is unjust to keep Helen according to the dual standard of the fixed moral laws of nature and the varying laws of nations. Nevertheless, despite the overwhelming weight of his own argument, Hector unexpectedly agrees to keep Helen and continue the war. Like the young Troilus, he puts truth, reason and the public good aside and places honor, the glory of the battle and the shame of returning Helen, their "joint and several dignities," above all else (II.ii.188–93). In fact, Hector has a plan predating the war council to achieve the two objectives he craves most of all: a reinvigoration of the action of the war and the consequent opportunity to win individual distinction. So, he has:

> . . . a roisting challenge sent amongst
> The dull and factious nobles of the Greeks
> Will strike amazement to their drowsy spirits.
> I was advertised their great general slept,
> Whilst emulation in the army crept.
> This, I presume, will wake him. (II.ii.208–13)

Hector's challenge to awake Achilles is a good idea only if war is for the sake of sport and honor, but not if the objective is justice or victory. It brings us back to Aristotle's *Ethics*. Aristotle says that knowledge and reasonable discussions about how to act are useful neither for the impulsive young man, such as Troilus, nor for those who lack self-restraint.[30] Hector is capable of exercising sound reason, but his actions are not guided by his reason. Hector's challenge to the Greeks for an individual duel with their best man, Achilles, reveals his impatience with the truce and an insatiable desire for action and honor. Honor can be a force for moral beauty, and an incentive to noble achievement when sought or awarded in the service of a worthy end. Hector does not believe in the justice of the war or that it brings any good to Troy, which means that he pursues the war for trivial ends, for action and for the accumulation of individual honor.

Aristotle does not describe Homer's Hector as, strictly speaking, a courageous man; instead, he possesses a characteristic that is most like courage. The truly courageous endure fear and pain and confront the possibility of death for the correct reasons and in the appropriate circumstances. Hector does not have the actual virtue of courage, Aristotle suggests, because he exercises courage for the sake of honor and to avoid shame and dishonor. He adds that men such as Hector are considered courageous most among those where "cowards are held in dishonor and courageous men in honor."[31] Such honor-induced courage is often useful in defense of the city, but is this true in the case of Hector and Troy? Or, does Hector, decent and chivalrous as he is, pursue individual honor to the detriment of the city? Shakespeare's Troy is clearly a city that rewards military might and displays of valor while reasonable men are, at best, disregarded, if not disdained. Hector displays the courage required of a good citizen but not the virtue of courage required of him as a military leader and a truly noble and good man. Instead, he behaves more like a follower in need of approbation. The result is that the entire city lives and dies under the tyranny of his passions and never receives the prudent guidance it needs.

During the debate over whether to continue the war, we noted that Troilus denounces the "reasons and fears" expressed by Hector about the war as small and petty things which should not weigh more heavily than "the worth and honor of a king" (II.ii.26). When Helenus argues that the king should guide the affairs of state "with reason" (II.ii.35), Troilus contends that "if we talk of reason / Let's shut our gates and sleep! Manhood and honour / Should have hare-hearts, would they but fat their thoughts / With this crammed reason" (II.ii.46–49). According to Troilus, reasoning is the pastime of unmanly dreamers, of fearful and inactive men. As such, reason is Troilus' adversary in his argument for continuing the war. The weakness of reason in Troy is indicated by Troilus' easy victory: his assault quickly silences Helenus, and easily overcomes Hector's initially rational opposition. King Priam contributes little to the discussion and says nothing at the conclusion of the war council. He thus allows that Troy be governed by private *eros*, youthful impetuosity and the excessive love of honor, rather than by wise planning and level-headed political leadership. Reason cannot rule when *eros* and the desire for action and distinction reign supreme. It is noteworthy that when Aristotle explains that the virtuous gentleman will endure his misfortunes gracefully, he identifies Priam as the example of a man whose misfortunes would be difficult to bear.[32] Perhaps Aristotle and Shakespeare draw our attention to Priam and Hector to indicate that sometimes we elevate the wrong qualities and invite our own misfortune.

Shakespeare makes clear that the problems confronting wisdom in politics are universal when he introduces us to the circumstances in the Greek camp. Ulysses' speech at the council of Greek leaders reveals that the Greeks too suffer from unwise and incompetent leadership. The contrast is striking. Hector provides reasonable counsel initially but his ultimate recommendation to continue the war is indicative of Trojan folly rather than a solution to its difficulties. In contrast to Hector, Ulysses provides a careful diagnosis of the malady afflicting the Greek camp which points towards a real solution, the restoration of "reason" as the guide for strength. Victory over the lackluster Trojans has eluded the Greeks only because "The specialty of rule hath been neglected" (I.iii.78). Wise leadership must be cultivated. Ulysses suggests that the natural order of leadership among human beings reflects the natural order of the universe that by necessity observes "degree, priority and place." When the sun rules the heavens, order is observed in nature. When the planets evade the sun's rule, evil mayhem prevails, producing plagues, earthquakes and the like (I.iii.85–99). Ulysses contends that like the disobedient heavens, the Greek camp has fallen into disarray by the "neglection of degree" (I.iii.127). The great Achilles lies lazy in bed with Patroclus maligning the leadership of Agamemnon and Nestor and neglecting his own battlefield responsibilities. Their disdain infects the camp as a whole, Ulysses contends, because they mock the Greek war policy as armchair strategy: "bed-work, mapp'ry, closet war." The real problem that Ulysses perceives is that they value only acts "of hand" but place no worth in "prescience," counting "wisdom as no member of the war" (I.iii.197–205). They dismiss wise leadership as cowardice and praise manly strength as the only means to success. Of course, in addition to wise leadership, the Greeks are still in need of Achilles' strength in battle. Ulysses, thus, recommends a plan to shame him into retaking the battlefield. The restoration of "degree, priority and place" in Greek rule requires the surreptitious assertion of Ulysses' wisdom over both Agamemnon's poor judgment and Achilles' irresponsible revolt. Whereas the order of the universe is impersonal and rational, order among human beings calls for the exercise of reason over impetuosity and passion. Ulysses does not speak to the audience in soliloquy, but his manipulative, covert tactics among men suggest that he is not awaiting the intervention of the gods to settle what he considers a frivolous dispute over a wanton creature like Helen. His speech and action reflect his understanding that it is human wisdom which creates order among human beings, according to the standards for degree that nature provides.

The Trojan court and the Greek camp have much in common. The military heroes on both sides, Achilles and Hector, pose a threat to the well-being of their own armies. Neither is dedicated to victory. Achilles is proud and ungovernable. He is concerned not with the Greek cause itself but with the promotion of his own reputation. It is the defense of his rank against Agamemnon's insults that keep him on the sidelines of the battlefield. Hector, while capable of reason, is also motivated and indeed governed by his desire for honor. Hector is a decent man while Shakespeare's Achilles is not, but both serve ultimately their own ends over those of the city. The only significant advantage in the politics of the Greek camp over the Trojan court is the cunning and wisdom of Ulysses.

In Troy, the examples of Hector's personal pursuit of honor and Paris' reckless *eros*, unchecked by Priam, set the standard for conduct. We observe the result through the divided behavior of Troilus. Troilus is either hopelessly in love and unwilling to fight on the Trojan battlefield, or he is zealously

ambitious for honor. His love of honor might surpass Hector's in public spiritedness in that he explains it wholly in terms of the glory of Troy and King
Priam, but it nevertheless has the effect of leading Troy in the direction of
self-destructive tragedy instead of happiness.

Troilus, Cressida and the Problem of *Eros*

Troilus and Cressida's love story parallels Shakespeare's account of the Trojan
War. Individually, each displays the characteristics of the leading Trojan
players in the war. Like Paris and Hector, the younger Troilus is reckless in
his love of Cressida and his desire for honor. Cressida, like Helen, the object
of a Trojan prince's affections, becomes a political subject, to be negotiated
away. Like Helen, she has only her feminine wiles and beauty at her disposal
to assert her power. While in Troy, Cressida seeks to secure Troilus' love
beyond one night's fulfilled passion through the manipulative strategy of
withholding her affection. Troilus pursues Cressida in Troy and in the Greek
camp as an exotic and forbidden love but his unwillingness to challenge her
exchange for a Trojan knight, when the whole world fights for Helen, raises
doubts in Cressida's mind about how true Troilus is. In the end, Shakespeare
shows us that just as Troilus subjected himself partly to political necessity,
but even more so to his desire for personal and national glory, in allowing
the transfer, Cressida follows a similar necessity and not her heart when she
chooses a new Greek lover over Troilus. But Cressida more than Troilus understands and explains to us the sacrifice she is making. The youthful Troilus
believes until the end that he can have it all: forbidden love and eternal
glory. Shakespeare's realist about romance here is Cressida. She calculates
what is good for her on the basis of reason rather than pursuing passions that
aim at potentially destructive illusions of love and honor.

W. W. Lawrence argues that Shakespeare could not make Cressida
"pure and noble" with the tradition of Chaucers' false Cressida so firmly
entrenched in the minds of his audience.[33] Yet, while Shakespeare may not
present an entirely sympathetic Cressida, he ensures that we understand her
motivation. Cressida offers explanations for her actions, which are mostly
the result of reason and sometimes the result of desire overwhelming reason.
Her position in Troy and then in the Greek camp is difficult: her father is a
Trojan traitor and he has left her in Troy to fend for herself, with only her
lascivious uncle Pandarus to speak for her. Instead of defending her virtue,
Pandarus seeks actively to corrupt it by persuading her to satisfy the longings
of the amorous Troilus. Even prior to our first encounter with Cressida, we
know from the exchange between Pandarus and Troilus that she has resisted

Pandarus' efforts to arrange a meeting for Troilus with her. We soon discover from Cressida that she has purposely concealed her desire for Troilus. In her soliloquy, in which she acquaints the audience with her theory of men and love, Cressida exhibits a certain jaded, worldly wisdom. She has learned that men are not trustworthy in matters of love. "Men prize the thing ungained more than it is," she explains. Men love women sweetly as long as they are pursued, but not yet caught. Perhaps Cressida's theory explains the causes of the war: honor is in possession. The Greeks value "the merry Greek" Helen so highly because she is no longer theirs, while the Trojans fight because her possession is insecure (I.ii.105). Once won, Cressida continues, women are no longer prized or sweetly loved. Because "Achievement is command," Cressida teaches all women who would be loved to hold off revealing the contents of their hearts to lovers (I.ii.280–84). From this, Bloom concludes that Cressida's speech "is a parody of a serious woman's reflections on her vulnerability" and "an exercise in sexual economics," that the "disguising of her desires is only the better to satisfy them."[34] But perhaps Cressida's reflections on sexual politics are more serious than Bloom allows. Certainly, Cressida is no innocent in matters of love and desire but her speech reveals that she has observed and reflected upon the mores regarding love that prevail in Troy. Her conclusion is that men's professions of love and fidelity are unreliable and her conduct in the play conforms to the principle implied in that rational observation. It might be accurate to say that Cressida exercises a calculative *eros*. In a world bereft of real chivalry, she must defend herself through careful speech and calculation.

Nevertheless, the next time we see Cressida, we find that she has succumbed to her "heart's contents" and agreed to meet with Troilus. Earlier Cressida had acted and spoken with a convincing degree of determination to conceal her affection for Troilus but the force of Cressida's reason and self-control turn out to be weaker than the power of her youthful passions. Indeed, she tells Troilus candidly, contrary to her own policy regarding men, that she had loved him "night and day for many weary months" but feared that if she were won too easily, he would "play the tyrant" (III.ii.110–11, 115). Despite her fears, however, her thoughts became "like unbridled children, grown too headstrong for their mother" (III.ii.118–19). Cressida recognizes her open confession of love for Troilus as a sign of her imprudence but she admits that her bold actions are born of frustration (III.ii.110; 124–29, 133). She confesses "though she loved" Troilus, she did not woo him because she could not: "I wished myself a man, / Or that we women had men's privilege / Of speaking first."[35]

Cressida longs for the independence that she believes her merit should permit and that men possess. Instead, she finds herself at the mercy of men's passions and in need of their protection. Cressida rebels against the idea of belonging to another and becoming his dupe or his fool. She confesses her dilemma to Troilus: she is with Troilus but she also seems to predict her departure: "I have a kind of self resides with you, / But an unkind self that itself will leave / To be another's fool" (III.ii.143). Cressida has clearly understood the conventions of courtly love. It is possible that she is trying to break free of them to establish a rational relationship through an honest assertion of love to Troilus. Nevertheless, she treads with trepidation towards consummation, which she fears will be the death knoll of Troilus' desire and perhaps also her own. One could say she gives Troilus fair warning.

It may be the anxiety in both Troilus and Cressida that leads them at this point to exchange their vows to be faithful and yet their vows ring of distrust.[36] He swears to be true, "As true as Troilus" (III.ii.177). Cressida, for her part, prophesizes accurately that if she is ever false, all false maids will take her name and be called "As false as Cressid" (III.ii.177, 191). But why are they so distrustful? Bloom argues that Troilus trusts Cressida because he is "a very moral man," but Troilus himself is not entirely innocent in matters of love: as Benedict reminds us in *Much Ado About Nothing*, Troilus was "the first employer of panders."[37] Troilus has pursued Cressida through a lascivious, obsequious, go-between. Furthermore, he expresses his own theories of love which amount to doubt that women are capable of constancy and yet he hopes that Cressida will match his love with equal "integrity and truth" (III.ii.156–60).[38] Cressida, too, has her doubts, we know, for she has also admitted her belief that "to be wise and love exceeds man's might" (III.ii.152). Cressida suspects that love and reason are incompatible and that men are more often crafty than they are true lovers. What is clear, in the end, is that both doubt the possibility of fidelity in love, perhaps a result of the example set by Paris and Helen, and perhaps a self-fulfilling prophecy.

No sooner is the lovers' first night together over than the news arrives from Aeneas that Priam and the Greeks have agreed on an exchange: the Trojan soldier Antenor for Cressida. Cressida is truly distraught to find that she is to be traded like a pawn to the Greeks and she swears "she will not go from Troy" (IV.ii.91). Again, we sense her frustration with the paucity of tools available to her as a woman. When she looks to Troilus to speak on her behalf, however, she is clearly disappointed. All of Troy fights for the Greek Helen, but Troilus will not speak for the Trojan Cressida. Cressida repeatedly asks Troilus whether she must leave Troy, as if repetition of the question rephrased will bring a new response: "is it true that I must go from Troy?" "What, and from Troilus too?" "Is it possible?" "I must, then, to the

Grecians?" (IV.iv.28–54). Troilus' responses must leave her cold; he too is pained but resigned to the political rules of Troy.[39]

The question is why Troilus is so compliant with the edict from Priam to exchange Cressida? There are at least two possible reasons. First, the conflict between Troilus' public silence and what he says to Cressida in private conversation parallels the conflict between public and private goods in the play as a whole. O'Rourke argues that Troilus' compliance results from "his belief that the political system in which he lives is beyond question."[40] O'Rourke's point is supported by Aristotle's argument that the young are unwilling to challenge the rules of the society in which they have been educated.[41] Troilus is willing to speak out fiercely at court on behalf of Trojan glory but he is ashamed to defend his private love before Priam and Hector. Instead, he endeavors to hide the liaison from view and promises to meet with Cressida clandestinely in the Greek camp.[42]

A second possible reason presents itself for Troilus' silence: with Troilus' promise to Cressida to "grow friend with danger," we are reminded of his earlier tendency to imagine Cressida as exotic and unattainable (IV.iv.69). His youthful spiritedness may be attracted to the romantic possibility of an illicit and dangerous erotic pursuit that Cressida's exile to the Greek camp makes necessary. Troilus perceives love as an incentive for sport and fails to perceive the tension between his pursuit of personal pleasure in the Greek camp and his desire for glory against it. Moreover, none of this is comforting to Cressida and only serves to support her earlier observation that "men prize the thing ungained." Worse still, Troilus leads her to doubt the quality of his own love with his persistent demands that she be true of heart (IV.iv.53).

With each insistence on her fidelity, Cressida responds with greater concern: "I true? How now, what wicked deem is this?" and "O heavens! 'Be true' again?" and finally, "O heavens, you love me not!" (IV.iv.58–82). Troilus reiterates that he will be true but confesses that his own fidelity is like a "vice" or a "fault;" he is incapable of cunning and hence compelled to be "plain and true" (IV.iv.101). One might argue that Troilus' insistence on this difficult loyalty is admirable in contrast to Cressida's confessed wandering eye or Achilles' unprincipled slaying of Hector, but is the only alternative to infidelity and deceit willful noble failure? Troilus' vows are clearly insufficient to alleviate Cressida's own insecurity and misery. He has promised to be true but he is the first to fail the love test, it must seem to Cressida. Her obvious pain evokes our sympathy at the time of their parting, though perhaps insufficiently to soften the blow of her later betrayal.

It is paradoxical that although Troilus and Cressida part with desperate promises of fidelity, Troilus' silence in response to her implicit pleas that he speak up for her serves only to remind Cressida, as Gil argues, "that her entire social viability depends on appealing to powerful male protectors."[43] This scene offers the serious sentiments that Bloom found lacking in Cressida's earlier reflections but, despite her promise to be true to Troilus, Cressida quickly commits herself to Diomedes, one of the Grecian youths who, Troilus' fears, will seduce Cressida because they "Are full of quality; / Their loving well composed with gifts of nature, / And flowing o'er with arts and exercise" (IV.iv.75–77). Troilus' insecurity about how he matches up against the Greeks, who reveal no greater refinement with arts and exercise than do the Trojans in Shakespeare's play, reflects the shallow rivalry between the two sides that culminates in the war over Helen.

Cressida immediately becomes aware of her precarious position in the Greek camp when upon her arrival Ulysses proposes that Cressida be welcomed and "kissed in general" by all the Greek leaders. The generals line up to take their kisses until she insists that Ulysses beg for his. Perhaps it is in part for this reason that she earns Ulysses' scorn. He dismisses her as a woman of "wanton spirits" and later comments to Troilus that she "will sing any man at first sight," a remark made to provoke Troilus' jealous rage, but perhaps proven untrue by her unwillingness to kiss Ulysses (IV.v.57). Ulysses clearly classifies Cressida as he does Helen, "sluttish spoils of opportunity / And daughters of the game," the pointless fight for whom keeps him so far away from home from his own virtuous wife, Penelope (IV.v.63–64). In light of such a reception from the Greeks, it may then be rational that Cressida accepts the protection of Diomedes, a "sweet guardian," who rescues her from the kissing generals (V.ii.9; V.v.53).[44] Gil argues that it is surprising to see Cressida struggle so profoundly with her betrayal and that she comes dangerously "close to holding out," which he believes "would surely be something of a suicidal gesture."[45] Strangely, Cressida seems to agree more with Ulysses: she attributes her betrayal not to fear but to her own weakness and to the weakness of the female sex generally: "Ah, poor our sex! This fault in us I find, / The error of our eyes directs our mind. / What error leads us err. O, then conclude, / Minds swayed by eyes are full of turpitude" (V.ii.106).

Cressida blames her eyes for her betrayal. She argues with herself that her heart is ultimately led by her eyes and her desires, and not by her mind. Should we discount Cressida's self-assessment? Perhaps she comforts herself with the explanation that her infidelity results from a weakness in the nature of women. Yet, we have observed that in principle she does not expect fidelity from others and that, for the same reason, she may not expect it from herself, despite her heartfelt pledges (V.ii.88). Troilus judges Cressida's behavior false by the standards of love but perhaps she demonstrates judgment about her own good, given her circumstances in the Greek camp that Hector and the other Trojan leaders lack. It is also true that Troilus, led by Ulysses, secretly watches Cressida's exchange with Diomedes without acting or speaking to her. Instead, he takes the part of the Greeks: Ulysses, and the scurrilous Thersites who, aside, judges Cressida a "whore" (V.ii.116). Troilus is betrayed by Cressida but in his youthful naiveté also manipulated by the cunning Ulysses who engineers Cressida's betrayal and, then, deliberately leads Troilus to witness it, apparently to ignite his passion for the battle with the hope of bringing the war more swiftly to an end (V.i.86). Ulysses alone perceives the distortion in Trojan rule and exploits it to conclude the war successfully for the Greeks.

The Triumph of *Eros* and Honor over Reason

Through Shakespeare's portrayal of Troilus and Cressida individually we see how the greatest passions may come to rule the souls of human beings. Through their love affair we witness the effects desire may have upon reason and virtue. It is important to note, however, that Shakespeare is not a moralist but a philosophic poet. In *Troilus and Cressida* his philosophic guide is Aristotle. In his *Nicomachean Ethics*, Aristotle explains that pleasure generally accompanies virtue but that the gentleman must conduct himself with regard to pleasure with moderation. The pleasure to which the gentleman may be drawn most of all is that which accompanies honor. For Hector and for Troilus, the attractions of honor are blinding and their reason is weak. This defect in Hector's reason in particular contributes to the defect of reason in the rule of Troy. Shakespeare's Troy falls by its own sword; it trivializes the ends of the city and thus sacrifices its true good, its very existence in fact, for light causes. Reason and moderation have no place in the highest towers of Trojan rule. Instead, unrestrained desire, the love of honor and the shame of dishonor hold sway in a manner that distorts political priorities. The priority of defending Helen aims at the glory of Troy but flies in the face of reason. Instead of reason, it is the tyranny of the passions that prevails. It is, thus, the absence of reasonable, prudent, political leadership that leads to the fall of Troy. Hector's death comes as a tragic shock to the Trojans who had frolicked and dueled their way through the stalemated war. Shakespeare's point is not to denigrate truly honorable action in a necessary and noble cause, but he judges that there is nothing noble about the Trojan pursuit of war as heroic sport. For this reason, the play is anti-heroic. Hector and Troy are undone by imprudence: gentlemanly chivalry, as Troilus in his darker mood points out, is no match for the desire to win once a war begins.

Troilus and Cressida ends on a still darker note. While the Trojans, led by Troilus, are lamenting the death of Hector, Shakespeare has Pandarus conclude the play with a bawdy little song. Pandarus is a base character who exists solely for the sake of pleasure. In fact, Pandarus seems practically oblivious to the tragic events occurring all around him. In his song, he exhibits only self-concern and the belief that the fall of Troy may be permanent but not the self-indulgence Pandarus represents. Before long, Pandarus will be able once again to practice his trade. The existence of a character like Pandarus, whose purpose is to serve the passions, is a symbol of Troy's decadence and perhaps the resilience of the passions in general. The fact that Shakespeare has Pandarus conclude the play as he does suggests that he is realistic about the difficulty of subjecting the passions to the rule of reason. Through Ulysses, the chief voice of reason and successful political calculation in the play, however, Shakespeare points to the solution he may have in mind. The Greeks have allowed the love of honor and power to rule without the guidance of wisdom. Thus, they have neglected the proper hierarchy of rule. To restore this, reason must guide and control the mighty and the passionate. Ulysses controls the Greek camp throughout the play, but he must use deception and persuasion to influence the minds of the warriors who pursue their own ends at the expense of a swift resolution to the war. Ulysses, too, has a private end—his desire to return home—but he never sacrifices the Greek objectives to his own desire. He finds a way to make them compatible.

Notes

1. All references to the text of *Troilus and Cressida*, ed. David Bevington (Arden, 1998).

2. James O'Rourke, "Rule in Unity" and Otherwise: Love and Sex in Troilus and Cressida," *Shakespeare Quarterly* 43 (1992) 141; Linda Charnes, "So Unsecret to Ourselves': Notorious Identity and the Material Subject in Shakespeare's *Troilus and Cressida*," *Shakespeare Quarterly* 40/4 (1989) 423; Daniel Juan Gil, "At the Limits of the Social World: Fear and Pride in *Troilus and Cressida*," *Shakespeare Quarterly* 52/3 (2001) 349.

3. W. Elton does argue that there is "a particular pattern of parallels with Aristotle's *Nicomachean Ethics* regarding ethical-legal questions": "Aristotle's *Nicomachean Ethics* and Shakespeare's *Troilus and Cressida*," *Journal of the History of Ideas* 58/2 (1997) 331. Elton (331n2) also establishes firmly that Shakespeare had access to Latin and an abridged English version of the *Nicomachean Ethics*. See also Christopher Crosbie for an explanation of the influence of Aristotle's *Nicomachean Ethics* in early modern England: "Fixing Moderation: Titus Andronicus and the Aristotelian Determination of Value," *Shakespeare Quarterly* 58/2 (2007).

4. Shakespeare relies on the traditional story of Troilus and Cressida, derived from Homers' *Iliad* and the contemporary accounts and translations available to him, for example: George Chapman's translation Seven Books of the *Iliad of Homer, Prince of Poets* (1598) and William Caxton's *Recuyell of the Historyes of Troye*, expanded by Benoit de Sainte-Maure in his *Roman de Troie*, followed by Boccaccio's *Filostrato*, which gives us the first full account of the Troilus and Cressida love story, and finally Chaucer's poem *Troilus and Criesyde*. On Shakespeare's sources for Troilus and Cressida, see Bevington 1998, 375.

5. Aristotle, *Rhetoric* 1390a 4–5.

6. Phebe Jensen, "The Textual Politics of Troilus and Cressida," *Shakespeare Quarterly* 46 (1995) 422.

7. James O'Rourke contends that "In a sexual economy the names of master-slave are 'men' and 'women,' and the greatest prestige accrues to the 'men' who can keep possession of the most, or the most valued, 'women'": "Rule in Unity" and Otherwise: Love and Sex in Troilus and Cressida," *Shakespeare Quarterly* 43 (1992) 143.

8. Homer, *Iliad*, tr. Richard Lattimore (University of Chicago Press, 1951) XXIV.257.

9. Richards argues that Shakespeare's Ulysses serves "as head of an Intelligence Service" in the play. As a result, Richards designates him as "the supremely well qualified man to describe Troilus to Agamemnon." See I. A. Richards, *"Troilus and Cressida* and Plato," in *Troilus and Cressida*, ed. Daniel Seltzer (Signet Classic, 1963) 241–42.

10. Aristotle, *Rhet.* 1389a25.

11. See Cathy Callaway, "Three Unsworn Oaths," *American Journal of Philology* 119/2 (1998) 167.

12. Allan Bloom, "Troilus and Cressida," *Love and Friendship* (Simon and Schuster, 1993) 362. O'Rourke notes: " It has often been noticed that there is no mention of marriage between Troilus and Cressida, but this omission should not be referred to a realistic economy of representation, where it can serve as a source of suspicion about the character of Troilus . . . the text does not support such a suspicion." In fact, the "absence of a public contract suggests rather the romantic wager that the couple could sustain itself without the support of the symbolic order that is in fact hostile to it" (1992, 146). It is true that the adolescent sincerity of his love is not in doubt, but Troilus' language suggests a romantic escapade rather than a lifelong commitment.

13. Aristotle, *Rhet.* 1389a4–9.

14. The reasons for this are speculative but chiefly the scarcity of money reduced the force size, and compelled the Greeks to pursue piracy and farming as means of support rather than prosecute the war in full force. See Thucydides, *History of the Peloponnesian War* I.11.

15. Bloom argues that Priam seems anxious to take the Greek offer to cease hostilities in return for Helen, but the playful tone of his censure of Paris (II.ii.160) calls this into question. Nor does Priam make any effort to influence the outcome of the discussion.

16. Aristotle, *Rhet.* 1389a29–32.

17. See Pericles' Funeral Oration for the connection between battlefield honor and immortal glory (Thucydides II.43). See also Plato's *Symposium* (208c–d) for Diotima's lessons to Socrates about the relationship among honor, *eros* and immortality.

18. Richards 1963, 242.

19. Homer, *Odyssey* XI.467–540.

20. Aristotle, *Nicomachean Ethics* 1116a25

21. Troilus' argument seems to undermine the assertion by Gil (2001, 345) that "competition for Helen is merely a vehicle for desire between men," unless what Gil suggests is that the *eros* in men culminates in the desire for honor.

22. Aristotle, *Rhet.* 1389a33.

23. Aristotle, *Nic. Eth.* 1116b10–15.

24. Bloom 1993, 358.

25. Aristotle, *Nic. Eth.* 1095a.

26. Ulysses, having judged Troilus' young and potentially vindictive nature (IV.v.97–113), ascertains his love for Cressida through slyly posed questions (IV.v.278–94) and has Troilus follow his rival, Diomedes to Cressida's father Calchas' tent (V.ii.8).

27. Richards 1963, 248–50.

28. Aristotle, *Rhet.* 1389b1–3.

29. Bloom offers a compelling explanation of the exchange between Achilles and Odysseus in 3.3 in which Odysseus persuades Achilles that the reputation for honor is what counts, through whatever means necessary (1993, 364–65).

30. Aristotle, *Nic. Eth.* 1095a.

31. Aristotle, *Nic. Eth.* 1115b, 1116a.

32. Aristotle, *Nic. Eth.* 1101a.

33. W. W. Lawrence, "Shakespeare's Problem Comedies," in Seltzer 1963, 197.

34. Bloom 1993, 352.

35. Cressida is like Beatrice in Shakespeare's *Much Ado About Nothing*, who longs to be "a man" so that she might avenge the villainy against her cousin Hero (IV.i.300–20).

36. Troilus tells the audience he is "giddy" with expectation of the pleasures he anticipates from his night with Cressida but also fearful "that I shall lose distinction in my joys" (III.ii.14–25).

37. *Much Ado About Nothing* V.ii.31.

38. Bloom 1993, 359.

39. Linda Charnes argues (1989, 423) that Troilus "hurries away from Cressida after their love making" and "immediately accepts the verdict that she must go to the Greeks," because he knows how the story ends: Cressida will betray him; hence, he is enervated by this self-conscious knowledge. But while Shakespeare is working within a tradition, he is a critic of that tradition.

40. O'Rourke 1992, 152.

41. Aristotle, *Rhet.* 1389a27–28.

42. Gil argues (2001, 349) that "Like Troilus, Cressida experiences desire as dangerous to her social standing and dignity."

43. Gil 2001, 349.

44. Note that Thersites, "a deformed and scurrilous Greek," who plays the wise fool in the Greek camp, observes that "Diomed's a false-hearted rogue, a most unjust knave," who will not keep his word to anyone. Thersites concludes his remarks with the observation that in the Greek camp, much like in Troy, there is "Nothing but lechery! All incontinent varlets!" (V.i.86–96)

45. It is also worth noting that in contrast to Shakespeare's Lucrece's choice to avenge her rapist politically and defend her honor and virtue personally through suicide, Cressida makes the private choice for survival (V.i.250).

6

~

Friendship and Love of Honor

The Education of Henry V

Bernard J. Dobski

Power is a poison well known for thousands of years. If only no one were ever to acquire material power over others! But to the human being who has faith in some force that holds dominion over all of us, and who is therefore conscious of his own limitations, power is not necessarily fatal.

—Aleksandr Solzhenitsyn, "The Bluecaps"[1]

In *The Case for Greatness: Honorable Ambition and Its Critics*, Robert Faulkner argues that statesmen like George Washington, Abraham Lincoln, and Winston Churchill stand apart from the tyrants and demagogues of political life because they managed the unique combination of goodness and greatness, that is of "sober respect for the law with honorable superiority."[2] As such, they were able to employ their considerable political talents and energies in the effort to create or restore lawful political orders whose enduring power reflected their own brilliance. But such men also inherited traditions of republicanism, liberal constitutionalism and a Christian ethos that upheld the rights and dignity of the individual; they could be conscious of their own limitations because they could acknowledge the political and religious traditions that existed independent of their making and outside of their control. These traditions were the preconditions of their greatness, providing them with a moral horizon that could ennoble their already considerable virtues. But what of the founder or restorer of a great political order who appears to enjoy no such advantages? Can one achieve that combination of goodness and greatness absent such conditions?

In Shakespeare's presentation of King Henry V one finds just such a "restorer"—a monarch who, through almost entirely his own efforts, manages to invest his throne and his country with a sense of national unity and greatness. In bringing together English, Welsh, Irish and Scottish soldiers in his conquest of France, Henry V manages to unite them as one people, giving them a sense of national pride that extends through the ages.[3] Through his military genius at Agincourt, Henry V not only brought order to the British people but restored legitimacy to a crown that had been undermined by his father's usurpation of Richard II. It is true that Henry V's conquests dissolved after his untimely death, and that his passing made possible the War of the Roses whose final issue was the abominable Richard III. But one must not forget that the tarnished crown whose luster Henry V restored so brilliantly was able to protect his infant son's claim to the throne until he, coming into his majority, repeatedly demonstrated his unworthiness for the "golden rigol." Despite these failings, Henry V's seemingly miraculous victory over the French, like those of Edward III and the Black Prince before him, remained a dazzling star by which the British people and their sovereigns could navigate national greatness.

We can best appreciate how Shakespeare's Henry V was able to restore political authority to the crown of England by understanding Henry's own political education, one connected (but not reducible) to his friendly association with the monstrously lovable Sir John Falstaff. Indeed, as anyone familiar with the Henriad knows, one cannot hope to do justice to Hal's famous political career without an appreciation of his no less famous friendship with that "fallen knight" whose blistering wit and unfaltering devotion to the young Prince not only match his prodigious appetites for sack and sex, but incline so many to forgive and even celebrate his (not always minor) outrages against human decency. Shakespeare's artistry makes it nearly irresistible for his audience to link the form of love that is friendship to the seemingly boundless pursuit of honor that defines the future King of England. A proper understanding of Hal's view of honor is thus prepared by understanding the impact of one of the most memorable and most celebrated friendships in all of Shakespeare's work. Such at any rate are the views advanced by some of the most current scholarly treatments of Hal and Falstaff.[4]

The "Problem" of Hal's Political Education

Contrary to the these views, I argue that Hal parts ways with his porcine companion early in the Henriad and that he does so precisely over the proper understanding of honor, of the origins, character and value of a lawful order, sacrifice in the service of which yields the praise of men and the glory of nations. For Hal, contrary to Falstaff's famous battlefield "catechism" at Shrewsbury (1H4 V.i.127–40)[5] honor is not merely air. Hal's no less famous remarks before the battle at Agincourt—"If it be a sin to covet honor then I am the most offending soul alive" (H5 IV.iii.28-9)—could not have been learned at the feet of his so-called Socratic master.[6] Indeed, unlike the sensualist Falstaff, Hal repeatedly demonstrates a concern for more than material pleasure, a concern that leads him to pursue greatness at the peak of politics. For Hal, political life at its best can ennoble men, this despite—or perhaps even because of—the fact that he never expresses a belief in an immortal soul or a judgmental God who rules the afterlife. Hal's political conviction centers on the earthly dignity available to human beings through a properly ordered politics. While the experience with Falstaff certainly sharpened his wits and refined his rhetorical skills, Hal's genuine insights into those hidden springs that generate men's devotion to lawful political orders and to the kings who uphold them—that is, his true education in politics—derive from *his own* reflections on the nature of political life.

Much of the scholarly debate over the extent to which Hal is the creature of Falstaff takes the form of whether Shakespeare intends us to understand Hal as the ideal of the Christian King or the avatar of Machiavellian cunning.[7] Suffice it to say that there is ample evidence on both sides to suggest that Hal can be simply neither one nor the other, but in some way effects a combination of the two. Hal's deviations from traditional morality are sufficiently numerous to render problematic his candidacy for "mirror of Christian kings" (H5 II.Chorus.6)—whether it be his venial sins, like his toleration of theft and his utilitarian approach to friendship, or his larger perversions, like a war with Catholic France whose justice is questionable at best and a public rhetoric that would appear to corrupt his countrymen.

And yet Henry does not simply disregard political and ethical limits. He is the only king in this tetralogy who we see convene Parliament, that institutional symbol of British constitutional order (2H4 V.ii.134, V.v.103).[8] While on campaign in France, Henry urges "mercy" for the inhabitants of Harfleur (H5 III.iv.54), commands his troops not to steal from the villages, indeed, not even to abuse "the French . . . in *disdainful language*" (H5 III. vi.108–10, emphasis added); and he enforces the death penalty for those caught stealing (Bardolph and Nym, H5 III.vi.106, IV.v.72). In his last appearance in Shakespeare's drama he informs us that while he and his future Queen are "the maker of manners" they may not ignore all customs (just the "nice" ones; H5 V.ii.268–69). Lest we conclude that Henry simply wants to appear to take political and ethical limits seriously, we should note that his eulogy over Hotspur (V.iv.86–100), the bestowal of his favors on Hotspur's corpse (V.iv.95), his mourning over the death of his father (*2H4* II.ii.38–65, IV.v.82–87; cf. IV.v.36–39), and his prayer on the eve of Agincourt (*H5* IV.i.286–303), all occur without the benefit of a public audience; the Machiavellian concern to appear just does not apply here. Hal seems to be both Machiavellian Prince and Christian King without being fully one or the other.

To understand how Hal might combine a Machiavellian prudence with what one might call a Christian respect for the limits governing such prudence, I turn to *Henry IV, Part 1* and to a close study of Act 2, scene 4 and specifically the "prank" played by Hal on Francis the wine-drawer. This much neglected passage represents a decisive moment in Hal's political education, one whose proper recovery opens new interpretive vistas for the remainder of the Henriad. A close reading of this scene shows why Hal does not accept the Falstaffian critique of honor. It helps us understand why he does not think men's dedication to the law merely reflects concessions to force, fraud, or the deep-seated irrationality of people. On the contrary, the episode in question indicates that men's dedication to lawful orders finds its support in an order (be it natural or divine) that exists independent of human agency. As such, it not only shows us why Hal might banish Falstaff as he does but how he might understand the link between the cosmic order, which is not of our making, and the lawful order, which is at least partly of our making, to provide a path to his own pursuit of glory. Hal learns that the kind of honors that he seeks cannot be won without attending to and thus genuinely respecting those limits on the pursuit of self-interest that are external to human agency and which, when observed, can lend political life a dignity it might otherwise lack. These insights prove crucial to understanding both Hal's dedication to active political life and that St. Crispin's Day speech which so glitteringly crowns it.

Act II in *Henry IV, Part 1*: Lawful Orders

While we hear of Hal in *Richard II* (V.iii.1–22) we do not see him until *Henry IV, Part 1*. But when we finally do meet him—in fact the first two times we encounter Hal—we see him in the company of Falstaff with their comedic antics on full display (*1H4* I.i, II.ii). Such is Shakespeare's art that the impression cast by these initial pairings is virtually impossible to undo; the laughably outrageous Falstaff and the scandalously ambitious Hal seem forever linked in the minds of his audience as Shakespeare's representation of friendship. It is in Act 2, scene 4, however, where Shakespeare first addresses explicitly and at length the political consequences of their relationship. It is also the scene where he sketches the grounds of their break. To appreciate the significance of this passage, we must situate it within the Act as a whole. And a moment's reflection on Act 2 of *Henry IV, Part 1* will show that its theme is the status of the ties that constitute personal and civic duties in an England where respect for ceremony and long-standing custom has been overturned.

From the Carriers despairing of the death of the old ostler and the apparent inadequacies of his replacement that open the Act (II.i.1–34) to the mock trial between Hal and Falstaff that closes it (II.iv.363–465), Act 2 of *Henry IV, Part 1* reveals the strains newly placed upon men's attachment to lawfulness by Bolingbroke's usurpation of Richard II. But more than just legal authority was brought into question by the deposition of a divine right king. The discrediting of an order that enjoyed the sanction of both God's authority and human practice also makes vulnerable long-standing alliances (II.iii.1–33), marital duties (II.iii.36–115), contractual obligations (II.iv.33–91), filial piety (II.iv.363–465) and even the rights of friendship (II.ii.1–45; II.iv.242–71). If there is any truth to the old adage that "the owl of Minerva flies at dusk," then we may plausibly conclude that a study of Act 2, with its focus on England's diseased state, will shed light on the nature of those pillars required to uphold a healthy political order. As the opening scene indicates, England, with her old caretaker gone and her new one seemingly unable to learn the ropes of his position (II.i.1–31), has fallen ill. It is thus possible for one to wonder now in a way that might be more difficult under better circumstances if a new "ostler" (II.ii.40) can be found capable of restoring England to political health.

Shakespeare invites us to place our hopes for just such an "ostler" in the figure of Hal himself. For while the theme of this Act is the degraded state of England's political health, its dramatic sequencing reveals a counter-movement, one whose denouement suggests that a lawful order is (or will be) restored and that it will find this restoration in and through Hal. Following the Carriers bemoaning England's diseased state, the Act turns, first, to the plotting and, then, to the execution of a robbery (and counter-theft) by the prince and his companions. Scene 3 gives us the greatest political evil, the internal workings of the conspiracy against the crown. And yet it is an evil whose prospects are already beginning to unravel; we learn that Hotspur's allies are beginning to drop off from his cause. The prospects of political health continue to improve as we turn to the last scene of the Act. Here we see that scofflaw Falstaff unmasked as a liar and a cheat, we witness his mock trial with its guilty verdict before the "King" and we judge his subsequent banishment from Harry's side. The Act concludes with Prince Hal, England's new "ostler" (II.ii.40), abandoning Eastcheap to return to court and take up arms against the Hotspur-led rebellion.

Of course, while Falstaff is not formally banished by Henry until his coronation (2H4 V.v.47–72) thus making good on Hal's "I will," he *is* effectively banished from Hal's company here, revealing the moral severity of Hal's "I do" (1H4 II.iv.468). For with the exception of a brief chance encounter on the battlefield at Shrewsbury (which concludes with Hal throwing a bottle of sack at Falstaff; V.iii.57) and Hal's pathetic eulogy over a "dead" Falstaff later, we never see the two alone together again in *any of the plays*. If Hal has indeed effectively banished Falstaff from his life at the end of Act 2, and if he has done so on the basis of a new-found respect for a lawful order that leads him to reject Falstaff's critique of honor—that is, if respect for the lawful order has been restored not in England but in Hal himself—then we must wonder what happened in the preceding scene to effect such a revolution.

This question and the preceding treatment of the ties that bind men to each other are framed by reflections on time throughout the Act. That is, they are framed by a consideration of what rightly orders men's private and public affairs. For if carriers are to fulfill their charges (II.i.1), thieves to lay their traps (II.i.32, 50–61), rebels to manage their conspiracies (II.iii.11, 35, 65–66), kings to save their kingdoms (II.iv.282, 320–26), and princes to go to war (II.iv.92–97, 526) then all must take accurate measure of the time. To be sure, knowing when to spring a rebellion is no easy matter. But in this Act even the simplest effort to mark the time is difficult; both the Carriers and Hal are unsure of the correct hour (II.i.1, 34; II.iv.92) and Hal must remind the Sheriff that despite the darkness it is, according to the clock, morning (II.iv.510–12) and thus a new day. By raising the theme of political disorder within the context of difficulties telling the time, the reader is led to wonder if men should take their bearings from the movements of an eternal cosmic order (like the position of Ursa Major: II.i.2)[9] or by man-made conventions (like clocks):[10] Should the cosmos or man be the source of political order? The opening reference to Ursa Major as Charlemagne's wagon suggests a third possibility, one repeated, and picked up by Hal later on, in his exchange with Francis the wine-drawer ("Michaelmas": II.iv.53). Might it be possible for a figure, a la Charles the Great, to join the two authorities and, through his sheer greatness and the long habit of customary usage, fix his name to the enduring cosmic order that governs men? Given his own stated ambitions (I.ii.188–210), it is not unreasonable to expect that Hal would find in a disordered England the opportunity to bring political customs into line with a framework that exists independent of human agency. A man who finds his celestial parallel in the "Sun" may be inclined to establish himself as the arbiter (or even embodiment) of both the heavenly and customary orders, that standard by which both the heavens and men mark the time and govern political life.[11] It is thus tempting to look ahead to the defining moment of Hal's political career—his stunning victory over the French at Agincourt—and see in the political glories that he forever links to St. Crispin's day the kind of political calculation anticipated here in Act 2 of *Henry IV, Part 1*.

To see how Hal might understand the interplay between the cosmic and conventional orders to prepare a path for his own pursuit of glory, we need to turn to his exchange with Francis. While this passage has long been ignored, glossed as a prime example of Hal's "tricksterism"[12] and read as a sign of his sporting cruelty,[13] reconsideration of this episode suggests its relevance to those broader political themes whose treatment unites the Act as a whole and reveals it as an important step in the self-education of the Prince, what Hal himself calls a "precedent" and a "pupil age." In his exchange with the wine-drawer he engages in a close study of those hidden springs within his subjects that activate their devotional capacities. Through this engagement, Hal shows that he knows how to teach himself about the nature of his subjects' law-abidingness and their willingness to serve others. Indeed, he learns about more than just his subjects; Hal's interrogation of Francis helps to illuminate his own devotional capacities and thus his own dedication to politics.

No Joking Matter: Taking Hal's "Prank" Seriously

At first blush, the episode in question seems to justify its scholarly neglect. It is filled with non-sequiturs, conversational stops and starts, bizarre and difficult to understand comments, and seemingly inexplicable rhetorical twists. It never addresses the question that inspired it and ends abruptly with no clear or definable resolution. It is also one-sided, pitting the hopelessly overmatched Francis against the piercing wit and wily rhetoric of the young Prince. The prank ends when Francis' master, the Vintner, interrupts with news that Falstaff and company have arrived. The scene then turns to a lengthy—and at times hilarious—treatment of more obviously political themes. When one compares the scene's bizarre opening with the more explicitly political episodes that follow, we might be inclined to do as so many have done and dismiss it as a crass prank on Hal's part.

The funny thing is, as a joke, this stunt doesn't play very well. It certainly doesn't match the comedic heights reached by Hal and Falstaff when they are together. Even Poins, no slouch himself when it comes to a good gag (it was his idea for him and Hal to rob the robbers Falstaff, Bardolph, Gadshill and Peto: I.ii.155–60), is mystified by the stunt. Hal on the other hand seems quite taken with himself. In response to Poins's "what's the issue?" he remarks enigmatically, "I am now of all humors that have showed themselves humors since the old days of goodman Adam to the pupil age of this pres- ent twelve o'clock at midnight" (II.iv.89-91). Hal's apparent non-response merely heightens our curiosity as to what is going on here. The absence of humor in an episode that everyone takes to be a prank conducted by one of Shakespeare's consummate tricksters forces us to take another look at their exchange.

As it turns out, this episode takes up and explores the very same reflections that are treated throughout Act 2. Hal's so-called prank takes the form of a test of Francis' contractual fidelity, with the Prince inviting him to abandon his professional obligations. Not only must Francis respond to Hal's brow- beating, but with Hal right in front of him and Poins calling from off-stage, he is forced to choose between two masters. And yet to discharge successfully his duties to the Vintner, Francis must serve both customers. The question is, can he satisfy both the princely lord before his eyes *and* the unseen caller from without? Or will he have to choose to serve one over the other? Such questions as are occasioned by this exchange allow us to treat the passage as a piece of the broader investigation outlined above. But what is perhaps most important to note is that Hal's joke is intended to pass the time until Falstaff arrives for their agreed upon rendezvous (II.iv.27–30). And yet, just after the prank, when Sir Jack shows up, the Prince tells the Vintner to make Falstaff and company wait outside. With Falstaff's entrance now delayed, Hal first comments on the preceding exchange with Poins, then inquires about the time and *then* launches into an unprovoked and seemingly out of place tirade against the character of Hotspur. Only after this, does Hal return his attention to his friends standing outside in the late night air.

Falstaff's delayed entrance becomes all the more interesting in view of the peculiar rhetoric deployed by Hal here. For while the pretext of this experi- ment is to discover why Francis gave him a penny's worth of sugar, Hal never directly poses this question to his interlocutor; instead, he approaches his target obliquely, only explicitly addressing the tapster's contractual obliga- tions. Such rhetorical sleight of hand betrays the influence of the slippery "Sir Jack."[14] And all of the challenges that Hal poses in his interrogation of Francis reflect Falstaff's critique of morality, a Manichean view that pits an incoherent devotion to others against a thorough-going selfishness and which elevates the latter over the former. If Hal was Falstaff's royal student, then why doesn't the Prince welcome his teacher when he arrives? What happened in the discussion with the wine-drawer to drive a wedge between the future King and his so-called friend? To address these questions we must examine his various rhetorical sallies in detail.

Hal's Dialogue with Francis

Hal begins his interrogation by asking how long Francis is contracted to serve the Vintner, a question which receives a surprising "five years plus." Astonished that such a lowly task could require such a lengthy contract, Hal half teases the bartender's assistant, asking if he has the courage to break with convention, shun his contractual obligations and earn the reputation for cowardice. Hals' rhetoric here sets off a fiery denial by the bartender; Francis swears on all the Bibles in England that he would do no such thing! No mere slave to the customs of men, Francis' willingness to uphold his contractual obligations is supported by his belief in the divine. For the tapster, God's authority stands behind his dedication to the legal customs of his profession.

In response to such moral seriousness, Hal ratchets up the intensity of his questions; he now inquires about Francis' age. At first blush, this appears a non-sequitur. But it is virtually impossible to point to one's age without leading one to think of the years that have passed and, subsequently, how much life one has left. Francis' reference to Michaelmas here (his presumed birthday), drives this reading home. Coming as it does near the autumnal equinox, Michaelmas signals the onset of winter and the shortening of days. Hal thus introduces into their conversation, ever so subtly, the specter of death. From Hal's rhetorical perspective, the rationale for such a move should be clear: by getting Francis to think about his age Hal can hope to get him to reconsider the sensibility of his decision to spend five years or more of his life serving drinks as an indentured servant simply so that he may become, of all things, a bartender. Hal's question appears to touch a nerve for the wine-drawer however, for it is at this point that Francis, who put off the first three calls from Poins, *now* takes advantage of the fourth and tries to extricate himself from the Prince's interrogation, turning at long last to serve the unseen voice calling from without.

Faced with the premature end of his game, Hal must keep Francis' attentions squarely on him. He does so now by mentioning the sugar and inquiring into its worth. Given an opportunity to discuss his generosity, Francis stays put. Indeed, he does more than just stay—he trumpets his virtue, replying that he wishes he could have given two penny's worth of sugar! Such self-flattery provides Hal his new opening. For if attention paid to Francis' virtue will keep him at Hal's side, that is, if a return on his virtue is what he seeks and if such a return will delay his turn to that "other" competing authority, then Hal intends to do Francis one better. Instead of praising his kindness, Hal offers him a thousand pounds for a penny's worth of sugar. By doing so, Hal not only praises him for his virtue, but makes it financially possible for someone like Francis to leave behind indentured servitude for good. Hal thus aims to eliminate whatever material need that might have been the source of such dedication. Now Francis's immediate response to this offer ("Anon, anon") is ambiguous, intended more it seems for his unseen caller than it is for Hal. But Hal exploits this ambiguity to pretend that Francis has accepted this insanely large windfall. And it seems Hal employs this pretense because it allows him to push the rhetorical point he raised earlier. By pretending that Francis will take the excessive financial gift, Hal can, half-accusingly, ask if he will rob his master, the Vintner. Francis is confused; he doesn't know what to make of this sudden turn in the conversation.

Such confusion is understandable. Once again, Hal's sharp comments seem to come out of the blue. And yet, once again, placed in their proper rhetorical context, they afford the Prince an opportunity to explore more deeply Francis' willingness to serve others. Hal began by tempting Francis to abandon his apprenticeship; five years or more of menial labor hardly seemed worth the bartending payoff. While Francis rejected this offer in the strongest possible terms, we discover *here* that he gives away the Vintner's sugar free of charge. And he even seems willing to accept a massive gift for such minor kindness, one that he produced at the expense of his master. If Francis is willing to accept a gift out of all proportion with his minor decency, as Hal here seems to think, and if a return on his virtue is what will keep him at the Prince's side, then Hal might have good reason to suspect that what moves his interlocutor is not a concern with propriety as such but self-interest. But if Francis' good deed was motivated by a desire for a reward of some sort, then it is not so unreasonable to wonder, as Hal seems to, if it would be more sensible to just "go for the gold" without serving others. If what Francis really wants is a reward for his virtue, then he should just steal from the tavern owner and cut out the moral middle-man. The student of Falstaff seems to have learned his lesson well.

Hal's follow up remarks, where he rebukes the waiter for his mulish attachment to duty, confirm these observations as his own. For if Francis is *not willing* to steal from the Vintner (as it seems he isn't), then he might as well remain a waiter. If serving others is all he wants to do, then he should remain content with his lowly station and attend to Poins now. From Hal's Falstaffian perspective a more consistent, and thus more rational, approach would require Francis either to embrace service completely or to "be a man" and pursue gain limitlessly. There is then a *certain* justice in Hal here calling Francis a "rogue." For if the bartender's assistant is going to cling resolutely to the virtues of serving others while at the same time consistently refusing to serve his customer, Poins, then either he lacks the most basic self awareness or he is a hypocrite and a scoundrel. The scene reaches its denouement when both the Prince and Poins call Francis at the same time, rendering the poor man speechless and immobile. The tension is resolved by the sudden appearance of the Vintner who advises his apprentice to "attend to the guests within" (II.iv.79).

We are now in a better position to see how the exchange just studied constitutes a fitting substitute for the original interest in the "under-skinker's" generosity. Hal's line of questioning aims more at plumbing the depths of Francis's devotional qualities and exploring the motives behind such devotion than it does at playing a joke. It is precisely the capacity for selflessness that is at the heart of generosity and devotion to others. By exploring the latter, he can address his original stated interest in the former. And since Francis seems capable of articulating little more than "Anon, anon," Hal's indirect interrogation promises to be much more fruitful than a direct query of a man so verbally challenged. By studying what pressures will and won't work on Francis' attachments to the Vintner and to his sense of duty, by exploring what will keep him by the Prince's side and what may drive him towards his unseen caller, Hal can experiment with those psychological levers that all successful rulers need to master.

The Politics of Cynicism

In the most literal reading of the passage, Hal, as a customer, tests Francis' attention to his lowly duties and to his master, by having another customer call from a by-room. To fulfill his responsibilities, Francis must attend to both men without also somehow alienating them. To satisfy one at the expense of the other is to fail in his duties. But Francis is more than just the apprentice of the Vintner. He is also subject to the crown, the heir to which sits before him demanding—playfully to be sure, but demanding nonetheless—that he respond to his questions. Hal thus represents political authority in England at a time when the legitimacy of that authority is in question. Given his carousing in Eastcheap with the likes of Falstaff, this description seems all too apt for Hal. But if Hal is the stand-in for a disordered and distempered England, then what are we to make of Poins, his partner in crime? As the unseen caller constantly reminding Francis of his duties over and against those of a corrupt political order, Poins would seem to represent God. Shakespeare's use of religious imagery strewn throughout these hundred lines[15] invites his audience to think of the Almighty and to find Him symbolically represented in Poins' invisible but noisy presence.

Read this way, the scene seems to suggest a deeply cynical political lesson. It shows how the political order keeps men like Francis from turning fully to their ethical or spiritual duties by getting them to focus on the rewards for service. Hal demonstrates how he can keep his subjects bound to him when they are tempted by the calls of morality, law and duty to do otherwise. Perhaps even more troubling, the scene also shows us how Hal can manipulate religious authority (i.e., using Poins to "embody" the call of God) to serve his own interests. But in the end, it is not clear that Francis does completely side with Hal. For while Hal dominates the conversation, Francis' attention is clearly split. As the conclusion suggests, the tension between political and religious authority doesn't seem fully resolved in favor of either; by attending to the "guests within" Francis serves neither Hal nor Poins.

It may be that, as in the more literal reading, Francis cannot hope to fulfill his legal and ethical responsibilities without serving in some way both masters. After all, the political order, diseased as it may be, still has *some* claim on men's devotions. One would certainly be hard pressed to explain how the wholesale rejection of political authority, and the instability and insecurity that follow in its wake, could be consistent with what moral conduct requires. The abandonment of a political community, especially one in need of moral refurbishment, would be nothing less than an abdication of one's moral charge. And yet one cannot simply identify with and slavishly serve the corrupt ends of a corrupt community. Christian ethics would seem to require that one avoid the bad examples set by the new King and his rambunctious son while still preserving respect for a genuinely lawful order. As such, the various appeals designed to keep Francis from leaving Hal's side—appeals to money, shame, vanity, and fear—do not get Francis to drop his apprenticeship and set aside a life of service. The guileless Francis is not so willing to view fidelity to contracts and lawfulness as a means to some other end; he doesn't understand service to others to be merely instrumental.

By bringing Francis's moral stubbornness to light, Hal can see more fully the rootedness of customs and conventions within a human nature uncorrupted by the moral sophistry that he employs here and that Falstaff employs elsewhere. The insight into such rootedness seems to constitute a rare but important exception in Hal's political education. For while Hal's education—from his usurper father and his debunking teacher—has taught him the flexibility of human customs and conventions, the treatment of Francis here shows him the extent to which a nature impervious to his rhetoric doggedly clings to serving others as an end in itself. It shows him the need within human nature for a limit external to human agency, one that is sacred and which can serve as a legitimate restraint on what would otherwise be a limitless pursuit of self-interest. According to this insight, it is possible to concede that some of the laws that govern our political, moral, familial and spiritual lives may indeed be the product of human creation. But their very existence testifies to an enduring need for them, a need rooted deep within the human condition. One can thus see the psychological origins of the rhetoric used so convincingly at Agincourt where, as King, Henry appeals to immortal glory to inspire his men to defeat the vastly superior French forces.[16]

The Recovery of Political Devotion

One might conclude that all we have shown is that Hal has learned (or reconfirmed) a well-worn Machiavellian insight: most men are attached to some notion of justice and as such require their rulers to act, or at least appear to act, in accordance with such a moral understanding. Because men like Francis may stubbornly cling to the dignity of law, contracts, and religion, the man who would rule them must understand that he may not blithely do away with all moral pretenses. He must, at the least, appear to be just. But we would be remiss to conclude that the attachment to legal, ethical and spiritual authorities at play in Francis characterizes only blue-collar simpletons, and not, say, worldly wise royalty like Hal or even moral degenerates like Falstaff. After all, Hal, like Francis, gives away his sugar to "Sweet Ned" Poins (II.iv.21–22). Hal promises Francis a tip so large that to call it generous would be an understatement. And Hal, like Francis again, refuses to forego his political vocation—a life that requires him to serve others—in order to enjoy all the pleasures that come from friendship with Falstaff and a life of cavorting at the Boar's Head tavern.[17] Perhaps then for Hal, too, something divine authorizes his own dedication to a life spent in pursuit of political honor and glory.

But if, to one way of thinking, Francis might be said to represent "the Prince" here, then Hal, with his indecent temptations of Francis, his seemingly casual treatment of contracts and law, his emphasis on self-interest at the expense of moral duty, to say nothing of the fantastic rhetorical skills on display, calls to mind Falstaff. In this particular reading, "the Prince" is tempted by "Falstaff." Poins, on the other hand, with his persistent reminders that "the Prince" turn his attention to his responsibilities, clearly represents the demands of Hal's father, King Henry IV. Read in this way, Hal, playing

"Falstaff," can perhaps gain some insight into what it is within his own soul that allows him to resist the unrestrained pleasures afforded by the lawless life in Eastcheap; it allows him to see that his dedication to politics is not rooted simply in custom or accident—the adventitious consequence of being the great-grandson to King Edward III—but in a nature independent of human making. While "the Prince" may dally with "Falstaff" his attentions here are split and he is ultimately kept from embracing the Falstaffian critique of lawfulness by a nature that remains stubbornly dedicated to the active political life over and above the blandishments offered by Eastcheap. Hal thus investigates that Hotspur-like attachment to honor which prevents him from ever taking the Eastcheap gang too seriously (I.ii.185–207).[18]

In this reading of the passage, as with the previous two, Francis is torn because the figures represented by Hal and Poins both make legitimate claims on his attention: to perform his duties he has to serve both men. The Falstaffian concerns expressed by Hal legitimately claim his attentions because, as intimated by Hal to Francis, we have only one life to live on this earth. Given the certainty of our mortality here (and the uncertainty of what happens after) it seems positively inhuman to disregard all sensual and material concerns. When he is King, Hal will need to respond to such demands if he is to fulfill his responsibilities; after all, how can he hope to rule others well if he is insufficiently attentive to the needs of the body or the human concerns with the here and now? Indeed, Hal himself must address these concerns if only because the success of his political enterprises requires an heir who will preserve, consolidate and perhaps even extend his conquests (H5 V.ii.204–8). And that requires that he be around long enough to prepare such an heir for his considerable tasks; his mortality and thus what will happen after he dies looms as a concern for Hal in a way that it never does for the eternally youthful Falstaff.

It seems precisely this very anti-Falstaffian concern with life after one's death that proves so crucial to Hal's dedication to political activity and to his concern for the dignity that can be found in a restored political order. To be clear, Shakespeare gives us no clear evidence that Hal, like his father, believes in an immortal soul or a God who doles out rewards and punishments in the next world. The night before Agincourt, the English soldier Williams remarks to his fellow soldiers, Bates and Court, and to a disguised Henry that on that "latter day" the King shall bear responsibility for all those who might die on his behalf in an unjust cause (H5 IV.i.134–46). But Henry demurs; according to the King's carefully limited response, God judges men here, in this life: "War is his beadle, war is his vengeance; so that *here* men are punished" (IV.i.168–69, emphasis mine). In claiming that the King is no more "guilty of their damnation than he was guilty before of those impieties for which they are *now* visited" (IV.i.174–76, emphasis added), Henry does no more than to suggest that their damnation is the untimely deaths they suffer on the field of battle. And in his solitary prayer that follows, Henry distinguishes the "contrite tears" that he bestowed on Richard's *corpse* from those priests who "sing still for Richard's *soul*" (IV.i.299, emphasis mine). Finally, Henry prays that the "God of battles" will not punish him tomorrow for the sins of his father, a concern that would be groundless if he believed his father's soul was capable of paying for such sins after he died (IV.i.286–302). While Henry V never openly denies the possibility of divine retribution in the afterlife, his most explicit remarks on the subject reflect a studied ambiguity, limiting divine punishment to this earthly realm.

And yet even if Henry V does reject the soul's immortality, Shakespeare's presentation of this royal's famous career does not lead us to conclude that he thereby rejects a moral order circumscribed by certain sacred limits. After all, Hal remains attuned to the possibility that political greatness can lend an enduring dignity to the life of man. Thus in his St. Crispin's day speech we see King Henry V speak of the glory to be won and enjoyed by those who will live through the battle, a glory to be enjoyed by them while they are alive partly because they envision it lasting after they die; the very prospect of one's mortality makes attractive the immortal glory he promises. For Henry IV by contrast, a God who judges our immortal souls always overshadows the greatness of political life even at its peak. It is precisely this possibility which torments the King throughout both *Henry IV* plays, leading him at times to despair of "the crooked ways" by which he came to the throne, at other times to advocate such measures openly.

For Falstaff, the possibility that a moral order exists capable of ennobling men is simply derisible; despite all of his legendary intellectual firepower, Falstaff seems closed to certain human and political questions in a way that Hal does not. As a result he falls prey to the moral beliefs that he takes so much joy in deriding. Sir Jack bears the moral mark of a world class boaster— a man who debunks all that men admire so that he himself may earn their admiration. Falstaff's public critique of morality allows him to display his cleverness, his daring (see *1H4* II.iv.45) and thus, paradoxically, his ability to consult more than his own self-interests![19] There is perhaps no greater evidence of Falstaff's attachment to ordinary moral conventions than the discovery, at the close of Act 2 scene 4 of *Henry IV, Part 1*, that he carries on his person receipts for what he owes others (II.iv.516–22). These attachments resurface in *Henry IV, Part 2*, where Falstaff "valiantly" protects Doll Tearsheet from Pistol's rage (*2H4* II.iv.133–208), and in *Henry V* where

Hostess Quickly reports that on his deathbed Falstaff railed against the women and booze he spent his life chasing (*H5* II.iii.26–37). One has to wonder whether a man who claims to be liberated from the charade of human customs, who believes honor to be "air," and who is reputed to possess such intellectual clarity that he is likened by some to Socrates, would keep track of his debts, display chivalry at sword's point and denounce at the end of his life what he spent most of it pursuing.

In the end, the Prince is more aware of his political attachments than Falstaff and thus is more self-aware.[20] This is perhaps why he is able to learn from Francis and why Falstaff is unable to learn from Hal. This might also explain Hal's decision to delay Falstaff's entrance to the tavern; until he has concluded his experiment with Poins, his boisterous friends can wait outside a bit longer (*1H4* II.iv.81). And that means that Hal's famous break with Falstaff does not take place at the end of *Henry IV, Part 2*. It occurs here, in the wake of his much neglected experiment with Francis, an episode which anticipates the more celebrated theatrics between Falstaff and the Prince later in this scene (II.iv.366-468), a drama that itself ends with Sir Jack "banished" and with Hal somewhere between the worlds of Eastcheap and his father's royal court. It is perhaps worth recalling in this context that Francis, by tending to the "guests within," serves neither "Falstaff" nor "Henry IV"—Hal, it seems, must consult his own understanding of the dignity of politics. When it comes to the nobility of political life, Hal stands between Falstaff and his father. By doing so he stands above them.

Hal and Friendship

By the end of the opening of Act 2 scene 4 of *Henry IV, Part 1*, Hal has effectively banished Falstaff from his company and he has done so on the basis of his new appreciation of the rootedness of customs and conventions in a nature uncorrupted by Falstaff's moral debunking. Of course, Hal informs us early on that he will use the Eastcheap crowd to serve his broader political designs. Later he "honors" Sir John with a charge of infantry whose command is likely to risk the life of this obese, gout-plagued knight, an ugly speculation supported by his pathetic eulogy over a "dead" Falstaff (*1H4* V.iv.101–9). Finally, once crowned, he does not hesitate to banish Falstaff from his company and to order the Chief Justice to throw him and those with him into prison. Hal may have always enjoyed a kind of distance from Falstaff.[21]

But such questions about the sincerity this friendship do not entitle us to conclude that Hal has no friends. There is, after all, Ned Poins. Whereas Hal and Falstaff mix blistering insults with friendly banter, Hal and Ned only speak "sweetly" to each other. Of the three practical jokes we witness Hal perpetrate in Eastcheap—all of which come at the expense of Falstaff—Ned is the only one "in" on all three and is the architect of the first and the last. Perhaps most importantly, it is only with Ned that Hal, that consummate political actor, lowers his guard and unburdens himself regarding his concerns for his father's health, an opening prepared by an expression of intimacy that is so startling and so out of character that most scholars simply ignore it.[22] Unprovoked, Hal confesses to Poins that he is "exceeding weary" and that such

> humble considerations make me out of love with my greatness. What a dis-grace is it to me to remember thy name! or to know they face tomorrow! Or to take note of how many pair of silk stockings thou hast—viz. these and those that were they peach-colored ones! or to bear the inventory of thy shirts—as, one for superfluity, and another for use! But that the tennis-court keeper knows better than I, for it is a low-ebb of linen with thee when thou keepest not racket there; as thou has not done a great while. (2H4 II.ii.11–21)

The attention paid by the normally detached Prince to the minor details of Ned's wardrobe and tennis habits betrays an intimacy that is arresting. For not even at the deathbed of his father does the Prince offer such an open display of affection, choosing instead to weep in private. Rather, Hal confides to *Ned*: "Marry, I tell thee it is not meet that I should be sad now my father is sick; albeit I could tell to thee, as to one it pleases me for fault of a better to call *my friend*, I could be sad" (2H4 II.ii.38–41, emphasis added; see 2H4 II.ii.60). It is perhaps because Falstaff himself is aware of such intimacy that he tries to undermine Hal's affection for Ned (2H4 II.ii.119–23). In the end, Hal's true friend is neither his equal in love of honor nor his equal in the battle of wits.

That Hal discloses his grief over his father's mortal illness in the context of proclaiming his friendship for Ned is not surprising. Falstaff's materialism empties human relationships of their substance and meaning, making it im-possible for him to take seriously here Hal's private passions. Hal knows this, despite Falstaff's many proclamations of love for him. He is fully aware that Falstaff's rejection of the soul's immortality provides the basis for his shaky judgment that there is simply no soul and thus no dignity to human and political life. The only other time we see from Hal a spontaneous display of emotion—and perhaps the only time we see him angry—is when he throws at Falstaff the bottle of sack he had playfully given the Prince on the field at Shrewsbury; failure to take seriously politics at its most serious wins Sir Jack the wrath of the Prince. Of course, despite all of his mockery, Falstaff may genuinely love Hal. But Falstaff will never be fully aware of the depths or origins of such passion. The intellectual consistency demanded by his materialism will always force him to chalk up to "medicines" anything smacking of altruism.

It is not for friendship then, but for a kind of dialectical mastery, that the Prince serves as apprentice to his bawdy vintner. As Falstaff himself declares "I am not only witty in myself but the cause that wit is in other men" (*2H4* I.ii.8–9). He is indeed a world-class rhetorician, a master wordsmith whose medium is allusion and double-entendre, capable of inverting meanings, bending language and reworking literary allusions to suit the needs of the moment.[23] But it is not merely verbal dexterity that Hal picks up from "Monsieur Remorse." What he learns is *the* Falstaffian calling card—how to use speech to evade or conceal personal responsibility. Such rhetoric isn't simply to avoid trouble; it is, rather, the means by which he preserves and advances a restored reputation.[24]

But if the capacity for moral evasion is what the young Prince hopes to get from his verbal sparring with Falstaff, then what does he get, or hope to get, from his time with Poins? What is it that this particular friendship brings the future King of England? If the passage noted above provides any guidance, then we might conclude that Hal's friendship with Poins allows him to unburden himself, at least temporarily, of the pressures that come with his playing such a sustained and intricate ruse, albeit one designed to win him a fame that will last as long as the world (*H5* IV.iii.51–60). For the path to glory that Hal has charted for himself (*1H4* I.ii.185–207) and which he conducts over the course of three dramas, requires a dissembling whose on-stage duration enjoys no parallel in Shakespeare's dramatic corpus. To be sure, as both Prince and King, Hal seems to pull off his plan with considerable success. But Hal's "confession" to Poins here suggests that such a single-minded pursuit of his own glory comes at great personal cost to him; it requires that he deny to both his father and his friend the open acknowledgment of his attachments to them, that he refuse to discharge what human sentiment naturally demands of us. For if he weeps for his father, he will be called a hypocrite, a charge which would render suspect his long-planned self-revelation; thinking him disingenuous, people would assume that his personal transformation was mere spin, a ploy designed to win their approval. At the same time, if he were to give full rein to his friendship with Poins, he would be disgraced in his own eyes as an aspirant to political greatness; a man concerned with his own fame and the glory of his nation does not preoccupy himself with "small beer" or the tennis rackets, silk-stockings, and linen-shirts of others (*2H4* II.ii.1–27). And yet, it is precisely his friendship with Poins that allows him to set aside, if only momentarily, his self-interested pursuit of fame and to reveal, and thereby partially relieve, the wearisome situation that he has constructed for himself. Because of this there is something "sweet" to the relationship between Hal and Poins (*1H4* I.ii.107, 152, II.iv.20–21), something not unlike the gift of Francis' sugar to the Prince, especially insofar as such "sweet" generosity seems capable of producing a pleasure in both the giver and the recipient that can overpower considerations of low self-interest.[25]

These reflections on Hal, Falstaff and Poins suggest an important link between Hal's nearly scandalous political ambitions and the possibility of genuine friendship. For despite the fact that Hal's political pursuits and his friendships clearly serve his self-interests, they also require him to recognize a good outside of himself that he lacks and whose possession requires him to moderate his conduct, to consult the welfare of others and thereby avoid the solipsism that makes friendship impossible and turns statesmanship into tyranny. Hal's most private pursuits must necessarily possess a "public" dimension if they are to be fully satisfied, a seemingly paradoxical conclusion anticipated by his exchange with the tapster. For such an exchange shows us the need to resolve the apparent antinomies between the material and spiritual realms, the demands of family and friendship, the needs of the mundane and the sacred, and the claims made by public duties and private interests. And the suggestion is that we—whether we are a wine-drawer, subject to a lord or to the Lord, or even the King of England—resolve them not by sacrificing one to the other but by recognizing the inextricable link between all of them.

Hal's "Eureka" Moment and St. Crispin's Day

Hal must treat the customary order with dignity not because long-standing social norms require that he do so, but because it reflects a truth found in that horizon which encompasses and ennobles his political pursuits. The dignity of the customary and the lawful may not necessarily lie in its specific prescriptions but in its capacity to give word—however inadequate the expression—to that broader order that governs us. This insight may us help us to understand Hal's enigmatic remarks at the close of his experiment. Again, in response to Poins' "what's the issue?" Hal says (*1H4* II.iv.89–91),

> I am now of all humors that have showed themselves humors since the old days of goodman Adam to the pupil age of this present twelve o'clock at midnight.

In a statement whose time-related references recall the Act's broader themes, Hal seems to declare that he now grasps all of those human passions that have always moved men; the preceding exchange with Francis has revealed an enduring truth about human nature. Such a "eureka" moment naturally constitutes for Hal an educational one, for he calls it his "pupil age," an education conditioned by the "present 12 o'clock at midnight." Because Hal, in the very next line, asks Francis for the time, we can rest assured that he is not reading the clock on the wall.

Midnight, like dusk, evening, dead of night, and dawn, designates a natural nocturnal phase and not simply a point on the clock. "12 o'clock" however, represents the conventional effort to mark, in this case, the end of one day and the beginning of another. Such enigmatic phrasing might suggest that Hal's insight into human nature is best described by the marriage of the cosmic and conventional orders. Far from placing upon the text an interpretive burden that it could not possibly bear, this reading picks up on an image already mentioned in this scene: Francis tells Hal that he marks his age by Michaelmas, the feast of St. Michael celebrated on September 29. With its proximity to the autumnal equinox, Michaelmas, in addition to heralding the onset of winter, also calls to mind the perfect balance between night and day. Given this earlier reference to the equilibrium between two seemingly opposed elements, is it so incredible to think that Hal might have in mind the possibility of bringing together antinomies in a way that doesn't favor one over the other?

This reading becomes even harder to resist when we consider that this feast day not only brings together the divine, natural and customary orders, but does so to celebrate the most glorious of God's angels near a time when the forces of light and darkness are evenly balanced. Michaelmas may thus represent in fine the kind of glories that Hal seeks to carve out for himself when he finally ascends to the throne: to have his name take on almost holy significance by linking it to a convention that celebrates the balance of those forces that are independent of human making but which govern men's affairs. Far from reflecting the limitless Machiavellian pursuit of individual glory, Hal's education here suggests the need to do justice to the limits imposed upon us by a cosmic order, limits whose boundaries are brought into specific relief by the customary order which regulates human affairs. "Michaelmas"—like the references to "Charlemagne's wagon" earlier or that "goodman Adam" with whom both humanity and time originate—prepares us for Henry V's St. Crispin's day speech and his attribution of the victory at Agincourt to God.

In the first place, the victory at Agincourt becomes that single event by which the men who fought there and lived to "see old age" would order their lives. Because of their conquest over the enemy's overwhelming forces, those who fought with Henry win for themselves a sense of self-respect that allows them to "stand a little taller"—to rise above their low stations and to take pride in their manhood, lessons that such men can pass on to their sons and neighbors. It also becomes the event which brings political order to the life of the British people. For in a victory won by the united efforts of Irish, Welsh, Scottish and English forces, one discovers a British "nation certain of its ruler, possessing an absolute unity of purpose, animated by wartime camaraderie, the exhilaration of conquest, the pride of demonstrated superiority, and given over to the feeling that it lives in a blessed historical moment."[26] The triumph of Henry's forces here thus marks the birth date of the modern British nation, a birth date whose undying commemoration will perpetuate the national unity so daringly won.

But their victory and the national order born from it does not just reflect the triumph of secular politics. By repeatedly invoking Crispin Crispinus in his speech (six times in *H5* IV.iii.40–67, and once at IV.vii.89), Henry tries to link in the minds of his audience the military victory at Agincourt to the religious figures with whom it shares a date. That Henry ascribes the victory to God alone (IV.viii.107–121), that he orders his victorious forces to sing the *Non nobis* and *Te Deum*, and that he charges death for those who praise themselves for the victory just won (IV.viii.115–117) suggests that the King wants a feast day, which is to take on a radically new political meaning, to retain that broader religious horizon capable of ensuring its continued commemoration. Finally, as the leader of God's army in a miraculous win against the French, Henry lays to rest any doubt about the legitimacy of his claim to the throne. Though the credit must be given to God, everyone in England and France knows that the victory was achieved by the hands of the King and those with him. The apparent discrepancy between Henry's speech and the effect of his deeds, far from revealing an inconsistency in his rhetoric, suggests rather his fidelity to healthy politics by balancing the antinomies such politics requires. For if men simply wait for God's divine intervention and don't take up arms on behalf of what is just, noble and good, then they will always wait until it's too late; and yet to allow men to think of themselves as masters of their own fate is to abandon them to a politically unwholesome sense of freedom.

If Shakespeare intends his audience to understand Henry V's spectacular victory at Agincourt to reflect the moment in which he reconciled the competing demands made by the political and heavenly realms and reflected in the tensions between public duties and private interests, as I maintain, then he could have hardly picked a more symbolic day. While the date of Agincourt (October 25) will commemorate the birth of the modern British nation, the name of the feast day also calls to mind not one but two saints, brothers whose martyrdom for Christ won them immortality, a soul-salvation that mimics their shoemaking vocation, that is a "trade" one "may use with a safe conscience," which is to say "a mender of bad soles."[27] That the patron saints of shoe-makers are alleged to have been twins, two offspring produced by one birth,[28] and that this Catholic feast day allegedly belonged originally to a pagan deity, merely adds weight to the contention that this customary celebration, with its overlapping religious dualities, represented the opportunity by which King Henry V could, through force of his political will alone, bring together the natural, conventional and divine orders in a way that would preserve the immortal glory of the British people and their king. Of course, that King Henry V could glimpse such harmonization as the highway to the glories reserved for the likes of Charlemagne—or even St. Michael—in his princely exchange with Francis should heighten our appreciation for the essential unity of the Henriad, of the career of Henry V and of the best possible political ruler that Shakespeare could envision. Indeed, capturing this unity seems to be the hallmark of political life at its best even as it reminds of the limitations that govern, guide and restrain the best political orders and the statesmen who found and lead them.

Notes

1. Aleksandr Solzhenitsyn, *The Gulag Archipelago: An Experiment in Literary Investigation*, tr. Thomas Whitney and Harry Willets (Harper Perennial, 2007) 69.

2. Robert Faulkner, *The Case for Greatness: Honorable Ambition and Its Critics* (Yale University Press, 2007) 45.

3. Tim Spiekerman, in *Shakespeare's Political Realism: The English History Plays* (SUNY Press, 2001), notes that the victory at Agincourt gives the British forces "the exhilaration of participating in a phenomenal military and political victory. The sense of national pride he engenders is expansive" touching not only the combatants, but "their children and grandchildren as well" (148). See also Paul Cantor, "Shakespeare's *Henry V*: From the Medieval to the Modern World," in *Perspectives on Politics in Shakespeare*, eds. John A. Murley and Sean D. Sutton (Rowman and Littlefield, 2006) 11–31, esp. 16; and Constance Hunt, "The Origins of National Identity in Shakespeare's *Henry V*," *Perspectives on Political Science* 36/3 (2007) 133–40. Derek Cohen argues for the importance of Henry V's reign to "nation-building and history making" and thus "the fraught process by which history and . . . nationality are created": see Derek Cohen, "History and the Nation in *Richard II* and *Henry IV*," *Studies in English Literature* 42/2 (2002) 293–315, esp. 295.

4. See, for instance, Allan Bloom, *Love and Friendship* (Simon and Schuster, 1993) 401–10, esp. 405–6, 409; see also Cantor 2006. For Harold Bloom the

friendship is decidedly one-sided, but a friendship nevertheless: see Harold Bloom, *Shakespeare: The Invention of the Human* (Riverhead Books, 1998) 271–314.

5. References herein are from the Arden Shakespeare editions published by Thomson Learning.

6. Allan Bloom (1993, 407–8), Spiekerman (2001, 113), and Harold Bloom (1998) stand out among those who understand Falstaff to represent some version of Socrates.

7. Norman Rabkin's chapter, "Either/Or: Responding to *Henry V*," provides a useful review of both sides of the debate: see Norman Rabkin, *The Problem of Meaning in Shakespeare* (University of Chicago Press, 1981) 33–62. Of special interest is Rabkin's recovery of the reading of Henry V as the "mirror of Christian Kings," a reading that is increasingly out of fashion. Perhaps most notable in this respect is J. Dover Wilson, *The Fortunes of Falstaff* (Cambridge University Press, 1943). Rabkin's own view is that Shakespeare intends us to see both sides of Hal as equally supported by the evidence from the plays and thus both equally likely: "the inscrutability of *Henry V* is the inscrutability of history" (1981, 62). Rabkin also concludes that Hal has "incorporated Falstaff's clear-sightedness" regarding honor (1981, 47). For views on Hal's unique Machiavellianism, see A. Bloom 1993, esp. 408; Avery Plaw, "Prince Harry: Shakespeare's Critique of Machiavelli," *Interpretation* 33/1 (2005) 19–43; Spiekerman 2001. Harold Bloom (1998) echoes this assessment, reiterating throughout that the "murderous" and "aggressive" Hal has learned everything he knows from the Socrates of Eastcheap. For John Alvis, Hal's "personalization of providence" prevents any easy identification of Hal with Machiavelli, though Hal does link Falstaff's teachings to the moral corruption occasioned by Machiavelli: see John Alvis, "Liberty in Shakespeare's British Plays," in Murley and Sutton 2006, 33–45; see also Alvis' chapter on Henry of Monmouth in his *Shakespeare's Understanding of Honor* (Carolina Academic Press, 1990). Cantor argues that despite Hal's Machiavellian methods of deception, he does not "ignore or disrespect . . . entirely" the boundaries of morality (2006, 23; see 16, 19). By navigating the extremes of Christian idealism and Machiavellian realpolitik, Henry V "represents Shakespeare's model of kingship," not "in the sense of a perfect ruler" but "the most we could reasonably expect in an actual ruler" (2006, 15). Spiekerman anticipates this conclusion (2001, 149–52). For Hunt (2007), it is Henry's recognition of his subject's erotic self-sacrificing nature that distinguishes him from Machiavelli. Aysha Pollnitz situates Shakespeare's treatment of the young Prince within the context of sixteenth-century debates over the education of princes, specifically whether "carefully educated princes" could alleviate the controversies attending royal succession: "Educating Hamlet and Prince Hal," in *Shakespeare and Early Modern Political Thought*, eds. David Armitage, Conal Condren and Andrew Fitzmaurice (Cambridge University Press, 2009) 119–38.

8. Of the five references to Parliament in this tetralogy, three of them deal with Henry V (*H5* I.i.1–5, 60–72); the other two are in *Richard II*. On the place of Parliament in Shakespeare's political thought and its subsequent absence in his plays, see Alvis 2006, 33–47, 45; Oliver Arnold, *The Third Citizen: Shakespeare's Theatre and the Early Modern House of Commons* (Johns Hopkins University, 2007).

9. On the "order" supplied by Ursa Major even to thieves, see the references to the "Seven Stars" by Falstaff (*1H4* I.ii.16) and Pistol (*2H4* II.iv.183).

10. In pointing to the differences between things like clocks and constellations, Shakespeare does not draw a simple distinction between convention and nature. The mere invocation of natural phenomena is not sufficient to rule out the possibility that the cosmic order which enfolds them is quite literally a heavenly one. By employing "cosmic" to refer to that non man-made order by which we mark the time, I hope to preserve the ambiguity of its divine or natural status, an ambiguity reflected in Shakespeare's own presentation.

11. Cohen claims that Hal is "determined to direct the forces of history" and in so doing will gain "the power to define the English nation in terms he dictates" (2002, 303).

12. Alvis 1990, 207.

13. Such is the gloss by Spiekerman (2001, 110) and Allan Bloom (1993, 403).

14. See note 24.

15. Consider the references to "christen names" (II.iv.7), "salvation" (II. iv.9), "all the books in England"—that is, the Bible (II.iv.48), "Michaelmas"—the feast day of St. Michael (II.iv.53), "goodman Adam" (II.iv.90), and the interplay between "Lord" and "lord" throughout the scene.

16. Cantor observes that Henry is "willing to cross the conventional line between morality and immorality when political necessity demands it, but he tries to avoid doing so in a way that will permanently erase that line." Henry "does not want to establish a public precedent for disregarding morality and thereby smooth the way for other men to follow in his footsteps and commit evil with a clear conscience" (2006, 25). Cohen, by contrast, argues that while Hal "is subject to the symbolic order, which allots meaning to the orders he gives . . . he surrenders his absolutism by his transgression of the system of differences" (2002, 300).

17. Shakespeare validates this particular link between Hal and Francis in Act 2 scene 4 of *Henry IV, Part 2*. There Francis rules over other tapsters while Hal disguises himself as a drawer. Of this disguise Hal says "From a prince to a prentice? A low transformation, that shall be mine, for in everything the purpose must weigh with the folly" (*2H4* II.iii.166–69). Falstaff foreshadows this moment when he complains to the Chief Justice that quick intellect "is made a tapster and his quick wit wasted in giving reckonings" (*2H4* I.ii.169–70; Hal's attending to "reckonings," cf. *1H4* II.iv.113, with I.ii.47–8).

18. In addition to linking Francis to Hal, Shakespeare also links Hotspur to Francis: both are "parrots" single-mindedly devoted to their vocation (II.iii.82, II.iv.97).

19. If "careful liars are carefree about morality," as Spiekerman suggests about Hal (2001, 117), then we must also conclude that Falstaff, who is a wildly careless liar, cares about morality, and that he does so precisely along the lines I suggest.

20. Allan Bloom claims, on the other hand, that Falstaff is the "only inhabitant of the Boar's Head who has self-knowledge" (1993, 403).

21. This distance is not bridged by the new King's decision to support financially the Eastcheap gang (*2H4* V.v.66–69, 97–101).

22. One of the few works to appreciate the significance of this passage is Eric Auerbach, *Mimesis: The Representation of Reality in Western Literature*, tr. Willard Trask (Princeton University Press, 1953). In his chapter "The Weary Prince," Auerbach identifies this scene as a classic example of Shakespeare's interweaving of styles, of the tragic and comic, high and low, sublime and quotidian. Auerbach's treatment of Shakespeare's representation of reality, largely anticipates my own conclusion about the importance of the cosmic and conventional orders to Henry V's political ambitions and career. Norman Rabkin, by contrast, considers the "flyting he carries on with Poins" to be "unpleasant (1981, 41). True to form, Harold Bloom sweepingly declares that Hal is "ambivalent towards everyone and everything" (1998, 277).

23. On Hal and Falstaff's "intellectual relationship," see A. Bloom 1993, 402, 405–9; Cantor 2006, 16. There is perhaps no more effusive praise, nor no more poetic a statement, of Falstaff's verbal dexterity than that offered by Harold Bloom (1998, esp. 275, 282, 294).

24. As King, Hal employs this Falstaffian tactic many times: he uses both the Archbishop of Canterbury and the Salic Law to justify his going to war with France (*H5* I.ii.33–114); he traps his would-be assassins into convicting and condemning themselves to death, for which they actually thank him (*H5* II.ii; cf. *2H4* IV.ii.105–24); he "liberates" himself from responsibility for those of his men who might die uncharitably disposed in battle (*H5* IV.i.101–86); and he attributes the victory to God not to himself (*H5* IV.viii.107–27). Hal's strategic use of this tactic is best explored in Alvis 1990; Cantor 2006; and Pamela K. Jensen, "The Famous Victories of William Shakespeare: The Life of Henry the Fifth," in *Poets, Princes and Private Citizens*, eds. Joseph M. Knippenberg and Peter A. Lawler (Rowman and Littlefield, 1996) 235–70.

25. As Hal gives to Poins the sugar he had just received from the tapster, he says to his friend, "to sweeten which sweet name of Ned I give thee this pennyworth of sugar" (II.iv.20–22). Near the end of the Henriad, after he has "won" his first kiss from Princess Katherine, King Henry observes that a "sugar touch" of Katherine's lips is capable of achieving what the members of the French Council and a "general petition of monarchs" (*H5* V.2.274–7) could not—namely, to convince him to lay aside what were *his* terms for a peace treaty.

26. Spiekerman 2001, 149–50.

27. *Julius Caesar* I.i.13–14; cf. *H5* V.Chorus.26–28 and IV.i.176–84.

28. Hal refers to his own situation as King as a "hard-condition Twin-born with greatness" (*H5* IV.i.230–31).

∽

7

Love, Sex, and Shakespeare's Intention in *Romeo and Juliet*

David Lowenthal

We know from experience that love, which seems a perfectly natural and fixed thing, is in fact changeable, depending on our thoughts about it. It is true that what we call "sex" constantly remains part of erotic love, but how large a part, and how is it related to love? That the two are not synonymous is apparent from the words themselves. We used to think that sex was properly the accompaniment of love, and seeking it for its own sake vulgar and immoral. That limitation is no longer popular, and the emancipation of sex—making it a proper object in itself—has, to a considerable extent, been a victory over love, not for it. The assault of contemporary mass media on tradition, and especially on religion, has launched us on an experiment without parallel, portraying untrammeled sex as the very height and center of human bliss. (It's as if we have at last fulfilled the Declaration of Independence by discovering the happiness on the pursuit of which we can all agree!) But is this truncated view of love sound? Is it good for individuals or societies? What does Shakespeare teach us about the traditional or romantic view of love, particularly in a Christian context, and how well that view comports with life?

Romeo and Juliet is undoubtedly the best known and best loved of the three plays Shakespeare devoted to pairs of lovers. These three plays treat the form love takes in different historical settings, as ways of thought and life change. Love in its Christian setting is the subject of *Romeo and Juliet,* and the least known of the three, *Troilus and Cressida,* treats love in its ancient or pagan form. The transition from pagan to Christian love constitutes a major motif in *Antony and Cleopatra*. The plays about love are far from the only ones in which Shakespeare manifests his interest in the pagan world. Of his ten tragedies, five are set in the greatest centers of antiquity, four in Rome and one in Athens. Even *King Lear* is set in pre-Christian Britain, so that only the remaining four—*Romeo and Juliet* and *Othello*, in Italy, *Macbeth* and *Hamlet* in northern Europe—have Christian settings. We may find it surprising that Shakespeare should not only bring the pagan world to life in so many plays but evince a sympathetic understanding and appreciation of it—surprising, only if we assume, as it often is assumed, that he was merely a creature of his own time.

It is hard not to love the lovers in *Romeo and Juliet*, but it is equally hard to know what to make of the play as a whole, which, after all, ends in stark tragedy. Are we to think well of a love that shortly after its incandescent birth issues in the suicides of the lovers? Is it love or, more aptly, dotage—mere infatuation, based on good looks—that draws them together, so that the play is at the same time a celebration and censure of erotic love? And there are other questions: Why, in fact, are we never told the nature of the dispute that gave birth to the enmity between the Montagues and Capulets, both of whom seem equally high placed in society and unmoved by further ambition? Why the prominence given to Friar Lawrence and his counterpart, the nurse? In addition, and more generally, why so much bawdiness and downright vulgarity (to the extent that Shakespeare will allow this anywhere) in a play featuring the most romantic sentiments of the lovers themselves?

Erotic Love and Spiritedness

We begin by noting that the Prologue, like others in Shakespeare, does not tell the truth. The interest-arousing phrases there—"fatal loins," "star-crossed lovers," "death-marked love"—foretell a doom that, judged by what happens afterwards in the play, was not the necessary outcome of their love, taken by itself (Pro. 5–9).[1] Many other factors, many people, many decisions and actions, had to intervene for that doom to be brought about, and the interplay of all of them is the subject of the play.[2]

It is surprising, even shocking, to move from the Prologue to the first scene. The unnamed lovers of whose fate we had just learned are nowhere to be seen. Instead we have an extended and rather vulgar conversation between two Capulet servingmen spoiling for a fight and adding crude sexual remarks to their simple-minded pugnacity—a pugnacity equaled by that of the men of the house of Montague nearby. To give this popular introduction a serious reading, let us assume it is Shakespeare's way of telling us that the play will concern itself with the two basic human passions thus displayed in perhaps their crudest form: spiritedness, embodied in anger and warlike contention, or *thumos*—as the Greeks called it—and sexual passion, or *eros*.[3] These passions have this in common—that they are natural, that they occupy a high place in the pagan world, and that they are regarded by Christianity as requiring the strongest suppression. In the Sermon on the Mount, some of Christ's most memorable words are directed against both erotic love and the anger connected with hostility and war. "You have heard that it was said, 'You shall not commit adultery.' But I say to you that everyone who looks at a woman lustfully has already committed adultery with her in his heart." (*Matthew* 5:27–28) And also: "You have heard that it was said to those of ancient times, 'You shall not murder'; and 'whoever murders shall be liable to judgment.' But I say to you that if you are angry with a brother or sister, you will be liable to judgment." (*Matt.* 5:21–22)[4] Certainly these injunctions go to the heart of Christianity—to its greatness and its problems too in their application to life generally.

Introduced in a comic way by the coarse exchanges of underlings, it is the interplay of these two great passions—erotic love and spiritedness—that sets the play into motion. A spirited fracas or minor war breaks out between the men of the two families, and at one point Tybalt—the very model of pure undiluted spiritedness—enters the fray. Immediately afterward we learn of the lovesick Romeo's extreme and unnaturally distracted condition, brought on by the determination of the woman he loves to remain chaste. But at the Capulet's party that evening, *eros* redirects his arrows and makes Romeo fall instantly in love with Juliet, daring on the briefest acquaintance, but in mutual physical attraction, to hold her hand and kiss her twice. Spiritedness returns with Tybalt's attack on Romeo, Mercutio's equally aggressive defense of Romeo, and Romeo's own killing of Tybalt, thus setting the stage for the play's tragic outcome.[5]

Alternative Educations

Friar Lawrence's pivotal role is another sign that the play has much to do with Christianity and its effects. We learn that Friar Lawrence is Romeo's teacher, the one who told him to "bury love" (II.iii.84)—that is, to suppress it—and it is out of distinctively Christian motives that he helps the lovers take actions that are their ultimate undoing. Friar Lawrence is an expert on herbs, a man who views the world in moral terms and sees the good and evil of which all things are capable, a man of natural moderation and good sense who nevertheless is led into extravagant deeds by certain elements of

Christian belief itself. It is his Christianity that makes him think that at all costs the young couple must not sleep together unmarried, and even makes him optimistically anticipate from their union the bringing together of the feuding families. This same optimism, this faith in providence, later keeps him from considering the chance elements that might interfere with his intricate plan involving Juliet's feigned death. More generally, it is to his Christianity that we must trace his confidence that, in the name of doing good, he can contravene tradition, engage in massive deception, and encourage law-breaking as well. He can place himself above and beyond ordinary moral and political restrictions because he thinks of himself as working for, and part of, a higher authority, privileged to be a major figure in God's plan for man. It is paradoxical, but true, that this good man unintentionally facilitates the tragic end of the lovers.

The friar's counterpart is the nurse—certainly one of Shakespeare's most wonderful creations.[6] If he represents Christianity in the play, she herself makes it clear that she represents nature, for what other conclusion can we come to after her graphic (and repeated) description of the way she weaned Juliet by putting wormwood on her nipple? She's not a medical nurse but a wet nurse who nurses and nourishes babies. To draw attention to her occupation, she is the only one in the play whose only name *is* her occupation. Can there be any better symbol for nature than the conjunction of breast and the baby—a word that in its Greek origin (*phusis*) refers to growth, to causes that work from within living things especially, that make them what they are, independent of artificial, conventional, or external stimulation? The nurse gives milk by nature, and by nature the baby receives that nourishment and keeps growing as a human baby. The milk helps the baby become more of what it already is by nature.

The nurse's character is consistent with this natural view: she is very physical and down to earth, even vulgar, in her humor. She values sex and money, and takes them for granted as natural and proper ends. With Romeo banished, she advises Juliet to marry Paris, knowing perfectly well of Juliet's prior marriage to Romeo, since she helped arrange it. Her materialism, crass as it is, finds its expression in one short line: "Death's the end of all." (III. iii.95) And when, after a long and overly optimistic speech by the friar to Romeo, she says, "O Lord, I could have stayed here all the night to hear good counsel! O, what learning is!" (III.iii.162–63), we know that she is talking pure irony. Far from being the fool she makes herself out to be, the nurse is a consummate actress who must be watched with care.

So the protagonists have had very different educations. Juliet, we are to understand, was not only nursed by the nurse but left by an absentee mother to be brought up by her, just as Romeo was brought up by Friar Lawrence. True to her name, Juliet was born in mid-July, almost fourteen years earlier— again, a reminder of nature, in its summer heat and flaming fullness, and also of female nature becoming fully feminine. Just before falling in love with Juliet, Romeo had been feverishly in love with Rosaline, but unlike Rosaline, Juliet has taken no vow of chastity. At first, she appears timidly obedient to her parents in affairs of marriage, to which, she says, she has till then given no thought. At the party, however, she falls precipitately and unreservedly in love with Romeo and confesses as much in the balcony scene immediately afterward, when, thinking she is alone, she asks him to doff his name (because he is a Montague) and "Take all my self" (II.ii.50). Here she says nothing of parental consent, or even of marriage, as if the natural operation of love does not require either marriage or parental consent. And concerning her marriage to Romeo, once it is determined she never speaks a word to her parents, much less seeks their prior consent. She is a revolutionary for the natural as compared to the conventional. Ironically, she did not realize how receptive her father, at least, might have been to this match.

Having confessed her love for Romeo—in his hearing, as it turns out—she goes on, knowingly in his hearing, to call him "the god of my idolatry" (II.ii.117). She means her words. He is her god and she has no other god: what is this but a form of forbidden idolatry? When Romeo complains of being left unsatisfied she asks: "What satisfaction canst thou have tonight?" To which he replies: "Th' exchange of thy love's faithful vow for mine." (II.ii.130–31) And soon, after describing her love as boundless, Juliet wants him to show that his love is honorable and that he intends marriage by arranging "where and what time thou wilt perform the rite," after which she will "follow thee my lord throughout the world" (II.ii.150, 152). Juliet does not directly ask him to get Friar Lawrence to perform the rite of marriage, and her language allows the possibility that it is Romeo himself—her god—who performs it all by himself. But she does expect marriage, and we wonder why, with her less Christian upbringing at the hands of the nurse, this is her expectation. Unlike Cressida, who never speaks of marriage, and Cleopatra, who refers to Antony as her husband only at the very end, as she commits suicide, marriage comes almost immediately to Juliet's mind.

Juliet is not simply a replica of the nurse. It is likely that just being brought up as a Christian in a Christian family and society makes her insist on marriage, but it also seems demanded by Juliet's own virtue, which makes of love a much finer and nobler thing than the simple natural conjugation the nurse has in mind. Christianity's requirement of marriage may jibe with the purity of Juliet's own impulses—with the infinite bounty and depth of the love she confesses to Romeo. Nevertheless, she realizes that marrying Romeo would be impetuous, and Friar Lawrence himself realizes how precipitate this marriage would be. We must not forget that Shakespeare has them marry the afternoon after the evening they first meet, having known each other only for a few minutes at the party and a few more in the balcony scene shortly afterward. It is one of those many cases where Shakespeare exaggerates a reality in order to make a deeper point—or uses an untruth for the sake of a deeper truth. He has the lovers do something rather incredible: marry voluntarily after having known each other so briefly. So we cannot help but agree with the friar's initial assessment. He speaks very sensibly when he tells them to proceed much more slowly and carefully, but he ends up marrying them anyhow, and for the sake of preventing their sinning through fornication.

The character of Romeo is much more complex than that of Juliet. We meet him first through the account given by Benvolio and his father. His life is completely upside down. Walking abroad before dawn, in tears, he returns to shut himself in his room all day. The cause of this grief—this extreme, excessive, and unnatural grief—is Rosaline's effort to "merit bliss" by remaining chaste," whereby she "cuts beauty off from all posterity" (I.ii.213, 211). By this Romeo implies that he has no doubt Rosaline does merit the bliss (in the afterlife) she seeks, but by her chastity she also keeps herself from passing her beauty on, through reproduction, to her progeny. He fails to mention another consequence of her chastity—his own frustration, and the unnatural behavior that is the counterpart of hers. She voluntarily suppresses her own sexual nature; he suffers acutely and excessively from sexual deprivation. In this extreme form his lovesickness even becomes an object of derision to his friend Mercutio, who hardly places on love the high value both Romeo and Juliet do.

Romeo is a very unsteady person, quite different from both the exuberant Mercutio and his more moderate friend, Benvolio. Just as he had sped from depths of despair over Rosaline to ecstasy over Juliet, impulsively exchanging one love for the other, so in his spiritedness he lurches from one extreme to another. Trying to mediate the argument between Tybalt and Mercutio, and justifying his peace-keeping efforts by saying "I thought all for the best" (III.i.96), he unintentionally allows Tybalt to kill Mercutio. Whereupon, despite the likelihood that the prince would himself have had Tybalt killed as a murderer, he reverses his excessive passivity and rages for revenge, exclaiming that Juliet's beauty had made him effeminate. In this mood he kills the returning Tybalt, yet on learning of the prince's decision to banish him, this imprudent display of extreme manliness vanishes, and instead he is found groveling and weeping on the floor of Friar Lawrence's cell. Seeing him in this condition, it is the old nurse who first exclaims, "Stand up, stand up! Stand, and you be a man" (III.iii.91)—language echoed shortly afterward by Friar Lawrence, calling upon Romeo to show spirit, to act like a man, to cease acting like a woman (see III.iii.113-118)—that is, to act in accordance with his male nature.

Romeo also believes in dreams. He has a sense of doom (in one place, at the beginning of the last Act, it is temporarily transformed into wild unfounded optimism), and believes some power beyond him directs his fate. He has thought of suicide before, just as it is the first thing that comes to his mind when he learns of Juliet's supposed death, failing to ask even the most elementary questions about the circumstances of her death. Such is his eagerness to die with her that he kills Paris outside the tomb when Paris tries to arrest him for unlawfully returning from exile. Let us sum up Romeo's traits. First, far from "burying love" as he was taught by the friar, he has become excessively erotic. And his Christian education may also have been responsible for his wavering between too much and too little spiritedness, between excessive manliness and excessive womanliness. As he himself says when fury against Tybalt seizes him—"Away to heaven, respective lenity" (III.i.115)—he returns "lenity" or gentleness to the heaven from which it came. And it may have been the same teaching that led to his forebodings of evil, his unease at living (since this life is so temporary) and his sense of fore-ordained destiny. Driven by this combination of passions, he ends up exercising very little forethought or prudence. He is neither entirely Christian nor entirely pagan, being pulled either way by one element or the other. He is a kind of minor league Hamlet, more erotic, more lovable, much more active but lacking Hamlet's powers of thought and expression.

Old editions of Shakespeare's plays (meant for high school and college use) regularly contained time analyses of the action of the plays. Shakespeare often omits details of time, but when he wants us to know the duration of action, or the month, day, and even hour, or the year, the information will be there, sometimes quite plainly, sometimes less conspicuously. In *Romeo and Juliet*, not only are the lovers married the day after they meet, but the whole action takes less than a week to complete, beginning early on a Sunday morning in mid-July and ending early on the following Friday morning.[7] At one point, well into the play, Capulet—arranging the marriage of Juliet to Paris—asks him what day it is, and Paris replies: "Monday, my lord." (III.iv.18–19) Capulet decides the wedding will be Thursday, since Wednesday would be too soon to make the necessary preparations (III.iv.15–17, 20–33). The next day—Tuesday—he moves the wedding ahead to the next day, when the "peevish" Juliet seems to express a sudden change of heart about the marriage after her meeting with the friar (IV.i.90–91, ii.15–35). As her father races to prepare through the night, Juliet drinks the potion given to her by the "holy" friar—and is discovered "dead" by the nurse in the morning, as Paris waits. Here are the only indications we are given of the days on which the action of the play takes place. Working back from Monday, we learn that all the action so far has taken place in less than two days, while the remaining action takes three days more: the lovers meet Sunday night, marry Monday afternoon, and then are both dead by Thursday night.[8] It is mere speculation, but the time left in the week almost exactly coincides with the period in the Gospel of Matthew between the Friday of Christ's crucifixion and early Monday morning, when his body is discovered missing. If this is correct, it would be like an arrow pointing to the subject of the play—which is to say, the effect of Christ's life and teaching on the lives of human beings.

Political Consequences

What lessons can be drawn from Shakespeare's *Romeo and Juliet*? That young men and women should not fall in love? That they should have longer court-ships? That their families should not feud? That lovers should not consult friars? That friars should not accommodate impetuous lovers and preempt the role of parents, or create elaborate schemes that involve massive decep-tion and law-breaking? That they should not consider themselves above the law? The friar was right in thinking that by marrying the lovers he might ultimately unite the families themselves—but it was the death of their children, not their marriage, that finally brought the families together. The friar impresses us as a good man, a virtuous man, but at the end he shows himself to be much less admirable. Entering the tomb at night, while Juliet is still asleep, he discovers both Romeo and Paris lying there dead. Only mo-ments later she awakens from the drug he had given her, just as he had said she would. Seeing him, but not Romeo, she asks where Romeo is. The friar replies (V.iii.159–64):

> Come, come, away.
> Thy husband in thy bosom there lies dead;
> And Paris too. Come, I'll dispose of thee
> Among a sisterhood of holy nuns.
> Stay not to question, for the watch is coming.
> Come, go, good Juliet. I dare no longer stay.

Could his answer have been more blunt or shocking? And how quickly and neatly he has devised a solution for her woes: he will get her to a nunnery.

Juliet refuses to run; but to save himself the friar does, despite knowing how desperate she was. Perhaps he could not know she would kill herself with Romeo's dagger, but by leaving he bears some direct responsibility for her death.

Only this late in the play does one of its major themes reveal itself fully: the problem posed for political rule by Christianity. Escalus, the Prince of Verona, makes three appearances in the play—at the beginning, middle, and end. He has not been a strong ruler. We never learn the cause of the hostility between the Montagues and Capulets. We do learn from the Prince that this was their third fight, yet only now does he threaten them with death should any further disruption occur. So, including the brawl that has just occurred, three have gone unpunished. Not a very effective prince. It is not long before he gets a chance to show the new rigor he has promised. Romeo kills Tybalt, despite Tybalt's obvious guilt as the initiator of the fight and the killer of Mercutio. When old Montague pleads with the Prince for his son's life, this is the very point he makes in his defense, since by killing Tybalt Romeo only did what the law would itself have done. Nevertheless, Romeo is banished. The Prince must have accepted Montague's point in mitigation of Romeo's guilt, but he does banish him. He probably thought Romeo had to be pun- ished for taking the law into his own hands, and banishment, after all, as the friar attempts to persuade Romeo, is a good deal milder than death.

But the Prince's new-found rigor does not continue. Just before he ar- rives on the dismal graveyard scene, the Third Watchman reports a captive: "Here is a friar that trembles, sighs, and weeps." (V.iii.189) The friar had not succeeded in escaping, but precisely why he is weeping we are not told. He knows his scheme for the lovers failed, knows of their deaths and knows he himself must be a suspect, so his concerns are understandable. Nevertheless, when the Prince asks about suspects, he voluntarily steps forward: "And here I stand both to impeach and purge / Myself condemned and myself excused." (V.iii.231–32) He tells the whole story, and while he tells it accurately, he fails to make plain the enormity of his wrong-doing—that is, his lies, decep- tions, usurpations, and illegalities. He ends with the lines (V.iii.271–73):

And if aught in this miscarried by my fault,
Let my old life be sacrificed some hour before his time,
Unto the rigor of severest law.

There is really no "if" about the friar's fault, and, while expressing his will- ingness to die, he indirectly pleads with the prince not to take his life "some hour before his time"—that is, as an old man who hasn't long to live. The

Prince's response is astonishing. And it comes in a single, simple sentence: "We still have known thee for a holy man." (V.iii.274) Case closed. No inquiry into the bizarre series of events that left three people dead in the tomb. No punishment at all for the part Friar Lawrence played in the calamity. Gone is the rigor the Prince began by banishing Romeo, and we can guess why. He is in awe of the Church and thus bows to its higher authority. In effect, he allows the Church to rule even in secular affairs—to commit crimes, and get others to commit crimes, with impunity.[9] We must conclude that the biggest—but invisible—division in Verona and the greatest challenge to the Prince is not, despite all appearances, the antagonism between Montagues and Capulets, which actually shows signs of abating, but the much deeper antagonism between the temporal and spiritual authorities, which, as we can see from this retreat by the Prince, shows no sign of abating.

In the sources that scholars believe Shakespeare used for the play, going back to the late fifteenth century, the Italian names "Montecchi" and "Capelletti" are used for feuding families. But these names also appear in Dante's *Divine Comedy*, an earlier and much greater work than these other sources. In *Purgatorio*, Dante addresses "enslaved Italy, a place of great grief," like a "ship without a master in a great storm," where fellow-citizens "are always at war" and, "thrown together within the same wall," cannot live "without biting one another." "Wretched country," he continues, "look around your shores . . . and then into your heart . . . see if any part enjoys peace" (VI.76–87).[10] And after accusing the clergy—"you people who are supposed to be devout" and who allowed Italy to grow untamed and vicious, "not having been corrected by spurs" since they laid their "hands upon the bridle"—Dante assails the Holy Roman Emperor for abandoning the Italian saddle, permitting a "garden . . . to be turned into a desert," and calls for his return to Italy to quell the bitter feuding of its nobility (VI.106–10):

> Come and see, you who are negligent,
> Montagues and Capulets, Monaldi and Filippeschi:
> One lot already grieving, the other in fear.
> Come, you who are cruel, come and see the distress
> Of your noble families, and cleanse their rottenness.

Without imperial rule, according to Dante, Italy is riven by lawless dissension, even or especially within its cities. The "devout" should obey God's injunction to leave unto Caesar the things that are Caesar's, but instead they have deprived Caesar of his authority without being able to rule effectively themselves, while the temporal ruler, the Holy Roman Emperor, has permitted this usurpation of the civil power by the Church. Dante uses the names of the noble families, like the Montagues and Capulets, as examples of Italy's plight. By using these names as well, Shakespeare confirms the idea that the deeper source of disorder in Verona (and Italy) is the weakness of the secular or imperial power relative to the spiritual power. The feud between the families is more a consequence than a cause, for its root is the lack of a political authority sufficiently strong to keep them both in awe. This may also be the reason why Shakespeare refrains from specifying any particular grievances as the cause of their hostility.[11]

Love

Why do we love the lovers, and what makes the story of Romeo and Juliet tragic? We love the young lovers because they fall in love at first sight, infatuated with each other's beauty. We love to love love. We even approve of their possessiveness, of their wanting to remain in the presence of that beauty and keep it for themselves. They declare their love quickly, barred by no convention, with nary a word about offspring, or raising a family (though the nurse mentions these things), for that would dilute the passion of love itself, their devotion to each other alone. Our approving interest in their love continues, even as they manage to spend their wedding night together—an event distinguishing this play from *Othello*, for example, where it is doubtful that the marriage of Othello and Desdemona is ever consummated. With help from both the nurse and the friar—but in violation of the Prince's decree banishing him—Romeo surreptitiously mounts a ladder to Juliet's bedchamber and stays until the following morning, when he must perforce, surreptitiously still, depart from Verona and his new bride.

The lovers are measureless in their love, risking all for each other, and giving all too. After an inner struggle, Juliet overcomes her detestation of Tybalt's killer, who is her husband, and, of course, the lovers end up dying for each other. We are struck, in particular, by the purity and nobility of Juliet's character, and while we can hardly admire Romeo as much, his devotion to Juliet itself disposes us to think less harshly of him. But they have made the kinds of mistakes impetuous lovers will make. They have married too quickly and disregarded their parents, as if they had no need for parents or even of society at large. Nor were they mature enough to understand that the character of the beloved, much more than physical beauty, makes for a durable marriage. They are young and foolish. But such is the charm with which Shakespeare endows them that we find it impossible to hold their faults against them.[12]

A final reason for loving them is that in their last breaths they speak and think of almost nothing but love. Neither says a word about the afterlife.[13] Both seem to regard death as the end, just as the nurse had, thus making their sacrifice even greater. Mistakenly believing Juliet dead, and on the point of killing himself, Romeo is still struck by her beauty and imagines, rather grotesquely, that "Death is amorous" and keeps her as "his paramour." To protect her he will die and join the worms, her "chambermaids," setting up his "everlasting rest" right there and shaking off the "yoke of inauspicious stars" from his "world-wearied flesh" (V.iii.101–12). Gazing upon her one last time, embracing her, and with a final "Here's to my love!" he quaffs the poison and, "Thus, with a kiss," slumps down across her (V.iii.113–20). Juliet, for her part, must die in even greater haste, before the guards enter. Finding no "friendly" poison left in his cup, she kisses him—"Thy lips are warm"—and immediately kills herself with his dagger (V.iii.165–75). She does not imagine a role for herself after death, as he does; for her it is simply the end.

These are the reasons why we love them. The young lovers are heroes of love, made all the more admirable in our eyes by the brief duration of their love, which maintains its intensity from beginning to end. The tragedy is that such lovers should die by their own hand so soon, and by a series of mistakes, most of them made by Romeo. Jointly they erred in not appealing to their parents in the name of love and in marrying so swiftly. But it was Romeo alone who brought about his banishment by senselessly killing Tybalt. And it was Romeo who, disregarding his banishment, shot like an arrow to Juliet's side, intent (mistakenly) on dying along with her. By contrast, Juliet's merit shines so much more brightly. She refuses to marry Paris, despite intense urging from her parents and even the nurse. She is brave enough to accept the friar's terrifying plan to take his drug, seem to die, and be buried in the tomb of her ancestors. Finally, at the sight of her dead husband, she prefers death to life. In moral virtue and nobility Juliet—the child of nature—soars far above and beyond the low materialism of the nurse. Yet we cannot say that her intellect is mature or her choices wise. She is, after all, not quite fourteen years old. An older, wiser woman would not likely have been swept off her feet by Romeo or sought marriage so swiftly. It is possible, had she known him better, that she would even have found it unnecessary to die for him.

Conclusion

All in all, we love the lovers in *Romeo and Juliet*. And here we find the most important general object and effect of the play taken as a whole—one so obvious it is easily overlooked. It is to restore sexual love, the love of men and women for each other, to a very high place in life. A sign of why restoration was necessary is given in the play by the ideal of chastity that both Rosaline and the friar cherish. This Christian ideal is partly rooted in the fact that the love of the body, or erotic love, necessarily involves selfish pleasure-seeking, the very lust Christ strongly condemns. Juliet's speech from her balcony affords another reason: that idolizing the beloved deifies him, and at least detracts from, if it does not nullify, the worship of God. In effect, the beloved becomes our "lord and master" (see II.ii.115–18, 147–52). At any rate, for God's sake, highly Christian societies will tend to make chastity a general ideal not confined to abstinence before marriage, where it has a proper place.[14]

Today, it seems we have sunk so low that the words "chastity" and "virtue" make us blush and stammer, fearing the worst of all accusations: prudery. We have come to regard sex merely as an innocent and temporary, if not momentary, recreation—a thrill, and not much more. So common, accepted, and popular has this carnal view become that it is hard for us to regain the perspective from which Shakespeare wrote about love, where not the eman-cipation of sex without love, but its natural and proper connection with love had to be established against an excessive Christian asceticism. Indeed, while no one knew better than Shakespeare the wide range of misuse and abuse to which our sexual desires are subject, he made it one of the chief objectives of his work as a whole—including his sonnets and long poems—to help create a more natural and complete view of love than the one prevailing in his time, which was still heavily influenced by Christianity. This meant reviving the ancient Greek view of *eros*, but it also meant going beyond the value placed on sexual love by classical philosophers and celebrating a higher form of that love in a new way. In *Romeo and Juliet*, a low level of erotic love is represented by the crude sexual boasting of the Capulet servingmen; yet the attitudes of Mercutio and the nurse are only variations on the same theme. We scorn these, and love only the lovers and their true love. Yet the harm and danger that even true love can bring, we also learn from Shakespeare—which is why his plays about love, like *Twelfth Night* and *As You Like It*, can end very hap-pily, while others, like *Othello* and *Romeo and Juliet*, end very unhappily.

The unhappy ending of these lovers, which Christianity might be tempted to read as proof of the need to rein in or suppress erotic love, is neverthe-less far from outweighing, in our minds, the admirable and happy goodness of love itself. Indeed, it is hard to avoid the thought that the friar and his pupil, Romeo, are together primarily responsible for the tragedy. What they have in common, underlying or in some way causing their defects and mis-takes, is their Christian belief, whereas Juliet, representing nature in a more elevated form, is their victim. Broadly speaking, this is the essence of the play. How, then, can a play that is critical of Christianity still be salutary for Christians—even Christians today—to read? For one thing, Shakespeare generally is without peer in conveying a sense of the full depths and span of human life. In addition, they will learn much about their religion—more than they are likely to learn by themselves, especially in corrupt times. Christianity makes great demands on its believers. Christ commands: "Be perfect, therefore, as your heavenly Father is perfect." (*Matt.* 5:48) This is no matter of mere self-esteem; after all, self-esteem writ large is nothing more than sinful pride. And when Christ proclaims that his kingdom is not of this world, Christians must understand that it transcends this world and that they are to look to eternity, far beyond the reach of our material concerns.

Above all, Shakespeare is concerned with understanding the effect the Christian view of perfection has on human life. The earliest Christians expected the return of Christ imminently, and did their best to live the good life, to rise above our natural selves, to be perfect, in accordance with his precepts; once that return did not occur, life had to settle down, with all its natural problems and concerns returning. In his plays, if we look carefully, we can see that the standard Shakespeare uses to judge people—their goodness, justice, nobility, greatness—reflects something like the natural morality found in Aristotle's *Nicomachean Ethics*, along with the conception of political life found in his *Politics*. These are closer to what our nature requires. But his criticism of Christianity is quiet, not clamorous. Usually, unless we look with care, it is barely visible, hidden under the veil of an entrancing or gripping story. Shakespeare is no "Machiavel," nor one of his many descendants, making war on Christianity in order to destroy it. He has no ideology, presents no program. Shakespeare gives guidance by portraying better and worse people, better and worse courses of action, exploring the inner workings and outcomes of the vastest range of human possibilities. Like Socrates before him, but through the medium of drama and poetry, he brings the fundamental alternatives to life before us and even, by having us consider them seriously, helps us become better ourselves.[15]

Notes

1. Parenthetical references herein, unless otherwise indicated, are to the division of the play into Act, Scene, and Line numbers in William Shakespeare, *The Tragedy of Romeo and Juliet*, eds. Bernice Kliman and Laury Magnus, The New Kittredge Shakespeare Series (Focus Publishing, 2008). This edition follows the text of the Second Quarto.

2. See George Kittredge's Introduction, in Kliman and Magnus 2008, x: "The premonitions of disaster continue throughout the play, but they are interlaced with evidence of human shortsightedness and weakness."

3. Samuel Taylor Coleridge remarks that Shakespeare shows us in *Romeo and Juliet* "the fineness of his insight into the nature of the passions": see *Notes and Lectures on Shakespeare*, ed. H. N. Coleridge (London, 1849), Vol. 1: 155; and "The Lectures of 1811–1812," in *Romeo and Juliet*, ed. Sylvan Barnet, Signet Classics Series (Penguin Books, 1998) 134–42.

4. *The New Oxford Annotated Bible: New Revised Standard Version*, Third Edition, ed. Michael Coogan et al. (Oxford University Press, 2001).

5. See John C. Briggs, "*Romeo and Juliet* and the Cure of Souls," *Ben Jonson Journal* 16 (2009) 281–303, esp. 286: "The first scene of the play, which has no precedent in the sources is especially revealing, for it . . . is indicative of the erotic and thumotic . . . aspects of catharsis as they play out in a Verona of intense rivalry and powerful longing."

6. To one critic, the nurse is a "triumphant and complete achievement" who "lives and breathes in her own right from the moment she appears"—a portrait unsurpassed in its fullness of character "till [Shakespeare] gives us Falstaff." See Harley Granville-Barker, *Prefaces to Shakespeare* (Atlantic Publishers, 2007), Vol. IV: 71–73.

7. See the "Timeline" in Kliman and Magnus (2008, 127–29), which tentatively proposes that the play begins on Saturday. Most modern editors, including Kittredge, believe that Shakespeare plays "fast and loose with exact times" (2008, ix–x, 127), but there is evidence to the contrary that—when it suits his purpose—Shakespeare pays careful, though unobtrusive attention to the passage of time in his plays.

8. There is a parallel in Shakespeare's dark comedy, *Measure for Measure*, where it is possible (with somewhat greater difficulty) to track the time elapsed from a Tuesday—also mentioned once—through Wednesday and Thursday, a duration of only three days. On the significance of these three days, see David Lowenthal, *Shakespeare and the Good Life: Ethics and Politics in Dramatic Form* (Rowman and Littlefield, 1997) 251–57.

9. See Jerry Weinberger, "Pious Princes and Red-Hot Lovers: The Politics of Shakespeare's *Romeo and Juliet*," *Journal of Politics* 65/2 (2003) 350–75, esp. 373: "At the play's end, Friar Laurence is the one who really rules Verona."

10. *Dante: The Divine Comedy*, Oxford World Classics, tr. Charles Sisson, ed. David Higgins (Oxford University Press, 2008).

11. On the political problem posed by Christianity, see Lowenthal 1997, 32–36, 56–59; see also, Allan Bloom, "*Romeo and Juliet*," in *Love and Friendship* (Simon and Schuster, 1993) 277–78, 291–96.

12. See Bloom 1993, 275, 283: "Romeo and Juliet are the perfect pair of lovers." "The terrible consequences of their love could have been avoided at many points if either lover had been moderate or reflective, but this would have been like cutting the wings of birds and still expecting them to fly."

13. See Coleridge 1849, 160: "All deep passions are a sort of atheists, that believe no future." Coleridge's remark is a gloss on Romeo's exchange with the friar

(III.iii.9–72) that banishment is a fate worse than death: "There is no world with-out Verona walls, / But purgatory, torture, hell itself." "'Tis torture, and not mercy: heaven is here, / Where Juliet lives" (18–19, 30–31). In his despair Romeo rejects the friar's "armor" against adversity, the consolation of his "philosophy": "Hang up philosophy, / Unless philosophy can make a Juliet . . . / It helps not, it prevails not. Talk no more" (III.iii.59–62).

14. See Harry V. Jaffa, "Chastity as a Political Principle: An Interpretation of Shakespeare's *Measure for Measure*," in *Shakespeare as Political Thinker*, eds. John Alvis and Thomas West (ISI Books, 2000, second edition) 203–40.

15. In this respect, Shakespeare's intention is much like that of Abraham Lincoln, who continued to read and recall his Shakespeare all through the darkest days of his Presidency. See John C. Briggs, "Steeped in Shakespeare," *Claremont Review of Books* (Winter 2008/2009) 63–66.

∽

8

Macbeth's Strange Infirmity

Shakespeare's Portrait of a Demonic Tyranny

Carson Holloway

Why should contemporary political scientists study Shakespeare's *Macbeth*? Most obviously, the play merits our attention for its vivid and insightful depiction of an important political phenomenon—one that is no less important for being nowadays seldom investigated, or even named, by professional political scientists. I refer, of course, to tyranny. Macbeth is judged a tyrant repeatedly in the play by various characters with whom the reader is invited to sympathize. Moreover, there can be little doubt that Shakespeare intends for us to share—and shares himself—these characters' sense that in so naming Macbeth they are expressing a genuine insight into the character of his rule. It would seem that for Shakespeare, unlike for Hobbes, tyranny is more than just monarchy "misliked."[1] On the contrary, the play invites us to the conclusion that Macbeth's rule is a cause of "woe" not only to his victims because it harms their self-interest, but to any "mind that's honest"—to borrow an expression used by one character to describe perhaps Macbeth's most egregious crime (IV.iii.196–97).[2]

In fact, *Macbeth* can be understood in part as a dramatic enactment, and implicit analysis, of tyranny as it was understood by the classical tradition of political philosophy. Roughly the first half of the chapter that follows pursues this argument, seeking to show how Shakespeare's drama both illustrates the character of, and provokes reflection on the origins and consequences of, tyranny as it was understood by the classics. The second half of the chapter, however, proceeds to contend that the classical conception of tyranny does not fully comprehend the kind of evil to which Macbeth succumbs.

Macbeth's reign is to some extent recognizable as a classical tyranny, but it is also something more. In the end, Shakespeare's *Macbeth* offers us an account of demonic evil, of not just the ordinary vice that pursues self-interest at the expense of others, but of the mysterious human capacity for an irrational and self-destructive wickedness.

Macbeth as Tyrant

According to Aristotle's account in the *Politics*, tyranny is a deviant form of regime because the tyrant rules not for the well-being of the whole community but rather for his own interest.[3] This seems to be true of Macbeth. His desire to be king has no reference whatever to the common good. To be sure, one could contend that Macbeth, at least at first, deserves to be king. The play begins with the realm convulsed by a rebellion mounted by disloyal nobles and aided by the King of Norway. According to the reports King Duncan receives, his forces have overcome the worst that fortune could throw at them largely because of Macbeth's courage on the field of battle. Thus Duncan's messengers speak to Macbeth of the day's triumph as "thy success" (I.iii.90). Macbeth more than any other man is responsible for saving Scotland from defeat, humiliation, and foreign subjection. As Duncan himself says: "More is thy due, than more than all can pay" (I.iv.21).

Macbeth, however, is not Coriolanus. The two are similar in that they both appear to be indispensable men, men whose unequalled military prowess saves their communities from defeat. Unlike Macbeth, however, Coriolanus is convinced—as are most of his fellow citizens—that his valor entitles him to the highest office the city can offer. While Coriolanus is a citizen of a martial republic, Macbeth is the subject of a feudal monarchy. He thus inhabits a markedly different moral and political universe, one in which martial virtue is valued, but fealty is valued even more, where manly virtue compels admiration but creates no claim to office. Accordingly, in response to Duncan's gracious praise, and his suggestion that he is in Macbeth's debt, Macbeth proclaims the feudal understanding of the subject's duty: "Your Highness's part / Is to receive our duties: and our duties / Are to your throne and state, children and servants; / Which do but what they should, by doing everything / Safe to your love and honour" (I.iv.23–27). Of course, because Macbeth has already begun to desire the crown, one might suspect his sincerity. Nevertheless, even in his private ruminations Macbeth never says anything to contradict this view. It never occurs to him to think that saving the kingdom entitles him to be king. Rather, tyrant-like, he just *wants* it. Indeed, Macbeth practically names himself a tyrant, understood in classical terms, when he proclaims: "For mine own good / All causes shall give way" (III.iv.134–35).

Moreover, Macbeth's rule, once underway, bears all the hallmarks of tyranny as described by classical political philosophy. Unable to trust his subjects, he must spy on them. At one point, he remarks to his wife on the absence of Macduff from a royal banquet. Wondering if Macduff has refused an explicit summons, Lady Macbeth asks, "Did you send to him, sir?" Macbeth's response reveals the network of political espionage that he deploys against his own nobles: "I hear it by the way. . . . There's not a one of them but in his house / I keep a servant fee'd" (III.iv.127–31).

Moreover, Macbeth must, like a tyrant, destroy his best subjects. The good King Duncan *delights* in honoring the worthy. He loads Macbeth with praise and makes him Thane of Cawdor, remarking to Banquo that he is "fed" in "his commendations" of Macbeth: "It is a banquet to me" (I.iv.55–56). Macbeth, however, makes a striking contrast as king. He, too, has a subject of extraordinary virtue: Banquo. According to Macbeth's own assessment, Banquo "dares" much, and "to that dauntless temper of his mind, / He hath a wisdom that doth guide his valour / To act in safety." Such courage and prudence are praiseworthy and, one would think, useful in a subject. Yet Macbeth regards Banquo's "royalty of nature" not with admiration but with fear; and he accordingly arranges his murder (III.i.48–53).[4]

Macbeth and the Origins of Tyranny

Shakespeare's *Macbeth*, however, is more than just a depiction of tyranny in action. It also follows a particular tyrannical career from its beginning to its end. It in fact introduces Macbeth before he has become a tyrant and thus allows us to follow his descent into tyranny. The play's title identifies it as a tragedy, and its story conforms to the common tragic model: it shows us an otherwise admirable man brought to ruin by some flaw in his character. As the play opens Macbeth has won universal praise, but by its end he is the object of universal hatred. In addition, the play does not merely trace the external actions of the tyrant but also admits us to his inmost thoughts. Shakespeare therefore provides us an opportunity to seek the origins of tyranny in the soul of the tyrant and to consider the consequences of that tyranny for that soul.

What, then, are the origins of Macbeth's tyranny? Tyranny is characterized by violence: the tyrant does violence to politics by disregarding the common good and perverting rule to his own advantage. And, because most human beings will resist such attacks on the common good, or at least on that portion of the common good dearest to themselves, the tyrant must do violence in a more obvious manner. To quell the resistance provoked by his violence to principles, he must do violence also to living persons. *Macbeth* puts such violence on blazing display. The play, however, also suggests, more subtly, that tyranny originates in a less visible kind of violence: violence against one's own nature. Before performing any overt acts, Macbeth and Lady Macbeth take the first steps on the path of tyranny by doing violence to their own souls.

Macbeth experiences the murder of Duncan as an act of violence against himself. Indeed, he feels even the contemplation of such a murder as a kind of self-violation. Merely to entertain the "fantastical" murder in his "thought," he finds, is to be confronted with a "horrid image" that "doth unfix my hair, / And make my seated heart knock at my ribs, / Against the use of Nature." In passing from consideration of murder to the actual resolution to do it, he continues to experience the same sense of doing violence to self. In his first decision to proceed, Macbeth says to himself: "The eye wink at the hand; yet let that be, / Which the eye fears, when it is done, to see" (I.iv.52–53). That is, he will consent to the deed, even though he knows that he will not be able to approve it once accomplished. Macbeth later begins to recoil from this enterprise, but his resolution is stiffened by Lady Macbeth. Even here, however, he continues to view the act as something to which he must somehow force himself: "I am settled, and bend up / Each corporal agent to this terrible feat" (I.vii.80–82). And his repugnance certainly does not dissipate upon completion of the deed. Having come from killing Duncan, he speaks of his bloody hands as "a sorry sight": "They pluck out mine eyes" (II.ii.20 and 57).

One commentator has suggested, based on a soliloquy in which Macbeth dwells on all the dangers involved in killing Duncan and usurping the throne (I.vii.1–28), that Macbeth was "worried only by practical considerations."[5] This view is, I think, refuted by the passages cited in the preceding paragraph, as well as by developments throughout the course of the play. Macbeth is not an amoral man. He is rather a moral man who does violence to his own moral nature in order to achieve what he wants. It is true that in this soliloquy Macbeth dwells on the perils that are likely to beset a usurper. Here he displays better foresight than his wife, who anticipates no such evils. It is also true that, in the subsequent dialogue, Macbeth finally consents to the murder once Lady Macbeth has persuaded him that they can get away with it (I.vii.75–81). Such speeches and actions, however, do not preclude the sincerity of Macbeth's moral concerns. He is a complex man. Like anybody else he wants to preserve himself, but it does not follow that his moral qualms are superficial or mere pretense. In fact, such an account of his character is impossible to square with the facts that he is practically beside himself with grief after having killed Duncan, and that it continues to prey on his mind even after he is king, points to which we will return later. Indeed, were Macbeth simply an amoral pragmatist, it is difficult to see how he could be a fitting tragic subject, insofar as tragedy is thought to depict how an otherwise admirable man is brought to ruin by some flaw in his character. Macbeth is not only acceptable, but is so compelling as a tragic protagonist precisely because he is so morally sensitive yet at the same time so willing to do violence to his moral sensibilities.

Lady Macbeth presumably knows her own husband, and by her own words she affirms his moral seriousness, even as she views it as an obstacle to what they both desire. That is, she recognizes that violence will have to be done to his nature in order to carry out their project: "I fear thy nature: / It is too full o'th'milk of human kindness, / To catch the nearest way. Thou would'st be great; / Art not without ambition, but without / The illness should attend it; / what thou wouldst highly, / That wouldst thou holily; would not play false, / And yet wouldst wrongly win; thou'dst have, great Glamis, / That which cries, 'Thus thou must do,' if thou have it; / And that which rather thou dost fear to do, / Than wishest should be undone" (I.v.16–28). Lady Macbeth's willingness to do violence to her husband's nature in order to achieve her ends is, of course, unattractive. Her regard for what he *is* as a mere impediment to what she *wants* seems incompatible with any genuine love for him. On the other hand, she could be defended on the grounds that, after all, he, too, wants the end for which she is scheming. And, leaving aside all moral considerations, perhaps the violence she intends to perform on him could be understood as necessary to his own good, as a kind of surgery that will heal his incompleteness and satisfy his deepest longings. As she so accurately discerns, his nature is deeply conflicted: he wants incompatible things. If he is to enjoy *any* of the goods that he desires, violence will have to be done to *some* part of him. If he is to realize his desire to be kindly, holy, and true, he will have to mortify his ambition. If he is to realize his ambition, he will have to mortify his desire to be kindly, holy, and true. Therefore, in choosing to suppress some of his desires, she is acting, she believes, to secure what he most deeply desires. The tenability of such a defense of Lady Macbeth has to be judged in light of all that develops in the course of the play. For the moment, it suffices to note that it does not take long for signs to appear that she has misjudged her husband's nature and therefore underestimated the degree of violence it must undergo to gain the crown. In the speech quoted above, she speaks of the murder of Duncan as something Macbeth fears to do but would not wish undone (I.v.24–25). Yet, immediately after having done it, he *does* wish it undone. Startled by a knocking at the castle's south entry, he exclaims: "Wake Duncan with thy knocking: I would thou couldst!" (II.ii.72–73).

The tyrannical enterprise requires that violence be done to Lady Macbeth's nature as well. She in fact expressly wills it. Contemplating her plans, she wishes that she might be "unsex[ed]" and so filled "from the crown to the toe, top-full / Of direst cruelty." She wishes to stop in herself "th'access and passage to remorse; / That no compunctious visitings of Nature / Shake my fell purpose, nor keep peace between / Th'effect and it." She desires that in her "woman's breasts" her "milk" be replaced with "gall" (I.v.41–48). She evidently believes that it is part of a woman's nature to be tender and life-nourishing. She wills, in explicit violation of that nature, to be cruel and deadly.

One might doubt that here Lady Macbeth really does do violence to her own nature. She is not a very sympathetic character, at least at first; and she so eagerly calls for this ugly transformation that we may suspect that she has no womanly feelings of tenderness to begin with. Yet subsequent developments show that, while Lady Macbeth puts up a brave front, the bloody requirements of tyranny do in fact go against her grain. When they first begin to plan the murder, she tells Macbeth that he need only "look up clear," or keep his face free from any suspicious signs: "leave all the rest to me" (I.v.71–73). In the end, however, Macbeth has to do the actual killing, and Lady Macbeth must take to drink to fortify her determination to go forward with the plot (II.ii.1–2). When Macbeth begins to hold back from the murder, she claims for herself a willingness to outrage her deepest feelings in order to advance their project: "I have given suck, and know / How tender 'tis to love the babe that milks me: / I would, while it was smiling in my face, / Have pluck'd my nipple from his boneless gums, / And dash'd the brains out, had I so sworn / As you have done to this" (I.vii.54–59). This is so shocking that it tempts the reader to view Lady Macbeth as a monster devoid of normal human feelings. Yet it is mere boast. When it comes to actually performing the murder, she is daunted by the mere reflection of a bond less deep than that of mother and child. Having sent Macbeth to kill Duncan, she reflects, "Had he not resembled / My father as he slept, I had done't" (II.ii.12–13).

As the preceding discussion implies, the violence against oneself in which tyranny originates is not done for its own sake, but for the sake of an apparent good: the "golden round," as Lady Macbeth calls it, the crown (I.v.28). This physical object, of course, is not desired for itself but for what Macbeth and Lady Macbeth believe will accompany it: the greatness to which they both aspire. They are united in ambition. Macbeth understands "vaulting ambition" as the only "spur" urging him on toward regicide (I.vii.25–26). Lady Macbeth approvingly attributes "ambition" to her husband, and she speaks as if she shares his ambition, or possesses it even more perfectly than he does (I.v.19). In his letter to her about the possibility of his becoming king, he addresses her as his "dearest partner in greatness." He informs her of the "greatness" that is promised to her, advising her to "[l]ay it to thy heart" (I.v.11–14). He thus implies that the longing for greatness is something that lies close to both of their hearts.

The situation is more complex than these passages indicate, however, because Shakespeare's vision of tyranny is keener than a first reading of the play might reveal. For while the play depicts two tyrannical souls united in a love of greatness, they are in fact drawn into tyranny by two distinct understandings of what greatness is. Here we may introduce as most useful Saint Augustine's distinction between "the desire of human glory and the desire of domination."[6]

Although Macbeth's motivations are, again, complex, he appears to have much in him of the love of glory. This is the first consideration to which he turns when he tries to stop their conspiracy to murder Duncan: "We will proceed no further in this business: / He hath honour'd me of late; and I have bought / Golden opinions from all sorts of people, / Which should be worn now in their newest gloss, / Not cast aside so soon" (I.vii.31–34). Moreover, as his tyrannical career nears its close, Macbeth singles out his loss of glory for special lamentation: "I have lived long enough: my way of life / Is fall'n into the sere, the yellow leaf; / And that which should accompany old age, / As honour, love, obedience, troops of friends, / I must not look to have; but in their stead, / Curses, not loud, but deep, mouth-honour, breath, / Which the poor heart would fain deny, and dare not" (V.iii.22–28).[7]

In contrast, Lady Macbeth appears to be much more a lover of domination. In urging Macbeth forward, she predicts that their murder of Duncan "shall give to all our nights and days to come / Solely sovereign sway and masterdom" (I.v.69–70). When Macbeth later takes up her suggestion that it will be thought that Duncan was murdered by the grooms of his chamber, she responds: "Who dares receive it other, / As we shall make our griefs and clamour roar / Upon his death" (I.vii.78–79). As we have just seen, it pains Macbeth to think that others hate him but "dare not" curse him openly. Lady Macbeth, however, seems indifferent to who suspects them, so long as their public grief is so ostentatious as to prevent anyone from questioning their contrived account of the crime. For her, their performance need not be convincing so long as it is sufficiently intimidating. Indeed, her concern with domination over honor is revealed even more clearly when, in the sleepwalking scene late in the play, she repeats something she has no doubt said to Macbeth: "What need we fear who knows it, when none can call our power to accompt" (V.i.35–36)?

Macbeth and Lady Macbeth are thus led into tyranny by two separate desires. Yet they are not exactly led separately. That is, they are propelled toward this same goal not only by the independent operation of these different desires on each soul, but also by the interplay of these desires in their relationship. She dominates him by manipulating his love of praise, and he seeks to maintain her good opinion of him by submitting to her domination. The early scenes in the play contain ample evidence that Lady Macbeth desires to dominate her husband. When she first anticipates his reluctance to use murder to advance himself, she wishes him present so that she can "chastise with the valour of my tongue / All that impedes thee from the golden round"— "chastise," we note, and not persuade (I.v.27–28). Later she proclaims: "The raven himself is hoarse, / That croaks the fatal entrance of Duncan / Under *my* battlements"—a remark that says a good deal about who she regards as the master of the castle (I.v.38–40, emphasis added). Her willingness to dominate him, and her use of his love of praise as her primary weapon, are most obvious when she has to surmount his refusal to go forward with Duncan's murder. "We will proceed no further in this business," Macbeth resolves; yet his desire so to settle the issue does nothing to dissuade her. She responds by threatening to withhold her esteem, and implicitly denying his worthiness of the honor he has won in the recent rebellion. As a result of his military exploits, it has been said that Macbeth "deserves" to be known as "brave" (I.ii.16). His wife, however, rebukes him for being "afeard" to take what he wants, a failure for which he will have to recognize himself as a "coward." She suggests that one who will not dare to do what he wants does not deserve to be called a man. She exhorts him to "screw" his "courage to the sticking place" for their venture, noting that they will be able to do whatever they want to Duncan when he is "asleep / (Whereto the rather shall his hard day's journey / Soundly invite him)" (I.vii.39–64). Unable to bear such condemnation from his "dearest partner in greatness," Macbeth submits. Moreover, in so doing he surrenders not only his judgment about a particular course of action, but even his standards of judgment. When she had initially attacked his manliness, he had responded by arguing that true manliness must be in the service of what is fitting, and not just whatever one happens to desire: "I dare do all that may become a man; / Who dares do more, is none" (I.vii.46–47). In the end, however, he agrees to what she wants, failing to note the obvious perversity of the courage to which she calls him, a "courage" that will kill a tired old man in his sleep.

Macbeth and the Consequences of Tyranny

The classical political philosophers contend that tyranny is bad for the tyrant as well as for his subjects.[8] Macbeth bears out this understanding. As Macbeth and Lady Macbeth soon learn, and as Plato could have taught them, as tyrants they cannot even securely enjoy the external goods for which they stooped to tyranny in the first place. As we have already noted, Macbeth realizes near the end of his reign that love and honor are things that he "must not look to have." Moreover, not even the power they win can be possessed in peace. Having become king, Macbeth reflects that "[t]o be thus is nothing, but to be safely thus" (III.i.47). Shortly, Lady Macbeth similarly laments, "Nought's had, all's spent, / Where our desire is got without content: / 'Tis safer to be that which we destroy, / Than by destruction dwell in doubtful joy" (III.ii.4–7). Paradoxically, this concern to secure their position drives Macbeth to even greater crimes, which in turn leads to his overthrow.

The argument developed in the course of this chapter, however, suggests an even deeper difficulty. Macbeth and Lady Macbeth have done violence to their own natures, to their own souls or selves, to win external goods. This appears on its face to be a fool's bargain, and so their experience of tyranny confirms. Alienation is one of the play's themes. In doing violence to themselves, they alienate themselves from things with which they desire communion. At the same time, they cannot alienate these desires for communion, so that they experience their alienation as a lack, an incompleteness, and their lives as increasing emptiness and misery. They learn that they cannot simply switch off the parts of their souls that impede them from gaining what they want. The play suggests that one cannot do such violence to oneself without paying a dear price, a price dearer, perhaps, than that paid by the tyrant's victims.

To begin with, tyranny estranges Macbeth and Lady Macbeth from each other. To be sure, this alienation is already implicit in the selfishness of their tyrannical desires. As we saw earlier, she begins her part in the play by regarding his nature—that is, himself—as a mere impediment to her quest for power. Later, Macbeth says, in his wife's presence, "For mine own good / All causes shall give way"—a remark at odds with his earlier sense that she is his "dearest partner in greatness" (III.iv.134–35, I.v.11). At the same time, neither Macbeth nor Lady Macbeth is characterized simply by these selfish, tyrannical desires. On the contrary, as we have noted, they both possess deep moral inclinations that they violate by their actions. Yet, because of their crimes, the persistence of their moral natures serves only to deepen their estrangement. Again, Lady Macbeth failed to understand how deeply her husband would wound himself in murdering Duncan: "th'attempt and not the deed / Confounds us," she says while waiting for Macbeth to return from his bloody work (II.ii.10–11). Yet subsequent events show that, contrary to her expectations, the deed itself continues to confound Macbeth, even after it is done, and this keeps them apart. After they have won the crown, they cannot enjoy sharing their high position, because Macbeth keeps to himself, brooding on his crime (III.i.8–12). Moreover, because they retain their essential moral natures, defiled but not destroyed, they find they cannot approve each other's characters any longer. Macbeth's disapproval of his wife appears after he has been terrorized by the ghost of Banquo, which he assumes she has seen as well. She rebukes him for his fear, and he responds: "Can such things be, / And overcome us like a summer's cloud, / Without our especial wonder? You make me strange / Even to the disposition that I owe, / When now I think you can behold such sights, / And keep the natural ruby of your cheeks, / When mine is blanch'd with fear" (III.iv.109–15). The "disposition" he owes, of which he speaks here, is one of love for her. That is, her apparently heartless indifference to such a grievous spectacle estranges him from his love for her. He begins to find her hardness repellent. And Lady Macbeth apparently experiences a corresponding revulsion for him. Having arranged Banquo's murder, Macbeth announces to his wife that during the coming night there shall be done "a deed of dreadful note." She asks what it will be, and he responds with a chilling speech calling for darkness to come, when "Good things of day begin to droop and drowse, / Whiles night's black agents to their preys do rouse." Lady Macbeth says nothing in response to this, yet she must react somehow with her face. For, observing her, Macbeth continues: "Thou marvell'st at my words: but hold thee still; / Things bad begun make strong themselves by ill" (III.ii.44–55). Given the hardness to which she had earlier urged him, we may be tempted to assume that here she is marveling with approval at the change in him. Yet the words of the speech cannot sustain this interpretation. Seeing her face, and apparently noting that she is about to say something, he tells her to keep still, and claims that things begun in evil make themselves stronger through more evil. It would make no sense for him to say such things to her unless he had detected a reluctance on her part to approve the dreadful deed that he is planning. She has sought to harden him, yet in the end she cannot approve the change she has wrought in his soul.

In addition, they are both haunted by their sense of alienation from God. This is true even of Lady Macbeth. She begins the play by disdaining her husband's desire to act "holily," and by wishing that the smoke of Hell might conceal her from the eye of heaven (I.v.21 and 50–54). By the end of the play, however, she is unburdening her troubled soul in sleep, revealing, among other fears, that "Hell is murky" (V.i.34). Similarly, when weighing the possible cost of murdering Duncan, Macbeth indicates that, if he could be assured of success, he would "jump the life to come" (I.vii.7). This remark expresses a willingness to disregard the afterlife, and hence God's judgment on his actions; but at the same time indicates that Macbeth cannot leave these considerations completely out of his deliberations. He would not need to resolve to jump the life to come unless it were something he had hitherto taken with some seriousness. Moreover, subsequent events demonstrate that despite this desire to ignore the possibility of divine judgment, he cannot in fact do so. Immediately after the murder, he expresses his torment over this very question. Stealing away from the scene of his crime, he has overheard the sons of Duncan, one perhaps disturbed by some nightmare, wake in the next room, one crying, "God bless us," and the other, "Amen." Macbeth relates his reaction to his wife: "List'ning their fear, I could not say, 'Amen,' / When they did say, 'God bless us . . . wherefore could not I pronounce 'Amen'? / I had most need of blessing, and 'Amen' / Stuck in my throat" (II.ii.24–32). Here Lady Macbeth advises him to leave off such thoughts, since they will "make us mad"—indicating, again, that the idea of alienation from God is not one she disdains so much as one she cannot afford to confront (II.ii.33). Moreover, this fear of alienation from God continues to dog Macbeth after he has become king. Even while planning his murder of Banquo, he realizes that he has already given his "eternal jewel" to "the common Enemy of man"— that is, given his soul to the devil (III.i.67–68).

Finally, Macbeth's tyranny alienates him from himself. In the first place, he is estranged from his own virtue. Macbeth is nothing if not a courageous man, as the reports of his martial heroics indicate. Nevertheless, by the end of the play he lives in constant fear of violent death (IV.i.82–100). His courage, moreover, is that of the straightforward man of action. The accounts of his deeds in the rebellion that opens the play contain no mention of any ingenious stratagems, but only of his dauntless heroism, his ability to prevail by attacking in the face of all possible misfortune. Tyranny, however, calls for guile and cunning. Macbeth is not suited to such things, and his need to attempt them goes against his grain. To Lady Macbeth's disapproval, he leaves the supper they hold for Duncan just before they are to murder him (I.vii.29). He apparently cannot sit and make merry with a man whose murder he contemplates. Later, when he must conceal his hatred of Banquo, he complains of the necessity to "lave our honours in these flattering streams, / And make our faces vizards to our hearts, / Disguising what they are" (III.ii.33–34).

Ultimately, Macbeth's self-alienation takes the form of an estrangement from the very possibility of self-knowledge. He cannot afford to know himself, so terrible are his crimes. Having killed Duncan, he forgetfully brings the daggers with him out of the chamber. When Lady Macbeth notices and asks him to return and plant these weapons with the sleeping stewards, he flatly refuses: "I'll go no more: / I am afraid to think what I have done; / Look on't again I dare not" (II.ii.50–51). At the end of the same scene, he adds, "To know my deed, 'twere best not know myself" (II.ii.72).

The classical political philosophers teach that, among the external goods, honor is more dignified than power. Macbeth's thirst for honor, however, wins him only a kind of power that denies him the honor he seeks. More profoundly, the classical political philosophers teach that the goods of the soul are more dignified, and more productive of genuine happiness, than external goods. Yet Macbeth's quest for honor, and his acquisition of power, deprive him of the very goods of the soul that he, too late, implicitly recognizes as essential to his happiness. He attains a kind of greatness within his community, but at too great a cost within himself. He cannot be himself or know himself, and he cannot enjoy friendship with God or his own wife. As Plato's *Republic* suggests, and as Macbeth's career amply demonstrates, a man with power to rule a kingdom, but with no power to be happy, has nothing.

The Demonic Origins of Macbeth's Tyranny

Although Macbeth's career is to this extent recognizable as an example of classical tyranny, it cannot be fully understood simply in terms of the classical account. The tyranny diagnosed by the ancients is said by them to be unnatural in one sense, insofar as it perverts rule from its natural purpose: securing the common good. In another sense, however, such tyranny is perfectly natural. It is, after all, a commonly encountered political phenomenon, and to that extent a familiar aspect of the order of nature. Tyranny as the ancients understood it, moreover, has natural causes that we can readily grasp. It arises from the tyrant's mistaken or unjust preference for his own self-interest over that of his community. But since, as Plato's Socrates observes, the inferior parts of the soul are typically bigger and more powerful than reason, it is understandable that many human beings will have tyrannical desires and predictable that some will succeed in acting on them. On the ancient account, tyranny is like disease: it is a corruption of nature that nevertheless commonly occurs in nature and is intelligible in terms of natural causes. *Macbeth*, however, depicts a tyranny whose causes and character cannot be wholly understood in such terms. Rather, some supernatural evil appears to be at work in Macbeth's tyranny.

After all, the play famously begins not with any choice of Macbeth's but with the resolution of the three "weird sisters" to meet with him in order to tempt him with their prophecy that he will be king. Although their nature and motivations are never made entirely clear, it is reasonable to take them as agents of some kind of demonic evil. The text identifies them as "witches," and in Shakespeare's time a witch would be understood to be one who traffics with devils. Certainly Banquo suspects that they have diabolical connections (I.iii.107). In any case, the witches are presented as a force for a kind of inhuman evil. That is, they are characterized by a malice that seeks evil for no discernible human motive. From their very first appearance, the witches betray a strange detachment from ordinary human allegiances. They agree to meet "When the hurlyburly's done, / When the battle's lost and won" (I.i.3–4). Ordinary human beings do not think of a battle as being simultaneously "lost and won," because they experience some tie of loyalty to one side or the other that leads them to view the outcome as *either* a victory *or* a defeat. The witches appear to acknowledge no such ties. As they conclude this first appearance, they announce that "Fair is foul, and foul is fair" (I.i.11–12). This remark bespeaks not the commonly experienced human evil that chooses bad means to attain good ends, nor even a nihilism that denies the distinction between good and evil. It rather expresses a desire to make the bad the good and vice versa. It is the expression of a mind in rebellion against the good, or one committed to evil for its own sake. Thus we find the witches, much later in the play, egging on Macbeth's tyrannical inclinations— conjuring up apparitions that advise him to "take no care" who "chafes" or "frets" under his "bloody" rule—and doing so for no discernible benefit for themselves (IV.i.78–92).

Moreover, the witches cannot be written off as mere figments of Macbeth's fevered imagination. True enough, Macbeth is given to seeing things that his other senses, and the senses of others, fail to register: the famous "air drawn dagger," and the ghost of Banquo. One might accordingly suspect that his visions are mere projections of his own guilty mind. One cannot entertain such suspicions, however, in the case of the witches. In addition to being shown to the audience when Macbeth is not even present, they are seen by, and vanish before the eyes of, both Macbeth and Banquo at the same time (I.i, I.iii, III.v, IV.i). Whatever they are, the witches represent something other than Macbeth, a force acting on him from the outside, and animated by a malicious will.

The Demonic Character of Macbeth's Tyranny

Macbeth's tyranny is unusual not only in its origins but also in its character, which also seems to go beyond the usual classical diagnosis. In his *A Century of Horrors*, French historian Alain Besançon contends that Soviet and Nazi leaders cannot be accurately understood as examples of the usual "criminal tyrants" of which "history offers numerous examples." Rather, "as the most lucid people knew," in these cases "the so-called tyrant was not a tyrant because he did not act with his personal good in mind. He was himself tyrannized by something of a higher order."[9] On this basis Besançon entertains (without embracing) the idea that such regimes were manifestations of demonic evil. Similarly, Macbeth's violence is never directed by any sober assessment of his own interests. That is, Macbeth's tyranny is irrational not only in the sense—developed earlier in this chapter—that it is ultimately incompatible with the full well-being of his soul. It is also irrational in the sense that his tyrannical actions are never calculated to reliably secure even his interests as they relate to his ambitious desires. He is aware that his tyrannical actions will sacrifice some of his desires to others; yet those very actions are not reasonably ordered to satisfy even the desires he chooses to pursue.

Shakespeare was aware of Machiavelli and of the character of his teaching.[10] Moreover, there are recognizable echoes of Machiavelli in *Macbeth*. For example, after the murder of Duncan, his sons decide that they will be safer if they flee, recognizing, as Donalbain says, "the near in blood, / The nearer bloody" (II.iii.138–39). This remark manifests the Machiavellian sense that a new prince seeking to supplant an old one will need to see to it that the blood or the "line" of the previous prince be "extinguished."[11] When she is warned that she is in danger, Lady Macduff protests that she has "done no harm." She immediately corrects herself, however, remembering that "I am in this earthly world, where, to do harm / Is often laudable; to do good, sometime / Accounted dangerous folly" (IV.ii.73–76). This speech recalls what is perhaps the core of Machiavelli's teaching: that those who wish to preserve themselves must be able "to be not good," that strict adherence to virtue may lead to one's "ruin."[12]

Macbeth himself, however, is no Machiavellian. His most fateful—and most wicked—decisions are taken without any sober calculation of his own interests. As was just observed, Donalbain expects that whoever is responsible for his father's murder will also have a plan to extinguish Duncan's

"blood." In fact, however, Macbeth has no such plan. When Duncan publicly proclaims his eldest son, Malcolm, as Prince of Cumberland and hence
his successor to the throne, Macbeth recognizes it as an impediment to his
aims (I.iv.48–49). Nevertheless, he never deliberates about this problem,
and, indeed, never mentions it again. He instead proceeds with a murder
that cannot of itself win him the kingship. In the event both of the sons of
Duncan flee, thus calling suspicion upon themselves for their father's murder,
so that Macbeth is named as king. This outcome, however, is not one upon
which he could have reasonably depended, and the play gives us no reason
to think that he expected it. In Machiavelli's terms, he owes his success more
to fortune than to virtue, and he experiences the insecurity that necessarily
results. Moreover, his failure to extinguish Malcolm leaves in place a legitimate successor to Duncan who desires the throne for himself and revenge for
his father's death, to whom dissatisfied subjects can appeal for aid, and upon
whom foreign powers can bestow their support.

There is a similar, or even greater, irrationality in Macbeth's decision
to kill Macduff's family. Visiting the witches for the last time, Macbeth is
told that Macduff is, as he had suspected, a threat to him. He resolves to
kill Macduff, but learns that he has gone to England. Macbeth then decides
instead on the following course of action: "The castle of Macduff I will surprise; / Seize upon Fife; give to th'edge o'th'sword / His wife, his babes, and
all unfortunate souls / That trace him in his line" (IV.i.150–53). It makes no
sense from the standpoint of Macbeth's own interest in securing his rule to
destroy the family if he cannot also destroy Macduff at the same time. On
the contrary, if he cannot reach Macduff, who therefore still poses a threat,
Macbeth would surely be wiser to take Macduff's family hostage, using the
threat of their deaths to deter Macduff from any hostile action. To kill them
while Macduff lives can only strengthen Macduff's enmity and, moreover,
strengthen his position by creating sympathy for him among his countrymen. As the story plays out these murders achieve for Macbeth nothing
but these worse than useless ends. Macbeth, it seems, fails to appreciate
the crucial Machiavellian distinction between cruelty well and badly used.
His violence is not done at a single stroke in order to establish his rule, but
it starts small and then grows. He has not reasoned out in advance all the
harm that needs to be done in order to secure his position, but he improvises
on the basis of hopes and fears that are fed by the witches' prophecies. His
career bears out Machiavelli's claim that those who pursue such a course cannot maintain themselves.[13] Indeed, as his career progresses, Macbeth more
and more openly disclaims, in both word and deed, any kind of rationality
in his actions. For example, in apparently first conceiving a plan to murder

Macduff, he tells Lady Macbeth: "Strange things I have in head, that will to hand, / Which must be acted, ere they be scann'd" (III.iv.138–39). And later, reflecting on Macduff's flight and deciding to kill his family, Macbeth vows that "From this moment, / The very firstlings of my heart shall be / The firstlings of my hand. And even now, / To crown my thoughts with acts, be it thought and done" (IV.i.146–49).

Macbeth's deeds, too, bespeak a radical repudiation of reason, insofar as many of his key actions not only are done without reasoning, but cannot even be reconciled with reason. This is most evident in his second consultation with the witches. Macbeth greets them as enemies—hailing them as "secret, black, and midnight hags"—while, they, for their part, openly mock at him during their meeting (IV.i.48). The supernatural counsel that they conjure up for him is self-contradictory, telling him both to "beware Macduff" and to "scorn the power of man," assuring him that his reign is secure, yet advising him to bold action apparently with a view to securing himself (IV.i.70–80). Finally, disappointed by their confirmation that Banquo will father a line of Scottish kings, he pronounces a curse on the witches: "Infected be the air whereon they ride; / And damn'd all those that trust them" (IV.i.138–39). Yet Macbeth does trust them— despite all these signs of their untrustworthiness, and in defiance even of his own sense that they do not merit his trust. And this blind, irrational trust is followed by his decision, noted before, to lash out at Macduff in a blindly irrational manner. In sum, Macbeth's violent career has a kind of desperation about it. It is based on a desperate belief in the prophecies by which he is manipulated. The character of his actions therefore differs considerably from those of a Machiavellian prince or classical tyrant. The latter must, admittedly, be a gambler. A taker of calculated risks, he must resort to crime in order to succeed, yet he knows he cannot have certainty of success. Macbeth, in contrast, resorts to crime without any reasonable hope of success. He acts not upon calculation but, one might say, upon inspiration—inspiration that is clearly not of a divine sort.

Macbeth's crimes appear demonic not only in their irrationality—and hence their pointlessness—but also in their willfulness. As we noted earlier, Macbeth is not insensitive to the distinction between good and evil. Rather, he does violence to himself by choosing to do things he knows are morally repugnant. This knowledge of the true character of his deeds is present not only at the outset of his tyrannical career, but all the way through it, to its very end. To be sure, the play does record the desensitization of Macbeth's moral feelings. He does not experience the same grief in murdering Banquo or the Macduff family as he did in killing Duncan. In fact, he acknowledges his loss of moral sentiment near the end of the play (V.v.8–15). This decline in moral *feeling*, however, does nothing to obscure his moral *knowledge* of the nature of his acts. Thus, even at the close of his tyrannical career, even after he has brutalized his soul by repeated acts of the utmost wickedness, he recognizes his crimes as crimes. Accordingly, just before his death, and as his tyranny is crumbling around him, he acknowledges that his "soul" is "charg'd" with the blood of Macduff's family (V.viii.5–6).

There is a final sense in which Macbeth's tyranny can be understood as demonic in character: not only does Macbeth clearly understand his crimes as crimes even as he is planning and executing them, he even acknowledges them as a kind of war against the cosmic order itself. Thus, in his final meeting with the witches, he commands them:

> . . . answer me: Though you untie the winds, and let them fight / Against the Churches; though the yesty waves / Confound and swallow navigation up; Though bladed corn be lodg'd, and trees blown down; Though castles topple on their warder's heads; Though palaces, and pyramids, do slope / Their heads to their foundations; though the treasure / Of Nature's germens tumble all together, / Even till destruction sicken, answer me / To what I ask you. (IV.i.51–61)

That is, Macbeth will have what he wants, even if it requires all manner of violence to nature, and even if it unhinges the intelligibility of nature itself—confusing "Nature's germens," or the seeds of its various kinds of beings—thus making universal chaos out of universal order. Indeed, Macbeth has already indicated that even this account does not fully capture the astonishing extent of his rebellion. Earlier, contemplating his need to eliminate Banquo, he exclaims: "But let the frame of things disjoint, both the worlds suffer, / Ere we will eat our meal in fear" (III.ii.16–18). Macbeth is thus willing to tyrannize not only visible Nature itself, but even the invisible order supporting it—not only this world but the next. There is, of course, a deep irrationality in the will to such a tyranny. Like any man, Macbeth is a dependent, contingent being. He has his existence only within the "frame of things" that he is willing to "disjoint." He is willing to harm the world itself as a means to his own good, but insofar as he is part of the world such harm can only result in harm to him as well.

Accordingly, as his story plays out, Macbeth suffers the most dire consequences of his demonic tyranny. As we have already seen, Macbeth understands himself to have gained nothing by his crimes. He had desired honor, but finds in the end that neither honor nor the other goods he had cherished are available to him. Although he clearly fears death, he admits to himself that he does not want his life to go on (V.iii.22). Yet it is in considering the demonic aspect of Macbeth's tyranny that we come to appreciate more fully the nothingness to which it brings him: his striving for cosmic tyranny leads him to a sense of cosmic desolation. Learning of his wife's death, he concludes that life is "a tale / Told by an idiot, full of sound and fury / Signifying nothing." Learning moments later that the witches' prophecies appear to be turning against him, he exclaims, "I 'gin to be aweary of the sun, / And wish th'estate o'th'world were now undone" (V.v.25–50). In the end, Macbeth concludes not only that he cannot have the good things of nature, but that nature has no good things to offer. He is haunted by a sense of the unintelligibility of things, and he wishes not just to leave the world, but for the world itself to end. As we have seen, Macbeth has himself gone so far as to will the sense of cosmic unintelligibility from which he now suffers. Moreover, this sense of the meaninglessness of things is necessarily implicit in his desire to subordinate nature itself to his desires. Again, Macbeth, like any man, is a contingent and dependent being. He is by nature a mere part of a larger whole. As such, any goods he can enjoy are only available to him in the context of the larger nature of which he is a subordinate element. He can only possess what is truly good for him by respecting his own nature, that of other natural beings that are distinct from him though related to him, and that of the natural whole to which they all alike belong. Put another way, the very possibility of goods to which he can aspire, and with which he can achieve the communion he desires, depends on the existence of an intelligible order of things that are good and meaningful precisely because they have an objective value apart from, and even superior to, himself. By subordinating the cosmos to himself, by turning it into a mere tool to gratify his desires, Macbeth drains it of all real meaning and goodness and thus leaves himself devoid of any possibility of happiness. Or rather, since the cosmos is in fact impervious even to the most powerful man's attempts to do violence to it, Macbeth, by his futile yet determined will to tyrannize it, obscures its true nature in his own mind, leaving himself desolately cut off from the world of meaning and goodness that is actually there.

Conclusion

This chapter began with the question: why should contemporary political scientists pay serious attention to Shakespeare's Macbeth? We found the initial answer to this question in the play's exploration of a political phenomenon of enduring importance that is nevertheless often neglected by contemporary political science: tyranny. Macbeth's tyranny, however, finally turns out to be like, but at the same time something more than, the tyranny that was diagnosed by the classical pioneers of political science, for whom even contemporary political scientists maintain some residual respect. By the end of this account of *Macbeth*, therefore, our opening question seems to be even more in need of an answer than it was at the beginning. Contemporary political scientists, after all, believe in witches and demons even less than they believe in tyranny. We are then led to ask whether such a depiction of demonic evil can possibly be of interest to a contemporary political science that is overwhelmingly secular in its assumptions. I think that it can. For whether or not one believes in demons, the ancient and popular belief in such malicious beings, and in their ability to influence human affairs, can be understood as a reflection of something very real indeed: the mysterious human capacity for irrational and self-destructive evil. The greatest dramatist of the human condition evidently believed at least this much, and thought the lesson worthy of his art.

Notes

1. Thomas Hobbes, *Leviathan*, ed. Richard Tuck (Cambridge University Press, 1991) 130.

2. Parenthetical references are to the Arden Shakespeare edition of *Macbeth*, ed. Kenneth Muir (Thomas Nelson and Sons, 1997).

3. Aristotle, *Politics* 1279a25–1279b10.

4. On this point compare Xenophon's *Hiero*, in Leo Strauss, *On Tyranny*, eds. Victor Gourevitch and Michael Roth (The Free Press, 1991) 12. Also consider Aristotle, *Pol.* 1311a15–20.

5. See Muir 1997, 36, note on lines 1–28.

6. Saint Augustine, *The City of God*, tr. Marcus Dods (The Modern Library, 1993) 171–72.

7. Compare the similar complaints of Xenophon's Hiero: Strauss 1991, 5, 7.

8. Consider the contention in Xenophon's *Hiero* that the evils of tyranny are hidden in the soul of the tyrant (Strauss 1991, 8), as well as Plato's famous account of the misery of the tyrant in Book X of the *Republic*.

9. Alain Besançon, *A Century of Horrors*, trs. Ralph Hancock and Nathaniel Hancock (ISI Press, 2007) 55.

10. Consider *Henry VI, Part 3* (II.ii).

11. Niccolo Machiavelli, *The Prince*, tr. Leo Paul S. de Alvarez (Waveland Press, 1978) 12.

12. Alvarez 1978, 93–94.

13. Alvarez 1978, 54–55.

9

~

Beyond Love and Honor

Eros and Will to Power in *Richard III*

Leon Harold Craig

The Tragedy of King Richard the Third, widely regarded as Shakespeare's first masterpiece,[1] is his only play that commences with a soliloquy. Moreover, it is a soliloquy of a special kind, very different from those he has provided Hamlet, for example, or Macbeth: devices whereby we eavesdrop on a character's own ruminations, an inner dialogue in which, often enough, he or she acknowledges being confused, perplexed, of divided mind, conflicted. Whereas, with but one exception (the last), Richard's soliloquies reveal a mind composed and clear of purpose, albeit predominantly villainous. Moreover, they are tacitly addressed not to himself but to the audience, seemingly taking us into his confidence and thereby inviting us to share his perspective.[2] To the extent his appeal is successful, he induces our passive complicity in his schemes.

This compromising relationship is initiated by his opening soliloquy, one of the most dramatically engaging, most memorable Shakespeare ever crafted:

> Now is the winter of our discontent
> Made glorious summer by this son of York;
> And all the clouds that lour'd upon our house
> In the deep bosom of the ocean buried.
> Now are our brows bound with victorious wreaths,
> Our bruised arms hung up for monuments,
> Our stern alarums chang'd to merry meetings,
> Our dreadful marches to delightful measures.

Grim-visag'd War hath smooth'd his wrinkled front:
And now, instead of mounting barbed steeds
To fright the souls of fearful adversaries,
He capers nimbly in a lady's chamber,
To the lascivious pleasing of a lute.
But I, that am not shap'd for sportive tricks,
Nor made to court an amorous looking glass;
I, that am rudely stamp'd, and want love's majesty
To strut before a wanton ambling nymph:
I, that am curtailed of this fair proportion,
Cheated of feature by dissembling Nature,
Deform'd, unfinish'd, sent before my time
Into this breathing world scarce half made up—
And that so lamely and unfashionable
That dogs bark at me, as I halt by them—
Why, I, in this weak piping time of peace,
Have no delight to pass away the time,
Unless to spy my shadow in the sun,
And descant on mine own deformity.
And therefore, since I cannot prove a lover
To entertain these fair well-spoken days,
I am determined to prove a villain,
And hate the idle pleasures of these days.
Plots have I laid, inductions dangerous,
By drunken prophesies, libels, and dreams,
To set my brother Clarence and the King
In deadly hate, the one against the other:
And if King Edward be as true and just
As I am subtle, false, and treacherous,
This day shall Clarence closely be mew'd up
About a prophecy, which says that 'G'
Of Edward's heirs the murderer shall be—[3]
Dive, thoughts, down to my soul: here Clarence comes. (I.i.1–40)[4]

Having shared his stratagem with us, the mock-surprise / mock-sympathy / mock-indignation with which Richard then greets Clarence—"Brother, good day; what means this armed guard / That waits upon your Grace?"— elicits a frisson of anticipation, whatever else. And as we follow Richard's further machinations, and share in the amusement with which he plots the ruin of those he beguiles, we find that something in us is secretly cheering him on, as it were, despite recognizing him to be evil, a monster even. But ever so fascinating! Why the fascination?[5] Admittedly, the political environment in which he operates makes it that much easier for us to indulge a grudging admiration for him, since there's almost no really attractive, "good" character to root for.[6] As Richard's mother laments, the very age is "accursed" (II.iv.55). But surely our savoring of Richard's villainy bespeaks some deeper truth about *our* natures, that something in us enjoys his clever scheming, his witty irreverence, his malicious toying with people, his willful displays of power, very much as he does.[7] And consequently, Shakespeare, through Richard, is toying with *us*, albeit for the higher purpose, perhaps, of promoting self-knowledge.

But Richard's opening soliloquy is more than simply a display of the ruthless ambition and rhetorical power with which Shakespeare has invested him. First of all, embedded in it is an ambiguity that points to what would seem an important *metaphysical* issue raised by the play: "Therefore, since I cannot prove a lover . . . I am *determined* to prove a villain." (I.i.29–30) As spoken by Richard, he is almost surely to be understood as meaning "*self*-determined"— that this is the role he has chosen for himself. After all, it's not as if Lover and Villain are the only two options in life, such that if one is foreclosed, logical necessity dictates that a person pursue the other. As crafted by Shakespeare, however, the line in question presents rather different possibilities that cannot be ignored, since they connect with what strikes me as another dramatic high point of the play, namely, old Queen Margaret's great curse-off in the third scene. What I have in mind is the fact that the evils she wishes upon the other seven characters present, and upon Richard in particular, are for the most part fulfilled.[8] Why so? That is: How so? By what agency? Likewise fulfilled is Anne's cursing of any future wife of Richard, which so ironically reverts upon herself. We are not allowed to ignore this facet of the drama, since all of the characters affected—save only Richard—recur to these curses upon their realization (e.g., III.iii.15–20, III.iv.92–94, V.i.25–27). Lady Anne's more ample recollection has a special pertinence (to be examined later), as in a different way does ex-Queen Elizabeth's when she again meets old ex-Queen Margaret, and begs of her: "O thou, well-skill'd in curses, stay awhile / And teach me how to curse mine enemies" (IV.iv.116–17).[9] Nor is Richard altogether exempt from the effects of fateful predictions, anxiously recalling a disturbing pair of prophecies, one by the late King Henry, the other by "a bard of Ireland" (IV.ii.94–105).

So, would Shakespeare have us regard the outcomes of human affairs as somehow pre-ordained—that perhaps "There's a divinity that shapes our ends, / Rough-hew them how we will" (as he has Hamlet assure Horatio)?[10] Or is it only the consequences of choosing Evil that sooner or later follows of necessity, that people in effect curse themselves by such choices?[11] Shakespeare has this possibility be suggested by pious-seeming Richard, referring back to the curses his father laid on then-Queen Margaret for the killing of his "pretty Rutland," supposedly but a boy (though, historically, seventeen at the time): "His curse then, from bitterness of soul / Denounc'd against thee, are all fall'n upon thee, / And *God*, not we, hath plagu'd thy bloody deed" (I.iii.177–80). Queen Elizabeth immediately adds, "So just is God, to right the innocent"—ironic words, to say the least, given what seems to be the future fate of her own two boys.[12] Then Hastings, Rivers, Dorset, and Buckingham each in turn denounce the deed. To all of whom old Margaret rejoins, "Did York's dread curse prevail so much with heaven . . . ? / Can curses pierce the clouds and enter heaven? / Why then, give way, dull clouds, to my quick curses" (I.iii.191–96; cf. IV.iv.150–51).[13]

The opening soliloquy raises other issues, however, that are more immediately germane to the themes of this volume. As Richard sees it, war, the traditional arena of honor and bloodlust, has moved from the battlefield to the bedchamber, and changed its demeanor accordingly. More to the point, this change of venue entails a radical revision in the taxonomy of qualities that favor victory. Those that best fit a man for mounting and using fearsome war-horses are not the same as those most suitable for a very different kind of mounting, satisfying a different kind of lust (or love, if you prefer). But however nimble the capering characteristic of weak, piping times of so-called peace, it is still war. Politics is simply the continuation of war by other means, whether in the boudoir or the boardroom, pulpit or council chamber. Life is war, because life is competitive. And in the final accounting, the only thing that matters is who wins, hence rules.

If Richard is to be taken at his word, this change in the locale of war has left him profoundly disadvantaged since his body is not shaped for the sportive tricks of courtship and love-making, being such an ugly cripple. Shakespeare has him provide a more expansive description of his deformity upon his full dramatic debut in Part Three of *Henry VI*. In an even longer soliloquy at the very center of that play, young Richard of Gloucester (The late Richard of York's third surviving son) first admits an ambition to wield England's sovereign power; then seems to concede its impossibility, since so many legitimate heirs stand between him and the crown; he then considers what other pleasure the world might afford him, such as to make his heaven in a lady's lap—a possibility he immediately rejects:

> Why, Love foreswore me in my mother's womb,
> And, for I should not deal in her soft laws,
> She did corrupt frail Nature with some bribe
> To shrink mine arm up like a wither'd shrub;

To make an envious mountain on my back
Where sits deformity to mock my body;
To shape my legs of an unequal size;
To disproportion me in every part,
Like to a chaos, or an unlick'd bear whelp
That carries no impression like the dam.
And am I then a man to be belov'd? (3H6 III.ii.152–63)

Thus he returns to his earlier thought: "since this earth affords no joy to me / But to command, to check, to o'erbear such / As are of better person than myself, / I'll make my heaven to dream upon the crown." (III.ii.165–68) He then rehearses the many difficulties that stand in the way of his gaining supreme *power*, but concludes he is more than a match for them:

Why, I can smile, and murder whiles I smile,
And cry 'Content!' to that which grieves my heart,
And wet my cheeks with artificial tears,
And frame my face to all occasions . . .
I can add colours to the chameleon,
Change shapes with Proteus for advantages,
And set the murderous Machiavel to school.[14]
Can I do this, and cannot get a crown?
Tut, were it further off, I'll pluck it down. (III.ii.183–95)

So, to summarize, Richard claims that Love for him is out of the question *because* he's such a deformed, physically repulsive cripple as to be unlovable; and that, consequently, he'll seek *power* over all those more handsome fellows by way of consolation (while, not incidentally, *hating* the sort of world that normal people prefer, that in which one is free to idle away one's time pursuing life's pleasures).

In the very next scene, however, we are given some reason to doubt these confidences he has so enjoyed sharing with us, his conscripted accomplices. First of all, how physically handicapped is he really? Apparently not so badly as would preclude his being a *very* fearsome warrior. When he halts the funeral cortege of the late King Henry, commanding that the corpse be set down and threatening to make a corpse of anyone who disobeys him, he is sufficiently intimidating that even the honor guard of professional soldiers quake with fear at the prospect of challenging him—or so Lady Anne implies: "What, do you tremble? Are you all afraid? / Alas, I blame you not, for you are mortal" (I.ii.33–44).[15] And though in the play's finale Richard is slain at the battle of

Bosworth Field, it is not before he has once more proven himself among the most formidable fighters there engaged. As the loyal Catesby attests in urging Norfolk to his rescue: "The King enacts more wonders than a man, / Daring an opposite to every danger. / His horse is slain, and all on foot he fights, / Seeking for Richmond in the throat of death." Then when Richard himself comes upon the scene, shouting his famous "A horse! A horse! My kingdom for a horse!" and Catesby urges him, "Withdraw, my lord; I'll help you to a horse," Richard responds, "Slave! I have set my life upon a cast, / And I will stand the hazard of the die. / I think there be six Richmonds in the field: / Five I have slain today instead of him" (V.iv.1–12).[16] How likely is it that a limping hunchback with only one good arm would be such an effective killing machine?

This leads me to question Richard's second claim, that his bodily condition precludes his proving a successful lover of women, and therewith to the primary theme of this chapter. Richard's seduction of Lady Anne is a dramatic tour de force—indeed, to my mind, having few rivals in the entire canon for sheer theatricality—and not least because Shakespeare has Richard emphasize its prima facie unlikelihood. However, the episode also makes manifest the key mystery of the play, and as such points to its deeper understanding. Shakespeare has this puzzle be posed with unusual explicitness by Richard in the soliloquy that concludes the play's very rich first scene.[17] He has been conversing with Lord Hasting about the state of King Edward's health. Upon Hasting's leaving to visit the ailing King, Richard muses, "He cannot live, I hope, and must not die / Till George be pack'd with post-horse up to Heaven." That is, Richard, having persuaded the King to issue a writ ordering the execution of brother George, he wants it carried out *before* Edward dies, for thereupon the writ would be vacated. So Richard continues:

> And if I fail not in my deep intent,
> Clarence hath not another day to live:
> Which done, God take King Edward to his mercy,
> And leave the world for me to bustle in.
> For then I'll marry Warrick's youngest daughter—
> What though I kill'd her husband and her father?
> The readiest way to make the wench amends
> Is to become her husband, and her father:
> The which will I, not all so much for love
> As for another secret close intent,
> By marrying her which I must reach unto. (I.i.145–59)

What *is* Richard's secret intent in marrying the young widow, Lady Anne—which surely must constitute the primary, if not the exclusive, motivation behind his spectacular display of will to power: her unlikely seduction?[18]

One might begin by eliminating what was instrumental for the historical Richard: that she was an heiress of very considerable *wealth*, not only from her disgraced father, Warwick, the erstwhile "King-maker," but from her mother as well.[19] However, inasmuch as there is no mention in the play of her being wealthy, this is not a plausible candidate for Richard's secret motive. Nor does there seem to be any clear answer in the seduction scene itself, which instead simply compounds the puzzles that the play presents. It consists (first of all) of the Lady Anne halting the procession by ordering the bearers to "Set down, set down your honorable load / (If honor may be shrouded in a hearse) / Whilst I awhile obsequiously lament / The untimely fall of virtuous Lancaster" (I.ii.1–4). And lament she surely does, both the death of her father-in-law (the hapless King Henry VI), and of his "slaughter'd son," her short-term husband, Prince Edward, "Stabb'd by the self-same hand" as killed Henry. Her grieving, however, is generously punctuated with curses upon that hand, as well as upon any wife and child that he might come to have.

It is at this point that Richard enters—or perhaps one should say, reveals himself—commanding the cortege to halt and again set down the coffin. Given that we know he has some secret intention in marrying, hence first wooing, the fair lady, we can be pretty sure that he hasn't simply happened upon this funeral train by chance; that he has, rather, lain in wait for it at what might be a likely, or perhaps the usual, resting place for such processions. But this suspicion no sooner occurs than it raises further questions: *why in the world* would he choose this time and place to begin a courtship that would seem to be doomed from the get-go! Who in his right mind would choose to woo a grieving widow and daughter *in public*, at a *funeral*, much less at one of which *he* was the *cause*? One can readily imagine fifty more congenial situations that might enhance his slim chance of success. There must be some reason that Richard has chosen this, seemingly so unpropitious circumstance.

And even if he didn't overhear the rant of damnation she wished upon his head, he could hardly have failed to anticipate the several earfuls of anger and hate and disgust she now bestows upon him. But after allowing her time to vent her initial hostility, he draws her into a contest of clever repartee, wherein she is allowed to insult and accuse him, while he parries her accusations and flatters her person, at last leading up to Richard's indecent rejoinder to her assertion that he is "unfit for any place but hell": "Yes, one place else, if you will hear me name it . . . Your bed-chamber." He then proceeds to blame *her* for all the misdeeds that she has accused him of: "Your beauty was the cause . . . / Your beauty, that did haunt me in my sleep / To undertake the death of all the world, / So I might live one hour in your sweet bosom" (I.ii.125–28). She continues to insult, and he to cajole. He offers to let her kill him if her "revengeful heart cannot forgive," then to kill himself if she so bid him, whereupon "This hand, which for thy love did kill thy love, / Shall for thy love kill a far truer love" (I.ii.176, 193–94). She weakens, then relents, accepts his ring, and allows him—crediting his ironic admission that he "hath most cause to be mourner"—to take charge of the late King's funeral procession to Chertsey Monastery (Richard promising to "wet his grave with . . . repentant tears"). Whereupon, joyfully persuaded that he has "become so penitent," she leaves for Richard's Crosby Place, escorted by a pair of gentlemen. With her gone, Richard orders Henry's body be taken, not to Chertsey, but to Whitefriars priory. Why does he do *that*?

Richard, now left alone, treats us to another of his mocking soliloquies, in which he confirms that his design on Lady Anne is indeed motivated "not all so much for love." If we had not previously been privy to his having a secret purpose for wedding her, and had heard only *this* soliloquy, we might suppose he seduced her just for the fun of it, for the sheer challenge of it, an expression of his will to power.

> Was ever woman in this humour woo'd?
> Was ever woman in this humour won?
> I'll have her, but I will not keep her long.
> What, I that kill'd her husband and her father:
> To take her in her heart's extremest hate,
> With curses in her mouth, tears in her eyes,
> The bleeding witness of her hatred by,
> Having God, her conscience, and these bars against me—
> And I, no friends to back my suit at all
> But the plain devil and dissembling looks—
> And yet to win her, all the world to nothing! . . .
> My dukedom to a beggarly denier,
> I do mistake my person all this while!
> Upon my life, she finds—although I cannot—
> Myself to be a marvelous proper man. (I.ii.232–59)

How *are* we to explain his success with Lady Anne—bearing in mind what he so graphically insists upon: that he's hardly blessed with movie star looks. Even if he's not as ugly as he pretends, we are not to imagine him a natural heartthrob—after all, other characters attest to his disfigurement, including Anne herself ("thou lump of foul deformity"; I.ii.57); most persistently, old

Queen Margaret ("Thou elvish-marked, abortive rooting hog," "poisonous bunch-backed toad"; I.iii.228, 246). So, what *does* he have going for him? And what would Shakespeare have us learn from his, and her, examples?

But to return to the question of what motivates Richard, someone might suggest that I am overlooking an obvious explanation: plain old everyday animal *lust*. We must imagine Lady Anne to be at least somewhat attractive. Richard would have sacrificed all credibility with *Anne herself* in going on so about her bewitching beauty if she actually *looked* like a witch. And to be sure, if we were considering King Edward here rather than Duke Richard, lust would top the list of likely explanations. There is ample testimony in the play as to *his* lustful disposition; it suffices to mention the notorious Mistress Shore (famously the most significant Shakespearean character never to have actually appeared on stage), whose charms the ailing King now shares with his Chamberlain, Lord Hastings, and perhaps also with her husband. In fact, Richard alludes to the effects of Edward's voluptuous lifestyle in our first indication of his failing health: "O, he hath kept an evil diet long, / And over-much consumed his royal person; / 'Tis very grievous to be thought upon" (I.i.139–41). And later, instructing "cousin Buckingham" what to tell those assembled in the Guildhall in order to persuade them to declare for Richard:

> Infer the bastardy of Edward's children; . . .
> Moreover, urge his hateful luxury
> And bestial appetite in change of lust,
> Which stretch'd unto their servants, daughters, wives,
> Even where his raging eye or savage heart
> Without control lusted to make prey. (III.v.74–83)

The point of making these charges against "insatiate Edward"—the credibility of which rests on what those assembled already know, or at least believe, about him—is to make Richard shine by comparison: *he's* not lustful, *he* doesn't prey upon good citizens' servants, daughters, wives; you've never heard anyone accuse *him* of luxurious living. Buckingham will subsequently make this point explicitly to the assembled Mayor and Aldermen when Richard refuses to come forth to hear their plea that he become their king, being so preoccupied (supposedly) in pious exercise with a pair of priests:

> Ah ha, my lord [mayor], this prince is not an Edward:
> He is not lolling on a lewd love-bed
> But on his knees at meditation;
> Not dallying with a brace of courtesans,

But meditating with two deep divines;
Not sleeping, to engross his idle body,
But praying, to enrich his watchful soul. (III.vii.70–76)

If a lust for Anne *were* a factor prompting Richard's designs upon her, surely
we would expect some indication to that effect in at least one of the soliloquies that frame her public seduction. It needn't be as blatant as that of Lord
Angelo's private confession of his lust for Isabella in *Measure for Measure*
(II.ii.163–87; II.iv.1–17); but surely some hint of sexual feeling would be
only natural in the circumstance . . . if it existed, that is. And as is shown
in his risqué bantering with Brackenbury about Mistress Shore (I.i.98–102),
Richard is adept enough at sexual innuendo if it serves his purpose.

I suspect that his Grace, the Duke of Buckingham provides a partial clue
to the answer when he and Richard are discussing the charade that they will
stage for the Mayor and Aldermen, with Richard seemingly determined to
decline the crown offered him, and Buckingham insisting that he accept it:
"And be not easily won to our requests: / Play the maid's part: still answer
nay, and take it." Richard's rejoinder, as if simply agreeing to 'play the maid's
part,' is nicely ironic in light of his subsequent dealings with cousin Buckingham: "I go, and if you plead as well for them / As I can say nay to thee for
myself, / No doubt we bring it to a happy issue" (III.vii.49–53). When their
pantomime is actually staged, Buckingham again employs 'trans-gendering'
language in playing his manly part of leading the Londoners' insistence that
Richard assume the kingship. Richard, having declined yet again in favor
of his dear nephew, Buckingham warns him in terms the irony of which he
could but half appreciate:

If you refuse it, as in love and zeal
Loath to depose the child, your brother's son—
As well we know your tenderness of heart,
And gentle, kind, effeminate remorse,
Which we have noted in you to your kindred,
And equally indeed to all estates—
Yet know, whe'er you accept our suit or no,
Your brother's son shall never reign our king. (III.vii.207–14)

"*Effeminate* remorse"—why would such a term even occur to him, unless . . . ?
I do not mean to suggest that Buckingham has accurately assessed Richard's
nature. For in believing that he (Buckingham) is actually going to be the
dominant partner in their relationship—being the stronger, tougher, more
resolute—he is quite mistaken (as he will learn to his eternal regret). But
he may have noticed things about Richard that made him suspect that the

Duke of Gloucester is not altogether what he would call 'a man's man.' For example, Richard is reputedly rather easily moved to weep (e.g. I.iv.234–35; II.ii.23). His cousin knows nothing, of course, about Richard's privately boasting of an ability to "wet his cheeks with artificial tears," as well as frame his face however would suit a given occasion—most convincingly, according to the doomed Hasting: "I think there's never a man in Christendom / Can lesser hide his love or hate than he, / For by his face straight shall you know his heart" (III.iv.51–53). And Richard did express what might seem an effeminate willingness to subordinate himself to Buckingham: "My other self, my counsel's consistory, / My oracle, my prophet, my dear cousin: / I, as a child, will go by thy direction" (II.ii.151–53). Whereas we know Richard includes Buckingham as well as Hastings among the "many simple gulls" his machinations misdirect (I.iii.328–29). When the two of them put on their show for the Lord Mayor, pretending to have but narrowly escaped an extreme danger posed by the popular—but now decapitated—Lord Hastings, Buckingham readily plays "bad cop" to gentle, kind Richard's "good cop":

> So dear I lov'd the man that I must weep.
> I took him for the plainest harmless creature
> That breath'd upon the earth a Christian;
> Made him my book, wherein my soul recorded
> The history of all her secret thoughts. (III.v.24–28)

Whereas Buckingham bluntly pronounces, "Well, well, he was the covert'st shelter'd traitor," and then, "I never look'd for better at his hands / After he once fell in with Mistress Shore" (III.v.33, 49–50).

Let me state the matter simply: there is a pattern of evidence that suggests Richard's true deformity is not so much that of body as it is of *soul* (which is not to say that the one has no bearing on the other). More precisely, he is defective sexually—but not simply in the way that Buckingham presumes would explain the radical *contrast* between "puritanical" Richard and his voraciously womanizing elder brother, the late King. True, women have no appeal for Richard. And quite apart from his sexual indifference, he despises them ("shallow, changing woman!"; IV.iv.431). However, beyond his not being sexually attracted to women himself, he is contemptuous of men who *are*—who in effect are ruled by women because they cannot rule their own passions, and so seek to please women by doing their bidding: "Why, this is it, when men are rul'd by women" (I.i.62). There's more to be said about the deformation of Richard's *eros*, but this much shows through in his opening soliloquy, does it not? How must we suppose he regards smooth-faced courtiers whose preferred pastime is capering in ladies' chambers to lascivious flute music? And which do we suppose he holds in greater disdain: "wanton ambling nymphs"? or the men who "strut" before them, trolling for their favors, (when not preening in mirrors)? Seen in this light, one supposes he especially enjoys the irony of his musing in the wake of seducing the Lady Anne, "Upon my life, she finds—although I cannot— / Myself to be a marvelous *proper man*" (I.ii.258–59, emphasis added). He cannot, because he knows better.

As I acknowledged above, there may well be a connection between Richard's bodily deformities and those of his psyche. Indeed, the latter may have its origin in his birth and childhood, which is repeatedly the subject of comment. There is not a lot of textual evidence upon which to base a diagnosis, but perhaps just enough. Meeting him in adulthood, we see he does not have a genial relationship with his mother—to say the least—and there are grounds for suspecting that this may be as much her fault as his. The first indication of her attitude is in response to Clarence's son's revealing that his "good uncle Gloucester" told him that the King, provoked by the Queen, is to blame for his father's death: "And when my uncle told me so he wept, / And pitied me, and kindly kiss'd my cheek; / And bade me rely on him as on my father"[20]—to which the Duchess replies, "Ah, that Deceit should steal such gentle shape, / And with a virtuous vizor hide deep Vice! / He is my son, ay, and herein my shame; / Yet from my dugs he drew not this deceit" (II.ii.20–30). And moments later, upon learning that King Edward has just died, she laments:

> I have bewept a worthy husband's death,
> And liv'd with looking on his images:
> But now two mirrors of his princely semblance
> Are crack'd in pieces by malignant death;
> And I, for comfort, have but one false glass,[21]
> That grieves me when I see my shame in him. (II.ii.49–54)

To be sure, her attitude towards Richard—one of *shame*—may have formed only in recent years, having observed various indications of his vicious nature. Then again, maybe not.

More revealing, I suspect, is the second scene in which we see the old Duchess, this time with the late King Edward's son (and Richard's namesake), the young Duke of York. He is telling his grandmother why he hopes he has not outgrown his elder brother, now the King designate, since his uncle Gloucester taught him the proverb, "Small herbs have grace; great weeds do grow apace." She replies:

Good faith, good faith, the saying did not hold
In him that did object the same to thee!
He was the wretched'st thing when he was young,
So long a growing, and so leisurely,
That if his rule were true, he should be gracious. (II.iv.16–20)

When this draws from the Archbishop of York the polite rejoinder, "And so no doubt he is, my gracious madam," her response is guarded: "I hope he is, but yet let mothers doubt." Do we normally associate mothers with some special privilege of *doubting* the goodness of their own offspring? Apparently ignoring what he has just been told about Richard's childhood, it occurs to the young prince that he could have made a clever joke at his uncle's expense concerning a rumor he'd heard: "Marry, they say my uncle grew so fast / That he could gnaw a crust at two hours old: / 'Twas full two years ere I could get a tooth. / Grandam, this would have been a biting jest!" To which the Duchess queries, "I prithee, pretty York, who told thee this?" Pretty York replies: "Grandam, his nurse." Duchess: "His nurse? Why she was dead ere thou wast born." York: "If 'twere not she, I cannot tell who told me." Why has Shakespeare included this exchange, which leaves really *two* questions hanging in the air? First, and seemingly of less importance, from whom in particular *did* young York hear this tale. But second, who was the *original* source of such a symbolically fitting claim, which it seems has circulated widely? Notice, old ex-Queen Margaret later uses this same story to berate the Duchess, that she has borne a monster: "From forth the kennel of thy womb hath crept / A hell-hound that doth hunt us all to death: / That dog, that had his teeth before his eyes" (IV.iv.47–9).

In any case, we are invited to wonder, are we not, whether Richard's mother the Duchess became ashamed of him only in his later years—or, was she ashamed of him from the first time she ever set eyes on his misshapen infant body, regarding him as a reproach to the womb that had already borne three handsome boys, including "pretty Rutland," captured and killed in the Lancastrian victory at Wakefield? Does not Shakespeare intend to suggest this possibility by having Lady Anne (to her eventual regret) curse any future wife and child of Richard: "If ever he have child, abortive be it: / Prodigious, and untimely brought to light, / Whose ugly and unnatural aspect / May fright the hopeful mother at the view" (I.ii.21–24)? And was his mother's shame, and consequent resentment of him, evident to Richard, and everyone else, throughout his childhood and youth—the disdain in which she held him, ever comparing him with his well-shaped brothers (to his chagrin, needless to add)?

Richard, for his part, maintains a proper public posture towards his mother, but privately never expresses any particular affection for her—*nor any dislike*, interestingly. So, for example, when he arrives ostensibly to commiserate Edward's death with his widowed Queen, and only belatedly notices the presence of the Duchess (or claims to), he kneels, saying, "Madam my mother, I do cry you mercy: / I did not see your Grace. Humbly on my knee / I crave your blessing." She obliges: "God bless thee, and put meekness in thy breast; / Love, charity, obedience, and true duty." To which Richard pronounces "Amen," then wryly adds to himself, "and make me die a good old man— / That is the butt-end of a mother's blessing: / I marvel that her Grace did leave it out" (II.ii.104–11). The one other time in which his mother figures substantially in his activities is when he is briefing Buckingham on what to tell the Guildhall assembly that would persuade them to prefer the crown go to Richard rather than to Edward's heir:

> Tell them, when my mother went with child
> Of that insatiate Edward, noble York
> My princely father then had wars in France,
> And by true computation of the time
> Found that the issue was not his-begot;
> Which well appeared in his lineaments,
> Being nothing like the noble Duke, my father— (III.v.85–91)

Then, with barely a token regard for his mother's reputation, he blithely adds, "Yet touch this sparingly, as 'twere far off; / Because, my lord, you know my mother lives." Imagine: "In furtherance of my political ambitions, claim my mother was an adulteress—a whore—but do so with some delicacy out of respect for her feelings!"

Later, when the Duchess along with Elizabeth and Anne are on Richard's orders denied access to the Princes in the Tower, and then learn he has usurped the crown, she exclaims, "O my accursed womb, the bed of death! / A cockatrice hast thou hatch'd to the world" (IV.i.53–54; cf. IV.iv.137–39). Still later, she and Elizabeth intercept Richard as he is hurrying with his army to confront the rebellious Buckingham. And though he warns he's in no mood to indulge her railing—having, as he so intriguingly puts it, "a touch of [her] condition, / That cannot brook the accent of reproof"—she pleads that he hear her one last time: "Art thou so hasty? I have stayed for thee, / God knows, in torment and in agony." Richard cannot resist tweaking her with "And came I not at last to comfort you?" Her Grace is not amused:

No, by the holy rood, thou know'st it well:
Thou cam'st on earth to make the earth my hell.
A grievous burden was thy birth to me;
Tetchy and wayward was thy infancy;
Thy school-days frightful, desp'rate, wild, and furious;
Thy prime of manhood daring, bold, and venturous;
Thy age confirm'd, proud, subtle, sly, and bloody:
More mild, but yet more harmful, kind in hatred. (IV.iv.166–75)

This, their final encounter concludes with her visiting upon him her "most grievous curse," wishing for his defeat and victory to his enemies, whereupon she turns her back upon him and leaves (IV.iv.188–96). Richard makes no reply either to her curse or her departing, but immediately addresses Elizabeth, intent on persuading her to smooth the way to his marrying her daughter. For true to his word, he had the poor Lady Anne but did not keep her long. We do not know for sure her cause of death, but having heard Richard order Catesby to spread the rumour "That Anne, my Queen, is sick and like to die," we are justified in fearing the worst. Be that as it may, Richard's attempt to reprise the seduction of Lady Anne, this time with ex-Queen Elizabeth, reveals that he has lost a bit of his magic.[22]

Before returning to the puzzles which attend that earlier episode, however, let me again register this curious fact, for it bears repeating: Shakespeare has given a certain prominence, subtle but unmistakable once noticed, to Richard's nativity and childhood. Since the poet can craft the play however he pleases, one must suppose that this feature of his drama somehow bears importantly on its proper understanding. Of course, we beneficiaries of post-Freudian enlightenment are hardly apt to be shocked by the suggestion that a boy subjected to maternal rejection may suffer sexual irregularities in adulthood, that it may even sour him on women in general. And I do believe Shakespeare anticipates Freud with respect to this and other insights about the effective, and defective, nurture of children. But this is by no means the whole explanation of Richard. I suspect Francis Bacon may be more helpful than Freud. I have in mind especially his Essay 44, "Of Deformity":

Deformed persons are commonly even with nature; for as nature hath done ill by them, so do they by nature; being for the most part (as the Scripture saith) *void of natural affection*; and so they have their revenge of nature. Certainly there is a consent between the body and the mind; and where nature erreth in the one, she ventureth in the other. . . . But because there is in man an election touching the frame of his mind, and a necessity in the frame of his body, the stars of natural inclination are sometimes obscured by the sun of discipline and virtue. Therefore it is good to consider of deformity, not as a sign, which is deceivable; but as a cause, that seldom faileth of the effect. Whosoever hath any thing fixed in his person that doth induce contempt, hath also a perpetual spur in himself to rescue and deliver himself from scorn. Therefore all deformed persons are extreme bold. First, as in their own defence, as being exposed to scorn; but in process of time by a general habit. Also it stirreth in them industry, and especially of this kind, to watch and observe the weakness of others, that they may have somewhat to repay. Again, in their superiors, it quencheth jealousy towards them, as persons that they think they may at pleasure despise; and it layeth their competitors and emulators asleep; as never believing they should be in possibility of advancement, till they see them in possession. So that upon the matter, in a great wit, deformity is an advantage to rising. . . . Still, the ground is, they will, if they be of spirit, seek to free themselves from scorn; which must be either by virtue or malice.[23]

Since he cannot prove a lover, deformed as he is in both body and soul, he has elected to prove a villain.

Shakespeare has certainly invested his Richard with great wit, and spirit, and boldness. Moreover, he has provided him a keen eye for the weaknesses of others—especially for detecting what they prefer to believe, hence are predisposed to believe, and the gullibility that results: not only young, naïve Lady Anne, but his own brothers,[24] first George, who almost to his bitter end prefers to believe Richard loves him; then King Edward, who wishfully believes he can and has made peace between Richard and the Queen's Woodville clan; also Lord Rivers, taken in by Richard's professed piety (cf. I.iii.316); Lord Hastings, who scoffs at Stanley's dream-induced fear, so sure that Richard loves him well (III.iv.14); manly Buckingham, whose own ambition to rule inclines him to exaggerate his own political shrewdness and underestimate Richard's. But perhaps the most important respect in which Shakespeare's Richard conforms to Bacon's profile is in his being "*void of natural affection*"—or *un*natural affection, for that matter. That is, he neither loves nor hates; thus, he is subject to neither envy nor jealousy, feels neither indignation nor admiration—and is the clearer thinker for it. This is basic to the superiority he believes he enjoys over everyone else, and is for him a source of endless amusement: the superhuman perspective whence he looks down on everyone, so susceptible to his artful manipulations.

Returning now to the puzzle with which the play practically begins: Richard's "secret close intent" in his marrying the grieving Lady Anne, recently widowed and left fatherless—thanks at least in part to him. I do not claim to have solved it with such certainty as would put the question beyond dispute, but venture here merely what I regard as the most plausible hypotheses. It seems safe to presume that Richard's hidden motive has something to do with how he goes about effecting the desired result, since he appears to have deliberately chosen the worst possible circumstance in which to begin his wooing of the girl.[25] That said, we needn't further presume that his hidden motive is his sole motive. For Richard is a man who specializes in killing several birds with one stone. So what can we be reasonably sure of?

First of all, that marriage to Anne in particular must somehow fit in with his confided ambition to become King, once both elder brothers have conveniently left this world for him to bustle in: "For *then* I'll marry Warwick's youngest daughter," albeit "not all so much for *love*." Second, that he wishes this *not* be seen as a marriage forced upon the girl, but rather willingly accepted by her. Third, that her 'seduction' be done in public is somehow important. Fourth, that the sheer implausibility of the attempt—which he emphasizes in both framing soliloquies, and would be obvious to all who witness it—is also somehow important. Fifth, he must be fairly confident that his attempt will be successful, and that even if it isn't, may provide some benefit, or at least do no harm (though he is a man who is prepared to take risks).

Given only these points, even bearing in mind what is revealed in the balance of the play, any explanation of Richard's secret intention is bound to remain speculative. But suppose that Richard believes his reputed *lack* of interest in women heretofore is a political liability, rendering his manliness suspect, especially among ordinary soldiers who judge manliness *per se* by their own.[26] People naturally presume that a man who does not desire women must, then, sexually prefer men. And since that often carries a stigma amongst decidedly heterosexual men, one avoids needless complications if one is regarded as a woman-lover also. Still, we also know that Richard disdains the very idea of men being *ruled* by women, which is more correctly understood as men failing to master their own passions for women, thus inclined to do their bidding in order to enjoy their favor—as, supposedly, Edward first had Hastings imprisoned to please his wife, then had him released to please his mistress (I.i.71–80). Richard, not being susceptible to the blandishments of the fair sex, doesn't have the problem, but he wants to appear as if he does, while also displaying an enviable self-mastery. Thus, having once won over the young Lady Anne—and, not incidentally, proven himself possessed of lady-killer charms despite his physical disabilities—he blatantly does *not* do her bidding. That is, he does not proceed with the late King's body to Chertsey, as he implored her to allow him to do ("For diverse unknown reasons": I.ii.221), and she assented, presuming he would abide by her intention. Instead, once she's gone, he orders the corpse taken to Whitefriars priory. His callous disregard for her wishes is all the more effective, given the intensity with which he professed his love for her.

This, then, is presumably what is 'secret' about Richard's 'close intent': that he means to mask his sexual deformity with an appearance of hyper-normality—to conceal the monstrous fact that his *eros* inclines him to *neither* women nor men, but is simply pure lust for power,[27] whereby he receives as much gratification in dealing death, *thanatos*—perhaps more—as in serving life. He seems amused whenever contemplating those whose deaths he ar-ranges, even inspired, to offer his victims ironic salutations: "Simple, plain Clarence, I do love thee so / That I shall shortly send thy soul to Heaven / If Heaven will take the present at our hands" (I.i.118–20). And when his namesake, the young Duke of York, requests Richard's dagger, he replies, "My dagger, little cousin? With all my heart" (III.i.110–11). Equanimous with respect to death, he is quite at home on the battlefield, not for the sake of honor (which has no intrinsic value for him, since he despises those who would presume to bestow it), but simply as an unfettered arena in which to discharge pent-up power.

But since courting and wedding any noblewoman might serve the purpose of establishing the appearance of his sexual normality, why has Richard fas-tened upon Anne? We must presume that her being pointedly identified as *Warwick's* daughter is germane, as that name comes trailing endless political implications. Anyone at all familiar with England's preceding history would recognize the title of the infamous "Kingmaker," Richard Neville, and the vast, still powerful Neville clan with which it is associated. Similarly, by virtue of her previous marriage to the Lancastrian Prince Edward, albeit short-lived, she could be seen as representing all those who had previously supported the House of Lancaster in its wars with the Yorkists—that long Winter of Discontent—and for whom the outcome of those wars, the Summer of York rule, still rankled. The more emphatically Anne declares both her grief for her dead husband and father-in-law, and her seemingly implacable hatred for their killers, the stronger is her identification with the Lancastrian cause. And the stronger that identification, the more valuable to Richard is her being won over to him, being a potent symbol of reconciliation and acceptance. And to use her for this purpose, he need not keep her long; that she be wooed, won, and wed is all that matters. Nor need Shakespeare have his Richard point explicitly to this implication, since Shakespeare's Richmond does so in his final victory speech. Himself claiming descent from the Lancaster branch of great Edward the Third's feuding family,[28] and now betrothed to the daughter of late King Edward, that glorious son of York, Richmond proclaims, "We will unite the white rose and the red. / Smile, heaven, upon this fair conjunction, / That long have frowned upon their enmity" (V.v.19–21).

For the wooing of Anne to serve this double purpose: that is, create a false appearance of Richard's sexual normality, and placate Lancastrians in preparation for Richard's usurping the Kingship—it is imperative that her unlikely seduction, his masterful display of seemingly 'benign' personal power, resting purely on friendly persuasion, not coercion—be *publicly witnessed*. For then he can be sure that it will be gossiped all over London by the morrow, and eventually filter throughout the country. Nor is it difficult to see why Richard would wish to do whatever might facilitate the unification of the Kingdom: only a united England can serve his purpose of pursuing still more power. Scotland begs to be finally conquered, granting Richard thereby mastery over the entire island, while eliminating both a potential beachhead for enemy States (especially France) and a chronic irritant to England's northern shires. Ireland likewise. But the big prize would be France, providing a powerful base for further expansion on the continent. Richard need not remind us of this perennial English ambition, since here, too, Shakespeare has another character—in this case, young Edward, the doomed Prince of Wales—do so for him: "And if I live until I be a man, / I'll win our ancient right in France again, / Or die a soldier, as I liv'd a king" (III.i.91–93). Had Richard only dealt more effectively with Lord Stanley, step-father of Henry Tudor, how differently might have been subsequent history.[29]

Be that as it might have been, the scarcely restrained exuberance with which Richard celebrates his seduction of Anne—"Was *ever* woman in this humour woo'd? / Was ever woman in this humour *won*? . . . To take her in her heart's extremest hate, / With curses in her mouth, tears in her eyes" and make her forget "that brave prince, . . . whom I, some three months since, Stabb'd in my angry mood at Tewksbury" (I.ii.227–41)—such private reveling suggests that he takes a deep personal satisfaction in his implausible success, this proof of both his extraordinary spiritual power and his superior prescience regarding the inclinations of human souls. Men who preen themselves as great conquerors whenever some woman surrenders her body are comically mistaken. Physical dominance over some woman or other is a paltry matter, within the capacity of almost any man. Meanwhile, truth is, women are the real conquerors, holding men's souls in subjugation. Establishing a genuine ascendancy over a woman means taking possession of her soul, not her body. Ironically, it is Anne herself who unwittingly points to this, though speaking with regard to the dead King she is attending: "Avaunt, thou dreadful minister of hell! / Thou hadst but power over his mortal body: / His soul thou canst not have" (I.ii.46–48). One can imagine Richard's inner reply: "O, but my dear, it's not *his* soul I'm after."

Why *has* Anne succumbed to this psychic assault on her? Later, sadly recalling the circumstances of her fatal seduction, she offers only this by way of explanation: "Within so small a time, my woman's heart / Grossly grew captive to his honey words" (IV.i.78–79). But surely it is not that simple, even giving full marks to the rhetorical power Shakespeare has bestowed upon this unhandsome Prince Charming. For the power that Richard radiates is not merely that of words. It includes, first of all, the evident *fear* that she sees he arouses in *other men*, such as her attendants in the funeral procession ("What, do you tremble? Are you *all* afraid?"). This is a power he offers to place at her disposal. So what if she's a physically weak woman; she may command a physically dominant man. But he is no brute—quite the contrary. As their extended repartee reveals, he is highly intelligent, every bit as quick-witted, and witty, as she. And he seems even-tempered, not easily riled despite the litany of abuse she heaps on him, but is instead patient, not hasty and impulsive as so many men are. His imperturbability bespeaks deep-seated self-confidence, psychic strength. Then, having proposed a halt to their "keen encounter of ... wits," he proceeds to eulogize her power—her ravishing *beauty* that did haunt him in his sleep—which he transforms into an appeal to justice: "Is not the causer of these [untimely] deaths / . . . As blameful as the executioner?" (I.ii.121–23). This man has *killed for her*. Think of it! How many women could claim as much?[30] Then, as *coup de grace*, he offers to let her kill him, if that be her pleasure, and even to kill himself at her bidding if she prefers not to bloody her own hands. Whereupon she capitulates behind a fig leaf of equivocation ("I would I knew thy heart," etc.; I.ii.196ff). Finally, to seal the deal, he begs as a *favor* to him the opportunity to relieve her of her sad funereal duty.[31] Does Richard know women! He could set the envious Sigmund Freud to school. Of course, we're not here talking about Richard, Duke of Gloucester, are we? We're talking about Shakespeare.

Notes

1. Expressly characterized as such by, among others, Richard Courtney, in *Shakespeare's World of War: The Early Histories* (Simon and Pierre, 1994, 21). It is generally recognized that the play taken as a whole represents a quantum advance over the *Henry VI* trilogy. Thus H. R. Richmond, in his *Shakespeare's Political Plays* (Peter Smith, 1977, 75), contends that with *Richard III*, "we are confronted by a work that, while it is still dependent in detail on the traditional forms, involves a resynthesis of the raw material in so powerful and brilliant a way as to earn it the title of masterpiece." John Julius Norwich, who has written a useful comparison of English history as understood by modern scholarship with that depicted by Shakespeare in his plays, judges *Richard III* to be "the greatest play" of the entire history

canon: *Shakespeare's Kings* (Viking, 1999) 10. Considered simply from the standpoint of dramatic qualities, I would readily agree; with respect to philosophical depth, its primacy is not so clear. Be that as it may, Shakespeare has endowed its eponym, who dominates the play to an extent comparable to that of Hamlet, with a level of poetic expression unsurpassed by any other character in his histories (including Prince Hal/ Henry V). However, Shakespeare's depiction of King Richard as the royal villain nonpareil remains highly controversial, with defenders of the historical figure rejecting it as merely so much Tudor propaganda.

2. Much as does Iago, a character with which Richard shares certain similarities, not the least being a strong sense of intellectual superiority over everyone else in their respective plays—and well deserved, one might add.

3. This is our first exposure to Richard's taste for irony; whereas "G" is the initial of the Duke of Clarence's Christian name (George), it is, of course, also that of Richard's own title (Gloucester). Hence, the 'prophecy' that Richard has somehow engineered is valid. It is notable that in a play filled with numerous characters making pious vows only subsequently to break them, Richard never breaks any—because he never makes any, though he seems to make many. When what he says is carefully considered, however, one discovers that they are illusions created by his irony. For example, the promise he merely seems to make Buckingham:

Rich: And look when I am king, claim thou of me
      The earldom of Hereford, and all the moveables
      Whereof the King my brother was possess'd
Buck: I'll claim that promise at your Grade's hand.
Rich: And look to have it yielded with all kindness. (III.ii.194–98)

So, while Buckingham is left with the clear impression that the earldom was in fact promised to him (thus IV.ii.87–90ff.), he was merely granted permission to claim it, and (further) to expect its being kindly granted.

4. The text is taken from *Richard III*, Second Arden edition, ed. Antony Hammond (Routledge, 1981).

5. Robert B. Pierce's observation, in *Shakespeare's History Plays: The Family and the State* (Ohio University Press, 1971, 103), is no doubt germane: "Richard is a very special kind of monster, the monster as humorist. To him the code of traditional morality and bonds of social affection are not a hated enemy but an amusing tool. He uses them to play with other people's emotions, both to attain his secret ends and out of sheer virtuosity."

6. Thus Henry Goodman, *Players of Shakespeare 6: Essays in the Performance of Shakespeare's History*, ed. Robert Smallwood (Cambridge University Press, 2004, 203): "Unlike the men and women around him, . . . hypocrites one and all who 'smooth, deceive, and cog' (I.iii.48) but are shown to have feet of clay, Richard is at least self-conscious and consistent—honest, indeed—about his own duplicity."

7. Richmond (1977, 79) contends: "Richard surpasses any earlier Shakespearean character in hypnotic power." Implicitly offering insight into the play's continuing

popularity, Richmond observes that "Richard's cheerful and efficient villainy, far from repelling the audience, delights it, [which shows] Shakespeare's power to break through the crust of rationalizing moral prejudice and respect for decorum to the disruptive inner springs of human motivation. Richard has the fascination of the superman—intelligent, witty, superior to human limitation and virtues. More seriously, he is the focus for the vicarious release of all the repressed resentments and desires that men share in a complex, organized society." However, as this author notes (94), we eventually become disenchanted with Richard, the turning point being "Tyrrel's pathetic description of the murder" of the innocent Princes in the Tower, an account "carefully calculated to alienate the audience's sympathy from Richard, and to lessen their delight in his wit, which is thereafter no longer allowed the same virtuosity."

8. The entire role of old ex-Queen Margaret, hence the major parts of scenes I.iii and IV.iv are frequently cut from performances of the play, *Richard III* being second in length only to *Hamlet*. Suffice it to say, such amputations greatly diminish the philosophical value Shakespeare has invested in the play.

9. Including its cognates, the term "curse" occurs some forty-four times (including the five occurrences of "accursed"). Moreover, these explicit mentions are augmented by other verbal equivalents, such as praying and beseeching God to visit evil upon someone in revenge (e.g., I.ii.62–65, I.iii.111, 137, II.ii.14–15). Thus Lily B. Campbell, in *Shakespeare's Histories: Mirrors of Elizabethan Policy* (Methuen, 1964, 313), can plausibly contend that "the plot of the play is woven as a web of curses and their fulfillment, and the sense of a divine vengeance exacting a measured retribution for each sin is ever present." But about that divine vengeance: it seems guided not merely by *Romans* 12:19: "Vengeance is mine: I will repay, saith the Lord" (Geneva Bible); but more disturbingly—bearing in mind the entire portion of English History treated by Shakespeare in his two tetralogies—by *Numbers* 14:18 as well: "visiting the wickedness of the fathers upon the children, in the third and fourth *generation*."

10. *Hamlet* V.ii.9–11.

11. As Hobbes affirms, *Leviathan* XXXI.40: "seeing Punishments are consequent to the breach of Lawes; Natural Punishments must be naturally consequent to the breach of the Lawes of Nature; and therfore follow them as their naturall, not arbitrary effects".

12. Careful consideration of the reports of their supposed murder by the "flesh'd villains, bloody dogs" hired by Tyrrell (whom Richard recruited for the task), leaves open the possibility that one or both princes actually escaped death at this time (IV.iii.1–30). Thus Shakespeare subtly allows for those embarrassing episodes of Richmond's reign as Henry the Seventh, famously involving not one, but two imposters claiming to be one or the other of the survivors (Perkin Warbeck posing as Prince Richard; and Lambert Simnel, supposedly Prince Edward)— but also for the rumour that, not Richard, but Richmond once he was King actually had the Princes, still captive in the Tower, murdered (as he and his heir are known to have systematically eliminated the progeny of George, Duke of Clarence, and anyone else who might be regarded as having a legitimate claim to the throne).

13. I merely mention these matters (determinism, fate, curses, divine justice) as part of a constellation of issues—including, most importantly, the nature of Evil and the status of the inner moral monitor we call 'conscience'—that pervade the play; I do not intend a systematic treatment of them in what follows. Most of these issues figure also in *Macbeth*, which I have discussed at some length in my treatment of the play in *Of Philosophers and Kings* (University of Toronto Press, 2001) 51–76. Mary Ann McGrail, in *Tyranny in Shakespeare* (Lexington Books, 2001, 60–64) has an especially useful discussion of the conscience-theme in *Richard III*.

14. Richard is often treated as Shakespeare's paradigmatic Machiavellian, with the corollary that his fate implies Shakespeare's judgment on this approach to political life. Suffice it to say, this view is superficial. For a superior treatment of the issues, see Tim Spiekerman, *Shakespeare's Political Realism: The English History Plays* (SUNY Press, 2001). Although Spiekerman does not separately treat *Richard III*, the play and its eponym are referred to extensively by way of comparison with other Shakespeare characters, notably Henry V.

15. Richard's prowess was established with his first appearance in Shakespeare's account of English history. The old Earl of Salisbury credits young Richard with having "three times" defended him "from eminent death" in the day's desperate battle (*Henry VI, Part 2* V.iii.18–19).

16. And are we not meant to note the contrast Richard makes to Henry Tudor (the future Henry VII), who is provided no comparable report of his battlefield behavior, and who has sent out at least five decoys to engage Richard in his stead? True, Shakespeare departs from the historical record in order to make Henry the slayer of Richard, and Norwich (1999, 366) defends his doing so on grounds of "dramatic license": "We shall never know at whose hands [Richard] met his death; we can be confident they were not those of Richmond, since if he had personally struck the fatal blow the fact would almost certainly been recorded." Suffice it to say, those who regard the play as but a piece of propaganda that eulogizes the ascension of the House of Tudor must ignore some of its finer subtleties.

17. For explicitness, its only rival is the mysterious identity of the third murderer in Macbeth.

18. It is remarkable that most scholarship on this play does not so much as mention this question, much less attempt to answer it. Alexander Leggett, in *Shakespeare's Political Drama: The History Plays and the Roman Plays* (Routledge, 1988, 35), does note it, but only to dismiss it as unanswerable: "The warning signs come early. In the middle of one of his breezy, information-packed soliloquies, there is a small touch of darkness. . . . What is that 'secret close intent'? Is it some political advantage, otherwise unrevealed? A need to degrade in Anne's bed the sexual love he professes to despise? We may speculate but we never know." True, like most interpretive puzzles Shakespeare poses, certitude is not to be had. However I do believe that he always has definite answers in mind, and that he supplies sufficient textual evidence for inducing them.

19. In the England of those days, primogeniture operated solely with respect to sons; if there were only daughters to inherit, estates were to be divided equally between them. Clarence had married Warwick's eldest daughter, Isobel, for her half of the money and properties, but he wanted it all. And according to the Croyland Chronicle

(which modern historians regard as generally reliable, and which Shakespeare may or may not have read), Clarence managed to get physical possession of the other daughter, Anne, and in order to prevent Richard from marrying her (and thus claiming her share of the wealth), hid her away as a scullery maid in the kitchen of one of his retainers. Richard, however, tracked her down, rescued her from her captivity, and placed her in sanctuary until arranging to marry her. Now, there's a story with possibilities.

20. One must regard this as further evidence of Richard's charm and plausibility, as children tend to be sensitive discerners of who does and doesn't like them.

21. This is an ironical lament—though the irony is surely unintentional on her part, and just possibly also on Shakespeare's, but not likely so (cf. III.v.90–91; III. vii.11–14)—in that of the elder Duke of York's four sons, the historical Richard most closely resembled his father.

22. I mean by this, the quality of his rhetoric and repartee is not quite up to the standard he set in seducing Lady Anne. But even if he had surpassed it, the likelihood of success would be infinitely less, given the radical difference in what he is attempting: to persuade a young woman that he is so in love with her that he has killed for the opportunity to make her his wife *versus* persuading a middle-aged woman, whose sons and brother he has killed, to become his mother-in-law by facilitating his marrying her daughter. If he really believes that he's convinced her—"Relenting fool, and shallow, changing woman!" (IV.iv.431)—rather than just elliptically expressing a wan hope, his power of judgment has declined more than his verbal dexterity.

23. *The Works of Francis Bacon*, eds. James Spedding, Robert Ellis, and Douglas Heath (Longmans, 1870), Vol. VI: 480–81. If only the dates permitted, one might reasonably suspect that Shakespeare had consciously modeled his Richard on this Essay. A quarto version of King Richard the Third was first published in 1597, though it may have been written as early as 1591. Bacon's essay 'Of Deformity' was first published as number 25 in the second collection of his Essays or Counsels, Civil and Moral (1612), and became number 44 in the third (1625).

24. Of course, they never heard his final soliloquy in the preceding play:

I that have neither pity, love nor fear . . .
I have no brother; I am like no brother.
And this word 'love', which greybeards call divine,
Be resident in men like one another
And not in me: I am myself alone. (3H6 V.vi.68–83)

25. It is actually Shakespeare, however, who has chosen this bizarre situation as ideal for a display of Richard's black magic—for there is nary a hint in the historical sources of anything remotely like this happening. That the scene is not merely believable, but dramatically unforgettable, attests to its creator's superior talent.

26. The dismal fate of King Edward the Second might be interpreted as a cautionary tale to this effect. Moreover, homosexual kings (as, reputedly, was "lion-hearted" Richard the First) invite political conflict upon their death should they have fathered

no legitimate heirs. And while Richard may not care what happens in or to England once he's shuffled off his mortal coil, he knows that this is a vital consideration for everyone else, especially for those who risk much whenever obliged to take sides in a disputed succession: the magnates.

27. In this, I agree with the actor Henry Goodman, in Smallwood 2004, 202: "Freud's . . . suggestion that Richard's will to power derives from his frustrated will to sexual power, seemed to me too simplistic. Murray Kreiger's notion . . . that Richard's will to power is a perversion of his sexual need for power I found more convincing."

28. Albeit *via* the Beaufort line that John of Gaunt fathered on his mistress, Catherine Swynford, and which Richard II belatedly legitimized, but which Henry IV attempted to have declared ineligible for the succession, though this was never ratified by Parliament.

29. In both Shakespeare's play and England's history, Stanley's betrayal of Richard at Bosworth Field determined the outcome of that pivotal battle, bringing to an end over three centuries of Plantagenet rule. The puzzle is: why did Richard rely on Stanley's support despite ample evidence that he was not reliable? Richard obviously did not trust him, but neither did he take the same "prophylactic" action against him as he did Hastings—despite Catesby's warning that Hastings will oppose Richard's usurpation, and that Stanley "will do all in all as Hastings doth" (III.i.168). Presumably, Richard believed that Stanley (unlike Hastings) was nonetheless manipulable, that he would side with whoever wields superior power, and that the Earl of Derby thus remained useful for the forces he could muster from his estates in the North. Hence, Richard grants him permission to muster his men, but only upon his leaving his son George Stanley as surety for his loyalty: "Look your heart be firm, / Or else his head's assurance is but frail." Stanley's reply is coldly ironic: "So deal with him as I prove true to you" (IV.iv.56–97). Holding the Earl's son hostage is the only guarantee Richard provides himself for the father's dependability; and perhaps he had no other options. He needs the forces—the "tenants and followers"—that only the Earl in person can raise. But Richard is in effect relying upon the strength of the father's attachment to the son. In Stanley's case, this was problematic. According to historical sources, the Earl was heard to remark that George was not his only son, that he had others. As Shakespeare often does, he leaves a character's rationale unspoken, challenging the reader to see it for himself.

30. Richmond (1977, 88–89) likewise observes: "Flattered by the thought that their beauty could drive men to crime, both Isabella (in *Measure for Measure*) and Anne can pardon that crime." He goes on to note, however, "The *coup de theater* by which Richard wins Anne establishes us also as his victims, for if intellectually we see a little deeper into him than she does, we are still prone to view his victims from his own merciless perspective, at least unconsciously." Thus, "Whatever its roots in history, this second scene . . . establishes the rhetorical seductiveness by which evil insinuates itself."

31. Somewhere, Nietzsche says something like: "You want to incline someone to you? Request a favor of him."

1 0

~

Taming *The Tempest*

Prospero's Love of Wisdom and the Turn from Tyranny

Dustin A. Gish

Happy day, when, all appetites controlled, all passions subdued, all matters subjected, MIND, all-conquering MIND, shall live and move the Monarch of the World.

—Abraham Lincoln, *Temperance Address*

And they feared exceedingly, and said one to another:
"What manner of man is this, that even the wind and the sea obey him?"

—Gospel of Mark

Omnipotence seems to me evil and dangerous in itself. Its exercise seems to me above the strength of man, whosoever he may be, and I see only God who can be omnipotent without danger because his wisdom and his justice are always equal to his power. There is no authority on earth therefore so respectable in itself or vested with a right so sacred that I should wish to allow to act without control and to dominate without obstacles.

—Alexis de Tocqueville, *Democracy in America*[1]

The title of this play, arguably Shakespeare's finest work, refers to the intense storm or "tempest" conjured by Prospero at the beginning.[2] This "tempest" threatens, or seems to threaten, the lives of all aboard a royal vessel at sea, itself an image of a mutinous Ship of State.[3] "All but mariners" plunge into the "roaring" sea, Ariel reports to Prospero, abandoning the sinking ship in desperation, with little or no hope for survival. Cursing the devils apparently loosed upon them by the storm, the spirited Prince Ferdinand was "the first man that leapt" into the sea, having assumed their prayers had not been answered, and that every man must fend for himself in order to escape an ignoble death in a watery grave (I.i.50–53, ii.206–15; V.i.178–79).

With his tempest, Prospero initiates the endgame—the play itself—by seizing control of those who until now have treated him as a pawn in their political chess match. Alonso, the king of Naples, and his entourage, including Antonio, the brother who usurped Prospero's dukedom, suddenly find themselves castaways on the island where Prospero has lived in exile since his expulsion from Milan. The tempest, then, is a sign of the power Prospero exercises over all those who pass within his sphere of influence; a power so extraordinary, so strange and unnatural, that their bodies and minds both are subject to his potent art. In this endgame, all of the moves on the board are foreseen by Prospero; almost all are made by him.[4] His strategy for concluding the game opens with a policy of divide and conquer (I.ii.219–20), and is followed by a series of moves executed or performed by Ariel. Prospero alone authors the action of the play. Openly or from behind the scenes, he dominates the play and its action from beginning to end; his rule is absolute. The one question that animates the action is not *whether* or *when* Prospero's "project" will succeed, but *how*.[5]

Prospero, it would seem, owes nothing to fortune, other than the occasion to exercise the virtue of his mind.[6] The action of the play reveals that every character is subjected to his will, or more precisely, to that "potent art" with which he is armed. Prospero's command of the play, we are led to believe, derives somehow from his study of nature and his possession of a knowledge about the fundaments of nature which in turn gives him power over natural elements as well as human beings. His power may be rooted in the cherished books associated with his secret study of "the liberal arts"—books which he happens to have with him on the island due to the gracious generosity of one good man. But his pursuit of knowledge is limited neither to his "study" in the ducal palace of Milan, nor to those books which once preoccupied his mind. The liberal arts that he once pursued failed to protect him from political intrigue and overthrow, but by means of his new "art"—which he has learned and practices on his island—Prospero reigns supreme.[7] Once the nature and power of that art are understood, we begin to see that Shakespeare directs our attention to how the unbounded exercise of such a potent art or science—even by such a rare person as Prospero, who merits rule on account of his love of wisdom and superior reason—can inevitably tempt a human being to tyranny.

Prospero's Love of Wisdom and its Coincidence with Power

In retelling for his daughter the near-tragic ending of his expulsion from Milan, we hear how the "retired" Prospero became "rapt in secret studies" so completely that he, "transported" thus, "grew stranger" to his own "state." To devote himself fully to the study of the liberal arts, he willingly "cast" the "government" of his dukedom and "the manage[ment] of [his] state" upon his brother, Antonio. Turning his back on ruling and high office, Prospero liberated himself from the drudgery and distraction of the political life: for in "neglecting worldly ends . . . [his] library / Was dukedom large enough" (I.ii.66–74). Prospero's life in Milan, it would seem, was defined by an overwhelming love of wisdom, which he pursued through his devoted study of "the liberal arts." Recent commentators on *The Tempest* whose interpretations have been informed by their study of political philosophy have viewed Prospero as a "philosopher" and the play as a representation of the rule of Socrates' philosopher-king. While this interpretation deepens our reading of the play, it rests upon a judgment which is in tension with the action of the play before the final Act. If indeed Prospero is a philosopher, he *becomes* one through the action of the play itself.[8]

Prospero is disinclined to rule in Milan because his studies seem to him the pursuit of the highest good, in light of which ruling necessarily becomes an unsavory burden, even an injustice. Prospero's liberal studies distanced him from his state and citizens, and appear to have cultivated in him a critical perspective from which to reject politics and political life as insufficiently good, when compared to the contemplative life. Such a perspective aligns Prospero with the portrait of the philosopher in Plato's *Republic*. As the capstone of this image of philosophy in the dialogue, Socrates establishes a philosopher's curriculum (*Rep.* 521c–34e), a course of studies intended to turn the philosophic soul away from the political realm toward an ascent to *what is*, thus drawing the lover of wisdom above and beyond the confines of the dark Cave into the luminous presence of the Good itself. The world of politics, once escaped, must be viewed ever after with disdain by the philosopher as a realm of illusion and vulgarity. No desire to descend back into the Cave—to live or to rule—tempts the philosopher whose soul knows the Good and flourishes in the truth. No thoughts of a return taint the enlightened mind, hence the compulsion to return there and rule as "philosopher-king" is rightly perceived as an obligation no less abhorrent than it is necessary (519c–21b, 539e–40b). For this reason, according to Socrates' argument, the philosopher alone is incorruptible, immune to the corrosive effect of power on the one who wields it—and so must be the one compelled to rule, if politics is to be just.[9]

In Milan, Prospero played the role of the a-political philosopher, a retiring humanist-scholar aloof from the practical affairs of state. This way of life led him in effect to abdicate his dukedom to his brother and other ministers, whom he apparently believed could be trusted not to abuse the power associated with ruling (I.ii.93–97). His disregard of the duties and problems associated with the political life rendered Prospero vulnerable to the deceit practiced on him by an ambitious brother whose nature, Prospero claims, was awakened to "evil" because corrupted by political power. Prospero's imprudence in this regard also helps to explain his friendship with the "good" but hopelessly idealistic Gonzalo, who envisions an island-commonwealth under his benign government as a golden age of innocence, leisure, and natural abundance, utterly lacking in displays of "sovereignty" (II.i.144–70). This naïve love of humanity dispenses with politics and resembles the retiring philosophy of Prospero in its neglect of the inevitably unpleasant and sometimes harsh necessities which attend political life. It is no wonder that good men, like Prospero and Gonzalo, fall prey to cunning and ambitious men, like Alonso, Antonio, and Sebastian, who they mistakenly consider "gentlemen" (II.i.174, 182). Such men do not adhere to honorable or noble distinctions when it comes to ruling—failing, for example, to distinguish tyranny from kingship, or to limit their choice of means and ends with an eye to justice; crucial distinctions that good men take for granted. If the best regime in theory or speech is to become a viable regime in deed, and if good men are to secure themselves and their rule against those who are not good, then those who are devoted to virtue must learn to recognize and defend themselves from assaults by those who lack virtue (see II.i.203–97).

Once cast out of Milan and isolated on his island, Prospero perfected and transmuted his studies into an "art" with worldly effect. His life on the island is an ascent beyond the political, not merely an exile from it, and the means to discover in the natural world a power sufficient to protect against the vulnerability associated with the contemplative life. Armed with this new art, Prospero transcends the liberal studies, which are "dedicated" only to the "bettering of [his] mind" (I.ii.89–90). The art to which he now devotes his attention, and which seems to be a form of philosophy, is no longer limited to books; it is partly derived from Prospero's study of nature itself. His study and conquest of the natural realm makes Prospero god-like in knowledge and power, an apotheosis without parallel in Shakespeare. The full power of this art is unveiled in the tempest which opens the play. With it Prospero demonstrates a capacity to vex and calm the natural realm at will, usurping the role of chance, fortune, and providence in human affairs, and setting aside conventional claims of authority. The perspective of Prospero in the play is like that of the omniscient narrator, and as the author of its action he has the power to determine the unfolding events in the dramatic narrative. Whereas others see the work of divine beings, or of chance, we know that all unfolds according to Prospero's will.[10]

Upon reflection, Prospero's "art" seems to be more closely identified with the theoretical knowledge acquired through the inherently progressive and non-teleological project of modern natural science. His power over the natural world, and human beings within it, is diametrically opposed to the vulnerable life that accompanied his study of the liberal arts. Indeed, in the action of the play, Prospero approaches omnipotence through the rule of reason. His rule over his island is based on knowledge, and it is absolute. In *The Tempest*, it seems, Shakespeare has brought to the stage for our consideration the rule of a philosopher-king, in whom we see the coincidence of philosophy and power, the necessary and sufficient condition for establishing justice and the best regime, according to Plato's Socrates:

> For unless those who are by nature philosophers rule as kings, or those now called kings genuinely and fully philosophize, such that political power and philosophy coincide in the same place . . . there will be no rest from ills for the cities, nor I think for humankind; nor will the just regime we have described in speech come forth from nature, insofar as is possible, and see the light of the sun (*Rep.* 473c–e).

But it is neither by chance nor by compulsion, as in the *Republic*, that Prospero rules. And there's the rub: having seized the occasion, he rules by choice—and he does so not only with *knowledge* but also with a *power* that renders him superior to the human beings who, willingly or not, live under his rule. Prospero is even more completely in command of his subjects than the philosopher-king, who Socrates says must rule in the just city-in-speech.

By bringing the philosopher-king to life before our eyes, and delivering him the power to accomplish the ends that he seeks, Shakespeare allows us to watch and reflect upon the character of such a regime, thereby exposing the temptation to rule absolutely—that is, as a tyrant, albeit a benevolent one—to which an extreme love of wisdom, coupled with a desire for justice, naturally inclines human beings. *The Tempest* thus represents Shakespeare's subtle critique of this regime and the means required to make it possible, thus raising the question of the desirability of rule by one who seems to embody the qualities of a philosopher-king.[11]

Tyranny as an Aspect of Rule

Prospero is, without question, the "master" of the play. Without even a hint of a true rival on the island, he stands above the others as the undisputed central character of the play. Prospero is literally in command of the play.[12] Moreover, he conducts its action; so much so that he seems to be more the author of the play than a character within it. After the opening scene, we immediately learn that the tempest has been conjured by Prospero, and that the fate (collectively and individually) of all aboard the unnamed vessel rests firmly in his hands. His dominance is shown to extend well beyond the material well-being of the other characters; he masters minds as well. Ariel describes Ferdinand's distress as more psychological than physical: no souls "so firm, so constant" that Prospero's "tempest" cannot vex their minds and warp reason (I.ii.207–10). Whereas others are moved by him, in body and soul, Prospero himself seems to remain steadfast, to be "unmoved" (Sonnet 94). He alone appears to possess a soul sufficiently well-ordered and ruled by reason: he is the lord and owner of others, because the master of the tempest.[13]

Prospero's mastery of Caliban is well known and has been the subject of much work by scholars eager to deduce a wide variety of popular pathologies at work between them. Be this as it may, it is clear that Prospero does not so much rule Caliban, as master him. His heavy-handed mastery of the unrepentant Caliban may be required, even to the extent that he is forced to work for the good of the others by supplying their needs as part of his punishment (I.ii.311–14). It may be necessary at times to rule harshly and by force, lest harm befall innocents; such rule might require imposing penalties of imprisonment or even of death. Justice would seem to demand, nevertheless, that the punishment fit the crime or that precautions be commensurate with threats.[14] But it is quite another thing to imagine as legitimate rule without consent over free beings—capable of self-motion, speech, and reason—who have not forfeited their natural right to liberty on account of some extraordinary vice or criminal behavior. Caliban admits no wrong, denies that he deserves the status of slave, and declares that his master Prospero is a tyrant and usurper of natural right.[15] But as much as he longs to be free (III.ii.174–82), he is nonetheless eager to enslave himself. What Caliban understands by liberty is nothing but license, and so he is willing to genuflect before a new "master" provided that he is allowed to indulge in his pleasures without restraint (cf. II.ii.174, 180, with II.ii.114–16, 122–23, 159–61, 179–82). Since Caliban appears incapable of ruling himself or his passions, Prospero's mastery over him looks both necessary and legitimate. But what of Ariel?

Prospero's rule over Ariel is more revealing than his rule over Caliban. Both are ruled by Prospero unwillingly, yet forced to submit to his superior power. Ariel, however, acknowledges that obedience to Prospero results in part from obligation—although it is not clear why assisting one who is in distress, or liberating one unjustly imprisoned, obligates that one to servitude. But this is precisely what Prospero asserts when Ariel tests his patience by insisting on the recovery of what was once a natural state of liberty (see I.ii.242–300; IV.i.264–66; V.i.86–96, 318–19). A complaint or two aside, Ariel's service to Prospero looks voluntary. Whereas Caliban stubbornly resists and must be threatened with corporal punishment before he will obey (I.ii.368–375; see II.ii.1–14), Ariel hangs on every word of Prospero, "correspondent to [his] command" (I.ii.297), like an extension of his will and mind (IV.i.164–65).[16] Ariel never calls Prospero a "tyrant" but frequently refers to him as "master" (I.ii.216, 293, 296, 300; III.ii.115)—a "potent" (IV.i.34), yet "noble" and beneficent one (I.ii.300, IV.i.48). Ariel's opening lines herald Prospero, and his rule, as such: "All hail, great master; grave sir, hail!" (I.ii.189; cf. *Macbeth* I.iii.47–50).

In the end, however, Prospero's rule over Ariel depends not on Ariel's willingness but on an explicit threat of corporal punishment: Prospero threatens to bind Ariel in matter—a sentence that is "torment" for a "spirit" (I.ii.274–81, 286–96).[17] Thus the brilliant Ariel, too, is mastered, no less than the vulgar Caliban, serving Prospero only under compulsion. They are indentured servants, enslaved and governed by the will of a benevolent master, their liberty duly circumscribed by Prospero's rational view of justice.[18] His rule over the native inhabitants of his realm is thus despotic, not political. Prospero calls both Caliban and Ariel his "slave" when each one first appears on stage.[19] He rules without laws or the consent of the ruled, which is the mark of despotism; his possession and use of Caliban and Ariel as "living tools" and instruments for accomplishing his will exhibit the science of mastery (*despotikê*).[20]

Prospero's mastery and enslavement of both Caliban and Ariel might be explained as an outward expression or manifestation of his own extraordinary virtue and self-control, which is to say, of his rule over himself and his body through the mastery of his own passions by reason.[21] Natural slavery may befit beings less than human, just as a well-ordered soul is naturally fit for ruling by nature over the body which it literally possesses.[22] If Caliban and

Ariel are interpreted as being other than human, this line of argument might hold. Prospero himself speaks of them as elemental beings—Ariel as "spirit" (I.ii.194) and Caliban as "earth" (I.ii.315; cf. *Genesis* 2:7). But despite appearances and smells to the contrary, Caliban's humanity cannot be ignored. If he is to be understood as a natural slave, it is at best on account of his willingness to enslave himself to bodily pleasures and desires. In this respect, though, he is all too human.[23]

While despotic rule over Caliban is an affront to the dignity of his humanity, on account of which he deserves some respect, despite his vices, Prospero's despotic rule over the inhuman, but natural Ariel poses a graver threat to his own humanity, more than to Ariel. In either case, we must wonder whether the play as a whole, insofar as it escapes the control of Prospero, offers a critique of that perfect rule which is so appealingly represented in *The Tempest*. Wisdom might be a sufficient ground for the natural authority to rule; but this does not settle the question of whether the means employed to secure and perpetuate that rule over unwise or irrational human beings, or the natural realm, is ultimately just. What are the limits of ruling, even for the one who is naturally best suited to do so? To answer this question, we must examine the nature—and the potentially tragic effect—of Prospero's rule over the other human beings on his island.

Prospero's Mastery over Enemies and Friends

The Tempest comes nearest tragedy at the moment when Prospero's control over the play seems most secure. At the summit of his power, we glimpse the tragic darkness that accompanies the use of it without restraint. His triumph over his enemies occurs at the end of the central Act, after Ariel has performed a fantastic spectacle harassing the conscience of the criminals (Alonso, Antonio, and Sebastian) with providential retribution for their crimes: a wrathful and "ling'ring perdition, worse than any death" awaits them (III.iii.53–82). The good Gonzalo bears witness to the guilt and "desperate" state of all three men, but especially Alonso, who is provoked by this haunting specter to contemplate suicide (III.iii.58–60, 95–102, 105–10). Prospero, content that he has his enemies right where he wants them, says nothing as to what he now intends to do with them: "My high charms work, / And these mine enemies, are all knit up / In their distractions. They now are in my power; / And in these fits I leave them" (III.iii.88–91). Instead, he turns his attention elsewhere. When he sees fit to think of his enemies again, at the start of the final Act, Prospero asks Ariel for their whereabouts and is duly informed: they are "just as you left them; all prisoners, sir," for "they cannot budge till your release"—hence "abide all three distracted," with Gonzalo and the "good" ministers "mourning over them" (V.i.6–17).

While he has reduced his enemies to prisoners who suffer constant "fits" of punishment, more mental than physical, Prospero's labors are not yet ended. He turns his attention in the fourth Act to accomplishing his intentions with regard to the mutual love and all-but-solemnized marriage of Ferdinand and Miranda (IV.i.1–22). The proper arrangement of their marriage depends upon his restraining the lovers' passions. To do so, Prospero calls for Ariel to bring forth "the rabble" (Ariel's "meaner fellows," the rude natural elements which also serve Prospero) to "bestow upon the eyes of this young couple / Some vanity of mine art" (IV.i.40–41). This vanity proves to be an enchanting display of Prospero's power to command nature and the divine. Inasmuch as he has knowledge of the procreative art, Prospero claims to be able to bless or curse the consummation and "fair issue" of marriage (IV.i.22–24, cf. III.i.74–76; Plato, *Rep.* 545d–547a). His power to deny the lovers those "prosperous" gifts that "the heavens let fall" to make unions "grow"—and instead to "bestrew" their wedding bed with "weeds so loathly" that both will come to "hate" it— gives real force to his advice to prince Ferdinand to "take heed" that he not undo Miranda's "virgin-knot" before the "sanctimonious ceremonies may / With full and holy rite be ministered" (IV.i.14–23). The taint of illegitimacy, in other words, must not cast a shadow over the natural title and claim of their "issue" to rule over both Milan and the kingdom of Naples.

This vanity of "potent" Prospero, orchestrated by Ariel (IV.i.33–37), delivers up the play-within-the-play which represents the pinnacle of Prospero's art: the subordination of the human, natural, and cosmic realms to his will. By his command, the deities perform before the eyes of the astonished lovers, including Juno, the "Highest queen of state" and patroness of marriages.[24] Prospero also takes care to remind the young prince and his beloved that this "most majestic vision" (IV.i.118) is composed of heavenly spirits that he himself—through his art—has confined and commands according to his "present fancies" (IV.i.120–22). If indeed "they may prosperous be"—as Juno wittily puns (IV.i.104)—it will be by virtue of that same art of Prospero which has thus far arranged their falling in love and desire for union. The natural order and the attendant images of the divine in the masque are subject to Prospero's power. Ferdinand, duly impressed, forgets his recently lost father and newly acquired kingdom (perhaps even his bride-to-be), and proclaims devotion to Prospero: "Let me live here ever! / So rare a wond'red father, and a wise / Makes this place paradise" (IV.i.122–24; see V.i.194–96).[25]

Prospero's intention is to mesmerize and overawe his future son-in-law with the power of his art in order to insure that Ferdinand will remain true to his word, and so curb his erotic desire ("not give dalliance / Too much rein"), lest his passionate longing for Miranda, or hers for him, lead him to violate his vow and break the "contract of true love" being celebrated (IV.i.51–56, 82–86). Their youthful "ardour," kindled by Prospero, has inflamed their passion and conquered them, such that each has become a willing "slave" to the other. Because they are ruled by passion rather than by reason, Prospero "abates"—that is, intervenes to restrain—their erotic longing.[26] Whereas the primitive erotic longing or lust in the unruly Caliban had to be suppressed by force and threats of punishment, the young lovers are taught moderation and the virtues of chastity and marital love.

The proper ordering of their souls rests not on the threat of force alone, but on their belief in the providential character of the divine, such that the gods are held to govern the natural order of things, rewarding virtue and punishing vice. Thus, an inherently intelligible vision of nature and the cosmos is invoked to support, as its foundation and capstone, the moral education of Ferdinand and Miranda by Prospero, including especially his taming of their *eros*, an important part of his project for a political restoration.[27] For the union of the two young lovers in the bonds of a proper marriage is the means to satisfy his obligation to his daughter (one-third of his life: IV.1.1–5) as well as to prepare the way for his resurrection and his recovery of that authority which his beloved studies once caused him to neglect and lose.

Prospero's triumphal masque ends abruptly, however, when he recalls to mind, suddenly, "that foul conspiracy / Of the beast Caliban and his confederates / Against my life. The minute of their plot is almost come" (IV.i.139–42). He shouts "Avoid, no more!" to his performing spirits and the "insubstantial pageant" dissolves before the eyes of Ferdinand and Miranda. His charms are broken and his "spell is marred" (IV.i.127), though not because their gazing on the spectacle in silence is interrupted (as anticipated) by Ferdinand's impetuous speech (see IV.i.59, 124–27). Instead, it is Prospero who has interrupted the masque. Startled by the realization he has (almost) forgotten the conspiracy, Prospero experiences a moment of anger.[28] Miranda professes that she has never before seen her father so strongly moved by such a passion—"Never till this day / Saw I him touched with anger so distempered!" (IV.i.143–45) In an earlier scene, when Prospero had appeared to be angry, acting and speaking sternly to them, Miranda had assured Ferdinand that, despite appearances, her father was "of a better nature" (I.ii.496–499); that his anger was not the defining quality of his character. Here, though, Prospero runs the risk of letting anger overcome his better nature.

Noting their distress, Prospero, in a famous flourish of eloquence, reassures his audience, first, that his power commands not only "all spirits" ("our actors") but all of the grand ephemera passing in and out of existence on the stage of life. In this, his finest speech, Prospero establishes himself as the wise man whose "vision" grasps the world and all within it as it is, from a properly philosophic perspective, *sub specie aeternitas* (IV.i.148–58): "We are such stuff / As dreams are made on, and our little life / Is rounded with a sleep." His effort to remain calm before his pupils, however, cannot conceal the fact that he is deeply "vexed" and "troubled," so he hastens to point out that this too shall pass— "Bear with my weakness / . . . Be not disturbed with my infirmity. / . . . A turn or two I'll walk / To still my beating mind." (IV.i.158–63).

What is the cause of Prospero's anger? Is it the plot of Caliban and his fellow-drunkards? Or does Prospero's reference to a "weakness" within himself hint at a deeper cause for his very spirited response? It is unlikely that such vexation in Prospero would stem from his sense of any real threat to his life or his project posed by the conspiracy of a Caliban and two bumbling fools, the drunken god-king Stephano and the trivial Trinculo (IV.i.225, 231). Indeed, there is no hint of dramatic tension associated with this comic attempt at a coup, for their absurd "project" is ill-conceived, well known to Prospero, and foiled with ease—requiring nothing more than some "stale" bait and "trash" to distract them and arrest their plans (see IV.i.186–87, 225). Prospero's anger, then, more so because we know that it is rare, seems strangely at odds with his otherwise complete control of events on the island, events which he has thus far engineered and continues to direct. Perhaps what angers Prospero is the thought of Caliban's recidivism. But the fact that Caliban desires to escape from Prospero's control, and to have his way with Miranda, cannot be a revelation to Prospero, who—like the virtuous Miranda—finds his former pupil's depravity to be repulsive (I.ii.309–11, 345–72). Who would expect anything other than hatred from such an "abhorred slave" and a "savage" named "malice" (I.ii.352, 356, 368)? Because of the persistent problem posed by Caliban and his base desires, the reminder of his incompetent plot is not likely to be the cause of this sudden and uncharacteristic display of anger by Prospero. What, then, has aroused his anger?

This "foul conspiracy," or more precisely his forgetfulness of it, may remind Prospero of something far more disturbing. The drunkards' plot to take his life and his rule of the island must be a reminder to Prospero of Caliban's first rebellion: his original assault on Miranda and his fall from Prospero's grace. But, what is perhaps even more infuriating, Caliban's conspiracy is also a comic imitation of the successful conspiracy of his brother which had thrust him (and Miranda) from his state in Milan. Such a sudden reminder of the ingratitude that he and his daughter have suffered more than once, especially at the hands of someone (the young Caliban or Antonio) who should have been particularly disposed to treat him and his own with gratitude and kindness, may have struck Prospero to the quick with anger—not so much at the present plot, but at the thought of the actual injustices that it called to mind. Prospero's anger, understood in this way, no longer seems strange, for it arises out of a spirited indignation at having suffered injustice, at his having been denied what he, on account of his virtue, rightly deserves. This desire for justice vindicates his display of anger against those who have committed or planned injustice against him.

Even though his desire for justice is admirable and his anger at having suffered injustice is reasonable, it remains to be seen whether Prospero fully understands the hidden springs of the anger which has been aroused in him, or whether this very anger, while justified, has blinded him to his own complicity in their injustice. Both the conspiracy of Antonio and the two rebellions of Caliban, while unjust, were precipitated by his preoccupation with his private studies and neglect of worldly affairs. Just as at this moment in the play when he becomes angry, Prospero's failure on those earlier occasions to have paid prudent attention to the potential or likely threats against himself and his daughter, especially from those close to them whose natural inclinations should not have been trusted, casts a dark shadow over his claim to wisdom. Most importantly, it is unclear that Prospero even now acknowledges that his own tendency to lose sight of the world around him as it really is, while engaged in contemplating beauty and enjoying the pleasures of the life of the mind, partly occasioned the unjust acts of others against him and his own. Having failed to anticipate and guard against the threats posed to him and his daughter by an ambitious and usurping brother, whom he wrongly entrusted with his powers as Duke, Prospero appears not to have learned from his mistake. He repeated it on the island, when he neglected to take certain precautions to protect his adolescent daughter from the (not unnatural) desires of a lusty Caliban. The fall of Antonio to his lust for power, no less than the eagerness of the young and uncivilized Caliban to grasp rudely at the fruit of sexual temptation, is as understandable as it is vicious.

To return to the question of his anger, and its cause, we must ask: Does Prospero even see that the injustices committed by his brother and Caliban have something in common, insofar as both seem to derive from his own, perhaps overly optimistic view of human nature—a defective perspective that plagued him in Milan and seems to have followed him to the island? Is the anger of Prospero, in other words, adequately buttressed by self-knowledge, and a proper awareness of both the human limitations that must circumscribe our expectations for achieving justice and the rational obligations imposed even, or especially, upon those virtuous and good souls who above all desire it? The vexation of soul and mind that Miranda observes and Prospero confesses seems to be beyond measure for a figure who, of all the characters in Shakespeare's works, appears to reflect the philosophic life. Being "touched" so by worldly matters, Prospero's anger would seem to belie his possession of a self-sufficient wisdom and philosophic detachment from human life and its affairs.[29] It remains to be seen whether his anger is partly derived from his own sudden realization of such a persistent "weakness" in himself.

At this point, it docs not at all seem to be the case that Prospero is angry with himself for being distracted from practical affairs requiring attention, but that he is angered by the injustices committed against him. Only if we are confident that his desire for justice and his powerful art remain guided by wisdom and self-knowledge are we then able to gauge the fittingness of the punishments meted out against his enemies. If his anger betrays in Prospero the same all-too-human and unreasonable tenacity that can distort the proper order of the soul and cause blinding ignorance with respect to self-knowledge, then his soul—and therewith his natural right to rule over others—must be judged to be deficient in a decisive respect. Justified anger, in particular, can taint reason by its very presence in the soul and prevent us from seeing the world around us with clarity, including the limitations of our own desire for justice. If Prospero does lack self-knowledge in this regard, then the political alternative he embodies in *The Tempest* must be seen to perpetuate a fundamentally tragic misconception of human wisdom and its limits. Inasmuch as his ascent beyond the cave of political life prompted by his love for wisdom may be viewed as a kind of comedy, his descent in the action of the play from high to low—from his contemplative life before "the tempest" down into the political life of the cave (first on his island, and perhaps then back in Italy) as a ruler with extraordinary power and knowledge, a descent initiated in anger and necessitating punishments of the unjust—approaches a kind of tragedy.[30]

The Tragic Action of the Play

Prospero's anger marks the beginning of a critical turning point in the play. At this point, the only moment in the play when he seems not to be fully in control of the action, Prospero is visibly distressed by the thought that he has come close to reenacting his previous errors as the Duke of Milan and father of Miranda. This anger puts Prospero into an agitated state and draws a "dismayed" look from Ferdinand. To his credit, Prospero appears only momentarily transported by his anger; he immediately recovers his sense of composure and seeks to assuage his troubled "son" and daughter with a show of confidence (IV.i.146–48): "Be cheerful, sir. / Our revels now are ended." If such reveries must be "ended," it is because Prospero has caught himself dreaming once again. He must awaken to the world as it actually is, including a scrupulous appraisal of his own soul and the cause of his anger, if he is to finish his "project" of re-fashioning the world with his potent art—and to do so in accordance with justice and the limits of knowledge.

Having been awakened suddenly from his dream, Prospero proceeds to deal with Caliban and the would-be assassins and usurpers. But rather than take some responsibility for his failure to attend to present circumstances, Prospero blames Caliban's nature as the cause of his villainy: "A devil, a born devil, on whose nature / Nurture can never stick; on whom my pains / Humanely taken—all, all lost, quite lost!" (IV.i.188–90) He thus refuses to admit that his failure to educate Caliban sufficiently when he had the chance, to liberate him from the tyranny of his baser desires by teaching him restraint in light of the good, may be partly to blame. This inclination to accuse "nature" rather than himself is also evident in his accusation of his brother, whose "evil nature" is said to be the cause of his corruption and the conspiracy (I.ii.92–93, 97–105, 111–16).

While little else in the play eludes his control, Prospero declares that the "nature" of both Caliban and Antonio is incorrigible, beyond the reach of humane efforts to improve or reform it. Prospero argues that the matter of Caliban's body is itself defective and base, invulnerable to education: as "with age his body uglier grows," so too Caliban's "mind cankers" (IV.i.191–92). The corruption of mind by recalcitrant flesh is what the enlightened, rational Prospero despises, and what—he thinks—justifies his treating Caliban as both "slave" and "beast."[31] His opinion of Antonio hardly differs. Stephano and Trinculo as well, each in his own indulgent way (not unlike Miranda and Ferdinand, with their erotic desires), prove no less enslaved to their bodily passions than Caliban.[32] Hence, all three are wracked with torments brought on by Prospero's art. Without thought for the reformation of souls through education, Prospero promises, as the punishment for their absurd insurrection, to "plague them all, / Even to roaring" (IV.i.192–93).

What is most disturbing about the punishment of Caliban and his fellow conspirators is the degree to which Prospero is willing to torment them to "roaring." This last touch suggests that they are being compelled to descend into an inarticulate condition which is less than human. Indeed, the word "roaring" signifies a loss of speech, when in the grip of an overwhelming pain or grief, and a turn toward beast-like cries of agony or the cacophonous din of crashing waves in a tempestuous sea.[33] On this harsh note, Act IV suddenly ends, as the conspirators are "hunted" off-stage by demonic hounds conjured up and unleashed by Prospero, and whipped to a frenzy in the chase: "Fury, Fury! There, Tyrant, there!" (IV.i.257) Here, at the peak of his power, Prospero is content to declare (again) that "At this hour / Lies at my mercy all mine enemies"—conquered by his potent art. The final Act begins in a similar vein with Prospero expressing his view that all goes according to his plan: "Now does my project gather to a head. / My charms crack not; my spirits obey" (V.i.1–3). Soon, he proclaims, "all my labours" will come to an end. What precisely it is that Prospero intends to do remains a mystery; but there is no doubt that his mastery over the play and its action is absolute.

While his need to punish the foolish conspirators seems justified, one wonders about the harsh means he has used to do so. Though the villains here are comical, their punishment is real; they are physically battered, bruised, and beaten. Are we to believe that their physical torments, which are not insubstantial, will cure them of their disordered souls or reform their licentious behavior by leading them to moderate or restrain their passions? What prospects for self-control or at least for becoming more reasonable are likely to emerge from such pains? In what sense, if at all, can such punishments be judged in accordance with the ends of retributive justice—to say nothing of corrective justice? In exercising power over them, Prospero insists on mastering them, rather than undertaking to rule them in a non-despotic sense—that is, in accordance with justice, reciprocity, and the rule of law.[34] Prospero seems to deny that justice demands he rule over even his enemies politically, because he views them as incurably base and irredeemable, as slavish in their behavior and less than human. The names of his hunting hounds are revealing; for "tyrant" is what Caliban already perceives Prospero to be, and "fury" is what Prospero himself will soon say must be restrained in himself. Indeed, it is striking that the word "justice" itself never occurs in *The Tempest*, though it appears to be a play about the rule of a true philosopher-king.

We are reminded by such reflections of Prospero's punishment of his actual enemies who no longer pose a threat to him, but who are still afflicted with pains more of the soul than body: "a ling'ring perdition, worse than any death." We may wonder if the line that separates natural justice from mere retributive violence has become blurred for Prospero, especially if the torments they suffer at his hands are not attended by his awareness of limits which a proper understanding of the human condition must impose upon our desire for justice. The severity of their punishment is in fact known to Prospero. When his enemies are reintroduced in the final Act, he realizes that "heavenly music" must be played to "cure" their "brains" which he admits, being "boiled" within their skulls, are now "useless." "Their clearer reason," that part of the soul which should be the light guiding our actions, is shrouded in "ignorant fumes" and "darkness" (V.i.51–54, 58–68).

Their minds, in other words, like "foul and muddy" stagnant waters or a tide withdrawn far from the "shore" of reason, lack "understanding" or even the power to recognize what is right before their eyes (V.i.79–84).[35] A state of "madness" grips the usurpers and would-be tyrants because of Prospero's punishments. More psychological than physical, their torment causes pain also in those who witness the punishment: The "good" Gonzalo, we are told, "brimful of sorrow and dismay," laments with his tears the suffering of his fellows. So "strongly" do the "charms" of Prospero work the ruin of his enemies that Ariel—the only character in the play who is fully aware of their crimes and of what Prospero has wrought in them through his art—is compelled (despite a lingering fear of his anger: IV.i.166–169) to appeal to Prospero on their behalf to end their suffering: "if you now beheld them, your affections / Would become tender" (V.1.17–19). Even a "spirit" like Ariel finds something inhumane about punishments that manage to drive those subjected to them literally "mad" (I.ii.208–10; II.ii.3–14; III.iii.53–58; V.i.115–16). With the help of Ariel here, Prospero first begins to confront the tragedy implicit thus far in the action of the play. Prospero, it seems, must relearn or rediscover his humanity; he has been playing the role of a god far too long.[36] His knowledge and absolute power, especially with respect to nature, has propagated in him the illusion of self-sufficiency, as a result of which he has become pitiless—as Miranda feared (I.ii.447, 475). When it comes to ruling over others, Prospero has abandoned the political art and become a tyrant, for while his rule may be that of a wise man over both fools and criminals, it is nonetheless accomplished by force.

The peculiar character of his tyranny and the potential tragedy of the play derive from the fact that Prospero appears to have elevated the state of the tyrant to a level beyond the political. His conquest of nature and his domination of the human beings who fall under the sway of his art reflect a tyranny of reason itself, over the body and its related passions, both ennobling and base. With his knowledge, Prospero has acquired the means, in addition to the natural right,[37] to rule over human beings, as the soul by nature "rules" over the body—through mastery; just as reason, according to nature and the proper order of the soul, rules over the sub-rational and irrational aspects of human beings. But an empire of reason is still an empire, not a political association. The tragic character of this rule and what it entails becomes most evident when extended beyond the domination of one's own body and soul, beyond self-control, to an absolute command over the bodies and souls of others in any human community To reduce the unwise to subservience, to enslave them—even "for their own good"—destroys the possibility of pursuing any common good between ruler and ruled; hence, no politics—to say nothing of friendship. The tyranny of reason over desire, justified in an individual soul by nature, becomes unjustifiable tyranny when exercised without limit by one human being over another: "O, it is excellent / To have a giant's strength, but it is tyrannous / To use it like a giant" (*Measure for Measure* II.ii.108–10).[38]

Prospero secures mastery over Caliban and Ariel, as well as the others, by means of his potent art; that is, his knowledge of the world and how natural elements can be controlled and used for good (or ill) to serve his rational will. The decision taken by Prospero, presumably at some point soon after his arrival on the island, to alter his "liberal studies" in such a manner as to cultivate a "potent art" seems to be a direct response to the loss of his dukedom and his suffering injustice at the hands of others. Judging from its powerful effect, his new art differs in kind from the studies previously undertaken, aiming at the acquisition of useful knowledge, particularly about the natural world, its material and immaterial causes; knowledge which can be used to control or harness that which exists in nature, including human beings. This knowledge became for Prospero (eventually and in its fullness) not only a means to conquer nature, and so provide relief from the misery of his estate, but also the basis for his domination rather than "rule" over other human beings who lack knowledge, and who are unwilling or unable to be self-governed, that is, guided in their actions and restrained in their desires by the dictates of reason. But the rise of a "fury" within Prospero himself, although associated with a sense of justice and strong indignation at unpunished acts of injustice, risks tainting the rational faculty which is the basis of Prospero's natural right to rule. All desires in the play, licit or otherwise, are held in check by his command. It is the unexpected intervention of Ariel that finally draws Prospero's attention to his own tyrannical desire to rule others through his reason, to establish a "best" regime of the wise over the unwise. This radical political founding has been brought within the horizon of human possibility, and removed from the hands of fate or chance, by the confluence of knowledge and power in the hands of Prospero.

On Wonder and the Limits of Prospero's Art

What Prospero has been doing throughout *The Tempest* was once reserved for the divine. While others perceive what is happening to them without understanding causes, his intervention in the action of the play is inexplicable (*alogon*).[39] Prospero's control of the natural elements is what has liberated him from the need to exercise prudence or cultivate the virtues associated with ruling and being ruled in turn, that is, with living politically.[40] What once was left in the hands of the gods, Prospero seizes as his own. He acts as both punishing deity and providential *deus ex machina* in the play (cf. V.i.104–6, with I.ii.388–90, V.i.187–89, 200–4). With his power, Prospero acknowledges no natural or human limits; he controls both realms, and can even raise the dead. His "potent art" makes him omnipotent, and is the foundation of his dominion.

But what exactly is his art? How has this art, by which he governs the action of the play, become the source of this potential tragedy? As his abrupt speech to the young lovers dismissing his "vanity" makes clear, Prospero manages to suppress admiration or wonder for anything other than his own power.[41] Miranda and Ferdinand are in awe of his anger and his art. What may be even more deeply disturbing is the fact that Prospero himself has ceased to wonder (see I.ii.5–15; III.i.31–32). Whatever his study of "the liberal arts" once was, Prospero has turned on the island to natural philosophy, or rather natural science, in its distinctively modern sense. Having rejected classical teleology, with its view of the cosmos as inherently intelligible, modern natural science—like Prospero—trusts in the power that derives from the knowledge which unlocks the secrets of the natural world and proceeds to construct rather than to admire the world. Science knows no limits and so dispenses with the pursuit of wisdom which, finally resting in essences and beings, lies beyond knowledge. Prospero, too, dissolves forms and treats all as a spectacle (IV.i.151–58) that answers to his command.

Modern natural science thus seeks to surpass that wonder which is the only beginning of philosophy in order to accumulate sufficient knowledge for the conquest of nature and relief of our estate. The impetus of that wonder which animates philosophy is lost when the philosophical disposition is replaced by an immoderate science, which concentrates intently on progress and the advancement of useful knowledge. The rational activity of modern natural science becomes its own end—the ceaseless pursuit of knowledge for its own sake, rather than for the sake of wisdom:

> 'we wonder too much . . . And this may entirely prevent or pervert the use of reason. That is why, although it is good to be born with some inclination towards this passion, because that disposes us for the acquisition of the sciences, we must at the same time [after we have turned toward science] try to free ourselves from [wonder] as much as possible.' If we already have the framework in which all truth is to be found, wonder is at best superfluous, and at worst subversive.[42]

It is more efficient and profitable, from the perspective of science, to leave the liberal arts and wonder behind us and to discipline reason to the task of pursuing knowledge through science. Here we see the intellectual temptation to use science to master nature and ameliorate, if not perfect, our human condition—hallmarks of modern thought. To be tempted thus is to reject the classical or Socratic sense of wonder that reminds us of the need to temper our desires, even for justice and wisdom, as we inquire into "the human things" (Xenophon, *Memorabilia* I.1.16).

Returning to the ship of state image at the beginning of the play, Prospero emerges as the natural ruler and master of the vessel, not because he possesses the human art of politics which, in the crisis of a storm, knows how to "Play the men!" His rule rests upon his capacity to raise and quiet tempests, to command the winds and thus to forego the need to row, to resolve a crisis with the wave of his hand or a thought (see V.i.314–19; Gospel of Mark 4:41). Prospero's "rule" throughout the play, in other words, is not political; it is equivalent to despotic mastery—a mastery perfected by the practice of modern natural science. For Plato and Aristotle, navigation and the art of sailing, and by analogy, ruling and the art of politics, requires at best wisdom, but next best is prudence; for Prospero, sailing the ship of state is a matter of science which furnishes knowledge sufficient for the conquest of nature and chance. From the perspective of classical political philosophy, the political art of ruling takes its bearings from the pursuit and possession of knowledge of justice. With the advent of modern natural science, ruling comes to depend not on distinguishing the just from the unjust, or upon knowing which laws would be fitting for a given people, or on the art of persuasion about the beneficial and the harmful, but upon the possession of a science that is the mother of power. Modern political science, like modern navigation, in other words, partakes of a certain utopian conceit, which sees nature and chance as subject to reason itself.[43]

Prospero's willingness to abandon the liberal arts, in favor of a philosophy defined by the project of modern natural science, can be said to be the "missing of the mark" (*hamartia*) that threatens to transform the action of *The Tempest* as a whole into a tragedy about the despotic rule of Prospero's reason. Were the play to end without his having come to grips with the unnatural and inhuman sway his "rough magic," and seemingly limitless art (V.i.41–50), has over human beings, or with the impact of the exercise of that art upon his own soul, Prospero's knowledge of himself would have been defective in a critical sense. His decision to break his staff and charms, to drown his book, and to abjure his potent art (V.i.50–57) is his "turn" in the play away from the tyranny of reason and the empire made possible by his studies on the island, his natural science and its conquest of nature. In so turning, Prospero recognizes the distinctive nature of the human, and recovers prudence and the art of politics, or political rule.[44] Though he chastises Miranda for her lack of self-knowledge (I.ii.17–18), the action of the play reflects Prospero's own defect in this regard and, most importantly, his recognition of that defect within himself. The action of the play in the final Act, in which Prospero suddenly becomes gentle and frowns no further (V.i.28–30) with torments upon his enemies, confirms this turn. But what, we must wonder, has occasioned his decision to turn away from his potent art?

The Voice of Ariel and Prospero's Turn from Tyranny

Wonder may be the end or issue of tragedy, but Prospero recovers his sense of wonder at the start of the last Act. The tragic motion of the play is thus averted when Prospero, prompted by Ariel, begins to pity his enemies—the very ones driven to madness by his torments (V.i.7–17). Such is their plight that Ariel takes it for granted that no human being, including Prospero, could look on their suffering without being moved to compassion: "Your charm so strongly works 'em / That, if you now beheld them, your affections / Would become tender." (V.i.17–19) Prospero, curtly, perhaps with a hint in his voice of that anger to which he has hitherto been prone (see I.ii.14–15, 294–96, 365–72, 468–78), completes Ariel's line: "Dost thou think so, spirit?" (V.i.19) Ariel, in response, only speculates about the response which the sight of such suffering must—or ought—to elicit from another human being: "Mine would . . . were I human." (V.i.20)

Prospero's sharp reply, not unlike his earlier retorts to Miranda's expressions of pity and wonder for the sinking ship or for Ferdinand, can be read with a tone of indignation and sarcasm, for Ariel of course is merely a "spirit" without humanity or a sense of moral indignation, a slave to Prospero's will. But his words can also be read with a genuine tone of wonder and reflection, as when one is struck suddenly by an unexpected thought; Ariel's rather innocent observation in fact may have caught Prospero off-guard. Prospero seems genuinely surprised by Ariel's remark; perhaps he is intrigued and prompted to reflection, as if to say: "Could it really be true that Ariel, who is not human, can yet sense what I should feel for good Gonzalo and the others, but do not?" Such a possibility surely warrants further examination, especially given the sudden change in his demeanor as well as in his actions toward his enemies in the final Act.

In his immediate answer to Ariel, as if finishing the thought himself,[45] Prospero seems to reverse course, suddenly concluding:

> And mine shall.
> Hast thou, which art but air, a touch, a feeling
> Of their afflictions, and shall not myself
> (One of their kind, that relish all as sharply,
> Passion as they) be kindlier moved than thou art? (V.i.20–24)

This reversal seems to rest on the acknowledgment that he is human, not divine; that he shares in the nature of those on the island, even Caliban, whom he now rules. He is no spirit, like Ariel, or a god—though his absolute command over the natural elements argues otherwise. Ariel, lacking the material substance essential for feeling pity as much as anger, perhaps unwittingly shows Prospero the way to feel pity, not to be like stone (cf. Sonnet 94). The severity with which he has pursued justice gives way to "kindlier" thoughts and a sense of compassion.[46] Here, in his turn, which he strikingly puts in the form of a question, Prospero recovers his humanity. What he has learned from Ariel, he might also have learned from Miranda, who had tutored him on the need for compassion on earlier occasions, although he ignored her pleas. Soon enough, she will naively remind him of the beginning of philosophy, and the significance of our nature as human beings as the subject of contemplation, in her most famous lines in the play: "O wonder! / How many goodly creatures are there here! / How beauteous mankind is! O brave new world / That has such people in't." (V.i.181–84) Moved by Ariel's empathy, Prospero turns away from any further temptation to use his art in a manner which denies his enemies'—and his—humanity.

Turning to an examination of the soul begins with reflecting upon one's own. In doing so, Prospero renounces the anger that distorted his reason; he thus calms the tempest in his mind (see *King Lear* III.iv.6–25) and announces that he will "release" his enemies:

> Though with their high wrongs I am struck to th' quick,
> Yet with my nobler reason 'gainst my fury
> Do I take part. The rarer action is
> In virtue than in vengeance. They being penitent,
> The sole drift of my purpose doth extend
> Not a frown further. Go, release them, Ariel. (V.i.25–30)

Prospero ceases to "frown" upon his enemies, and instead smiles upon them, offering his pardon for their crimes—both committed and intended. It is worth noting, however, that we have had no indication up until this moment about Prospero's intentions; which is to say, whether or not his "project" from the beginning has been to offer his "penitent" enemies forgiveness. In the case of his brother, at least, we have no reason to believe that Antonio deserves pardon, for he does not show signs of penitence or remorse; his relative silence throughout the last scene betrays no sign of inward contrition or a confession of guilt (see V.i.264–66). His spirited reaction to the Furies and his cold silence here must not be taken as an acknowledgement that justice might set a limit on his ambition and actions in the future—a fact which Prospero prudently foresees and counters with a threat to reveal his conspiracy against the king (V.i.74–79, 130–32, cf. 126–30). In the case of Alonso, who, unlike Antonio or Sebastian, openly confesses his guilt, Prospero promises to make amends to the king by rendering an account that will satisfy his desire to make sense of the bewildering "maze" of events through which he has been helplessly wandering.[47] Whereas before his commands were authoritative and binding over those under his sway, Prospero now shifts at the end of the final Act to the power of speech, persuasion and exhortation as well as warnings, to appeal to the desires and passions, in addition to reason, of even the most recalcitrant of those who surround him: Antonio, Sebastian, even Caliban (V.i.290–98).

The potential tragedy enacted by the despotic rule of Prospero's reason over both friends and enemies by means of his potent art is thus overcome. But compassion alone is not sufficient. Since the temptation to act tyrannically would be perpetuated in him if he maintains possession of this "so potent art"—indeed, may even be necessitated by the envy of ambitious men who will observe his power and desire to possess its source—the instrumental cause of his tyranny must be renounced. He must leave his powerful art, and his command over nature and human beings, on the island where he first acquired and perfected it. In having him do so, Shakespeare indicates that it is not Prospero's nature, strictly speaking, which has come to light as tyrannical, but rather that potent art of which—in the name of justice—he has made such "tyrannous" use.[48] What he has come to realize is that the desire for wisdom must be tempered by self–reflection; that science and the conquest of nature and human beings (which science sees as not different in kind from other organic beings), which scientific knowledge makes possible, cannot be the foundation for his political rather than despotic rule after his restoration. His art must be buried "fathoms in the earth" (V.i.50–57). With this conclusion to the turn which began with his reflection on Ariel's tender affections and which now ends in a soliloquy, Prospero concedes that his power, once he returns to Italy, will be "most faint"—yet, because less strong, more humane, in accord with human nature and what is fitting: "my charms are all o'erthrown, / And what strength I have's mine own." (Epilogue 1–2)

The Argument of *The Tempest* and the Limits of Philosophy

In the final scene, good Gonzalo proclaims that "all of us [have found] ourselves, / When no man was his own" (V.i.212–13). He cannot know how true it is to say that Prospero has not only found his dukedom (V.i.211), but himself in a profoundly Socratic sense; that he has come to know his soul more fully, and so acquired self-knowledge. What his recent journey down into the cave, so to speak, as a philosopher-king has taught him is this: that the domination of human beings by force, like the domination of one part of the soul over another, even if that ruling part is reason itself, is tyranny—perhaps benevolent, if it is grounded in a genuine concern for virtue, but tyranny nonetheless. A regime founded or patterned on such mastery, while rational, is unjust because it offends the dignity of those on whom it is unwillingly imposed.[49]

The temptation which attends the immoderate desire for justice—that is, the temptation to have perfect justice on earth, to construct a political regime based on the order or structure of the best soul by nature—must be resisted, and especially so by those who can see what is, or seems, "best" about such an order. Back in Milan, where he will presumably take care to rule, at least in some respect, Prospero will no longer have the power to act despotically as he has on the island: he shall "want / Spirits to enforce, art to enchant;" instead, he must learn to rely on more than the unbounded exercise of his reason, and the power of his most potent art, if he is to hold together that political order (with its orientation toward limited political goods) which will continue to demand his attention, human beings being what they are by nature.

We trust that Prospero's new-found respect for, and knowledge of, politics and the good (or goods) that political life makes possible, will not fade from his thoughts. If indeed one-third of his thoughts are reserved for contemplating death and dying, and another third dedicated to his daughter and her happiness (V.i.308–12), then we must assume that he intends to hold in mind for the portion that remains the practical obligations related to the active life and political rule of his restored dukedom, a third that bridges the gap between the distinct engagements with nature represented by the other two portions: philosophic contemplation and familial responsibilities.[50] The knowledge Prospero attains on the island, though potent, fell short of a philosophy grounded in the pursuit of self-knowledge and aiming at wisdom regarding the nature of things, above all human nature. His knowledge over the course of the play has deepened or ripened to wisdom, it seems, as he acquires a genuinely philosophic view of his soul and the human condition, a condition he now sees that he shares with those around him. Only near the end of the play, when Prospero makes his turn away from the tyranny of reason toward prudence, does his pursuit of wisdom finally begin. If he was not a wise man before, there is some ground to think that he is now. Having come to understand the false hopes of the private and public extremes to which the life devoted to knowledge necessarily inclines—the a-political retreat of the scholar into his study, or the philosopher-king in whom knowledge and power coincide—Shakespeare's Prospero has learned to moderate his longing for wisdom as well as for justice.

The action of *The Tempest* thus dramatically represents the motion of Prospero's soul in its shift from his belief in self-sufficiency and possession of wisdom to an awareness of the limits of his knowledge, especially with respect to human beings and himself. Whatever he may have had in mind at the beginning of the play may have been different, even radically different, from what finally occurs by the end. With the beginning of the final Act, Prospero turns away from the power of his art, with its illusion of knowledge and omnipotence, and its affinity with the project of modern natural science, toward a proper study of the human soul and hence human nature, that part of the cosmos which his study of nature thus far had neglected. By rejecting "fury" and the alliance within him between justified anger and a powerful art, and embracing a "nobler reason," Prospero releases his tormented enemies from his control, thereby restoring to all those in his realm, himself included, a dignity appropriate to their nature—regardless of whether or not they happen to possess the wisdom or moderation to live their own lives fully in accord with "the better angels" of our nature (Sonnet 144).

To judge from the action of *The Tempest*, Shakespeare's views of human nature and the prospects for ruling in accordance with perfect justice lead us to conclude that the coincidence of politics, power, and philosophy—even if it is, at least on this dramatic stage, possible to attain—is undesirable. Philosophy, love of wisdom, as a life of self-examination in pursuit of knowledge not simply aimed at the perfection of science, must resist the temptation to justify its rule in terms of efficiency or justice, which leads us to turn away from the pursuit of knowledge to the exercise of it for political purposes. However just their rule might be, the wise would be compelled to exchange their love of wisdom for the pursuit of perfect justice through the exercise of power, by force if necessary, over both the unwise and those unfit for self-rule. The action of the play, and therewith its argument, is a reflection of the extraordinary motion of Prospero's—perhaps even Shakespeare's—own soul. Having turned, therefore, from the tyranny of reason toward the pursuit of that knowledge and common good which is the proper end of the political art, Prospero (or is it the retiring Shakespeare?) abandons his potent art, and so is ready to go home. To that end, he begs pardon for his "faults" and "crimes" (Epilogue 15–20) from those judges he had dominated throughout the play with his charms, charms which had almost imprisoned him, even more so than those over whom he had ruled by means of his art.[51]

Notes

1. Mark 4:41; Tocqueville, I.2.7. See Luke 8:25, 21:25–28; Matthew 8:27; Mark 4:33–40. All references herein, unless otherwise indicated, are to the Arden edition of *The Tempest*, Third Series, eds. Virginia Vaughan and Alden Vaughan (Thomson Learning, 2005).

2. *The Tempest* holds pride of place in the Folio of 1623 and is Shakespeare's only play to exhibit classical ideals about dramatic unity with respect to time, place, and action. See Vaughan and Vaughan 2005, 14, 89, 124–25.

3. Ship of State: Plato, *Republic* 487b–89d; Xenophon, *Memorabilia* III.5.5–6; Aristotle, *Politics* III.4 (1276b16–35); Norma Thompson, *The Ship of State* (Yale University Press, 2001) 167–72; David Keyt, "Plato and the Ship of State," in *The Blackwell Guide to Plato's Republic*, ed. G. Santas (Blackwell Publishing, 2006) 189–213. Aristotle appropriates the ship of state image in discussing the necessity for a "second sailing" in politics, when natural beneficence fails: *Pol.* III.13 (1284a3–b23); cf. Plato, *Phaedo* 96a6–100b3. See Paul Cantor, "Prospero's Republic: The Politics of Shakespeare's *The Tempest*," in *Shakespeare as Political Thinker*, eds. John Alvis and Thomas West (Carolina Academic Press, 1981) 239–56, 241.

4. The "endgame" refers to the final stage in a chess match, when few pieces remain on the board, pawns becoming important and kings much more active, even aggressive. Chess is an allegory for both courtship and government: Vaughan and Vaughan 2005, 274n. The chess board in *The Tempest* (V.i.167–77) must have been made by Prospero.

5. Prospero mentions his "project" twice (V.i.1, Epilogue.12; see II.i.300; cf. IV.i.175), but never articulates its substance. The word rarely appears in Shakespeare; when used as a noun, it always refers to a dangerous or concealed plan. The emphasis on "now" in the play points to the urgency of Prospero's project: see, e.g., I.ii.187; I.ii.22, 33, 36, 136–37, 169, 178–84, 187; III.iii.90; cf. IV.i.148, with V.i.1; Epilogue 1, 3, 13. See Paul Cantor, "Shakespeare's *The Tempest*: The Wise Man as Hero," *Shakespeare Quarterly* 31/1 (1980) 64–75, esp. 64, 67–68 [reprinted as Cantor, "Shakespeare's *The Tempest*: Tragicomedy and the Philosophic Hero," in *Shakespeare's Last Plays*, eds. Stephen Smith and Travis Curtright (Lexington Books, 2002) 1–16].

6. Virtue opposed to fortune: I.ii.178–84; cf. I.ii.154, 159; see Machiavelli, *Prince* VI.

7. Prospero refers to his studies in Milan as "the liberal arts" (I.ii.72–74)—a phrase that appears nowhere else in Shakespeare (cf. *Measure for Measure* I.iii.7–10;

Taming of the Shrew I.i.1–40, I.ii.70). Hereafter, Prospero speaks only of his "art" (singular, not plural): I.ii.1, 25, 28, 291, 373; II.i.298; IV.1.41, 120; V.i.50; Epilogue 14.

8. There is no mention in *The Tempest* of philosophy or philosophers; indeed, such references are rare in Shakespeare, and often used condescendingly. There is a tradition of reading Prospero as a philosopher/philosopher-king in the Socratic sense: Howard White, *Peace Among the Willows* (Martinus Nijhoff, 1968) 98–99; Howard White, *Copp'd Hills Towards Heaven: Shakespeare and the Classical Polity* (Martinus Nijhoff, 1970) 12, 19–20, 24, 113–33; Cantor 1980; Cantor 1981, 239–40, 242–43, 253–55; Harry Jaffa, "The Unity of Tragedy, Comedy, and History: An Interpretation of the Shakespearean Universe," in Alvis and West 1981, 277–304, 281–82; Barbara Tovey, "Shakespeare's Apology for Imitative Poetry: *The Tempest* and *The Republic*," *Interpretation* 11/3 (1983) 275–316; Barbara Tovey, "Wisdom and the Law: Thoughts on the Political Philosophy of *Measure for Measure*," in *Shakespeare's Political Pageant*, eds. Joseph Alulis and Vicki Sullivan (Rowman and Littlefield, 1996) 61–76; David Lowenthal, *Shakespeare and the Good Life* (Rowman and Littlefield, 1997) 21–70; Leon Craig, *Of Philosophers and Kings* (University of Toronto Press, 2001) 390n107; Nathan Schlueter, "Prospero's Second Sailing: Machiavelli, Shakespeare, and the Politics of *The Tempest*," in Smith and Curtright 2002, 178–95; but cf. Patrick Coby, "Politics and the Poetic Ideal in Shakespeare's *The Tempest*," *Political Theory* 11/2 (1983) 215–43; Peter Lawler, "Shakespeare's Realism in *The Tempest*," in Smith and Curtright 2002, 91–109. Prospero's attachment to the world and fear of death (I.ii.153–58), prior to acquiring his "art," seem un-philosophic. Philosophy as learning to die: Plato, *Phaedo* 64c–68b; *Apology* 28b–30b, 38d–39b, 40a–41d; Xenophon, *Apology of Socrates* 4–9.

9. On the insufficiency of Socrates' argument here, as well as the political problem posed by the philosopher's desire for a Good beyond politics and the subsequent tendency to neglect matters deemed intrinsically unworthy, see *Rep.* 519b–521b, 540a–b, 592a–b; Craig 2001, 242–43.

10. The revolution on the ship in the opening scene points to a re-founding of the political order on the basis of natural right: Cantor 1981, 241–42, 247. As conventional authority collapses under the pressure of natural necessity and self-interest during the tempest (I.i.14–26, 35–36), the true master of the ship (I.i.9–13) and the play becomes evident. See White 1970, 132.

11. In this way, *The Tempest* supplements the teaching about the proper order and hierarchy of the human soul in Plato's *Republic*. See White 1970, 120; John Alvis, *Shakespeare's Understanding of Honor* (Carolina Academic Press, 1990) 32.

12. One-third of the lines in the play belong to Prospero, four times the lines (and twice as many speeches) as belong to Caliban, his nearest challenger. Alonso the "King" has the fewest lines, as is fitting for a ruler shown to be completely at a loss (I.i.9–10, V.i.312–14).

13. Ariel is the efficient cause of the storm (I.ii.194), but "the tempest" belongs to Prospero, who alone refers to it as such (I.ii.194; V.i.6, 153; see I.ii.1–2, 175–77). See Jaffa 1981, 282n1.

14. There is reason to think that Prospero, for the sake of Miranda, has no choice but to imprison or enslave Caliban, if not kill him (I.ii.345–52). See White 1970, 88. But Caliban has not always been viewed as a threat (I.ii.345–68). Prospero's education of young Caliban, not unlike that of Miranda, may be seen as both a success and a failure (cf. V.i.181–84, with 261; cf. I.ii.409–20, with the central lines of the play: II.ii.114–16).

15. Two of three uses of the word "tyrant" in this play are by Caliban in describing Prospero's rule (II.ii.159, III.ii.40, cf. IV.i.257). The line separating just rule and tyranny is thin: See *Macbeth; Winter's Tale* II.iii.112–23; *Measure for Measure* I.iii.31–39, II.ii.91–111. Caliban's argument for his rule of the island by natural right: I.ii.332–45, III.ii.41–42, 50–51; cf. Hobbes, *Leviathan* II.19.

16. Ariel performs Prospero's commands "to th' syllable" and "article" (I.ii.195, 500–501; cf. I.ii.285–300). Given the ease with which Ariel accepts being mastered, it seems odd to speak of Ariel as "spiritedness" in the classical Greek sense of *thumos*; cf. Cantor 1981, 246.

17. The word "torment" is repeated three times by Prospero in describing Ariel's condition when embedded in matter. Caliban refers four times to the physical pains imposed on him by Prospero as "torment" or "torments" (II.ii.15, 55, 63, 70; see Cantor 1981, 244). Even Gonzalo senses that the island is a place of "torment" (V.i.104). These words appear more frequently in *The Tempest* than in any other play, but the word "torture" (which occurs elsewhere) is never used here.

18. On the subordination of the liberty of others to Prospero's justice, see Lawler 2002, 96–97.

19. Ariel: I.ii.270; Caliban: I.ii.309, 314, 320, 345, 352, 375. After these first seven uses, the word "slave" reappears only once: when Ferdinand describes his love for Miranda (III.1.66). Prospero calls Ariel "servant" twice, including the first time he commands Ariel to come (I.ii.187, IV.ii.33; cf. I.ii.271). The word reappears only once, when Miranda describes herself and her affection for Ferdinand (III.ii.85). See note 26.

20. Xenophon, *Mem.* IV.6.12–13; Aristotle, *Pol.* I.3–7, esp. I.4 (1253b23–1254a7).

21. Prospero's reason stands against passion's storms—no soul but his is "so firm, so constant" as to seem immune to winds that buffet the mind. But the conquest of his passions may prepare the way for a rational indignation that desires and demands perfect justice.

22. See Aristotle, *Pol.* I.5 (1254a28–b1).

23. To declare Caliban less than human, or utterly incorrigible, would be to deny that he is capable of being educated at all, seemingly justifying his treatment as a natural slave. But slavery is not a natural condition for Caliban, who is human and "first was mine own king"—he wants to be free and knows that he is not (I.ii.332–33, 342–43). Ariel, on the other hand, is explicitly said to be other than human (V.i.19). See Tovey 1983, 296; cf. Cantor 1981, 246–47. If it is justice to treat Caliban as a slave, then Prospero would be justified also in treating harshly (by denial of liberty

and perpetual servitude) all those who prove unrepentant or irrational. The same argument thus would justify the philosopher's absolute rule over non-philosophers as a natural master over natural slaves.

24. Juno presides over the masque to "bless this twain" with prosperity and honor in their issue. Prospero is here the power staging Juno's appearance; cf. Juno's role in Virgil, *Aeneid* I and IV.

25. Some editors change "wise" to "wife" although the First Folio prints the former: Vaughan and Vaughan 2005, 136–38.

26. Ferdinand and Miranda fall in love at first sight: I.ii.409–31, 441–48, 451–53. Ferdinand confesses he is a "slave" to (his love for) Miranda; she requites his love with her own confession to be his "servant." Both speak of their "bondage" as pleasant: I.ii.484–95; III.i.1–15, 63–67, 83–90. In this respect, they are not unlike Caliban, Trinculo, Stephano, Antonio, and Sebastian, all of whom are in some sense slaves to their desires. See note 32.

27. On the poetic representation of a cosmic order that supports justice through a system of reward and punishment, see Plato, *Republic* X; Allan Bloom, *The Republic of Plato* (Basic Books, 1968) 434–36; Craig 2001, 243–48, 385n84; Lawler 2002, 97–99.

28. Cantor (1980, 65–67; 1981, 243–44) argues that Prospero only pretends to be angry here. But while he does seem to feign anger at other times (I.ii.441–67), this is not one of those occasions. The scene only works if he is angry, and if his anger is directed at himself: Alvis 1990, 256–257. Having a soul immune to anger or indignation might even be considered a flaw that renders one unfit for political rule: Tovey 1996, 63; Craig 2001, 384n78.

29. See Cantor 1981, 254–55.

30. White 1970, 19–20. See Bloom 1968, 355: "Anger . . . is closely allied with the sense of justice and injustice. Unfortunately, it is unreasoning . . . Spiritedness is the only element in the city or man which by its very nature is hostile to philosophy." *The Tempest* has affinities with many of Shakespeare's tragedies: Cantor 1981, 240.

31. Prospero refers to Caliban as a "beast" only once, here when angered by his recollection of the conspiracy (IV.i.139–141). Trinculo, on discovering Caliban, asks if "this monster" and "strange beast" is a man; he eventually decides that he is one, though not one blessed by fortune (II.ii.24–39). Trinculo and Stephano refer to Caliban often as "servant–monster" (three times) and "monster" (thirty-nine times)—by far the most usages of this word in any of Shakespeare's plays. But their opinion of Caliban as less than human can hardly be accepted as authoritative.

32. Caliban, Trinculo, and Stephano all appear naturally slavish, with irrational, insatiable desires for sex, sack, and silk; their subjection of reason to the pursuit of material pleasures renders them incapable of that self-control necessary for ruling or governing themselves.

33. The words "roar" (I.ii.1–2, I.ii.371, II.i.316, IV.i.261) and "roaring" (I.ii.204, IV.i.193, V.i.44, V.i.233) appear more often in *The Tempest* than any other play, often

comparing the lamentable cries of a character to natural tumults (I.i.16–17, I.ii.149; see I.ii.286–90, 294–96).

34. Lawler 2002, 95–96: "Prospero's rule . . . is the dream of the tyrant." See Plato, *Rep.* 576a–b. Justice and the political art: Plato, *Gorgias* 464b–c, 480a–481b, 500b–501c, 504c–e, 521d; Aristotle, *Nicomachean Ethics* V.6 (1134a25–b18). Prospero's rule may be rational, but it is hard to see how it can be called political: cf. White 1968, 98–99; White 1970, 47.

35. Prospero can undo the damage of his first "charm" (V.i.17, 64) by means of another (V.i.54), which distinguishes his art from that of Sycorax (see I.ii.263–81, 289–93; cf. I.ii.341–42, with I.ii.373–75). Charms are mentioned more frequently in this play than any other.

36. Prospero's misanthropy: Lawler 2002, 95.

37. See Plato, *Rep.* 473c–d, 499b–c; White 1968, 98; White 1970, 48.

38. See Mary Ann McGrail, *Tyranny in Shakespeare* (Lexington Books, 2001) 117–63.

39. See Aristotle, *Poetics* 1454b6, 1460a12.

40. White 1970, 11.

41. White 1970, 60.

42. Descartes, *The Passions of the Soul* (Part II, Article LXXVI), quoted in the "Introduction" to Aristotle, *Poetics*, tr. Joe Sachs (Focus Publishing, 2006) 16, see 13–17. Wonder as the beginning of philosophy: Plato, *Theaetetus* 155c.

43. With the advent of modern natural science, the art of navigating by the stars ceased (cf. Plato, *Rep.* 488a–89d), and the allegorical use of travel by sea as an image of philosophy took on new meaning: Keyt 2006, 192–93; White 1968, 93–99; White 1970, 102–3. See Machiavelli, *Prince* XXV.

44. White 1970, 11.

45. Shared half-lines reflect "a dialectical intimacy" between characters defined by "being bound together in a common action": Scott Crider, *With What Persuasion: An Essay on Shakespeare and the Ethics of Rhetoric* (Peter Lang Publishing, 2009) 131n. Such lines comprise one-fifth of the play (Vaughan and Vaughan 2005, 22), hastening the pace of the dialogue and the action.

46. White 1968, 101: "The world of the *Tempest* is severe, with the very severity that comes when the heart is dominated by the mind. It must give way to greater compassion, and lesser justice."

47. Prospero hints that he will provide an account of all that has transpired on the island, but we do not expect that he will reveal all he knows, which would tempt others to acquire his art.

48. See *Measure for Measure* IV.ii.77–83; cf. White 1970, 48: "man becomes a despot by chance; he becomes a tyrant by nature." Kinship of philosopher and tyrant: Bloom 1968, 422–24.

49. Prospero's return to and rule over the "cave" of politics is not a matter of compulsion, unlike that of the philosopher-king. It is a second sailing of sorts, for without the use of his "potent art," he must acquire prudence and the arts appropriate

to politics. See Abraham Lincoln, fragment on slavery and democracy (1858?): "As I would not be a *slave*, so I would not be a *master*."

50. See Alvis 1990, 260–61.

51. With gratitude, I thank those who have read and commented on this chapter: Ashley Adams, George Anastaplo, Paul Cantor, Tobin Craig, Scott Crider, B. J. Dobski, Lawrence Greene, David Lowenthal, Mary Ann McGrail, Bill Morse, and Laurence Nee. The flaws that still remain I acknowledge mine.

11

~

A Motley to the View

Staging Tragic Honor

Glenn Arbery

I

Shakespeare's depictions of theater, amateur and professional, from *Love's Labors Lost* and *A Midsummer Night's Dream* through *Hamlet* and *The Tempest*, have been understood for centuries in terms of the *theatrum mundi*. The common Renaissance metaphor—"All the world's a stage"[1]—underlies not only the work of worldly playwrights, but even the thought of John Calvin.[2] Imagining the world as a great theater allows one to think of the "exits and entrances" of historical personages, the many parts played by each individual, and the passing show of appearances. Shakespeare uses the idea of the stage everywhere: disguises, plays within plays, lying performances such as Richard III's affectation of reluctance to take the crown, and various near-theatrical manipulations of appearance (such as those by Iago and Edmund).[3] But even apart from these are other glancing references to playing that seem to be more telling clues to Shakespeare's self-understanding.[4] They hint that this way lies Shakespeare himself: here he reflects on his practice; here he must be showing something of what he really thinks about staking his livelihood and reputation on a profession long considered dishonorable. For example, Sonnet 110 begins,

> Alas, 'tis true, I have gone here and there
> And made myself a motley to the view,
> Gored mine own thoughts, sold cheap what is most dear,
> Made old offenses of affections new. (110.1–4)

A motley: a fool, a jester, someone who wears motley clothes made of various colors. Nietzsche thought that Shakespeare was full of self-contempt for being a poet at all, a "jigging fool," as Brutus calls a poet in Julius Caesar, and that "before the whole figure and virtue of Brutus, Shakespeare prostrated himself, feeling unworthy and remote."[5] These lines from Sonnet 110 have been taken as Shakespeare's lament that his world-historical mind has been reduced to displaying itself before an uncomprehending audience (and perhaps professors are naturally sympathetic to this perspective). The following sonnet (111) seems to underscore Shakespeare's distaste for the general ignorance, since the speaker complains that fortune "did not better for [his] life provide / Than public means which public manners breeds" (111.3–4). His nature is almost "subdued / To what it works in, like the dyer's hand" (111.7).

There is good reason from his other works for thinking that Shakespeare viewed his career in the theater with some distaste. "A Never Writer to an Ever Reader" introduces Troilus and Cressida with an appeal to the discerning reader rather than the public: "Eternal reader, you have here a new play, never staled with the stage, never clapper-clawed with the palms of the vulgar."[6] Is it Shakespeare's opinion that to stage a play is to "stale" it by submitting it to the opinions of those who lack judgment? As Allan Bloom says, Shakespeare is no democrat, and certainly the common people—those who make up much of his audience—rarely appear to good advantage in his plays, largely because their shortsightedness makes them vulnerable to manipulation by would-be tyrants. In fact, they prefer tyrants, as audiences (or actors like Bottom) do. In the uprising led by Jack Cade in the Second Part of King Henry VI, one of Shakespeare's earliest plays, his followers give him absolute sway of the kind that the conspirators fear in Julius Caesar: "Away!" Cade commands his mob. "Burn all the records of the realm. My mouth shall be the parliament of England" (2H6 IV.vii.13–14). One remembers Coriolanus' harsh judgment of the many in Shakespeare's last tragedy. If the people gain power, then "gentry, title, wisdom, / Cannot conclude but by the yea and no / Of general ignorance" (Cor. III.i.143–45).

But if the theater is the sphere where the vulgar rule, Shakespeare is like Coriolanus having to show his scars; he has to gore his thoughts because he needs popular approval to be able to exercise his excellence to the fullest extent. He is alive to the question of honor, because praise lies at the heart of theater, which needs its audience, and praise also lies at the heart of honor considered as an external good—in good regimes, praise for virtue. To honor Shakespeare means to praise his work, not for satisfying the vulgar appetite that prefers a Herod to a Cato, but for fostering prudence and nobility of character in actions sustained by superb poetry. But despite the appeal in

Troilus and Cressida to the "eternal reader," Shakespeare took no care to establish definitive texts of his plays. It is as though the wealthiest man in history had died intestate. What Ron Rosenbaum calls "the wars" over such matters as the texts of *King Lear* and *Hamlet* continue to rage four centuries after Shakespeare's death.[7] Moreover, the man himself, unlike Coriolanus, never appears as himself, except in the variety of his characters and his actions. During his time in London, of course, he would have presented himself in person as an actor. World fame of the kind now universally accorded Shakespeare would seem to be at odds with his ever consciously being "a motley to the view"—an actor hooted at by groundlings, a playwright whose gorgeous lines for Cleopatra might be mangled in the mouth of an adolescent boy. Yet playing, with its depiction of heroism and disgrace, its existence on the stage where character is always a poetic fiction, is the very element of the art for which Shakespeare is honored, even when one encounters him primarily in reading him.

Shakespeare never unambiguously appears as the man he is, and in this respect, he fits what John Keats wrote about the "poetical character" as opposed to the "egotistical sublime" found in Wordsworth. Such characters as Coriolanus and Brutus—or Falstaff, for that matter—exhibit the sublimity of self-reference that Keats opposes to the poetic. This character "is not itself—it has no self—it is everything and nothing—It has no character—it enjoys light and shade; it lives in gusto, be it foul or fair, high or low, rich or poor, mean or elevated—It has as much delight in conceiving an Iago as an Imogen. What shocks the virtuous philosopher," says Keats, "delights the chameleon Poet." Keats tells his friend Richard Woodhouse, "not one word I ever utter can be taken for granted as an opinion growing out of my identical nature—how can it, when I have no nature?"[8]

Does Shakespeare have no nature? Needless to say, it would be foolish to try to account for the greatest playwright through the self-estimate of a lyric poet who died at twenty-five. On the other hand, Keats makes it possible to think about the sheer magnitude of Shakespeare's accomplishment, not in terms of presenting the systematic exposition of himself or his philosophy— George Santayana is surely right to deny the presence of any philosophical or religious *system* in Shakespeare[9]—but in terms of presenting many different characters, in many different regimes and situations, each of whom thinks from within the densely associative verbal complexity of a life in the process of being lived. In other words, Shakespeare seems capable of putting himself aside and letting what is base or noble be what it is, its own nature, without ever seeming to impose his nature on it, except to give it speech. When Keats describes himself as always being "in for and filling some other body" instead of "coming home to himself," he is also trying to understand Shakespeare, who has the capacity to cast his soul into the distinctive worlds of Othello, Iago, Cassio, Montano, Desdemona, and Emilia at the same time, making each verbally distinct, without any one of them carrying Shakespeare's own point of view. How is it that he can become other characters across an astonishing range of human possibility, from Doll Tearsheet to Coriolanus, through hundreds of personae, and never himself be identified with one in particular?[10] Taken together, however, the discrete plays grow to something "of great constancy," as Hippolyta puts it. The phenomenon of "the Shakespearean"—the shadow of the immense Shakespearean nature—emerges by inference and so does a characteristic identification of tragic honor with playing a part. Tragic honor stems from the absolute identification of oneself with a single role, an identification that Shakespeare absolutely avoided. Shakespeare's use of the stage metaphor for honor—by no means exclusively Roman—nevertheless centers on Rome, and the dramatic Roman practice of falling on one's sword becomes a gauge of other understandings of honor because of the close connection between honor, suicide, and acting a part in public.

II

But what is the stage metaphor? Early in *Othello*, when Brabantio's men come to arrest the Moor, the implicit question is why Othello does not have his sword drawn when everybody else does. He answers with a metaphor that converts everything around him to the stage on which he acts: "Were it my cue to fight," he says, "I should have known it without a prompter" (I.ii.83–84). To call it a "stage metaphor" does not quite capture the playfulness at the boundaries of illusion that Shakespeare indulges. The lines comment on what is actually happening on the stage as the audience watches, and for a moment, the actor who plays Othello seems to be breaking out of his role to speak to the expectation of the other actors and to insist that he would know if this were a fight scene. He has not forgotten what to do, like a poor player. Rather, he feels his importance, and he expresses it with a metaphor of performing against the grain of expectation and so controlling the stage like a great actor surrounded by neophytes. He understands being honorable, in other words, as setting the terms of his own staging. As a character, this is a serious man who understands himself as honorable. Othello, the principal actor of Venetian warfare, is looked *to* and looked *at* by other men, and he controls how he stages himself. At the same time, to be concerned with staging at all involves a reliance on the opinions of others. Othello, like Cassius, Brutus, Antony, and even Cleopatra with her "infinite variety," ends up killing himself as the only way to control his final scene and keep from being made a motley to the view, a public fool, "The fixèd figure for the time of scorn / To point his slow and moving finger at" (IV.ii.54–55).

Shakespeare uses such stage metaphors in similar ways in most of his tragedies, usually in situations when the protagonist reflects about finding himself put dramatically before others as the focus of their common attention. "I love the people, / But do not like to stage me to their eyes," says Duke Vincentio in *Measure for Measure* (I.i.67–68). Most of Shakespeare's tragic heroes have a certain relish for staging themselves, but even those who do not like it nevertheless invoke the stage metaphor. When Macbeth faces defeat, for example, this man who has described life as "a poor player / That struts and frets his hour upon the stage" refuses the role of the suicide: "Why should I play the Roman fool, and die / On mine own sword? whiles I see lives, the gashes / Do better upon them" (V.viii.1–3). If he killed himself, he would be "playing" the Roman, since Romans killed themselves for honor. The phrase "Roman fool" is charged, because it suggests that the tyrant Macbeth is contemptuous of Roman honor, which he sees as a kind of acting.

What kind of Roman fool might Macbeth have in mind? Of all the Roman suicides in Shakespeare, I would suggest Brutus, who has a blind spot when it comes to self-staging. Brutus allows Cassius to seduce him for the conspiracy against Caesar, on the one hand, but on the other hand overrules his seducer—disastrously, as matters turn out—on every major decision. Casca first introduces the metaphor of the stage in *Julius Caesar* when he describes the reaction of the crowd to Caesar: "If the tagrag people did not clap him and hiss him, according as he pleased and displeased them, as they use to do the players in the theatre, I am no true man," Casca reports to Brutus and Cassius (I.ii.258–61). Allan Bloom contrasts the relatively honest people of Coriolanus' earlier Rome with the people in Caesar's time, "a lazy, brutal populace, a real urban proletariat. They are accustomed to dominating, and they are insolent; they have the habit of being flattered . . . They are accustomed to bread and circuses; they change heroes according to how much is done for them."[11] For Brutus and Cassius, but especially for Brutus, Caesar's concern for whether he pleases the people is inherently dishonorable because he ought to want the approval of the best men whose praise means something. Caesar plays to the people as though the most important matters of state were theater and he were one of the Roman actors. The "tagrag people" have been corrupted into a political *audience* capable of being manipulated by his theatrics, and Cassius does not form part of this audience. Caesar warns Antony when he sees Cassius,

> He reads much,
> He is a great observer, and he looks
> Quite through the deeds of men. He loves no plays,
> As thou dost, Antony; he hears no music . . . (I.ii.202–5)

Caesar does not single out Brutus, who hears music later in the play and who several times speaks of plays. On the morning of the assassination, Cassius tells the other conspirators, "show yourselves true Romans" (II.i.222) and Brutus adds his own admonition:

> Good gentlemen, look fresh and merrily.
> Let not our looks put on our purposes,
> But bear it as our Roman actors do,
> With untired spirits and formal constancy. (II.i.223–26)

The shift is a subtle one. For Cassius, what should *show* is the aspect that makes them "true Romans," whereas for Brutus what should show is a theatrical surface that hides their purposes behind their merry looks. Anne Barton comments that "Brutus actually bids the conspirators model themselves on the players . . . Reality is enjoined to draw its strength from illusion, reversing the usual order. The actors are no longer the frail, shadowy figures of *Love's Labors Lost* or *A Midsummer Night's Dream*; they are the creators and also the guardians of history." In her view, the reference is honorific, and it reflects "an attitude toward the Elizabethan theatre itself."[12] Yet Brutus uses this figure because he is aware, perhaps for the first time, of a violation of the Roman principle of *honestum* memorably articulated by Cicero—that men should be what they seem. Actors set the standard for "untired spirits and formal constancy," not because they possess these things in fact, but because they are capable of hiding their personal anxieties and deficiencies. As Lucius Crassus remarks in *De Oratore*, the Roman actor Roscius became a paradigm for other arts, including oratory: "anyone who excels in any particular art is called a Roscius in his own profession."[13] Perhaps true Romans *are* actors, especially when a deed for the common good requires dissimulation.

Brutus understands himself as a true Roman who upholds a code of honor going back to the founding of the Roman republic. He satisfies his desire for distinction in the way the noblest Romans have always done, by subordinating his personal pleasures and ambitions to the good of Rome, confident that Rome will reward him with the fame it gives to those who do great deeds on its behalf. The problem is that Rome itself is undergoing a fatal shift away from Roman honor, and it seems poised to restore the monarchy it had abandoned at its founding and to bestow a unique honor on Julius Caesar. As Cassius puts it,

> Why, man, he doth bestride the narrow world
> Like a Colossus, and we petty men
> Walk under his huge legs and peep about
> To find ourselves dishonourable graves. (I.ii.133–38)

His fame threatens to consume the fame of all others:

> When went there by an age, since the great flood,
> But it was famed with more than with one man?
> When could they say till now, that talk'd of Rome,
> That her wide walls encompass'd but one man? (I.ii.150–55)

Brutus' new position in Rome under the threat of Caesar's tyranny resembles the situation of an intellectual in one of the "people's democracies" that Czeslaw Milosz describes in *The Captive Mind*. He wants to act on behalf of Rome by killing Caesar, because if Caesar lives, he will consume for himself all Roman honor, but Brutus has to pretend to be a friend of Caesar, because the Roman people love him. In order to serve the single, pure Rome, he has to hide his intentions from Rome. "Officially, contradictions do not exist in the minds of the citizens in the people's democracies," writes Milosz. "Nobody dares to reveal them publicly. And yet the question of how to deal with them is posed in real life. More than others, the members of the intellectual elite are aware of this problem. They solve it by becoming actors."[14] To describe the nature of this acting, which "one does not perform on a theater stage but in the street, office, factory, meeting hall, or even the room one lives in,"[15] Milosz uses the term *Ketman* from a work on Persian religion. It describes the practice developed by Persian philosophers under Islam, who hid their real beliefs under the guise of perfect piety and obedience to the authorities: the one who is "in possession of truth must not expose his person, his relatives or his reputation to the blindness, the folly, the perversity of those whom it has pleased God to place and maintain in error."[16]

Unlike the followers of Avicenna who practiced *Ketman* in fear of the mullahs, Brutus risks himself and his family to kill Caesar, but he practices *Ketman* until Caesar lies dead. He believes that the true Rome already supports his decision to kill Caesar—and expects his dissimulation—as long as he acts his part well. He calculates every gesture, every speech, almost every thought, with respect to two audiences. One is the Roman populace de-scribed by Casca as resembling the crowd at a theater; the other is that noble audience, the true Rome, formed in his imagination by the messages that Cassius has other people throw in his window. Brutus makes it clear in his soliloquy before the arrival of the other conspirators that he has never known Caesar to act the part of the tyrant; he feels the disjunction between what he actually thinks and what he thinks the true Rome wants. He makes much of having to "fashion"—we might say "spin"—the conspirators' motives for the assassination. Their reasons for killing Caesar must satisfy the support-ers of the true Rome who have to remain hidden (and practice *Ketman*) in Caesar's Rome, but they must also appear as publicly comprehensible, even praiseworthy, to the Roman people whom Caesar flatters. When the others suggest killing Marc Antony at the same time they kill Caesar, Brutus objects in a way based less on high-minded principle than on his concern with how their deeds will seem to the common people, their audience:

> Our course will seem too bloody, Caius Cassius,
> To cut the head off and then hack the limbs,
> Like wrath in death and envy afterwards—
> For Antony is but a limb of Caesar.
> Let's be sacrificers, but not butchers, Caius. (II.i.162–66)

He emphasizes that the conspirators need to make their purpose look "neces-sary and not envious; / Which so appearing to the common eyes, / We shall be called purgers, not murderers" (II.i.178–80).

By the time of Julius Caesar, the stage has become the governing meta-phor for political life, and, ironically, this is particularly so for men of honor like Brutus who apparently reject the theatrics of Caesar. One might expect Brutus and Cassius to proclaim the end of politics as theater while they stand over Caesar, whom they have just murdered: the tyrant's show is over, no more playing to the "tagrag" people. On the contrary, Cassius, who "loves no plays," has a keen sense of being at the center of a moment that will forever afterward be imitated *on the stage*—as it is being acted at that very moment, in his own lines, in Shakespeare's play. When Brutus says that they should bathe their hands and arms in Caesar's blood, Cassius says,

> Stoop, then, and wash.
> [They smear their hands with Caesar's blood.]
>   How many ages hence
> Shall this our lofty scene be acted over,
> In states unborn and accents yet unknown! (III.1.112–14)

The caesura after "Stoop, then, and wash" hints that in stooping to dip his hands in Caesar's blood—a self-consciously theatrical gesture—Cassius discovers the dramatic essence of their deed. In the discovery he finds the moment itself penetrated by its own future imitation and repetition. Brutus shares the dizzying image of theatrical reduplication:

> How many times shall Caesar bleed in sport,
> That now on Pompey's basis lies along,
> No worthier than the dust! (III.i.115–17)

On the surface of it, this is one of those moments when Shakespeare seems to give himself an acknowledgement from the characters themselves. They recognize, as it were, their future presence in his play, and at the same time, in the context of the action, they find a way to focus the historic momentousness of what they are doing by having it remembered from the future, like Agincourt in Henry V's St. Crispin's Day speech.

But if they regard themselves in this crucial moment specifically in terms of a theatrical repetition, age after age, then what *is* the original scene? Who *are* the real Brutus and Cassius? Their deed presents itself to these republicans, not as the restoration of Roman liberty per se, but as something already *being acted*. They have already distanced themselves from the historical moment in order to imagine their depictions as heroes of liberty "in sport" in a staged play. The characters Brutus and Cassius momentarily dissolve into the actors who play them: what they say *is* being said, from the perspective of ancient Rome, "In states unborn and accents yet unknown." Literally, the Brutus and Cassius onstage are actors in roles written by William Shakespeare, roles that take on reality only *through* the actors. But to the extent that the performance succeeds, the personalities of the actors disappear into the characters of these ancient Romans who reflect upon being proleptically brought *back into existence* by *being acted*. What keeps this play of perspectives from being mere cleverness is what it says about the nature of honor as a role that consumes the person who takes it on. To be a noble Roman means to be an actor who subordinates himself to his role like a great actor, because his lasting fame will come from the true Rome. Roman honor turns Romans into actors who have already put their private selves to death for the sake of their reconstitution by posterity.

If Anne Barton is right, Shakespeare finds the honor of the actor and the playwright to lie in bringing Roman honor to England and making it live. She reads the stage metaphor in this scene as glorifying the Elizabethan theater:

[I]t represents neither a sly, Plautine joke with the audience nor an excuse for any artificiality in the action. It serves, preeminently, to glorify the stage. The actors, Shakespeare's own companions and friends, have become the chroniclers of man's great deeds. It is in the theater that the noble actions of the world are preserved for the instruction of future generations.[17]

But in the play itself, explicit reference to the stage makes the assassination of Caesar a performance before the audience of posterity. Brutus and Cassius imagine that they will "be called / The men that gave their country liberty" (III.1.118–19). Like Othello, they seem to themselves to set the terms of their own staging far into the future. But to understand the situation of Brutus, one need only imagine him as a Roscius who must appear before an audience entirely made up of those who cannot appreciate the subtleties of his accomplishment. He hates to flatter, yet he knows that he would have no profession without his audience. As a compromise, he does not condescend to them in his performance; he attempts to please them by revealing his excellence before them. They are both aware of his greatness and intimidated by his assertion of it. For their part, they love actors who appeal to them directly on a level that does not make them suspect their own inferiority. But they have seen their betters understand and appreciate this Roscius, and they know his reputation. The best they can do is to affirm his superiority by giving him honor, but without much heartfelt gratitude for his portrayals. They know that he really acts for a different audience, and when they honor him, they imitate those more discerning than they are, but they do so with a residue of resentment.

So it is with the people and Brutus. His speech about the assassination—an appeal to the people to participate in the honor of the true Rome for which he acts—seems rhetorical and stagy. Mark Antony, of course, is not an honorable man, and he demolishes Brutus' awkward, if high-minded attempt to stage himself before the people by supplanting it with his own masterful theatrics. Brutus loses the audience because the theatrics of honor seem increasingly chilly and inhuman next to the warmth and pathos of Antony's love of Caesar. The true Rome that Brutus imagines dissolves into the mob that seeks to kill him. By the end of the play, when Brutus decides to kill himself, the implicit metaphor again seems to be staging. Philosophically, he opposes suicide, as he tells Cassius. But when Cassius asks him whether, if they lose the battle, Brutus will be "contented to be led in triumph / Thorough the streets of Rome," Brutus instantly abandons his philosophical conviction and takes up his role: "No, Cassius, no: think not, thou noble Roman, / That ever Brutus will go bound to Rome; / He bears too great a mind" (V.ii.107–13).

Part of traditional Roman honor came from staging the shame of defeated enemies in triumphs, but never before Caesar's triumph for defeating the sons of Pompey had Rome turned its own citizens into its victims. Brutus' use of the third person in rejecting his submission to this practice is telling. In himself, as the person who says "I," he finds suicide "cowardly and vile," but as Brutus—this character he plays—he cannot submit to be put in circumstances that display his impotence to control the scene in a Rome that has ceased to be Rome. Rather than lose his power to control the terms under which he and Rome appear, Brutus kills Brutus to preserve the integrity of the role for a Rome that now exists only theatrically. Roman honor turns the "noblest Roman of them all" into an actor who must die to secure his role. The character puts to death the actor, as the private man he might be or might have been outside this determining context of reputation. But in dying, the actor immortalizes Brutus.

III

Antony and Cleopatra both kill themselves as well, and for reasons that resemble those of Brutus in at least one respect: the fear of being staged. Mark Antony obviously is not concerned with honor in the same way that Brutus is. In fact, at the beginning of Antony and Cleopatra, his fellow Romans lament the scandal of his complete abrogation of Roman honor. He gives himself over to Cleopatra as if the love between them could overcome any possible concern with reputation in the ordinary sense. Antony is not free from the sense of honor as self-staging, but with Cleopatra he is staging a different kind of play full of excess and eros, characterized by an insistence on overflowing the measure set by Rome. It is not until he leaves the battle and follows Cleopatra at Actium that he recovers a Roman conscience through the acute sense of shame. But loyalty to Brutus' "true Rome" is hardly the dominant strain. Rather, it is his consciousness of having failed before his men in a great theater of action. Having escaped and exceeded Rome after his own fashion, he refuses to be brought back under its terms; he kills himself as much to defy Rome as to meet its measure of honor.

When he thinks that Cleopatra is dead and that Octavius will soon come to capture him, Antony asks Eros, who is reluctant to kill him,

Wouldst thou be windowed in great Rome and see
Thy master thus with pleached arms, bending down
His corrigible neck, his face subdued
To penetrative shame, whilst the wheeled seat

Of fortunate Caesar, drawn before him, branded
His baseness that ensued? (IV.xiv.72–77)

Like Brutus, Antony cannot abide the idea of being led in triumph, any more than he could stand being crucified like a slave: it is better to kill himself than to submit to being shamed as part someone else's spectacle. With his theatrical sense, however, Antony makes the scene much more vivid—almost cinematic. Brutus simply imagines going "bound to Rome," which would shame the very nature of Roman liberty, but Antony imaginatively situates Eros as a spectator safely "windowed in great Rome" like the nobler (or wealthier) part of the audience looking down on the stage, not the groundlings looking up. Displacing himself to this point of view, Antony sees himself in the third person, but in a way far removed from Brutus' self-respecting use of his own name. He pictures for Eros "His corrigible neck, his face subdued / To penetrative shame." The bent, "corrigible neck" might be becoming in a schoolboy, but for a man of Antony's accomplishment and age, it is an unbearable image. As Aristotle writes in Book IV of the *Ethics*, "we think it is necessary for [the young] to have a sense of shame because, since they live by feeling, they err in many ways but are held back by shame. And we praise those among the young who display shame, but no one would praise an older person for being filled with shame, since we think he ought not to do anything to which shame applies."[18] Much more keenly than Brutus, Antony dreads being displayed behind the "boy" Octavius in his "wheeled seat," and the audience he dreads is the one Brutus would have welcomed: men of honor who exercise temperance and prudence in addition to courage, men who do not continue to live by feeling into middle age. So vivid is this picture of great Antony being brought back within the Roman measure that Eros kills himself rather than his master, and Antony must take the job upon himself, though his botched attempt allows him to extend his theatrics.

After Antony's death, when Cleopatra imagines being led in triumph back to Rome, she has a different perspective from Antony's. He dreads the judgment of noble Romans out of a sense of self-condemnation, whereas Cleopatra exhibits not the slightest remorse or self-doubt about her deeds or her worth. What concerns her, as she tells Iras, is that they will be displayed to the common people—the groundlings, as it were:

Thou, an Egyptian puppet, shalt be shown
In Rome, as well as I. Mechanic slaves
With greasy aprons, rules, and hammers, shall
Uplift us to the view; in their thick breaths,

Rank of gross diet, shall we be enclouded,
And forced to drink their vapor. (V.ii.209–14)

"Uplift us to the view" recalls the language of Sonnet 110—"a motley to the view"—with the additional sense here of being raised above the common level and exhibited for mockery. Worse still in her imagination is the presence of actual theater in Rome:

. . . the quick comedians
Extemporally will stage us, and present
Our Alexandrian revels; Antony
Shall be brought drunken forth, and I shall see
Some squeaking Cleopatra boy my greatness
I' th' posture of a whore. (V.ii.217–22)

As with Othello and Cassius, but with a more pointed sense of irony, Cleopatra calls attention to the performance going on at the moment she speaks. She objects in advance to the fact that some *boy* plays her on Shakespeare's stage; in fact, the scene loses some of its pungency when a real woman says these lines, since the difference between what the boy actor is and what he *plays* is so extreme that only the poetry can make the character believable. Enobarbus says of Cleopatra earlier in the play, "Age cannot wither her, nor custom stale / Her infinite variety" (II.ii.245–46). The lines could describe Shakespeare's imagination. The worst threat to Cleopatra is to have her protean being reduced to a stale trope by some "squeaking" caricature. It is as though Shakespeare were forced to watch himself depicted as a Warwickshire bumpkin, an upstart from Stratford, a Dogberry savant—if such things even concerned him. To avoid this humiliation, which has less to do with shame than with disgust at the impotence of the audience's imagination, Cleopatra will kill herself in her own way, striking a last Egyptian pose before the mirror of Roman honor and the judgment of posterity: not the suicide of *eros*, but death as powerfully erotic—a swoon, a pun on orgasm, asp in hand.

IV

It is difficult to read Cleopatra's death and feel Shakespeare's moral condemnation, and it is impossible to find in the calculating but untheatrical Octavius broader or deeper nobility than Antony shows. In a sense, the great lovers seem to bring to an end the play metaphor of Roman honor, but Shakespeare returns to the theme in *Coriolanus* by going back to the early Republic and intensifying the question of the great man's relation to the vulgar. Even more than Brutus, Coriolanus seems to be at the furthest remove from identifying himself as an actor. He abhors the idea of staging himself to the people. Indeed, his reluctance to show his wounds to them in order to get their "voices" for his consulship stems from what he sees as ignoble dissimulation. When Menenius tells him that he should fit himself to the custom, he responds, "It is a part / That I shall blush in acting, and might well / Be taken from the people" (II.ii.142–44). He reasons that he is not simply being asked to demonstrate his service to Rome by letting them see what bodily price he has paid for the city; rather, he is being asked to act *a part* that belongs to them, a role that they insist all Roman leaders play. Anne Barton writes, "Gone completely are those noble actors of Rome upon whose style Brutus had once advised the conspirators to model themselves."[19] Oddly, Barton seems to ignore the fact that, in the early Roman Republic of Coriolanus, Rome had no stage of the kind it later inherited from Greece. Her thesis is that, over the course of his career, Shakespeare gradually becomes disillusioned with the powers of the stage, but it seems more fruitful to try to understand what Shakespeare understands honor to mean in a Rome without plays.

Coriolanus seems to embody Roman *honestum*. He wonders why even his mother insists that he humble himself to get the voices of the people: "would you have me / False to my nature? Rather say I play / The man I am" (III. ii.15–16). He tells Menenius that they have given him a part which he will never "discharge to th' life" (III.ii.106). When he imagines himself doing what Caesar and even Brutus (however awkwardly) do later in the history of Rome—play to the people—he satirizes it bitterly:

> Well, I must do't:
> Away, my disposition, and possess me
> Some harlot's spirit! My throat of war be turned,
> Which quired with my drum, into a pipe
> Small as an eunuch, or the virgin voice
> That babies lulls asleep! The smiles of knaves
> Tent in my cheeks, and schoolboys' tears take up
> The glasses of my sight! A beggar's tongue
> Make motion through my lips, and my armed knees,
> Who bowed but in my stirrup, bend like his
> That hath received an alms! (III.ii.110–20)

Then, unlike Cassius stooping to wash his hands in blood and discovering himself onstage, Coriolanus suddenly reverses himself when the caesura falls at the imagined (and perhaps mimed) bending of his knees:

> I will not do't,
> Lest I surcease to honor mine own truth
> And by my body's action teach my mind
> A most inherent baseness. (III.ii.110–23)

The idea of appearing to be anything less than he is strikes him as corrupting. The metaphor of playing or imitation presses forward insistently only to be condemned, as though Coriolanus had been reading Book III of the *Republic*;[20] but no Roman theater exists—as it obviously does in the Rome of Brutus and Antony—that might instruct Coriolanus in the subtleties of seeming and being. But why should he need instruction in dissimulation, since he already seems to have the insight of Rousseau in his *Letter to D'Alembert?* Rousseau writes that if the playwright neglected to flatter the passions of the people, "the Spectators would soon be repelled and would not want to see themselves in a light which made them despise themselves."[21] Coriolanus presents the people to themselves in just such a light. For Coriolanus, integrity consists of an absolute rejection of politics as show, except for one small and possibly fatal concession: he wants others to say that he *plays the man he is.* If he has to play someone, in other words, he wants to play the character of Coriolanus. But *playing* himself introduces a note of calculation about how he appears to others, like Brutus saying "Fashion it thus" about how to present the assassination of Caesar to the people, and this concern exposes what is in fact uppermost for Coriolanus: how he looks in the mirror of honor.

After he "banishes" Rome, disguises himself (in an apparent contradiction), and goes over to the Volscians, he becomes increasingly self-conscious about playing a role. When Valeria, Volumnia, and Virgilia approach to plead with him to spare Rome, the impossibility of simply playing "the man I am" becomes overwhelming. As in *Othello*, Shakespeare turns Coriolanus' disquietude into a moment of anxiety in the play as a play. Confronted by these women and his son, Coriolanus first says that he will "never / Be such a gosling to obey instinct," as though his emotions had already been scripted by nature. Rather he will "stand, / As if a man were author of himself / And knew no other kin" (V.iii.35–37). His language gives him away. Instead of asserting absolutely, as Caesar does, "the cause is in my will," the best he can do is the "as if" of self-authorship: he can stand as an actor stands, but he feels keenly the disjunction between his part and his "instinct" of pity. His very appearance becomes a kind of costume. He is never more an actor than when he claims the greatest autonomy.

When Coriolanus first appeared before the people, the tribune Brutus criticized him by telling Sicinius, "With a proud heart he wore his humble weeds" (II.iii.153). His outer appearance, in other words, was at odds with his obvious pride. Now Coriolanus tells Virgilia: "These eyes are not the same I wore in Rome" (V.iii.38). He means that he does not see his mother and his wife as he saw them in Rome; they should therefore see him in a different guise as well, almost as a different character. Virgilia responds that if he does not see them as the same women, the cause is the "sorrow that delivers [them] thus changed" (V.iii.39)—a sorrow that he himself has caused. She completely rejects the idea that he has become someone else, and he has no immediate answer.

Far from it. Instead, the text suggests, there comes the kind of dead silence that disquiets an audience and that a reader might miss entirely if he is not imagining the play on stage. For a moment, the player seems to have forgotten his lines. His dreadful lapse threatens the whole theatrical illusion, especially if the actor prolongs his silence a beat or two past conventional pacing. The audience's identification wavers for a moment between the character and the actor who plays him. Then Coriolanus breaks out of it: "Like a dull actor now, / I have forgot my part, and I am out, / Even to a full disgrace" (V.iii.40–42). The momentary break in the illusion onstage, which *must* be there for the lines to have their full effect, draws the audience into the simile of Coriolanus as an actor, whose full disgrace would lie in forgetting his part. The momentary illusion of a break onstage, when in fact there has been no such break, underscores what might be called the theatricality of honor, to the extent that honor always requires the sustaining expectation of an audience. Within the play itself, he has at least two audiences: the women and the Volscians. Unlike Brutus, he can no longer play to the true Rome, since he has claimed to *be* the true Rome. Yet to concede to the private pleas of his mother disgraces him before Aufidius, who later describes Coriolanus to the Volscian senate as a "boy of tears." At the end, he is trapped in a part he could never have conceived, the traitor to two cities at once, dependent upon an audience whose very inferiority to himself defines him in his own mind. He would never have been hemmed in and put to death in Corioles if he had had the slightest irony about himself in Rome. Refusing to be staged and made "a motley to the view" in Rome, incapable of staging himself, he works himself out of any part at all. Yet he remains magnificent.

V

If Shakespeare repeatedly and consistently presents tragic honor in terms of control over self-staging, several things seem to follow. The first is a practical matter having to do with reading Shakespeare. The very texture of his language, especially in the metaphors of the men most concerned with honor, repeatedly demands that these plays not be read as though their natural habitat were the printed page. The speeches of his characters always point to their performance, unlike, for example, the speeches in Thucydides that can be imagined back into a historical context without the intervening artifice of the stage. This consideration might not alter the content of the thought in the speeches, but it subtly changes what honor looks like. One does not, for example, think of Brutus or Coriolanus first of all in terms of their theatricality, but they themselves are haunted, if not dominated, by the metaphor of playing. Why? Because they, least of all, can accommodate themselves to the necessity of appealing to those beneath them, and they become obsessed with how they seem. They most resemble actors. Shakespeare's repeated insistence on this point also suggests that theater is most dangerous wherever high honor plays the foremost role in politics. The stage exposes the honorable man as a role by showing exactly how it can be acted. Antony's calculated, theatrically canny, extemporaneous play over the body of Caesar easily destroys Brutus and the old idea of Roman honor with him.

An even greater danger might come from the satirical "quick comedians" that Cleopatra fears—those who mock what is high for the benefit of common laughter. But as John Alvis has shown, the greatest danger to Roman honor comes, not from the stage per se, but from the two men who acted most consciously, one might argue, with the *theatrum mundi* in mind: Caesar and Christ. "As Caesar monopolized honor to the destruction of the Republic," writes Alvis, "much more decisively will the Church direct all praise unto Christ, thereby severely attenuating, if not extinguishing, the spirit of republicanism."[22] The theatricality of Caesar's assassination, staged—they think—by Brutus and Cassius, recoils on the perpetrators, since they cannot conceive how thoroughly Caesar had already appropriated the role of sacrificial victim they thought they were imposing. Because Caesar stages his own death, Antony can then interpret it, not as the restoration of republican liberty, but as an appeal to loyalty through the power of pathos and the claim of universal largesse. With Christ, theologically understood (especially from the Gospel of John), the playwright of the *theatrum mundi* appears among men in the Incarnation yet goes unrecognized in the world. Christ submits to the crucifixion of *thumos* in the shame of Roman staging and becomes "a motley to the view," a "fixèd figure for the time of scorn." He undergoes the full shame that Antony dreads and the mockery that Cleopatra fears. The scene can be understood as a self-staging in which Roman suicide for the sake of honor undergoes a transfiguration into the very different valence of martyrdom. As Alvis puts it, "Christ fulfills Caesar and establishes a universal church which promises to satisfy popular demands for a communal but non-political mode of life."[23]

The question is whether the protean Shakespeare, ranging among so many regimes and ways of being, ultimately prefers republican Rome to all other regimes—Brutus to Edgar, as it were, or Virgilia to Miranda. The art of playing seems to lie at the root of his universal imagination, a tireless act of attention to what Perdita in *The Winter's Tale* calls "great creating nature." Politics occupies him, not exclusively but certainly with unparalleled depth, as the art most like his own—most in need of a wise master of the stage.

Notes

1. All citations in the text are from *The Complete Pelican Shakespeare*, eds. Stephen Orgel and A. R. Braunmuller (Penguin, 2002).

2. Calvin understands "the heavens and the earth," in John T. McNeill's words, "as a theater (*theatrum*) in which we may behold the Creator's glory," John Calvin, *Institutes of the Christian Religion*, ed. John T. McNeill, tr. Ford Lewis Battles (Westminster Press, 1960), Vol. I: 61n27. In his commentary on Psalm 107, Calvin (1960, 61) specifically mentions such deeds as freeing prisoners, making barren ground fertile, and casting down the proud as acts of God visible to the elect, whereas "most people, immersed in their own errors, are struck blind in such a dazzling theater." The privilege to see the works of God rightly in this theater "is a matter of rare and singular wisdom, in viewing which they who otherwise seem to be extremely acute profit nothing."

3. Anne Righter Barton first called critical attention to the extent of Shakespeare's use of the "play metaphor" already ubiquitous in Renaissance Europe. Her book *Shakespeare and the Idea of the Stage* (Penguin Books, 1967) brilliantly traces the nature of stage interaction with the audience from its early form in the mystery plays to its use in Shakespeare and reveals a good deal about the extent of Shakespeare's attachment to or hope for the stage at various points during his career.

4. As James Calderwood puts it, "most men's professional concerns get smuggled into other areas of their lives by metaphoric conveyances. . . . It is hardly surprising that a playwright like Shakespeare would project his concerns about drama not only into life but even into the fictional life of his plays, where the world might become a stage, history a plot, kings dramatists, courtiers actors, commoners audiences, and speech itself the dialogue or script that gives breath to all the rest." See his *Metadrama and Shakespeare's Henriad: Richard II to Henry V* (University of California Press, 1979) 5.

5. Nietzsche, *The Gay Science*, tr. Walter Kaufmann (Vintage Books, 1974) 151.

6. Orgel and Braunmuller 2002, 482.

7. Ron Rosenbaum, *The Shakespeare Wars: Clashing Scholars, Public Fiascoes, Palace Coups* (Random House, 2008) 29–154.

8. John Keats, *Selected Letters*, eds. Robert Gittings and Jon Mee (Oxford University Press, 2009) 148–49.

9. George Santayana, "The Absence of Religion in Shakespeare," in *Interpretations of Poetry and Religion* (Charles Scribner's Sons, 1927) 147–65, 163.

10. It is dangerous to speak as confidently as Michael Gillespie does, for example, where he says that Hobbes shared "Shakespeare's conviction that a single man's passions cannot be that great a danger to the state." See his *The Theological Origins of Modernity* (University of Chicago Press, 2009) 243. In a footnote he cites Macduff's speech to Malcolm about the vices allowable in a sovereign (348n115), but one could multiply the counter-instances in plays from *Richard II* to *King Lear*.

11. Allan Bloom, "The Morality of the Pagan Hero," in his *Shakespeare's Politics* (Basic Books, 1964; University of Chicago Press, 1986) 81–82.

12. Barton 1967, 141.

13. Marcus Tullius Cicero, "On the Character of the Orator," in *The Basic Works of Cicero*, ed. Moses Hadas, tr. E. Moor (The Modern Library, 1951) 211.

14. Czeslaw Milosz, *The Captive Mind*, tr. Jane Zielonko (Vintage Books, 1981) 54.

15. Milosz 1981, 54.

16. Milosz 1981, 57.

17. Barton 1967, 141.

18. Aristotle, *Nicomachean Ethics*, tr. Joe Sachs (Focus Publishing, 2002) 78 (1128b).

19. Barton 1967, 170.

20. Barton notes that Coriolanus' attitude is "very much like the one Plato held in *The Republic*, banishing the actors from the state because men should not 'depict or be skillful at imitating any kind of illiberality or baseness, lest from imitation they should come to be what they imitate'" (1967, 170).

21. J. J. Rousseau *Citizen of Geneva to Monsieur d'Alembert.* in *Collected Writings of Rousseau: 10, Letter to D' Alembert and Writings for the Theater*, eds. Allan Bloom, Charles Butterworth, and Christopher Kelly, tr. Allan Bloom (University Press of New England, 2004), Vol. X: 263.

22. John Alvis, *Shakespeare's Understanding of Honor* (Carolina Academic Press, 1990) 163.

23. Alvis 1990, 162.

~

Epilogue

12

~

The Phoenix and Turtle and the Mysteries of Love

Who Wants What, Why, and To What Effect?

George Anastaplo

I

A distinguished student of William Shakespeare introduces our poem in this way:

> "The Phoenix and Turtle" first appeared in a collection of poems called *Love's Martyr: Or, Rosalins Complaint* by Robert Chester (1601). This quarto volume offered various poetic exercises about the phoenix and the turtle "by the best and chieftest of our modern writers." The poem assigned to Shakespeare has been universally accepted as his and is one of his most remarkable productions.[1]

It is suggested in what follows how remarkable this production is:

> With a deceptively simple diction, in gracefully pure tetrameter quatrains and triplets, the poem effortlessly evokes the transcendental ideal of a love existing eternally beyond death. The occasion is an assembly of birds to observe the funeral rites of the phoenix (always found alone) and the turtledove (always found in pairs). The phoenix, legendary bird of resurrection from its own ashes, once more finds life through death in the company of the turtledove, emblem of pure constancy in affection. Their spiritual union becomes a mystical oneness in whose presence Reason stands virtually speechless. Baffled human discourse must resort to paradox in order to explain how two beings become one essence, "Hearts remote yet not asunder." Mathematics and logic are "confounded" by this joining of two spirits into a "concordant one."

This introduction to the poem concludes with suggestions about its theological content and literary context:

> This paradox of oneness echoes scholastic theology and its expounding of the doctrine of the Trinity, in terms of persons, substance, accident, triunity, and the like, although, somewhat in the manner of John Donne's poetry, this allusion is more a part of the poem's serious wit than its symbolic meaning. The poignant brevity of this vision is rendered all the more mysterious by our not knowing what, if any, human tragedy may have prompted this metaphysical affirmation.

This poem has been identified here as made of "gracefully pure tetrameter quatrains and triplets." There are thirteen quatrains. These are followed by the five triplets identified as "Threnos" which Professor David Bevington explains as "lamentation, funeral song" (from the ancient Greek, *threnos*).[2]

The account of the traditional Phoenix in a standard reference work can make us wonder whether *it* could have ever properly been considered a "dead" bird (67):

> *Phoenix*—a fabulous bird connected with the worship of the sun especially in ancient Egypt and in classical antiquity. It was known to Hesiod, and descriptions of its appearance and behaviour occur in ancient literature sporadically, with variations in detail, from Herodotus' account of Egypt onward. The phoenix is said to be as large as an eagle, with brilliant scarlet and gold plumage and a melodious cry. Only one phoenix exists at any time. It is very long-lived; no ancient authority gives it a life span of less than 500 years; some say it lives for 1,461 years (an Egyptian Sothic Period); an extreme estimate is 97,000. As its end approaches the phoenix fashions a nest of aromatic boughs and spices, sets it on fire, and is consumed in the flames. From this pyre miraculously springs a new phoenix which, after embalming its [predecessor's] ashes in an egg of myrrh, flies with them [that is, the ashes] to Heliopolis in Egypt where it deposits them on the altar in the Temple of the Sun.[3]

This account continues with these recollections of the Phoenix legend: "Clearly the country of the phoenix, its miraculous rebirth, its connection with fire, and other features of its story are symbolical of the sun itself, with its promise of dawn after sunset, and of new life after death." This account concludes with what has been done with the Phoenix in the West:

> [T]he Egyptians associated the phoenix with intimations of immortality, and this symbolism had a widespread appeal in late antiquity. The Latin poet Martial compared the phoenix to undying Rome, and it appears on the

coinage of the Roman Empire as a symbol of the Eternal City. It is also widely interpreted as an allegory of resurrection and life after death. These were ideas which appealed to emergent Christianity; Church Fathers...used the phoenix as an illustration of Christian doctrine concerning the raising of the dead and eternal life.

II

The career of the Turtledove across millennia is far less spectacular than that of the Phoenix. But it, unlike the Phoenix, *is* sanctified by its appearance in the Bible. Thus, the "Turtle and Turtledove" entry in one dictionary of biblical terms opens with this description:

> A species of pigeon. It is gentle and harmless, fit emblem of a defenseless and innocent people (*Psalms* 74:19). It is migratory (*Jeremiah* 8:7), and a herald of spring (*Song of Solomon* 2:12).[4]

But however "gentle and harmless" the turtledove may be, it could evidently be dealt with mercilessly. The entry continues thus: "Abraham sacrificed a turtledove and other victims when the Lord's covenant was made with him (*Genesis* 15:9)." Perhaps this sacrifice anticipated what was attempted later by Abraham with the somewhat hapless ("gentle and harmless"?) Isaac. "Under the law," we are further told, the turtledove

> served as a burnt offering (*Leviticus* 1:14) and for a sin offering; and two turtledoves were prescribed for these two sacrifices in case a poor person was obliged to make a guilt offering, and for the purification of a woman after childbirth if she was poor, of a man or woman with an issue, and of a Nazirite (*Leviticus* 5:7, 11; 12:6, 8; 14:22, 30; 15:14, 29, 30; *Numbers* 6:10, 11). [The turtledove] was readily obtainable by the poor, for it abounds in Palestine and is easily trapped.

These, then, are the kinds of things long said about the Phoenix and the Turtledove and evidently were routinely available to Shakespeare and his contemporaries. How, then, might our most celebrated poem by Shakespeare about "these dead birds" (67) be understood?

III

Learned scholars seem to believe that Shakespeare considered his poetry more enduring, if not also more significant, than his plays. Efforts were evidently made by him to assure that his poems would be circulated among the more influential (as well as the more learned) readers of his day. His plays, on the other hand, seem to have been collected in print only by others.

Speculation abounds as to what personalities, and perhaps what events, are alluded to, if not even commented on, in *The Phoenix and Turtle*. But Shakespeare should have known that this poem might be read someday by thoughtful men and women who either would not know or would not much care about the "personalities" or events originally drawn on for its composition. How then would the poem have been intended by Shakespeare to be understood by such readers, especially by the more astute among them?

Indeed, it could be that the meaning available to a reader *without* knowledge of particular (or historical—that is, accidental?) allusions may even be superior. The "insider's" knowledge of particulars may interfere with the development of a sustained understanding of what the poet most wanted to say. This may be especially so if the "informed" reader recalls inconvenient facts about any of the historical personages alluded to, facts which may get in the way of grasping the enduring meaning of the terms used and the kind of event depicted.

IV

The reader can be expected, however, to know something of the more dramatic qualities traditionally associated with the Phoenix. Is there something divine in its reputed characteristics, especially its routines of self-destruction and immediate rebirth (or resurrection)? What do its unique attributes—that is, attributes *not* shared with the Turtledove or with "anyone" else—do to how thorough and enduring the love celebrated in the poem can truly be?

It might even be wondered what is being suggested by Shakespeare in this poem about the relation between the divine and the human that is at the heart of Christianity? A critical problem here may be illuminated by recalling Aristotle's suggestions (in the *Nicomachean Ethics*) about the relation of honor (or love?) to virtue. Honor may be sought, it is recognized, as a means for reassuring oneself of one's virtue.

But would that human being be significantly inferior, no matter how exalted he may be by his fellows, who has to rely upon such guidance? Would not that human being be superior who does *not* have to depend on what others may—or may not—happen either to know or to say about him? Related to this is what Aristotle suggests (also in the *Nicomachean Ethics*) about who can—and who cannot—truly be friends.

V

Further illumination here may be provided by considering the problem of the relation between such critically divergent lovers as Achilles' parents, mortal Peleus and divine Thetis, as indicated in Homer's *Iliad* and elsewhere. Did the immortal Thetis play the part of the Phoenix to the markedly deteriorating Peleus' Turtledove? And, for Shakespeare, how would the critical relations between the Divine and the Human in Christianity, with its self-sacrificing yet immortal divinity, be illuminated by the periodic "flaming" associated with the Phoenix?

It may also be wondered how well the Turtledove can ever know the particular manifestation of the Phoenix that he encounters, especially if the Phoenix is indeed anything like what scholars report about her repeated incarnations. It is also reported, we have seen, that the Phoenix legend was early pressed into the service of Christian teaching.[5] What comment, then, might the poet of *The Phoenix and Turtle* be making about critical theological doctrines of his day?

However all this may be, what *can* be expected of any love to be developed by and with the perpetually reincarnated Phoenix? It might even be wondered, on behalf of (or even by?) the Turtledove, what "mutual flame" had been "enjoyed" theretofore (and especially with whom) by the Phoenix, and whether any of the Phoenix's other partners in immolation had perished before their time for this privilege. Such inquiries need not endorse (even as they are aware of) the assessment of our poet voiced by George Bernard Shaw in his preface to *Man and Superman*:

> The truth is, the world was to Shakespeare a great "stage of fools" on which he was utterly bewildered. He could see no sense in living at all.[6]

VI

Or should we not make too much of the Turtledove's mortality? May there not be, after all, something special about *this* Turtledove? Is he, too, being immortalized, if only in sentiment?

Is the celebration of love here a likely, if not even a necessary, illusion that lovers are moved by, at least for awhile? It may be wondered whether the Phoenix, as lover, is somehow moved to believe either that she will truly die with the Turtledove or that the Turtledove will be resurrected with her. We can be reminded by the Aristophanes of Plato's *Symposium* of the errors about the currently grasped Other that Lovers are often inclined to embrace.

Another way of putting this inquiry is to ask whether the "eternity" to which the poem refers (58) can ever mean the same for both of such birds. Might at least the Phoenix know better how things stand—and are likely to develop—between them? Should we see here, therefore, that tension between *truth* and *love* which may be anticipated even in the most celebrated or exalted manifestations of True Love?

VII

We can wonder as well whether it is merely a matter of chance that *love* can be seen to be literally the central word in the text of the complete poem (33)? It can be noticed too that central to the first part of the poem (the quatrains) seem to be the words *one* and *two* (26–27), while central to the second part (the triplets, or Threnos) seems to be the word *married* (61). Is it suggested thereby that *love* should be understood as the sentiment or activity that can move a couple to marry, to be somehow united in an authoritative way?

May it be, furthermore, a matter of chance how love is regarded or what happens because of it (including, here and there, suicidal developments)? It may be critical what lovers can truly know not only about "the other" (36) but also about themselves. Do the illusions that many, if not all, lovers depend upon contribute to the "confound[ing]" of reason that is noticed in the poem (41)?

A critical illusion here, we have noted, may be the notion—insisted on at the very end of the poem—that both of these birds are "dead" (67). Should it be wondered whether the Phoenix, even if *she* should be resurrected after her fiery embrace of the Turtledove, somehow perishes with him? That is, did *this* particular encounter of lovers somehow make subsequent reincarnations by the Phoenix severely limited, a prospect that the dying Turtledove can properly anticipate with satisfaction?

VIII

Critical to how the poem should be read is how the fate of the incinerated Phoenix should be regarded. Although nothing is said explicitly in this poem about the traditional understanding of the routine revival of this unique bird after its death, such a cycle seems to be recognized in the writings of Shakespeare's contemporaries. This may be seen as well elsewhere in Shakespeare's own work, as in *Henry VI, Part 1* (IV.vii) and *Henry VI, Part 3* (V.v).

The most significant recognition of the traditional Phoenix in a work associated with Shakespeare (aside from "The Phoenix and Turtle") is seen in *Henry VIII*. There, Archbishop Cranmer can prophesy, as following upon the long and successful reign anticipated for the then-infant Elizabeth (V.v.40–43):

> Nor shall this peace sleep with her; but as when
> The bird of wonder dies, the maiden phoenix,
> Her ashes new-create another heir
> As great in admiration as herself . . .

These lines can remind us of the longevity, and hence at least a seeming immortality, that can follow from a political allegiance for which the greatest sacrifices may be made.

The importance of political rule, in "keep[ing] the obsequy so strict," is recognized in what is said about "the eagle, feathered king," of our poem (11–12). May the Phoenix, at least in the form noticed in the poem, be like the eminently successful political actor who goes out in a blaze of glory, so much so as to be periodically revived among its successors? Such an actor can well have (and may even need and treasure?) a companion whose devotion is so deep and so critical as *not* to require any public recognition, each being "the other's mine" (36).

IX

The "Threnos" (or lament), it is anticipated, will be provided by "Reason," after it has been "in itself confounded" (41). It is recognized, that is, that there are matters touched upon here that are difficult to understand, especially when the basis and extent of fidelity are considered. The illusions of perpetuity may be needed to sustain useful associations (as may be seen, perhaps, in the celebrated insistence that one's precious way "shall not perish from the earth").[7]

It is recognized as well that the lovers invoke and depend on a "logic" of their own. Sometimes, indeed, they even call into question obviously reasonable considerations that are generally accepted. What do suggestions in this poem about love, illusion, and confidence suggest about how the plays of Shakespeare should be read (and not only *Romeo and Juliet* and *Antony and Cleopatra*)?

The concluding stanzas of our poem include these ominous lines:

> Truth may seem, but cannot be;
> Beauty brag, but 'tis not she,
> Truth and beauty buried be. (62–65)

Even more ominous, perhaps, is the recognition (in the seventh stanza of the poem) that "Number there in love was slain." (28) Can there be, without a proper grasp of number, a reliable ability to *figure out* both how things *are* and (perhaps even more critical) how they *should be?*

Notes

1. David Bevington, *The Complete Works of Shakespeare*, Sixth Edition (Longman, 2009) 1698. Most of the line and other citations in this text as well as notes have been supplied by the editors.

2. The full text of Shakespeare's "The Phoenix and Turtle" as it appears in the Bevington edition is printed at the end of this chapter. Unless otherwise indicated all parenthetical references herein are to the line numbers of the poem.

3. "Phoenix" entry, *Encyclopedia Britannica*, Revised Fourteenth Edition (online).

4. *The Westminster Dictionary of the Bible* (Westminster Press, 1924) 615.

5. "Phoenix" entry, *The Oxford Classical Dictionary*, Revised Third Edition (Oxford University Press, 2003) 1174: The phoenix was "a potent symbol for both pagans and Christians."

6. George Bernard Shaw, Epistle Dedicatory to *Man and Superman* (Penguin Classics, 2000) 30.

7. On Lincoln's reading of Shakespeare, see George Anastaplo, *Abraham Lincoln: A Constitutional Biography* (Rowman and Littlefield, 1999); and "Shakespeare's Politics Revisited," in *Perspectives on Politics in Shakespeare*, eds. Murley and Sutton (Lexington, 2006) 197–242. For additional materials bearing on the discussion here, see: www.anastaplo.wordpress.com.

THE PHOENIX AND TURTLE

1   Let the bird of loudest lay
    On the sole Arabian tree
    Herald sad and trumpet be,
    To whose sound chaste wings obey.

5   But thou shrieking harbinger,
    Foul precurrer of the fiend,
    Augur of the fever's end,
    To this troop come thou not near.

9   From this session interdict
    Every fowl of tyrant wing,
    Save the eagle, feathered king;
    Keep the obsequy so strict.

13 Let the priest in surplice white,
    That defunctive music can,
    Be the death-divining swan,
    Lest the requiem lack his right.

17 And thou treble-dated crow,
    That thy sable gender mak'st
    With the breath thou giv'st and tak'st,
    'Mongst our mourners shalt thou go.

21 Here the anthem doth commence.
    Love and constancy is dead;
    Phoenix and the turtle fled
    In a mutual flame from hence.

25 So they loved, as love in twain
    Had the essence but in one,
    Two distincts, division none;
    Number there in love was slain.

29 Hearts remote yet not asunder,
    Distance, and no space was seen
    Twixt this turtle and his queen;
    But in them it were a wonder.

33 So between them love did shine,
    That the turtle saw his right
    Flaming in the phoenix' sight;
    Either was the other's mine.

37 Property was thus appalled
    That the self was not the same;
    Single nature's double name
    Neither two nor one was called.

41 Reason, in itself confounded,
    Saw division grow together,
    To themselves yet either neither,
    Simple were so well compounded,

45 That it cried, "How true a twain
    Seemeth this concordant one!
    Love hath reason, Reason none,
    If what parts can so remain."

49 Whereupon it made this threne
    To the phoenix and the dove,
    Co-supremes and stars of love,
    As chorus to their tragic scene.

    THRENOS

53 Beauty, truth, and rarity,
    Grace in all simplicity,
    Here enclosed, in cinders lie.

56 Death is now the phoenix' nest,
    And the turtle's loyal breast
    To eternity doth rest,

59 Leaving no posterity;
    'Twas not their infirmity,
    It was married chastity.

62 Truth may seem, but cannot be;
    Beauty brag, but 'tis not she;
    Truth and beauty buried be.

65 To this urn let those repair
    That are either true or fair;
    For these dead birds sigh a prayer.

13

∼

Love's Book of Honor and Shame

Shakespeare's Sonnets and Lyric Flourishing

Scott F. Crider

And as it is of speech, so of all other our behaviours.

—George Puttenham, *The Art of English Poesy*

One cannot, I suspect, build either a happy family or a just polity on the foundations of *Shakespeare's Sonnets*, even if one interpreted the sonnet sequence as a negative example—"Whatever you do, do not love like *that*"—but then neither the family nor the polity will satisfy all of the soul's longings.

The identity of the Speaker of *Shakespeare's Sonnets* is a famously vexed question, and I suspect we will never know whether he is the earnest autobiographical William Shakespeare himself, or the rhetorical ethos of William Shakespeare, or the fictional character "Will."[1] Whatever the case, our Speaker recognizes that time ultimately destroys all human beings and is, therefore, a danger to the honor paid to beauty—both the honored beautiful one and his honoring admirer. After all, one's beloved will age and die: Time is not providential in the sonnet sequence; it is destructive. Human beings are the most linguistic of creatures, and they are also the most conscious of mortality, so Davidic lamentation comes naturally to us, as we see early in the sequence in Sonnet 5's octave:

> Those hours, that with gentle work did frame
> The lovely gaze where every eye doth dwell,
> Will play the tyrants to the very same
> And that unfair which fairly doth excel:
> For never-resting time leads summer on

293

> To hideous winter and confounds him there;
> Sap cheque'd with frost and lusty leaves quite gone,
> Beauty o'ersnow'd and bareness everywhere. (5.1–8)[2]

Both beloved and his honor, then, must be transvalued to be redeemed from time, but that raises the following question: How? Through either the sexual procreation argued for in Sonnets 1–17 or the poetic recreation argued for and enacted in 18–126 (the two parts constituting the Fair Youth subsequence), both forms of which new life he figures in Sonnet 5's sestet:

> Then, were not summer's distillation left,
> A liquid prisoner pent in walls of glass,
> Beauty's effect with beauty were bereft,
> Nor it nor no remembrance what it was:
>> But flowers distill'd, though they with winter meet,
>> Leese but their show; their substance still lives sweet. (5.9–14)

The distilled flower here is the perfumed rose-water outliving the flower itself, and it is not difficult to see here a figure for both child and poem. Our Speaker recognizes that love must be secured against metamorphosis, not only from the beloved's changes in body through age and death, but also eventually even from those in soul through vice and betrayal; otherwise, the poet's act of praise will be undone by blame since the Speaker eventually discovers that his beloved is beautiful, but not true—a cankered rose without sweet smell, whose "sensual fault" (35.9) threatens to destroy the Speaker's love and poetry: "O how much more doth beauty beauteous seem / By that sweet ornament which truth doth give" (54.1–2), he pleads with his untrue friend.

Honor too must be transvalued, expanding the honoring audience across time to renew audiences, and the transhistorical character of that audience—readers of the book, *Shakespeare's Sonnets*, who dwell with him in the republic of letters—will alter the nature of the honor itself.[3] The double securing of love and honor takes place in and through the lyric form of the sonnet sequence itself. The speaker does not understand such lyric flourishing from the beginning; rather, he discovers it within the Fair Youth subsequence (1–126), then forgets it in the Dark Lady one (127–54).[4] Allow me to examine one moment of such discovery in Sonnet 25 in order to trace this transvaluation of love and honor by seeing them both in relation to beauty, an important term in the sequence's thesis, provided in the sequence's opening: "From fairest creatures, we desire increase / That thereby beauty's *Rose* might never die" (1.1–2). For Shakespeare's Speaker, human beings are not primarily rational animals; they are first and foremost beauty-desiring ones. Beauty's lyric flower here marries love and honor, but this is decidedly not Dante's Rose of salvific virtue from the *Paradiso*.

Sonnet 25 is less well-known than many others, but it explicitly addresses our volume's two topics together:

> Let **those** / who **are** / in fa/vor **with** / their **stars** >
> Of **pub**/lic **ho**/nor and / **proud ti**/tles **boast**,
> Whilst **I**, / whom **for**/tune of / **such tri**/umph **bars**,
> **Unlook'd** / for // **joy** / in <u>that</u> / I **ho**/nor **most**. (25.1–4)[5]

The Speaker allows those favored by public honor and proud title to enjoy and celebrate their favor, taking their orientation from the simple constellation of the stars of honor and title. The poem's first metrical substitutions emphasize the *hypallage*—"Of **pub**/lic **ho**/nor and / **proud ti**/tle **boast**"—so that we know that the title itself is not proud; the favored ones are. The coordination of prepositional objects—"stars of honor *and* titles"—leaves their relationship ambiguous: Are they honored because titled, or titled because honored? (This will be important in the second and third quatrains.) What we do yet know, though, is that the Speaker is somehow barred by fortune from "such triumph," lacking recognition and status since he is "unlook'd for." If he is denied both, what, then, is the source of his happiness? He does "joy in that [he] honor[s] most." His happiness is not that he is honored, but that he honors. Discussions of honor have a tendency, especially when oriented by ancient conceptions of honor, to neglect the good of honoring in their desire to elevate being honored. There is here an ambiguity so far, to my knowledge, unnoticed.[6] "[I]n that" may be a prepositional phrase, the "that" a demonstrative pronoun whose antecedent is his beloved; even so, it may be a conjunctive phrase specifying not *what*, but *why*: "I joy [since] I honor most." This ambiguity allows for diversity of scansion, as well: If one wishes to stress the former reading, the foot is iambic ("in **that**"); if the latter, pyrrhic ("in that"). That is, the joy may be due to the object of honor, but it may be due to the act of honoring itself. Honor as a human good may change after the advent of Christianity since honoring is a form of regard for the other that is at least proximate to love. Even after Christianity, I would suggest, a trace of charity remains in the regard of honor.

Interestingly, though, honoring may also better fulfill the ancient desire for self-sufficiency. Being honored is not as self-sufficient as honoring, for honoring itself may be free of the honored object's response. What is the tone of the Speaker's attitude toward this ordinary triumph over the mortal rage that destroys the honored beloved? The next two stanzas provide a clue:

Great prin/ces' fa/vorites / their fair / leaves spread
But as / the ma/rigold / at the / sun's eye,
And in / themselves / their pride / lies bu/riéd,
For at / a frown // they in / their glo/ry die.
The pain/ful war/rior famoused / for worth,
After / a thous/and vic/tories / once foil'd,
Is from / the book / of ho/nor ra/zéd quite,
And all / the rest / forgot / for which / he toil'd[.] (25.5–12)

The courtier relies on princely favoritism; the warrior, on a record of victory. Of course, honor as renown (as opposed to honor as integrity) depends on others to honor one, so it lacks what John Alvis designates as a necessary condition of happiness, "the complete self-knowledge which enables ordinate love of honor which, in turn, sustains self-sufficiency," the complex of which is Shakespearean "integrity."[7] Let me take up the courtier first. As the sun helps the marigold to open in display, the prince honors his favorites; so too, as the marigold collapses when the sun does not shine, the courtiers die when the prince frowns. The Speaker figures the favorite as a languid flower whose "**fair / leaves spread**," a spondaic flourishing dependant upon the prince, figured as the "**sun's eye**." Yet night will come and the courtier's flourishing "**die**." There is a natural inevitability to the caprice of the prince. The warrior is handicapped, though, not by the natural inevitability of princely caprice, but by the human impossibility of a perfect martial history. Though Katherine Duncan-Jones does not, editors have emended the text since Theobald, changing 1609 Quarto's "worth" to some other word that actually rhymes with "quite" (such as "might" or "fight"), but such emendation may miss the point. First, the stress in the poem is not what the honored one is honored *for*, but instead either that *he* is honored or *that* he is honored: the warrior is "famoused for worth." Honor has a dual character—the act of honoring and the standard by which and to what degree one honors, one's estimation of worth. As well, the loss of the rhyme word's sonic completion is jarring when the warrior is "from the book of honor razéd quite," the quite-ness of his razing shocking when denied rhyme's almost teleological completion.

Why are the quatrains in this order; why, that is, does the Speaker take up the courtier first, then the warrior? I would argue that they are ordered from the lesser to the greater, relative perhaps to self-sufficiency and certainly to justice. Their honorings are different: Both are dependent upon others for honor, but the courtier is more so since he has an audience of only one, and the prince's favor is less within his control, even if his art of the courtier were perfectly refined. The warrior has greater control. As well, even though there may be injustice in the prince's darkening, the Speaker does not emphasize it, whereas the fact that a warrior, even after a thousand victories, will lose fame with *one* loss is disturbingly unjust. The Speaker figures the loss of fame with the poem's most significant metaphor: the warrior's loss of fame is his razing or erasure from "the book of honor," a book written by others. His defense against oblivion—his own talent—is powerless to signify his worth, to write himself, or anyone else, into immortality. That requires another since the figure of self-praiser is the braggart, hardly an honorable figure. (Think only of Pistol.) The Speaker has a number of metaphors for his poetry, but he sometimes employs those from early modern manuscript and print culture. To cite only one example, the medium of the Fair Youth's miraculous immortality is ink: "in black ink my love shall still shine bright" (65.14). The Fair Youth's existence beyond death will be housed in that black ink, a book of honor.

The poem's *volta* comes with the couplet:

Then **hap**/py I / that **love** / and **am** / beloved >
Where I / may **not** / remove, / nor **be** / removed. (25.13–14)

Unlike the favored of court and battlefield, the Speaker depends upon a surer foundation for his flourishing: not the art of the courtier or warrior, but, surprisingly, that of the lover. Love has two characteristics, one of which will be exposed later as unreliable, while the other is sure—if anything in this life can be sure: love's reciprocity and its fixedness. The parallel instances of *polyptoton* of "love/bel*oved*" and "remove/*removed*" indicate that the Speaker's happiness starts with him and ends with his beloved. Although there is dependency here—and we know that the Speaker will, eventually, no longer be beloved by the Fair Youth, and will indeed be "removed" from him—there is also a powerful element of self-sufficiency; after all, it is the Speaker who decides whether he himself loves or removes. Notice that the lover self-sufficiently submits to dependency. There is here a kind of lyric Augustinianism without God. The character of that submission is crucial: Does the self-knowledge John Alvis demands attend this submission, or not? As the Speaker explains in Sonnet 116 (perhaps the most famous sonnet in our language) after the Fair Youth has rejected him,

Let me not to the marriage of true minds
Admit impediments. Love is not love
Which alters when it alteration finds,

> Or bends with the remover to remove:
> O no! it is an ever-fixed mark
> That looks on tempests and is never shaken;
> It is the star to every wandering bark,
> Whose worth's unknown, although his height be taken.
> Love's not Time's fool, though rosy lips and cheeks
> Within his bending sickle's compass come:
> Love alters not with his brief hours and weeks,
> But bears it out even to the edge of doom.
>   If this be error and upon me proved,
>   I never writ, nor no man ever loved. (116.1–14)

I have elsewhere argued that this poem's defense of the will to lyric bearing surpasses even Virgilian heroism.[8] Yet, as early as Sonnet 25, the Speaker recognizes that his flourishing is here, in part, contingent upon his own will to constancy, what John Alvis calls "integrity," though I wonder if Alvis has anything like our Speaker's love in mind given that he isolates the Speaker of Sonnet 94, during an especially Stoic moment, and *The Tempest*'s Prospero as exemplars of Shakespearean integrity (1990, 27–32, 251–61).

All of which brings me back to the question of the Speaker's tone in Sonnet 25 toward the fortunate courtier and warrior. Helen Vendler sees the couplet as "a private boast . . . , countering the public boasts of the stars' triumphant favorites" (1997, 145). I would suggest, though, that the tone is not the bitter boast of frustrated rivalry which results in proud confidence, but the sympathy of shared fragility which results in hesitant hope. By now in the sequence, we know enough of the Fair Youth to suspect that the Speaker's reliance on him is a dubious way to achieve happiness. Yet there is a self-sufficiency within the Speaker's own constant love since it is free of fortune's favoritism. Vendler argues that Shakespeare ironizes the Speaker's boast: "The implicit irony in the fact that the speaker-lover does not expect a reversal of fortune in his own case suggests that he thinks he can hide from the *stars*, which is the most foolish *boast* of all" (1997, 145). This is a helpful point, but it requires refinement, for, while it is true that half of his claim is ironized, the other half is not: he loses the Fair Youth's love, but the Fair Youth does not lose his, as we see as late as Sonnet 116, where the stars of honor and title yield before the star of constancy, "the star to every wandering bark / Whose worth's unknown, although his height be taken." Notice that the lover cannot know the essence of love, only orient his or her life by it. Hence, he "defines" love only by means of its activity of "bearing." After all, only with Sonnet 126 does the Speaker "remove" himself from the Fair Youth to write of another beloved, the devastatingly empty parentheses which close the poem's Fair Youth sub-sequence and remind all of what the Fair Youth will be without his poet:

Her audit, though delayed, answered must be,
And her quietus is to render thee.
(   )
(   ). (126.11–14)

Until then, the poet maintains his integrity by still loving his friend and may do so throughout both sub-sequences. The fact that the sub-sequence ends does not prove that the Speaker's will to constancy is a "foolish boast"; it proves that human beings are fragile and their loves incurable. The poet's love for the Fair Youth does not end; only the sub-sequence does. Though Shakespeare's later plays transform tragedy into romance, his sonnet sequence (published in 1609 during the period of romances) locates tragedy *after* romance, without, however, ever diminishing the romance. The ugly dispraise of the ugly does not undo the beautiful praise of the beautiful, even if it qualifies the soul's admirable longings with the body's foolish carnality: "Poor soul, center of my sinful earth" (146.1).

For 126 sonnets, the Speaker testifies to fidelity by doing what the warrior as warrior cannot do, writing, not merely being written; that is, the Speaker writes his own book of honor, love's book of honor, the sub-sequence of the sonnets themselves. While the Fair Youth, like the warrior, is written into immortality, the Speaker writes his beloved, himself and their love into it. Of course, some wag may point out that we do not even know the name of the beloved, but that only qualifies the exact character of immortality. Even when there is no caption for a photo and the subjects remain "unknown," they have a form of immortality. The Speaker joys in that he honors most, and what he honors most will shift from his beautiful beloved to his own attempt through lyric bearing to save that beautiful beloved from the mortal rage of age and death. Even so, it must be conceded that, with Sonnet 127, our Speaker abandons the Fair Youth to himself and takes up with the Dark Lady in an "expense of spirit in a waste of shame" (129.1), wherein the qualified, Petrarchan idealism of his friendship with the Fair Youth (qualified by the beloved's vice) becomes the anti-Petrarchan misogyny of "lust in action" with the Dark Lady (misogynistic since the Speaker scapegoats her for his own vice).[9] The Speaker acknowledges his "sinful loving" (142.2) only in the Dark Lady sequence. And, whatever failures one reads into the sequence's final antimetabole, the last line of *Shakespeare's Sonnets*—"Love's fire heats water; water cools not love" (154.14)—the Speaker believes those failures due only to his venereal lust for the Dark Lady, not to his lyric love for the Fair Youth. Shakespeare himself may see honor and shame in both sub-sequences, but the Speaker sees honor in one and shame in the other. Either way, *Shakespeare's Sonnets* is love's book of honor and shame—the flourishing and suffering of love.

Allow me to conclude by recognizing qualified Shakespearean wisdom in Sonnet 25 concerning honor and love in his Speaker's recognition that, if there is one foundation for human flourishing, it is this: the lyric will to constancy in love. That is why, only four sonnets later, we come upon a greater poem, one which we may, I hope, understand better when it is understood in relation to its lesser:

> When, in disgrace with fortune and men's eyes,
> I all alone beweep my outcast state
> And trouble deaf heaven with my bootless cries
> And look upon myself and curse my fate,
> Wishing me like to one more rich in hope,
> Featured like him, like him with friends possess'd,
> Desiring this man's art and that man's scope,
> With what I most enjoy contented least;
> Yet in these thoughts myself almost despising,
> Haply I think on thee, and then my state,
> Like to the lark at break of day arising
> From sullen earth, sings hymns at heaven's gate;
>   For thy sweet love remember'd such wealth brings
>   That then I scorn to change my state with kings. (29.1–14)

Arising from sullen earth, the Speaker sings a hymn of love's honor, an immortally lyric state bringing such wealth that he would disdain to rule an actual ship of state or to fight in its defense, preferring instead to pilot his ship of lyric on the sea of being, bearing it out unto the edge of human comprehension, to a point where no one other than he may remove his love.

Whatever the family and the city require, the soul requires something other. If for Dante and Petrarch that other is the beautiful lady incarnating divine love, for Shakespeare's Speaker that other is only the humanly lyric remnant of beauty's "increase" in the lyric love for untrue beauty, one which does not transfigure carnal love (nor is it corrupted by it): lyric love simply lives alongside carnal. This is neither pagan, nor Christian love, for neither the Platonic nor the Pauline conceptions of proper love "cure" human desire of its honor and shame.[10] *Shakespeare's Sonnets*, love's book of honor and shame, enacts a modern love.[11]

Notes

1. Both rhetoric and poetics recognize that the speaking subject—rhetor or character—is not strictly identifiable with the actual person speaking, whether public figure or actor. Because lyric is such apparently intimate discourse, it is difficult not to identify "Will" with William Shakespeare, but the urge should be resisted. Lyric allows for a discourse of lived experience without, however, reducing it to autobiography. For rhetorical poetics in the Renaissance and Shakespeare, see Heinrich Plett, *Rhetoric and Renaissance Culture* (Walter de Gruyter, 2004), and my review, with reference to *Shakespeare's Sonnets*, especially Sonnet 1, in *The Ben Jonson Journal* 14/2 (2007) 268–84.

2. All citations from *Shakespeare's Sonnets* are from Katherine Duncan-Jones' edition (Arden, 1997).

3. Discussions of honor would do well to attend to the rhetorical genre of praise and blame. On epideictic rhetoric, see O. Hardison Jr., *The Enduring Monument: A Study of the Idea of Praise in Renaissance Literary Theory and Practice* (University of North Carolina Press, 1962). On the subversive possibility that all praise is self-praise, see J. Fineman, *Shakespeare's Perjured Eye: The Invention of Poetic Subjectivity in the Sonnets* (University of California Press, 1986).

4. That these episodes *are* episodes is debated in Shakespeare Studies. For a critique of identifying and distinguishing the Fair Youth and Dark Lady sonnets as episodes of an emplotted whole, see Heather Dubrow, "'Incertainties now crown themselves assured': The Politics of Plotting Shakespeare's Sonnets," *Shakespeare Quarterly* 47 (1996) 291–305.

5. The sonnets are in iambic pentameter (usually): Stressed syllables are here in **bold** and unstressed ones not so, while debatable syllables are underlined; feet are divided (/), caesuras indicated (//), and enjambments suggested (>). On Shakespearean metrics in the plays and the poems, see George Wright, *Shakespeare's Metrical Art* (University of California Press, 1988).

6. I am indebted to the editions of *Shakespeare's Sonnets*, with commentaries on this sonnet, by Carl D. Atkins (Fairleigh Dickinson University Press, 2007), Stephen Booth (Yale University Press, 1977), Hyder Edward Rollins (J. P. Lippincott Company, 1944), Helen Vendler (Harvard University Press, 1997), and David West (Duckworth, 2007). There is, to my knowledge, only one, somewhat extended discussion of this sonnet in the secondary literature on *Shakespeare's Sonnets*: David Weiser, *Mind in Character: Shakespeare's Speaker in the Sonnets* (University of Missouri Press, 1987) 55–58.

7. John Alvis, *Shakespeare's Understanding of Honor* (Carolina Academic Press, 1990) 31 (hereafter, cited internally). I am indebted to the book throughout this chapter. For John Alvis' most recent reflections on honor in Shakespeare, see chapter 1 of this volume.

8. Scott Crider, "Lyric Bearing: Shakespeare's Sonnet 116, Virgil's *Aeneid* and the Ship of Metaphor," in *The Garden of Lyric*, ed. Bainard Cowan (Dallas Institute for Culture and the Humanities Press, forthcoming).

9. On Petrarchanism in Shakespearean comedy, see Paul Cantor's discussion in chapter 3 of this volume. On anti-Petrarchanism in the sonnet sequence, see Heather Dubrow, *Echoes of Desire: English Petrarchanism and its Counterdiscourses* (Cornell University Press, 1995).

10. There is no evidence that Shakespeare read Plato, but we do know that he read Castiglione's *Book of the Courtier* in Thomas Hoby's translation, especially Bembo's speech on love in Book 4, a reworking of Plato's *Symposium*. On Shakespeare's engagement with Platonism, see J. B. Leishman, *Themes and Variations in Shakespeare's Sonnets* (Harper and Row, 1963), esp. 149–77. For his engagement with Pauline theology, see Lisa Freinkel, *Reading Shakespeare's Will: The Theology of Figure from Augustine to the Sonnets* (Columbia University Press, 2002).

11. I would like to thank all the participants of the stimulating, collegial conference that was the origin of this volume's chapters, but especially its organizers and hosts, the editors of this volume: B. J. Dobski and Dustin Gish. This chapter is dedicated to my colleague, fellow-Shakespearean and friend, Gerard Wegemer.

~

Appendices

APPENDIX A

~

Shakespeare's Plays
First Folio Edition (London, 1623)*

A CATALOGUE
of the severall Comedies, Histories, and Tragedies
contained in this Volume.

COMEDIES.

The Tempest.
The two Gentlemen of Verona.
The Merry Wives of Windsor.
Measure for Measure.
The Comedy of Errours.
Much adoo about Nothing.
Loves Labour lost.
Midsommer Nights Dreame.
The Merchant of Venice.
As you Like it.
The Taming of the Shrew.
All is well, that Ends well.
Twelfe-Night, or what you will.
The Winters Tale.

HISTORIES.

The Life and Death of King John.
The Life & death of Richard the second.

The First part of King Henry the fourth.
The Second part of K. Henry the fourth.
The Life of King Henry the Fift.
The First part of King Henry the Sixt.
The Second part of King Hen. the Sixt.
The Third part of King Henry the Sixt.
The Life & Death of Richard the Third
The Life of King Henry the Eight.

TRAGEDIES.

The Tragedy of Coriolanus.
Titus Andronicus.
Romeo and Juliet.
Timon of Athens.
The Life and death of Julius Caesar.
The Tragedy of Macbeth.
The Tragedy of Hamlet.
King Lear.
Othello, the Moore of Venice.
Anthony and Cleopater.
Cymbeline King of Britaine.

*The First Folio of 1623 is the earliest edition of William Shakespeare's collected works. Sponsored by John Heminges and Henry Condell, two of his theatrical colleagues, this edition published thirty-six plays by Shakespeare, half of which had not been previously published. Shakespeare's works of non-dramatic poetry (published in his lifetime) and one play partly attributed to him (*The Two Noble Kinsmen*) were not included in the First Folio. One play on which Shakespeare is thought to have collaborated appears here (*Henry VIII*), while another attributed entirely to him does not (*Pericles, Prince of Tyre*). Absent from the "Catalogue" but included in the First Folio—inserted between the Histories and Tragedies, perhaps as a late addition—is *The History of Troilus and Cressida.*

APPENDIX B

Shakespeare's Works
*Arranged according to composition date**

1588-92	*Henry VI, Part 1* *Henry VI, Part 2* *Henry VI, Part 3*
1589-94	*Titus Andronicus* *The Comedy of Errors*
1589-98	*Love's Labor's Lost*
1590-94	*The Taming of the Shrew* *Two Gentlemen of Verona*
(1593)	Venus and Adonis
1592-94	*Richard III*
(1594)	The Rape of Lucrece
1594-96	*Richard II* *A Midsummer Night's Dream* *Romeo and Juliet* *King John*
1596-97	*The Merchant of Venice* *Henry IV, Part 1*
1597-98	*Henry IV, Part 2*
1597-1601	*Merry Wives of Windsor*
1598-1600	*Much Ado About Nothing*
1593-1603	Sonnets (1609)

1598-1601	*As You Like It*
1599-1600	*Henry V* *Julius Caesar*
1600-01 (1601)	*Hamlet* The Phoenix and Turtle
1601-02	*Twelfth Night* *Troilus and Cressida*
1601-05 (1609)	*All's Well that Ends Well* A Lover's Complaint
1603-04	*Measure for Measure* *Othello*
1605-06	*King Lear*
1605-08	*Timon of Athens*
1606-07	*Macbeth* *Antony and Cleopatra*
1606-08	*Pericles* *Coriolanus*
1608-11	*Cymbeline* *The Winter's Tale*
1611	*The Tempest*

*This arrangement is based on a survey of scholarly reconstructions (at times highly speculative) which consider literary style, textual references and allusions, and extant information about first performances or publication (here in parenthesis): *The Norton Shakespeare*, Second Edition, eds. Stephen Greenblatt et al. (W.W. Norton, 2008) Timeline; *The Complete Works of Shakespeare*, Sixth Edition, ed. David Bevington (Pearson, 2009) Appendix 1; *The New Cambridge Companion to Shakespeare*, Second Edition, eds. Margreta de Grazia and Stanley Wells (Cambridge, 2010) xv–xvi. Shakespeare arguably collaborated on two plays after *The Tempest*: *Henry VIII* (1612–1613) and *The Two Noble Kinsman* (1613–1614).

APPENDIX C

~

Shakespeare's Plays
Arranged according to political order*

Monarchy / Kingdom

Troilus and Cressida
The Winter's Tale

Cymbeline
King Lear

King John
Richard II
Henry IV, Part I
Henry IV, Part II
Merry Wives of Windsor
Henry V
Henry VI, Part I
Henry VI, Part II
Henry VI, Part III
Richard III
[*Henry VIII*]

Macbeth
Hamlet, Prince of Denmark
Love's Labor's Lost
All's Well That Ends Well

Empire

Antony and Cleopatra
Titus Andronicus

Republic / City

Timon of Athens

Coriolanus
Julius Caesar

Othello, the Moor of Venice
The Merchant of Venice

Principate / Dukedom

A Midsummer Night's Dream
The Comedy of Errors
Pericles, Prince of Tyre

Much Ado About Nothing
Romeo and Juliet
Two Gentlemen of Verona
The Taming of the Shrew
Twelfth Night
As You Like It
Measure for Measure

The Tempest †

---

*In some cases, like the English histories and Roman tragedies, the political order is relatively evident; but in other cases, as with many of the comedies, it is much more difficult to identify one political order as the setting. This arrangement of the plays is not intended to be definitive.

†The action of *The Tempest* takes place on an unknown island with few inhabitants. A variety of political orders may be represented by certain characters (e.g. Alonso: Kingdom; Prospero, Antonio: Principate/Dukedom).

APPENDIX D

~

Shakespeare's Plays
Arranged according to dramatic setting and date*

(Ancient Greek World)

A Midsummer Night's Dream	Athens	Heroic Age
Troilus and Cressida	Troy	Archaic Age[1]
Timon of Athens	Athens	Classical Age, 431-404 BC
The Comedy of Errors	Ephesus, Syracuse	*ca.* 220 BC
Pericles, Prince of Tyre	Tyre, Antioch, Ephesus	*ca.* 200 BC

(Ancient Roman World)

Coriolanus	Rome	Republic, 510-490 BC
Julius Caesar	Rome, provinces	Republic, 45-42 BC
Antony and Cleopatra	Rome, Egypt, provinces	Republic, 40-30 BC
Cymbeline[2]	Roman Britain, Rome	Empire, 5-40 AD
Titus Andronicus	Rome	Empire, 4th-5th centuries

(Britain)

Cymbeline[2]	Roman Britain, Wales, Rome	5-40 AD
King Lear	Prehistoric Britain	*ca.* 2nd-3rd centuries
Macbeth	Scotland, England	*ca.* 11th century
King John	England, France	1191-1216
Richard II	England	1398
Henry IV, Part 1	England	1398-1413
Henry IV, Part 2	England	1398-1413
Merry Wives of Windsor	England: Windsor	1400-1413
Henry V	England, France	1413-1422
Henry VI, Part 1	England, France	1422-1471
Henry VI, Part 2	England	1422-1471
Henry VI, Part 3	England, France	1422-1471
Richard III	England	1483-1485
[Henry VIII]	England	1520-1533, 1556
The Taming of the Shrew[3]	England & Italy	*ca.* 16th century
As You Like It	England?[4]	*ca.* 16th century?

*It is difficult to identify one setting or date in many cases, due to multiple or shifting dramatic locations and historical anachronisms in many plays. This arrangement of the plays is not intended to be definitive.

(Europe)

The Winter's Tale	Sicilia & Bohemia	?
Twelfth Night	Illyria (Adriatic coast)	?
Hamlet, Prince of Denmark	Denmark: Elsinore	*ca.* 1500-1550
Measure for Measure	Austria: Vienna	*ca.* 16th century
Love's Labor's Lost	France: Navarre (forest)[4]	1588-1592
All's Well that Ends Well	France, Italy	
Much Ado About Nothing	Italy: Messina	13th century
Romeo and Juliet	Italy: Verona, Mantua	13th-14th centuries
Two Gentlemen of Verona	Italy: Verona, Milan, Mantua	16th century
The Taming of the Shrew[3]	Italy: Padua & England	*ca.* 16th century
The Merchant of Venice	Italy: Venice & Belmont	*ca.* 16th century
Othello, the Moor of Venice	Italy: Venice & Cyprus[5]	*ca.* 16th century
The Tempest[6]	(Mediterranean island)	*ca.* 16th century

1. *Troilus and Cressida* appears to be a medieval recreation of the Homeric world.

2. Cymbeline appears twice, since its setting is both the late Roman empire and prehistoric Britain.

3. *The Taming of the Shrew* appears twice, since the "Induction" at the beginning takes place somewhere in England, while the action of the rest of the play occurs entirely in Italy.

4. The action of *As You Like It* and *Love's Labor's Lost* both take place mainly in natural settings. 5. Only the first Act of *Othello* occurs in Venice, thereafter the action takes place on Cyprus.

6. *The Tempest* is set on an unknown island in the Mediterranean sea somewhere between north Africa and the kingdom of Naples.

Index

Achilles, 5, 122, 124–25, 127–29, 131, 135, 140n29; in *Iliad*, 287; in *Odyssey*, 124–25

actors, 229n27; and *As You Like It*, 77, 83n26; and love, 99; political, 159, 289, 301n1; Roscius as, 266, 270; Shakespeare as, 263; and stage metaphor, 262, 264–67, 269–71, 273–79; and *The Tempest*, 240. *See also* Rome

adultery, 171

Aeneas: in *A Midsummer Night's Dream*, 92; in *Troilus and Cressida*, 122, 128, 134; in *Aeneid*, 24–25, 38n5

afterlife: belief in, 22, 145, 157; disregard of, 180, 195; and virtue, 174. *See also* Immortality

Aligheri, Dante. *See* Dante

Alulis, Joseph, 81n2

Alvarez, Leo Paul S. de, 115n23,115n29, 115n32, 116n33, 203nn11–13

Alvis, John, 12, 16n9, 17n13, 17n16, 18n19, 18nn21–22, 165nn7–8, 166n12, 167n24, 256n11, 258n28, 260n50, 277, 279nn22–23, 296–98, 301n7

Anastaplo, George, 14, 18n20, 260n51, 283–90, 290n7

ambition: and anger, 24, 27; and Christianity, 10–11; and common good, 21, 35, 37, 266; extreme forms of, 7, 28, 31, 32, 124, 148, 207–8, 221, 223; for honor, 25, 31; of Macbeth, 189–91; and justice, 252; as motion in the soul, 3, 6, 7, 170; political, 10, 13, 26, 44, 161, 167n22, 218, 220; and reason, 23; and shame, 31

anger: and Caesar, 29; and Christianity, 171; and love, 66, 91; and moderation, 49, 51n4; moral form of, 41; patriotic, 27, 159; and Prospero, 29, 240–44, 246, 248–51, 254, 258n28, 258n30. *See also* injustice; justice; *thumos*

Aquinas, Thomas, 36, 94

aristocracy: courtly, 85n53; App. C

Aristophanes, 287

Aristotle, 12, 21, 36, 38n5, 117, 120–21, 128, 249, 272; *Nicomachean Ethics*, 17n10, 18n19, 121, 125–26, 129–30, 137, 138n3, 140n20, 140n23, 140n25,

About the Contributors

John Alvis is professor of English and director of the American Studies Program at the University of Dallas, where he received his doctorate and has taught since 1969. His books include *Shakespeare's Understanding of Honor* (1990) and *Divine Purpose and Heroic Response in Homer and Virgil* (1995). He is the coeditor of *Shakespeare as Political Thinker* (1979; revised, 2005) and *Willmoore Kendall: Maverick of American Conservatism* (2006), and the editor of *Areopagitica and the Political Writings of John Milton* (1998). He has published numerous articles and book chapters on Shakespeare, John Milton, Herman Melville, Caroline Gordon, Eugene O'Neill, and American constitutionalism. His most recent book is on Nathaniel Hawthorne: *Revolutionary Principles Personalized and Domesticated: Hawthorne as Political Philosopher* (2011).

George Anastaplo is professor of law at Loyola University of Chicago, professor emeritus of political science and philosophy at Dominican University, and (for over fifty years) lecturer in the liberal arts at the University of Chicago. He has authored scores of book chapters, articles, and critical reviews, and his publications include more than fifteen books on constitutionalism, literature and the law, free speech, Abraham Lincoln, and political philosophy. He has published interpretations of almost all the works of Shakespeare, including in two law journals devoted exclusively to his writings: *Prudence and Mortality in Shakespeare's Tragedies* (1979) and *Law & Literature and Shakespeare: Explorations* (2001).

Glenn Arbery has taught literature at the University of St. Thomas in Houston, Thomas More College in Merrimack, New Hampshire, and the University of Dallas. He has also served as director of the Teachers Academy at the Dallas Institute of Humanities and Culture and senior editor for People Newspapers in Dallas. The author of *Why Literature Matters* (2001), he has edited *The Tragic Abyss* (2003) and *The Southern Critics: An Anthology* (2010). Currently the d'Alzon Chair of Liberal Education at Assumption College, he is working on two books: on the "ontological criticism" proposed by John Crowe Ransom, and on the literary fruits of the marriage of Allen Tate and Caroline Gordon.

John C. Briggs received his doctorate from the University of Chicago and is professor of English at the University of California, Riverside, where he received the 1995–1996 UCR Faculty Teaching Award. He teaches courses on American literature, Renaissance literature and Shakespeare, and on Lincoln and the history and theory of rhetoric and composition. His published articles and book chapters include studies of Shakespeare's *Romeo and Juliet*, *Timon of Athens*, *The Tempest* and *Macbeth*. He is the author of *Francis Bacon and the Rhetoric of Nature* (1989), which won the Thomas J. Wilson Award, and *Lincoln's Speeches Reconsidered* (2005), and is currently working on a book on Shakespearean catharsis.

Paul A. Cantor is Clifton Waller Barrett Professor of English at the University of Virginia. He is the author of *Shakespeare's Rome: Republic and Empire* (1976) and the volume on *Hamlet* in the Cambridge Landmarks of World Literature series (1989; revised, 2004). He has published widely on the subject of politics, film, and literature, as well as on Shakespeare, including essays on *The Merchant of Venice, King Lear, Othello, Macbeth, Henry V* and *The Tempest*. His most recent book, coedited with Stephen Cox, is *Literature and the Economics of Liberty: Spontaneous Order in Culture* (2009).

Leon Harold Craig is professor emeritus at the University of Alberta, where for more than thirty years he taught graduate and undergraduate courses on Plato, Shakespeare, Hobbes, Rousseau and Nietzsche, as well as on the history and philosophy of science. The author of *The War Lover: A Study of Plato's Republic* (1994), *Of Philosophers and Kings: Political Philosophy in Shakespeare's Macbeth and King Lear* (2001), and most recently *The Platonian Leviathan* (2010), he has published numerous scholarly articles on political philosophy and is currently writing a second book on Shakespeare.

Scott F. Crider is associate professor of English at the University of Dallas, where he teaches a wide range of courses, but especially in Shakespeare studies and rhetorical studies. He is the author of two books, *With What Persuasion: An Essay on Shakespeare and the Ethics of Rhetoric* (2009) and *The Office of Assertion: An Art of Rhetoric for the Academic Essay* (2005), and has published articles, review essays, and reviews in a variety of journals, including *American Catholic Philosophical Quarterly*, *Cithara*, *Modern Age*, *Studies in the Literary Imagination*, *The Ben Jonson Journal*, and *The Sixteenth Century Journal*.

Bernard J. Dobski is associate professor of political science at Assumption College, where he teaches courses in international relations, American politics, and political philosophy, including a course on Shakespeare's politics. He is the contributing coeditor of *Shakespeare and the Body Politic* (forthcoming). He has published articles on Mark Twain, Thucydides, and Xenophon in *The Review of Politics*, *Interpretation*, and *Polis: The Journal for Ancient Greek Political Thought*, as well as a book chapter on "Thucydides and the Soul of Victory." His book reviews on American foreign policy and classical political thought have appeared in *Society* and *The Review of Metaphysics*.

Dustin A. Gish received his doctorate from the Institute of Philosophic Studies at the University of Dallas and, since 2007, has been visiting assistant professor of political science at College of the Holy Cross. He is the contributing coeditor of *Shakespeare and the Body Politic* (forthcoming) and *The Political Thought of Xenophon* (special issue of *Polis*, 2009), and has published book chapters as well as articles, review essays, and reviews on classical political philosophy (Homer, Xenophon, Plato) and American political thought (Jefferson) in *The Journal of Politics*, *History of Political Thought*, *Polis: The Journal for Ancient Greek Political Thought*, *Perspectives on Political Science*, *The Review of Politics*, and *Bryn Mawr Classical Review*.

Carson Holloway is associate professor of political science at the University of Nebraska at Omaha, where he teaches political philosophy, constitutional law, and American government. He has edited a collection of essays on *Magnanimity and Statesmanship* (2008) and has authored several books, including *The Way of Life: John Paul II and the Challenge of Liberal Modernity* (2008), *The Right Darwin? Evolution, Religion, and the Future of Democracy* (2006), and *All Shook Up: Music, Passion and Politics* (2001). He has published numerous scholarly articles, including "Shakespeare's *Coriolanus* and Aristotle's Great-Souled Man" in *The Review of Politics* (2007).

David Lowenthal is professor emeritus at Boston College, where he taught in the Political Science Department for more than thirty years. He has held the d'Alzon Chair of Liberal Education at Assumption College and taught seminars on Shakespeare at College of the Holy Cross. He is the author of many scholarly articles as well as *Shakespeare and the Good Life: Ethics and Politics in Dramatic Form* (1997) and *Present Dangers: Rediscovering the First Amendment* (1997), a translation of Montesquieu's *Considerations on the Causes of the Greatness of the Romans and Their Decline* (reprint, 1999), and most recently *Abraham Lincoln's Twenty Best Speeches: Texts and Interpretations* (forthcoming).

Carol McNamara received her doctorate from Boston College in 1996, and is senior lecturer at Utah State University where she teaches courses on political philosophy, political theory and literature, and the American presidency. She is the author of several book chapters and articles, including "Men and Money in Tom Wolfe's America," "The Pursuit of Happiness, American Style: Tom Wolfe's Study of Status and Freedom" (*Perspectives on Political Science*), and "Socratic Politics in Xenophon's *Memorabilia*" (*Polis: The Journal for Ancient Greek Political Thought*). She is the contributing coeditor of *The Obama Presidency in the Constitutional Order: A First Look* (2011), and is currently writing *A Political Companion to Tom Wolfe*.

Laurence Nee is a tutor at St. John's College (Santa Fe); he holds a PhD from the University of Dallas and JD from Northwestern University. He is the author of several legal articles in the *Notre Dame Law Review* and *Law and Social Inquiry* as well as an article on Xenophon in *Polis: The Journal for Ancient Greek Political Thought*. In addition to teaching courses on Shakespeare's works at St. John's College, he also taught Roman histories and Italian comedies for many years during academic summer programs in Rome, Italy.